Canada:
The State
of the
Federation
1992

Edited by
Douglas Brown and
Robert Young

Institute of
Intergovernmental
Relations

Institut des
relations
intergouvernementales

Canadian Cataloguing in Publication Data

The National Library of Canada has catalogued this publication as follows:

Main entry under title:

Canada, the state of the federation

1985-
Annual.

ISSN 0827-0708
ISBN 0-88911-559-1 (1992)

1. Federal-provincial relations - Canada - Periodicals.* 2. Federal government - Canada
- Periodicals. I. Queen's University (Kingston, Ont.). Institute of Intergovernmental
Relations.

~~JL27.F42~~   321.02'3'0971   C86-030713-1

JL
27
.C466   /73409

The Institute of Intergovernmental Relations

The Institute is the only organization in Canada whose mandate is solely to promote
research and communication on the challenges facing the federal system.

Current research interests include fiscal federalism, constitutional reform, the reform
of federal political institutions and the machinery of federal-provincial relations, Canadian federalism and the global economy, and comparative federalism.

The Institute pursues these objectives through research conducted by its own staff and
other scholars through its publication program, seminars and conferences.

The Institute links academics and practitioners of federalism in federal and provincial
governments and the private sector.

L'Institut des relations intergouvernementales

L'Institut est le seul organisme canadien à se consacrer exclusivement à la recherche
et aux échanges sur les questions du fédéralisme.

Les priorités de recherche de l'Institut portent présentement sur le fédéralisme fiscal,
la réforme constitutionnelle, la modification éventuelle des institutions politiques
fédérales, les nouveaux mécanismes de relations fédérales-provinciales, le fédéralisme
canadien au regard de l'économie mondiale et le fédéralisme comparatif.

L'Institut réalise ses objectifs par le biais de recherches effectuées par son personnel
et par des universitaires de l'Université Queen's et d'ailleurs, de même que par des
conférences et des colloques.

L'Institut sert de lien entre les universitaires, les fonctionnaires fédéraux et provinciaux et le secteur privé.

CONTENTS

III Intergovernmental Issues

IV Chronology

PREFACE

This is the seventh in the annual series of the Institute of Intergovernmental Relations, *Canada: The State of the Federation*. This volume departs somewhat from the previous pattern in being so dominated by one set of issues, constitutional renewal. The "Canada round" is covered by two full-length chapters, followed by seven shorter commentaries. These are followed in turn by four more full-length chapters that deal with longer term constitutional and intergovernmental issues. Each of the full-length chapters has been reviewed by external referees, but the shorter commentaries, designed to be more current reflections on the results of this summer's negotiations, were only prepared in the past two months. As in the past, this volume includes a chronological listing of the most significant developments in intergovernmental relations over the year 1 July 1991 to 30 June 1992.

The editors would like to thank all of the authors for their contributions, and add a special thanks to the commentators for preparing texts within such a short time frame. We are also indebted to the following people, who read one or more of the contributions and provided comments to the authors: Ned Franks, Katherine Graham, John Meisel, John McDougall, Peter Neary, Hugh Thorburn and Robert Wolfe.

At the Institute, we would like to thank Valerie Jarus for text preparation and formatting, Daniel Bonin for preparing the "sommaires," Marilyn Banting for proofreading, and Patti Candido, Dwight Herperger and Mary Kennedy for their assistance. Through the exceptional efforts of this team we are able to meet our publishing deadline in this extraordinary year.

Douglas Brown
Robert Young
September 1992

CONTRIBUTORS

Thérèse Arseneau is Assistant Professor of Political Science at St. Mary's University, Halifax, Nova Scotia.

Daniel Bonin is Research Associate, Institute of Intergovernmental Relations, Queen's University.

Douglas Brown is Acting Director, Institute of Intergovernmental Relations, Queen's University.

Peter Clancy is Associate Professor of Political Science at St. Francis Xavier University, Antigonish, Nova Scotia.

Andrew F. Cooper is Associate Professor of Political Science, University of Waterloo.

Stéphane Dion is Associate Professor, Department of Political Science, Université de Montréal.

Alain-G. Gagnon is Professor, Department of Political Science, McGill University.

Roger Gibbins is Professor and Head of the Department of Political Science at the University of Calgary.

J.L. Granatstein is Professor of History at York University.

Guy Laforest is Assistant Professor, Department of Political Science, Université Laval, Québec.

David Milne is Professor of Political Science at the University of Prince Edward Island.

Anne Poels is Librarian, Institute of Intergovernmental Relations, Queen's University.

Douglas D. Purvis is Professor of Economics and Director of the John Deutsch Institute, Queen's University.

André Raynauld is Professor of Economics, Université de Montréal, and an associate with the Institute for Research on Public Policy.

John Richards is Professor, Faculty of Business Administration, Simon Fraser University.

François Rocher is Associate Professor, Department of Political Science, Carleton University.

Katherine Swinton is Professor, Faculty of Law, University of Toronto.

Robert Young is Associate Professor, Department of Political Science, University of Western Ontario, and in 1991-92 was Visiting Fellow at the Institute of Intergovernmental Relations and the School of Policy Studies, Queen's University.

I

Introduction

1

Overview

Robert Young and Douglas Brown

Comme lors des années précédentes, ce volume réunit plusieurs articles qui explorent en profondeur tantôt certains aspects de la fédération canadienne, tantôt les forces qui déterminent son évolution. Ainsi, l'accent est particulièrement mis cette année sur la ronde du Canada qui a marqué, au cours de la dernière année, le processus de renouvellement de la Constitution. Rétrospectivement, celui-ci apparaît avoir été mené rondement dans la mesure où les morceaux se sont ultimement mis en place pour produire l'entente de Charlottetown, le 28 août dernier. En fait, depuis que les propositions fédérales en faveur de modifications constitutionnelles furent rendues publiques en septembre 1991, en aucun temps la perspective d'un règlement imminent à ce chapitre n'est-elle apparue évidente, y compris pour les acteurs impliqués au premier chef dans ce processus.

Or, le résultat du 28 août a consacré une entente unanime intervenue entre le gouvernement fédéral, les premiers ministres provinciaux, ainsi que les leaders des territoires et des organisations autochtones sur des changements significatifs apportés à la constitution canadienne. Ceux-ci auraient pour conséquence de définir le caractère fondamental du Canada (incluant le Québec comme société distincte); modifier la répartition des compétences en faveur d'une plus grande décentralisation; reconnaître le droit inhérent des autochtones à l'autonomie gouvernementale; et d'entraîner une réforme du Sénat en modifiant l'équilibre entre celui-ci et la Chambre des communes.

Cet aperçu passe en revue ces changements et le processus auxquels ils ont obéi. Il analyse les gains obtenus par le Québec une fois que le Premier ministre Bourassa eut décidé de se joindre aux négociations multilatérales d'août 1992. Il évalue aussi les progrès réalisés par les autochtones ainsi que la participation des Canadiens ordinaires et des groupes d'intérêts au processus de renouvellement constitutionnel.

Néanmoins, le rôle le plus important que les Canadiens auront à jouer dans la détermination de leur avenir constitutionnel viendra précisément lors du vote référendaire du 26 octobre prochain: ils seront appelés à ce moment à endosser ou rejeter les changements constitutionnels que leurs leaders auront avalisé préalablement. Nous espérons que ce volume les aidera dans leurs réflexions et leurs choix.

INTRODUCTION

As Canadians approach the autumn of 1992, they are profoundly ambivalent about their constitutional future. On the one hand, the state of their federation hangs in the balance, supported by the sweeping constitutional accord reached on 28 August by the federal government, the provincial premiers, and the leaders of territorial governments and aboriginal organizations. This "Charlottetown accord" is the culmination of two years of consultations and negotiations which have involved concerned Canadians in unprecedented exercises in public participation, and it represents the best efforts of their elected leaders to reform fundamentally the country's constitutional framework. The changes envisaged are great, but the consensus of political leaders seems firm, and few voices other than those of the sovereignist groups in Quebec have yet emerged to challenge the accord. On the other hand, Canadians are weary of the entire exercise. They are distracted by the faltering economy, distrustful of their elected leaders, uncertain about aspects of the "deal" and unsatisfied by others, and unhappy about the process that has produced it. There is no ringing endorsement of the Charlottetown accord arising from any quarter in the land.

The essays in this collection reflect this ambivalence. This is the seventh volume in the Institute's annual series of commissioned articles on Canadian intergovernmental relations. Given that the year has been so dominated by the constitutional renewal process, we have chosen to depart from the standard format of the past. We did ask certain scholars to analyze long-term trends in the evolution of Canadian federalism. Hence, Peter Clancy surveys the various dimensions of the movement towards political autonomy in the north, Andrew Cooper analyzes the negotiations in the Uruguay Round of the GATT to show how the regional concentration of different agricultural interests in this country has led to inconsistency in Canada's position about liberalizing trade in agriculture, John Richards provides deep background on the currents within the New Democratic Party (NDP) that have shaped its constitutional agenda in the federal and provincial spheres, and Daniel Bonin depicts in Quebec one sector affected by the debate over the division of powers — culture — not only to describe that province's traditional position about this area of jurisdiction but also to show the complexity of the field and the diverse interests with a stake in both cultural policy and its constitutional location. Such contributions help realize the Institute's goal of deepening our understanding of federalism in Canada and the forces that shape it.

With respect to the Canada round itself, we took two approaches. The first was to ask two scholars to analyze a couple of its most intriguing features. So David Milne undertook to describe and assess a wholly new participatory and consultative mechanism, the Renewal of Canada conferences held between January and March of 1992. And Guy Laforest has provided a close analysis of the Quebec strategy that has driven the Canada round — that of contemplating sovereignty while awaiting offers from the rest-of-Canada on renewed federalism — and also of the politician, Premier Robert Bourassa, who has straddled these two processes, mastering time (perhaps!) in a fashion reminiscent of Mackenzie King.

We also aimed to cope with developments in the Canada round by assembling a group of seasoned scholars who generously agreed to stand ready to comment on any package that emerged from the process. To these seven people we are very grateful. Along with other Canadians, they endured the perpetual extension of the negotiations, and were ready to write, despite vacations and many other commitments, when we called on them in mid-July in order to meet our publication deadline. As a result of this decision, most of these authors do not comment on the final package of 28 August. But their comments remain quite pertinent to the debate. First the differences between the deal struck in Quebec's absence on 7 July and the Charlottetown accord are irrelevant to most of the commentaries. As well, each analyst brings to the volume some useful background material on the dossiers they chose to examine. Third, we have arranged the commentaries chronologically, roughly in the order in which they were written, and so some valuable sense is conveyed of how the debate unfolded during the summer of 1992. Because of these people's efforts, we hope that this volume will be of more interest than usual, and that it will be a timely contribution as Canadians debate their constitutional future.

THE CANADA ROUND: GROPING TOWARDS AGREEMENT

Strangely enough, this year has not been a tumultuous one in the Canadian federation. It has been a busy one, (and for the negotiators, an exhausting one). The progress towards a constitutional settlement has been slow but hectic. Indeed, this feature of 1991-92 may account for some of the public's ambivalence about constitutional renewal. When one looks *back* on the many stages and components of the process that produced the Charlottetown accord, one finds a pattern, a logic, that seems to have led ineluctably to the agreement. Yet the components were orchestrated by no one, and each stage was jury-rigged. The major players scarcely knew at any time what they would be discussing in two weeks, or with whom they would be discussing, or whether they would be discussing at all. It is this aimless, amoebic quality, this near purposelessness, that has tainted the year for many. And yet the participants, moving forward according to the niches open to them, have truly been making history. Although it speaks perhaps of little more than a collective determination to carry on, the amoebic quality of the year's negotiations may represent the essence of Canadian federalism and of Canada itself.

The collective groping towards a constitutional agreement has involved several milestones. It moved always within the setting of the failure of the Meech Lake Accord to be ratified (in June 1990), and, beyond that, of the patriation of the constitution in 1982 without Quebec's approval. With the collapse of Meech, sovereignist sentiments rose dramatically in Quebec. They were channelled by the Bourassa government into the Bélanger-Campeau Commission and the Allaire Committee of the Liberal Party.[1] The results were a formal commitment by the Quebec Liberals to the recuperation by the province, or by all provinces, of a long list of areas of jurisdiction, and the passage by the Quebec National Assembly of Bill 150. This bill obliged the Quebec government to hold a referendum on Quebec sovereignty by 26 October 1992, and it was this "knife-at-the-throat" bargaining position that consistently drove what Ottawa called the "Canada round" of constitutional negotiations. (As noted, Guy Laforest describes this strategy, and analyzes Bourassa's efforts to play it out, in his contribution to this volume.)

But negotiations came slowly. First, the Spicer Commission reported in June 1991, after its consultations with a wide cross-section of Canadians through a variety of traditional and innovative mechanisms. The Commission, essentially, was meant to lance boils of post-Meech resentment across the country; however skewed was its sampling of opinion, its chairman was nevertheless drawn to report that "there is fury in the land against the prime minister."[2] In the meantime, the Beaudoin-Edwards Committee toiled in relative obscurity on the intricacies of constitutional amendment, driven by Meech's demonstration of the pitfalls of elitism, delay and unanimity. The Committee produced some long-range recommendations in favour of a regional amending formula rather like that agreed at Victoria in 1971, but provided no solutions to the immediate problem: that Quebec's demands for a new deal contain "Meech at a minimum" would leave the rigours of unanimous ratification still to be faced, and that while a national referendum might speed the process, it could not circumvent it.[3]

After a summer's labour under Joe Clark, who was appointed Minister Responsible for Constitutional Affairs in April 1991, Ottawa officials produced the proposals for constitutional change made public on 24 September. (See the Chronology by Anne Poels, at the back of this volume, for an account of this and other events in the year dated 1 July 1991 to 30 June 1992.) The proposals, which were supported by several background papers, formed the starting-point for all subsequent discussions.[4] Constitutionologists hurried to divine which proposals were bargaining feints to be dropped in order to mollify powerful players (e.g., protection of property rights in the Charter), which were designed to buy off potential opponents (e.g, strengthening the commitment to equalization and regional development), and which gaps would inevitably be filled (e.g., the absence of a proposal for Ontario's favoured social charter).[5] Such interpretations certainly overestimated the coherence of the federal government's position. After all, the proposals envisaged both a reformed Senate and a new Council of the Federation (for joint federal-provincial decision making and policy harmonization), and they also aimed to strengthen the economic union through both inhibiting interprovincial trade barriers and conferring more power upon Ottawa for positive economic management (an issue taken up by Douglas Purvis and André Raynauld in their commentary in this volume). From beginning to end, the proposals were the product of a committee, and, issuing from a groping government, they were truly up for negotiation. One striking manifestation of this was in the area of aboriginal rights, where Ottawa informed the native leadership that it was open to any arrangement that could garner the requisite provincial support.

The proposals were directed to another Senate-House of Commons Committee, chaired by Dorothy Dobbie, MP, and Senator Claude Castonguay. This Committee soon broke down in confusion and overload, perhaps inevitably, as it attempted to combine Spicer-like popular consultation with reception of the measured views of significant interests. By early November, Ottawa seemed dead in the water, facing crises of competence and legitimacy. Paramount was the need for public consultation — perhaps the strongest lesson learned by those involved in the Meech Lake drama. At the provincial level, various committees and commissions were reporting as ordained, and one of Quebec's committees, the Committee to Examine Matters Relating to the Accession of Quebec to Sovereignty, was hearing in a measured fashion from experts and organized interests. But Ottawa was stuck.

Then came the idea of consultative conferences. These would be organized by non-governmental agencies, and would be a hybrid of Parliamentary committee hearings and constitutional conventions. David Milne, in his chapter in this volume, analyzes thoroughly this quite new consultative device. Here it is important to note only that the conferences demonstrated organizational competence, solved an immense logistical problem by allowing many interests to feel consulted about the proposals in a very short time, and instilled new momentum into the process by capturing media attention and by showing both that modifications to the proposals were desirable and probable and that Canadians were serious, committed, and capable of compromise in order to reach consensus.

It was through the conferences, too, that Aboriginals were brought into full participation in the Canada round. Some principal players, notably Premier Bob Rae of Ontario, had pressed hard for the round to address the basic demands of native peoples. The Royal Commission on Aboriginal Peoples made an unusual intervention in February 1992 to support the demand that the constitution affirm the inherent right of self-government of Aboriginal Peoples.[6] Ovide Mercredi, Grand Chief of the Assembly of First Nations, made a dramatic appearance before the Quebec Committee, and shocked the province by arguing that natives had a stronger claim than Quebecers to the appelation "distinct society," and, ultimately, to self-determination.[7] Initially, most Aboriginals had refused to engage in the conferences. Soon after their success became apparent, however, the aboriginal organizations demanded, and got, a special conference devoted to aboriginal issues. Thanks to this, and to the drive of Premier Rae and the acquiescence of Joe Clark, the four major aboriginal groups were included in the intensive negotiations that began in March.

There was one more stage to come first. The Beaudoin-Dobbie Committee reported at the beginning of March, after its members had attended the conferences, heard other representations, and, most important, discussed the fine points of the proposals among themselves. This Committee played an important role in setting the framework for the "multilateral talks" that followed.[8] First, it massaged the proposals, eliminating the unpopular Council of the Federation, for example, torpedoing the proposed new head of federal power for positive economic management, and supporting both a social charter and the Aboriginals' inherent right of self-government. Second, it refined the discussion of several topics, presenting many alternatives for Senate reform and suggesting the mechanisms for negotiating shared administration in those areas of jurisdiction which Ottawa had offered to leave to the provinces. (See Katherine Swinton's contribution for an analysis of the evolution of proposals about the division of powers.) Finally, with some exceptions, it embodied a consensus among the major national political parties. Throughout the constitutional rounds of 1991-92, partisan considerations lurked in the background. Impossible for any actor to transcend entirely, and extremely pressing for some participants, the imperatives of party and of electoral contests to come were softened at the federal level through intense discussions in the Beaudoin-Dobbie Committee.

On these foundations were negotiations launched by Joe Clark and the premiers (excepting Premier Bourassa) on 12 March 1992. This process broke new ground, not least by including Aboriginal Peoples. Not since the unsuccessful conferences on aboriginal issues in the mid-1980s had aboriginal organizations been a part of intergovernmental negotiations. They had never before participated in discussions of the full range of constitutional issues; indeed their absence from the Meech Lake process, and the neglect of their agenda, helped stymie the Quebec round. Their determination was also made evident at Oka. And in 1992, powerful Ontario was their champion. One strategic objective of that province was to ensure aboriginal participation from the beginning, in the knowledge that substance would reflect process and that the Aboriginals' objectives would finally be achieved. On 12 March, Premier Rae insisted and Ottawa and the other Premiers agreed. The "multilateral round" would include territorial governments and representatives of the four aboriginal organizations.

Always the participants confronted several tough issues — Senate reform, aboriginal rights, the economic union, the division of powers, Quebec's distinct society clause and its demand for a veto over changes to central institutions, and the social charter. Always the talks were hampered by the continuing refusal of the Government of Quebec to participate in the negotiations until the substance of the Meech Lake Accord, once more, had been accepted by Ottawa and the other provinces. Always they were bedeviled by the prospect that unanimity would be essential for constitutional amendments that fully satisfied this requirement, including Quebec's guarantee of three of nine Supreme Court judges and a veto over changes to federal institutions.[9] Always they were slowed by the inclusion of the territorial governments and aboriginal organizations, along with ten provinces and the multitudinous advisors to all parties. And yet always they were driven forward by the accommodating Joe Clark, by Quebec's referendum deadline, and by the sense that the public would forgive no participant for failure.

The negotiators divided up the labour among four working groups. These corresponded roughly to matters covered in major sections of the final agreement: Unity and Diversity, Institutions, Roles and Responsibilities, and First Peoples. The working groups proceeded to tackle the issues with varying degrees of coherence and dispatch. Some managed to commission studies and background papers. Others bogged down in a welter of textual details and alternatives.[10] The process had boundaries that were fuzzy if not non-existent. Aboriginal groups, for instance, recruited as advisors the representatives of many organized interests that had been excluded from formal participation, such as the National Anti-Poverty Organization and the National Action Committee on the Status of Women. Many academics were involved. Federal and provincial opposition parties were informed and consulted. Some sessions involved over four hundred politicians, civil servants and advisors. Another interesting feature of the talks was their perambulatory nature: they were held in Ottawa, Halifax, Edmonton, Saint John, Vancouver, Montreal, and Toronto. Wherever they took place, however, the fax machines and telephones worked overtime as the webs of conflict and consensus extended across the country, including Quebec. Despite the complexity of the material and the tight deadlines, Joe Clark ensured that sessions never extended through the night and that discussions were never prematurely curtailed. At times it appeared as though the essence of the federal strategy was to keep the parties talking and to avoid souring the mood with a trumped-up atmosphere of pressure and crisis reminiscent of Meech Lake.

By late June, the deadlines had been extended several times. Ottawa had introduced legislation allowing for a national referendum that, while obviously not binding, might provide a way to by-pass recalcitrant premiers through going to the people and which, therefore, might spur agreement. But still there was no consensus about the definition and implementation of the Aboriginals' inherent right to self-government, the accession to provincehood of the territories, and the division of powers. The main stumbling-block, however, was Senate reform. Alberta, Newfoundland and Manitoba, with British Columbia and Saskatchewan, were holding out for a genuine Triple-E Senate (elected, equal and effective), against the opposition of Ontario and presumably Quebec. The conundrum was how to reconcile a reformed Senate with Quebec's veto over changes to central institutions. To obtain the veto, unanimity would be required, but unanimous agreement would not be forthcoming until the Triple-E coalition had obtained assent to a Senate reformed to its desires. If, under the orthodoxy of provincial equality, each province then obtained a veto over central institutions, it would be impossible to change a Senate that turned out to work to the detriment of all provinces but one.

Many schemes were advanced to break this deadlock. Some were far too intricate to be explained to the public; they reflected no principle other than the need to end a standoff generated by the negotiators themselves.[11] The prime minister, who had held himself aloof from the discussions, signalled at a first ministers' meeting at the end of June that the end was drawing near, and then absented himself in Munich at a G7 meeting. At the beginning of July, there was movement towards a plan that would compensate for equal provincial representation in the Senate by enlarging the representation of the more populous provinces in the House of Commons.[12] And then, on 6 July, Ontario moved. Bob Rae accepted the principle of an equal Senate, one that would be elected (by the single transferable vote system), and that would have varying degrees of effectiveness.[13] (In his commentary, Roger Gibbins provides an account of how the west won this concession. Thérèse Arseneau analyzes how the single-transferable-vote system might affect the roles that Triple-E advocates and others expected the new Senate to fulfil.) The 7 July ("Pearson") accord was announced with much mutual congratulation. According to one report, the turning point came when Premier Getty of Alberta argued that the premiers could not read Quebecers' minds, and so should proceed to reach an agreement that suited the players at the table.[14]

If this package represented the rest-of-Canada's offer to Quebec, however, it quickly became apparent that it was inadequate. In their commentary, Alain Gagnon and François Rocher show why, from the perspective of nationalist Quebecers. The equal Senate represented the symbolic end to the "deux nations" concept of Canada as an ethnic partnership. And Quebec won nothing in the area of powers: Ottawa merely offered to withdraw from fields it had illegitimately occupied using the spending power. After some collective hesitation (not shared by Lise Bissonnette, editor of *Le Devoir*, who published a one-word editorial comment: NON), these views prevailed in Quebec. It was the Senate that seemed particularly offensive, although this could only be symbolic, because the reformed Senate could harm Quebec only by stopping federal-government initiatives favourable to the province (which, in the nationalist view, are rare). But the matter of powers had become symbolic, too, since Allaire's famous list of 22 — however much moderate nationalism really is fuelled in the province, as Stéphane Dion explains in his commentary, by linguistic insecurity rather than the drive towards exercising more powers for socio-economic development.

But the agreement ran into opposition in the rest-of-Canada as well. Jack Granatstein shows why in his commentary, from the nationalist perspective that he articulates so vividly. Under the Pearson accord, the central government would be too reduced in power to act effectively in the social or economic realm. As well, the Canada clause continued to define an array of special, collective rights which would inevitably divide, if not clash. (Ironically, some of the interests involved — women, the disabled, and visible minorities — began in July to take issue with the package as its contours emerged to view.)

In the end, though, it was the concern not to isolate Quebec that kept the talks moving. Prime Minister Mulroney inserted himself into the process, and, even as recriminations flew about whether Joe Clark or Bob Rae or anyone had misunderstood Quebec's position on the Senate, negotiations resumed informally with Quebec. The problem was how to re-start the multilateral round, which some participants declared could not happen without Quebec present.[15] Re-starting also threatened the Triple-E coalition, the Aboriginals and the territorial governments, all of whom sought to preserve the gains won in the 7 July package. After three weeks of reflection and pre-negotiation, the talks did resume on 4 August. At this first session, only the premiers met with Prime Minister Mulroney. But they included Bourassa, who had decided that the essence of Meech had indeed been offered to Quebec. He was not in Ottawa to "negotiate," however, but to discuss a process that might lead to a settlement. Encouraged, Bourassa agreed to return for more talks on 10 August. And this was the crucial point. It would then have been unthinkable for the Quebec premier to leave the negotiations without signing onto a final deal. The willingness to compromise was evident. Canada had made its offer to Quebec, and now its premier was coming to bargain. What would he win?

The negotiations took place in Ottawa, with the prime minister in the chair. Still looming was the threat of unilateral federal action through a national referendum — though this was not a very compelling threat because, as sceptics noted, Mulroney was so unpopular that he could never carry a referendum against campaigning premiers and other interests were they shortchanged in an alternative final package. In long negotiations between 18 and 22 August, a compromise was reached, and it was nailed down in Charlottetown on 27-28 August. The critical changes involved some constraint on the Aboriginals' inherent right of self-government and a new arrangement about the Senate, where equality was to be counterbalanced by an enlarged House with more seats for the populous provinces.

THE CHARLOTTETOWN ACCORD

In broad outline, the Charlottetown accord owes much to the September proposals, the Beaudoin-Dobbie report, and the 7 July multilateral agreement. It has five major elements.[16]

UNITY AND DIVERSITY

- A Canada clause defines the country's "fundamental characteristics," recognizing the Aboriginals, Quebec's distinct society, official-language minorities, and the equality of the provinces, along with liberal values and racial, ethnic and gender equality.
- The policy objectives (non-justiciable) of the social and economic union are laid out: a mechanism to monitor them is to be established later.
- The commitment to equalization is strengthened.

INSTITUTIONS

- The Senate is to be elected, under federal legislation written to accommodate provincial preferences about direct or indirect elections and gender equality.
- The Senate is to be equal, with six Senators per province and one from each territory. There will also be guaranteed aboriginal representation.
- The Senate's effectiveness will depend on the type of legislation. It cannot impede revenue and expenditure measures for more than 30 days. It can defeat fundamental tax policy changes regarding natural resources by a simple majority. Measures affecting French language or culture can be defeated, either by majority vote or by a majority of francophone Senators. Defeat or amendment of any other bills would trigger a joint sitting of the House and Senate, where a simple majority would decide the issue. The Senate can initiate legislation.
- The House of Commons would be expanded from 295 to 337 seats, with Ontario and Quebec each receiving 18 more, British Columbia 4 and Alberta 2. (A special redistribution after the 1996 census would produce 3 more seats for B.C. and Ontario and 2 more for Alberta.)
- Quebec is guaranteed 25 percent of the seats in the House of Commons.

- Section 51 of the *Constitution Act, 1982*, embodying the formula for redistribution, will be amended and entrenched in the constitution. (Currently it is amendable by the federal government.)
- The Supreme Court will be entrenched in the constitution. Of the nine judges, three must have been admitted to the civil law bar of Quebec. Judges will be named from lists submitted by the provinces and territories.
- There will be provision for aboriginal representation in the Senate, and perhaps in the House of Commons; as well there may be provision for aboriginal representation before the Supreme Court on certain cases.

ROLES AND RESPONSIBILITIES

- The provinces can opt out of new shared-cost programs in areas of exclusive provincial jurisdiction, with compensation, if they undertake a program compatible with national objectives.
- Agreements concerning immigration must be negotiated at the request of any province.
- Provincial jurisdiction is recognized over labour market development and training (except for unemployment insurance and the development of national occupational standards), culture (except for national cultural institutions), forestry, mining, tourism, housing, recreation, and municipal and urban affairs. In these areas, Ottawa could be obliged to negotiate its partial or complete withdrawal (with compensation), or its continuing presence.
- Intergovernmental agreements made to implement these arrangements cannot be altered for five years.
- The federal powers of disallowance and reservation are eliminated; use of the federal declaratory power would require provincial consent.

FIRST PEOPLES

- A new section 35.1(1) of the *Constitution Act, 1982* will recognize that the Aboriginal Peoples of Canada have the inherent right of self-government within Canada.
- A contextual statement describes generally how the right can be exercised to safeguard and develop their societies.
- Recourse to the courts to define the right is delayed for five years.
- Both the *Charter of Rights and Freedoms* and the notwithstanding clause will apply to aboriginal governments.

- The federal and provincial governments are committed to negotiate agreements for the implementation of the right, including "issues of jurisdiction, lands and resources, and economic and fiscal arrangements."
- Negotiations are to be triggered by aboriginal request, and result in self-government agreements.
- A dispute-resolution mechanism including mediation and arbitration will be established.
- Aboriginal governments are committed to providing public services at levels comparable to those available to other Canadians in the vicinity.
- The federal and provincial governments are committed to "the principle" of providing aboriginal governments with fiscal and other resources to help them meet those commitments.
- Four First Ministers' Conferences on aboriginal constitutional matters will begin no later than 1996, and will be held every two years.
- Ottawa, Ontario, Manitoba, Saskatchewan, Alberta, British Columbia and the Métis National Council are to enter an accord governing negotiations with the Métis Nation.

AMENDING FORMULA

- Amendments to the Senate will require unanimous agreement. So will those relating to the principle of proportionate prepresentation of the provinces in the House of Commons.
- New provinces can be established by an Act of Parliament. They will have no effect on the amending formula, however, without the unanimous agreement of the provinces and the federal government.
- When any amendment transfers legislative powers from the provinces to the federal government, a province may opt out, and compensation will be paid.
- There must be aboriginal consent to future constitutional amendments that directly refer to Aboriginal Peoples.

By the time this volume appears, these components will have been much debated. Our purpose in the rest of this Overview is simply to draw out several themes about the Charlottetown accord and the process that produced it.

UNFINISHED BUSINESS

One striking feature of the accord is its unfinished quality. At the time of writing, no legal text is available — even covering vital issues such as the

Senate and aboriginal rights. It will be particularly difficult to draft and to reach agreement on the new provisions about representation in the House of Commons and the permanent formula under which future redistribution must occur to capture the changing demographic composition of the country. Also widespread are the areas in the accord that must be fleshed out by negotiations. Some are simply noted in the text: a mechanism for monitoring the social and economic union must be established, for example, and a process for registering aboriginal consent to these and other constitutional amendments must be hammered out. Beyond these are, of course, the negotiations to be conducted with the provinces about the new divisions of responsibilities in those areas of jurisdiction from which Ottawa can be forced to withdraw (or to maintain its presence). The final agreements in these areas will very likely resemble the agreements under regional development initiatives, and those are complex enough.

Other matters, like the rules of Senate elections, will require federal legislation. Still others are to be more fully defined through the negotiation of "political accords." The constitutional status of such agreements is quite unclear. It is not known, for instance, whether all or some of them would be governed by the new five-year protection mechanism for intergovernmental agreements. In any case, a great many areas are to be subject to political accords. The 28 August document refers to no fewer than 29 of them. Many concern aboriginal matters, including some very important ones, such as the framework that will "guide the process of self-government negotiations." Others cover vital matters such as the principles and commitments relating to the Canadian common market, the extension of intergovernmental-agreement protection to the Canada Assistance Plan, the harmonization of federal unemployment insurance with provincial employment and training functions, and provisions in intergovernmental agreements about serving the public in both official languages.

On some of these matters, a lot of work (and drafting) has already taken place. But considering them as a whole, it is clear that politicians and officials have much more to do before the final package is fully cast in legal language, and even more to accomplish before governments turn to delivering services rather than negotiating the terms under which they will be provided.

QUEBEC'S GAINS

The Canada round was effectively driven by Quebec's strategy of non-participation. The province was to await binding offers from the rest-of-Canada on renewed federalism. And, in broad outline, this is what did occur: the 7 July package can be regarded as the offer, and the 28 August package as the compromise between Quebec and the rest-of-Canada. The question, then, is what Quebec managed to get, and this can be approached by comparing the two texts.[17] Of course, this presumes that only Quebec's impact produced change in the initial deal; more seriously, it presumes that the initial offer was not tailored with Quebec in mind, which it certainly was. Nevertheless, a comparison is instructive.

1. There is now no mention of Quebec's distinct society in the *Charter of Rights and Freedoms*. Instead it is mentioned twice in the Canada clause: once in a definitional sense, and again as "the role of the legislature and Government of Quebec to preserve and promote the distinct society of Quebec is affirmed." In this position, these clauses help courts interpret the whole constitution rather than the Charter alone. However, insofar as language is concerned, the "commitment" (in the English text) or the "attachement" (in the French text) to the "vitality and development of official-language minorities throughout Canada" has also been moved to the Canada clause.

2. Section 121 (on interprovincial trade) will not be replaced by a tough provision preventing the erection of interprovincial trade barriers by law or practice.

3. In the Senate there is no commitment to election by proportional representation. There is to be scope for the indirect election of Senators by provincial legislatures.

4. The provisions that ordinary legislation could be rejected by 70 percent of the Senators and that a joint sitting could be forced by a 60 percent negative vote are eliminated. Instead, any defeat or amendment triggers a joint sitting. In that sitting, Senators comprise 15.54 percent of votes rather than 21.75 percent (excluding any future aboriginal Senators or MPs).

5. The House of Commons is expanded to 337 seats rather than 312. Quebec receives 18 extra members rather than 3. Of the combined Senate and House of Commons (excluding the extraordinary "GST Senators"), Quebec currently holds 24.8 percent of members. In the 7 July arrangement, Quebec would have had 21.7 percent of the members, but the Charlottetown accord gives it 24.8 percent (excluding Aboriginals).

6. Quebec is guaranteed 25 percent of the House of Commons seats in perpetuity.

7. The federal spending power is further constrained in the Charlottetown accord by the requirement that a "framework" be developed to guide its use in "all areas" of exclusive provincial jurisdiction. This would require that such spending contributes to national objectives, reduces overlap and duplication, does not distort provincial priorities, and ensures equality of the provinces, "taking into account their different

needs and circumstances" (a modifying clause that has been inserted into several provisions of the accord concerning the division of powers). This framework could become a protected intergovernmental agreement (for five years).

8. There is a new provision about telecommunications, and a commitment by Ottawa to negotiate agreements with the provincial governments "to coordinate and harmonize the procedures of their respective regulatory agencies in this field."

9. A new section in the provisions regarding First Peoples stipulates that neither the inherent right of self-government nor the commitment to negotiate its implementation, including fiscal and other resources such as land, shall create new aboriginal rights to land (or derogate from existing rights).

10. Another new provision holds that a law passed by an aboriginal government, or an assertion of its authority based on the inherent right provision "may not be inconsistent with those laws which are essential to the preservation of peace, order and good government in Canada." This circumscribes considerably the exercise of the right in cases where aboriginal measures spill over to the territory or jurisdiction of one and maybe two of the other orders of government.

11. Unanimity is required to change not only provisions about the Senate but also about provincial proportionate representation in the House of Commons, including Quebec's 25 percent guarantee.

12. While new provinces can be created by Act of Parliament (rather than under the 7/50 rule), following consultations at a First Ministers' Conference, they will have no role in the amending formula without the unanimous consent of all provinces and the federal government. (The 7 July agreement provided that the general amending formula would change with the admission of new provinces from two-thirds of the provinces with 50 percent of the population to three-quarters of the provinces with 50 percent of the population.) As well, any increase in territorial representation in the Senate upon accession to provincehood also would require unanimous consent.

In summary, between 7 July and 28 August the distinct society clause has gained more precedence, the economic union provisions are weakened, Quebec's part of an enlarged House of Commons is guaranteed and the threat from an equal Senate is reduced, the spending power is further constrained, the likely impact of the aboriginal inherent right is lessened, and the veto over changes to national institutions (and the impact upon them of new provinces) is secured. Premier Bourassa undoubtedly had a major impact on the Charlottetown accord. In a very short time, Quebec received its offer, and came to the table to negotiate a new, pan-Canadian compromise. Whether Bourassa's impact was large enough to satisfy Quebecers, or too large for the comfort of the rest of the country, will soon be decided in the national referendum.

ABORIGINAL PEOPLE AND THE CONSTITUTION

A remarkable feature of the Canada round has been the inclusion of Aboriginal Peoples. None of the chapters in this year's volume addresses these issues at length, so it is important to review the main features of this part of the constitutional process and proposals.

The agreement that emerged in the summer of 1992 represents an impressive compromise between the federal and provincial governments and the aboriginal organizations. The most significant achievement may be the apparent level of mutual understanding and trust reached among the parties. While the accord's aboriginal elements are sweeping, it does leave to the future the main task — negotiating detailed self-government agreements appropriate to the particular circumstances of individual First Nations. Governments have committed themselves to negotiate, and Aboriginal Peoples have accepted that commitment as credible. It is unlikely this result could have occurred had not all parties been involved in the long multilateral process.

This is not to deny the substance of what has already been achieved. One by one the major constitutional issues affecting Aboriginals have been resolved. The centrepiece of it all, of course, is unanimous recognition that "the Aboriginal Peoples of Canada have the inherent right of self-government within Canada." The last two words may appear too constraining to the more fundamentalist sovereignists in the aboriginal communities, but the formulation still recognizes straightforwardly that the First Nations' basic right to govern themselves has always existed and is neither created by nor bestowed upon them by existing governments. Thus the renewed constitution truly enshrines a "third order" of government. It achieves what the frustrating negotiations of 1984-87 did not.

The right of self-government is not defined, nor is it contingent on negotiations. These were two big stumbling blocks to agreement in the past. Instead the accord will include a "contextual statement," a broadly worded description of aspects of self-government. This has some potential to circumscribe the right, because the courts would take it into account in interpreting self-government, (after a delay of five years), and also in determining whether negotiations had been conducted in good faith. But the right is very open-ended, and it drives future negotiations. The 28 August accord also includes provisions to the effect that the inherent right does not confer new rights to land and that aboriginal jurisdiction is subject to laws essential for the "peace, order and good government" of Canada. A few months ago these could be seen as potential deal-breakers, as was the proposal to have the *Charter of Rights and Freedoms* apply to aboriginal governments. Their inclusion as part of the overall compromise shows the accord was a victory for moderates within the First Nations as well in the rest-of-Canada.[18]

Despite these breakthroughs, much remains to be done. Many sections of the Charlottetown accord refer to political accords that have not as yet been released for public scrutiny. These will elaborate the commitment to negotiate, and will cover many aspects of implementation, financing and dispute resolution. So negotiations will continue throughout 1992. And — including conferences at the first ministers' level until at least 2002 — they will continue until every First Nation has reached a constitutionally entrenched self-government agreement with its partners in the federation. This will take a long time, but time is needed to make room for the third order of government. And it is also essential to allow consensus about priorities to take shape with the First Nations. There is a great deal in the Charlottetown accord for them to digest.

Given the political divisions (some of which have been imposed from without) and the conflicting interests among aboriginal groups, their unity throughout the negotiations has been impressive. This is not to say that either the process or the result has obtained unanimous support from all Aboriginals. Women's organizations have challenged their exclusion from the negotiations, and too late in the day for practical effect they won a victory in the Federal Court of Appeal.[19] Nor is it clear how the leadership of the rather loose coalitions which are the four national aboriginal organizations will organize the ratification of the accord in their communities. Some First Nations may refuse in the end to accept the accord, and this would create an interesting constitutional dilemma. Other Aboriginals may well ask what are the implications of the inherent right for the benefits they now receive from Canadian governments.

Other Canadians may be apprehensive about the recognition of a third order of government. No one is certain what self-government will cost or how existing interests will be affected by the negotiations to come. The fact that costs are deferred should make the package more readily accepted; for the basic principle of self-government there is probably broad, if uninformed, public support. Since the accord addresses the more troubling issues, like the application of the Charter and territorial concerns, it seems unlikely that opponents of the accord will focus on its First Nations' provisions. This has two implications. Even if the package as a whole is rejected, the aboriginal component could be resurrected intact at a later date (assuming anything constitutional could be retrieved later). Second, by reaching an historic compromise with the First Nations, the other governments have improved the chances for ratification, for they have gained in the campaign for constitutional renewal new allies who are interesting, legitimate, well organized, and politically imaginative.

PARTICIPATION IN THE CANADA ROUND

Another important aspect of the year's negotiations has been public participation in constitutional renewal. Since the battle over patriation and the Charter in 1981, it has been apparent that organized interests — groups representing categories of citizens — perceive that they have a lot at stake in constitutional matters. Supreme Court rulings in Charter cases have confirmed the significance of constitutional texts that constrain and guide the policies that governments can adopt towards these groups. These organized interests have not been absent from the debates of this year.

As Milne shows, the federal government took enormous efforts to involve them fairly in the Renewal of Canada conferences. They have also been engaged by some provinces and aboriginal groups in the multilateral talks. At the same time, as Spicer's Citizens' Forum showed and as negotiators have recognized throughout the year, ordinary Canadians watch constitutional debate with an ominous blend of boredom and distrust. The current of populism most clearly represented by the Reform Party contains a profound scepticism about the motives of politicians, and a strong demand for direct citizen involvement in government. To the extent that this demand is shared, it may mark a transition in Canadian thinking towards Lockean concepts of community, but its practical importance is to make a popular ratification of the 28 August agreement highly desirable.[20] In effect, the intricate machinations of executive federalism have been tolerated by a (bored and distracted) populace only in the expectation that the same (distrustful) populace will be able to pronounce on the final results of their leaders' labours.

Finally, those traditional mechanisms of participation (the political parties) have been relatively muted throughout the year. As John Richards shows in the case of the NDP, and as is undoubtedly true also in the case of the Liberals, this is caused by internal divisions about ideology and by the regionalized nature of each major party. The result, even within most provinces, has been that political leaders have colluded across party lines, and will continue to collude, to support the constitutional renewal package. Quebec, of course, provides the strong exception.

All these participatory elements will play out in the referendum campaign. All citizens will be able to pronounce on the same question on the same day: Canadians will have the chance to reconstitute their political community. But the rules governing the referendum will have different consequences in Quebec and the rest-of-Canada. In Quebec, provincial legislation forces all members of each side to coordinate their efforts within a single umbrella organization, which is firmly under the control of the opposing parties. This makes it difficult for members to defect. It also, however, inevitably divides the whole society into two opposing camps. In the rest of the country, there are no overarching umbrella organizations, but a multiplicity of organizations. Hence interest groups or coalitions of them may conduct their own campaigns, or their memberships may fragment to become involved in party or regional organizations. At the same time, the major parties are not forced to take an embarrassingly visible monopoly position within a single organization; nor must their members coordinate with those of other parties. Finally, the popular consultation will enable governments to short-circuit much of the normal public participation associated with constitutional amendment. If the Charlottetown accord is approved across the country, there will be little need or obligation to consult with organized interests about a "done deal." Ratification by Parliament and the provincial legislatures should be rapid.

THE FUTURE

Beyond the preoccupations of the Canada round, what forces will continue to affect the workings of the Canadian federation? One, undoubtedly, is globalization, the amorphous phenomenon of greater worldwide integration through accelerating flows of information, capital, technology, goods and services, and people. States are increasingly exposed to these forces. Andrew Cooper's article on the GATT is eloquent testimony to how difficult it is for Canadians to frame a coherent response to international forces. Another, concomitant trend is the universal drive towards autonomy, the manifestations of which are vividly described by Peter Clancy in the case of Canada's north, at the same time as the desirability of this evolution is unquestioned. Some analysts have linked these dual trends into an argument that the nation-state itself is tending towards desuetude, as functions of economic management are transferred upwards to the international level, and citizens in local communities are demanding more political control over the factors affecting the quality of their lives.[21] Whether this view holds in the Canadian case is not yet evident. Whether or not Canadians affirm their agreement to constitutional reform, they seem to believe that their central government has a function and a future. At the same time, the flexibility built into the new package may allow more scope for accommodating the distribution of responsibilities to both centralizing and decentralizing forces.

Two other considerations seem set to play a major role in the evolution of the federation. Had the Canada round not so dominated the year's events, each would have been treated in depth in this collection. One is the crisis in federal-provincial-municipal fiscal relations. At all levels governments are having to deploy shrinking resources to meet rising needs. The recession, of course, has affected the revenue side of every government's balance sheet, at the same time as demands for income support and many other services have risen. As well, Ottawa's efforts to bring its deficit under control have included reductions in transfers to the provinces, and some restrictions in program spending. In reaction to the "off-loading" of program and financial responsibilities, the provinces have had to borrow, to raise taxes, and to cut programs (including transfers to municipalities and health and education authorities). The tensions produced have been very great. Astoundingly, they have not much affected the content of the constitutional package or the tenor of the year's negotiations. But with fundamental questions settled, and elections imminent in several jurisdictions, these very contentious matters will certainly re-surface.

The other dossier that will occupy much intergovernmental attention is the environment. As a glance at the Chronology will show, conflicts over the environmental impact of public and private developments have become frequent and bitter. At issue is not only the impact of such developments beyond the borders of provincial authorities, but also their extra-jurisdictional effects, when they impinge upon areas of federal responsibility. Often, local groups prevail upon Ottawa to block provincially sanctioned projects and if Ottawa chooses not to act politically, these groups have used the courts to force its hand. These issues have affected the constitutional talks, and *vice-versa*. Ottawa has chosen not to intervene in western dam projects, while Quebec has developed considerable ill-will towards both Aboriginals, for helping delay the Great Whale project, and the federal government, for proceeding with a bill (C-13) that extends its power to conduct environmental hearings — a bill denounced as "totalitarianism" by Quebec's minister of the environment.[22] The environmental issue offers new opportunities for citizens' control over their living conditions; it also promises to generate much conflict between the priorities of the different orders of government.

Of course, it is possible that these deeper background issues will be pushed off centre stage once more in the year to come by immediate constitutional concerns. Canadians face a momentous choice in 1992 — to renew their federation according to the terms worked out by political and other leaders over the past two years, or to reject the Charlottetown accord. This is not the place to speculate about the consequences of a total or partial rejection of the constitutional package. But it is clear that the issue is not yet settled. As the summer swings past Labour Day into the autumn of 1992, Canadians, as ever, remain ambivalent about their community and the constitution that purports to enshrine it.

NOTES

1.   These events are described in various contributions to Douglas M. Brown (ed.), *Canada: The State of the Federation 1991* (Kingston: Institute of Intergovernmental Relations, 1991).

2. Canada, Citizens' Forum on Canada's Future, *Report to the People and Government of Canada*, (Ottawa: Supply and Services, 1991), pp. 6-7.

3. Canada, Special Joint Committee of the Senate and the House of Commons, *The Process for Amending the Constitution of Canada* (Ottawa: Senate and House of Commons, 1991).

4. Canada, *Shaping Canada's Future Together: Proposals*, (Ottawa: Minister of Supply and Services Canada, 1991). See also: Canada, *Responsive Institutions for a Modern Canada, Canadian Federalism and Economic Union — Partnership for Prosperity*; *Shared Values — the Canadian Identity, The History of Canada's Constitutional Development*; *Aboriginal Peoples, Self-Government, and Constitutional Reform*; Dwight Herperger, *Distribution of Powers and Functions in Federal Systems*; and Peter M. Leslie, *The European Community — A Political Model for Canada?* (Ottawa: Minister of Supply and Services Canada, 1991).

5. See, for example, Douglas Brown, Robert Young and Dwight Herperger (eds.), *Constitutional Commentaries: An Assessment of the 1991 Federal Proposals* (Kingston: Institute of Intergovernmental Relations, 1992).

6. Canada, Royal Commission on Aboriginal Peoples, *The Right of Aboriginal Self-Government and the Constitution: A Commentary*, 13 February 1992.

7. See *The Globe and Mail*, 12 February 1992, p. A-4.

8. Canada, Senate and House of Commons, *Report of the Special Joint Committee on a Renewed Canada*, 28 February 1992.

9. Ottawa had carefully framed the September proposals so that they could be accomplished under the 7/50 provisions of sections 38 and 42 of the *Constitution Act, 1982*, but Quebec had made it clear long before March that Meech was the "bottom-line starting-point," and so unanimity would be required on some matters.

10. See, for example, Continuing Committee on the Constitution, Group III [First Peoples], "Rolling Draft" fourth revision, 9 June 1992.

11. For example, at least one proposal was to have equal numbers of Senators from each province, but with their votes weighted according to the population of the provinces they represented.

12. *The Globe and Mail*, 4 July 1992.

13. Toronto *Star*, 9 July 1992, p. A-1. The Senate as envisaged could not initiate legislation. It could defeat legislation about the taxation of natural resources by a simple majority, and could defeat any legislation (except supply measures) by a 70 percent vote. Bills negatived by a vote of 60 percent to 70 percent of the Senate would be decided by a special joint sitting of the Senate and an enlarged House of Commons where a simple majority would prevail.

14. *The Globe and Mail*, 9 July 1992, pp. A-1, A-6.

15. *The Globe and Mail*, 15 July 1992, p. A-4.

16. The source is the text as printed in *The Globe and Mail*, 1 September 1992, p. A-1, with refinements reported in the *The Globe and Mail*, 5 September 1992, p. A-4. Our analysis is based on the text released in *The Globe and Mail*. Subsequently, the government participants released the document *Consensus Report on the Constitution*, Charlottetown, 28 August 1992, Final text.

17. The Charlottetown accord is taken from Ibid.; the July package is found in *Status Report — The Multilateral Meetings on the Constitution*, 16 July 1992, Final.

18. For an illustration of the range of positions taken by various aboriginal leaders and of the potential clash between these and the concerns of Quebec, the other provinces, and "Charter Canadians," see the summary of discussions and selected papers from a conference held in February 1992, in Douglas Brown (ed.), *Aborginal Governments and Power Sharing in Canada* (Kingston: Institute of Intergovernmental Relations, 1992).

19. This decision will be scrutinized closely by all potential participants in constitutional negotiations. The legal reference is *Native Women's Association of Canada v. Canada* (F.C.A.), 20 August 1992; [1992] F.C.J. No. 715.

20. See Peter H. Russell, *Constitutional Odyssey: Can Canadians Become a Sovereign People?* (Toronto: University of Toronto Press, 1992).

21. See Thomas J. Courchene, "Global Competitiveness and the Canadian Federation," in his *Rearrangements: The Courchene Papers* (Oakville: Mosaic Press, 1992), pp. 108-44.

22. *The Globe and Mail*, 18 March 1992, p. A-4.

II

The "Canada Round"

2

Innovative Constitutional Processes: Renewal of Canada Conferences, January–March 1992

David Milne

Le présent chapitre porte sur la série des six conférences constitutionnelles qui eurent lieu dans autant de villes canadiennes de janvier à mars 1992. Ces rencontres furent organisées dans le but d'amener le public canadien à réagir formellement aux propositions constitutionnelles déposées par le gouvernement fédéral en septembre 1991. L'organisation de ces conférences fut confiée à cinq instituts indépendants qui en profitèrent pour modifier, de façon substantielle, le profil de la représentation lors de ces réunions; on procéda, notamment, à une sélection au hasard des participants, et on fit en sorte de recruter les personnes présentes parmi une gamme exceptionnellement large de groupes d'intérêts. Les conférences se sont avérées être de puissants outils pour évaluer les propositions fédérales: de fait, plusieurs des recommandations gouvernementales furent rejetées et de toutes nouvelles propositions suggérées. Ces colloques ont conforté chez le public la conviction qu'il était nécessaire de réaliser une réforme constitutionnelle; de plus, les rencontres en question auront contribué aussi à freiner le cynisme du public, amenant celui-ci à une plus grande ouverture d'esprit. La démocratisation du processus constitutionnel canadien semble assez bien engagée; à preuve, la capacité des participants à délibérer autour de la constitution aura été bien démontrée lors de ces rencontres, de même que leur aptitude à pouvoir dégager des consensus (sauf pour la rédaction détaillée des recommandations constitutionnelles). Les diverses conférences offrent aussi des enseignements — positifs et négatifs — pour la mise sur pied, dans l'avenir, de rencontres similaires: on songe ici à l'importance d'éviter que de tels forums puissent être éventuellement contrôlés par des groupes d'intérêts bien organisés. La marge existant entre le contenu de l'entente constitutionnelle négociée et la teneur des échanges dans le cadre de ces conférences pourrait bien créer, toutefois, certaines difficultés pendant et après le processus de ratification de ladite entente.

Historians may one day write that the six publicly televised conferences of 1992 marked a critical turning point away from Canada's traditional model of constitution making through executive federalism towards broader public involvement in constitutional change. This transformation came about not only because Canadians had been gradually prepared over the previous dozen years to think and act as constitutional actors, but also because of the inability of governmental elites to work successfully the traditional machinery of constitutional consultation. Hence, governmental failures opened the door for the public to become directly involved in constitutional discussions in a way unthinkable in an earlier time. The public conferences, hastily erected to help save a narrow elite-driven constitutional consultation process that was in shambles, are splendid testaments to these themes.

It is fair to say, however, that governments did not at first warmly welcome these changes; nor did they expect much from them. The evidence suggests that they turned to public participation only as a last resort when the traditional machinery under their control failed to operate properly. To the practitioners of the art of executive federalism, only desperation could warrant resort to such risky ventures where the federal government would have to yield much control over its constitutional agenda *and* process. Yet, with a breakdown in the elite-driven system, those risks had to be assumed if any progress were to be made. In the end, the success of the public conferences in retrieving the constitutional process came as a considerable surprise to governmental actors, and helped compensate for some of the damage that the conferences inflicted upon the federal constitutional package. For the conferences made a significant contribution to the reshaping of the federal constitutional package, and ultimately to the debate over ratification. In fact, these conferences, begun as mere hasty elite afterthoughts yet portentous of much wider democratic change, pointed the way towards the full-scale participation of Canadians in deciding, through referenda, their constitutional future.

SAVING THE PROCESS:
THE HASTY BIRTH OF THE PUBLIC CONFERENCES

It was Arthur Kroeger, the experienced deputy minister in Employment and Immigration "invited" to assume responsibility for the proposed conferences, who first offered a bemused and understated retrospective on the origins of the conferences in a speech to the Institute of Public Administration of Canada.[1]

> On November 14 of last year, while attending a meeting in Toronto, I was called out to take a telephone call from Paul Tellier, the Secretary to the Cabinet. He informed me that it had been decided to hold a series of conferences on the Constitution and that he was calling to "invite" me (thus do we preserve civilities in the federal Public Service) to assume responsibility for this undertaking.

He went on in a suitably tactful vein:

> In September of 1991 the federal government made public a set of 28 proposals for constitutional revision. Its intention was that these proposals should be subjected to extensive public scrutiny, and for this purpose a Special Joint Committee of Parliament had been established. It was to hold hearings across the country and submit a report by February 28. The government would then make decisions about constitutional changes, taking into account the Committee's findings.
>
> The difficulties experienced by the Committee in its initial set of hearings in Prince Edward Island, Ontario, and Manitoba were widely reported in the media [prior to the Committee's return] from Manitoba in deadlock, and there was considerable doubt that the necessary agreements could be reached among the three parties to permit a resumption of its hearings.
>
> The government was therefore faced with a major problem. It needed to get a response from the public concerning its proposals, and the clock was running. The approach decided upon by the Prime Minister and the Minister of Constitutional Affairs, Mr. Clark, was that a series of public conferences should be organized to examine the government's proposals, with each conference being assigned a specific cluster of subjects. In the worst case, if the Committee remained deadlocked, the conferences would provide the government with some kind of reading of public attitudes; in the event that the negotiations among the parties permitted the Committee to resume its hearings, (which of course is how things turned out) the conferences could give the Committee some further insights into public attitudes.

This matter-of-fact account underplays significantly the extent to which the federal government's constitutional plans were imperilled by the Committee's carnival of blunders. After an ill-prepared plunge into "townhall" meetings in several provinces that seemed to offer either empty halls or ready platforms for redneck comments damaging to national unity, after consequent demands for the resignation of co-chairperson Ms Dobbie, and the departure of her counterpart, respected Quebec Senator Claude Castonguay, the Parliamentary Committee had literally sputtered to a complete stop. At that stage, the government needed to reassert its control over the constitutional process, or face irreparable damage to the constitutional package and its own reputation. Politically, the question was not simply one of finding some other vehicle for testing public attitudes, but rather of finding a means of restoring public confidence in the constitutional process itself.

As Kroeger acknowledged, the level of public suspicion and cynicism before the government's unfolding constitutional fiasco was considerable. On the one hand, there was the danger of ongoing "organizational failures or logistic break-downs," that could prove "fatal" given the exhaustion of "public tolerance after the well-publicized difficulties of the Spicer Commission and the Parliamentary Committee."[2] These dangers, noted Kroeger, were especially relevant given the tight time frame:

First, because of the February 28 deadline given to the Parliamentary Committee, there wasn't a lot of time: just nine weeks, as matters turned out, before the first conference opened in Halifax on January 17, with the next four taking place on successive weekends thereafter. Our schedule also meant that, from mid-January on, the execution of each conference would have to proceed in parallel with preparations for those which were to follow. At a maximum, we would have four clear days from the time each conference ended on a Sunday afternoon in one city until the next one would have to begin in another.

On the other hand, public exasperation with elite manipulation of the constitutional process, a deeply imprinted legacy from the failed Meech Lake Accord, was an everpresent threat to the government's revived attempts at constitutional reform. These sentiments were not likely to be mollified by the mere announcement of public constitutional conferences, as the many statements of suspicious and disgruntled commentators confirmed at the time.

Hence, there was evidence from the start of *competition* between the need for tight organizational control to avoid a repeat of logistic breakdowns on the one hand, and the need for public confidence in the independence of the consultation process on the other. While Kroeger's account acknowledges the government's willingness to reassure the public by assigning responsibility for the conferences to "credible independent organizations," it does not tell us that this policy choice actually came at the insistence of the institutes themselves and not as part of the original federal thinking. In fact, the original federal plan had been built on the primacy of the other need — to maintain control to avoid organizational messups — by assigning responsibility for each conference to a federal deputy minister. This plan went flatly against the preconditions considered essential by the independent institutes themselves.

The heads of the institutes invited to organize the conferences (the Atlantic Provinces Economic Council, the Canada West Foundation, the C.D. Howe Institute, the Niagara Institute, and the Institute for Research on Public Policy) had already caucused shortly after the announcement of the conferences by Constitutional Affairs Minister, Joe Clark. Most, if not all, had decided, prior to their first official meeting with federal officials, that their participation in the proposed constitutional conferences would depend on maintaining their own independence and control over the "organization, management, and final report of the Conferences," including the manner in which chairpersons, experts, and public would be selected. Since these were the only terms upon which the government could expect cooperation from these or other like-minded independent institutes, there was no alternative but to "swallow hard" and shelve the Ottawa-controlled plan. It was only later, after the success of the conferences both in avoiding organizational foulups *and* in winning public confidence in their genuine independence, that the political advantages of the original position taken by the institutes became apparent.

The government commitment to a genuinely open and meaningful process, however, entailed more than a formal ceding of control over the operation of the conferences to the institutes; it also meant accepting a very generous set of conference guidelines and objectives. These were:

1. to facilitate consultation among elected officials, constitutional experts, and the public on the 28 proposals for constitutional change contained in the Government of Canada's *Shaping Canada's Future Together*;
2. to increase public understanding of the proposals and/or alternative proposals for constitutional change;
3. to stimulate specific commentary on the viability of the specific proposals, and to identify viable alternatives;
4. to identify areas of broad agreement on principles, and to discuss possible tradeoffs;
5. to involve a broad and balanced cross-section of Canadians which reflect the make-up of the country.[3]

With this broad mandate, the conferences were given the latitude they needed to do serious work on the proposed constitutional package — to approve, delete, add and revise as they saw fit. These relatively unrestricted debating and recommending powers were in practice freer and wider than those of any legislative committee, necessarily entangled in party loyalties. Moreover, given their wide constitutive basis and high visibility, the conferences could be expected to command more public interest and attention than would any legislative hearing process. In accepting these conditions, the government assumed a risk that, in other circumstances it would probably have been unwilling to assume. Having done so, however, the question then became: how to make work credible conferences involving a "a broad and balanced cross-section of Canadians?"

REPRESENTATIVENESS

The conference planners took a giant stride towards achieving public confidence in that goal with their extraordinary decision to invite randomly selected participants (RSPs) to the constitutional conferences. But here again, this kind of daring initiative was very far from federal thinking at the outset. Government planners' first thoughts on how to represent the public spanned a more exclusive and apparently practical range of alternatives: drawing from recipients of the Order of Canada; from among high achievers in Canadian society; from attenders of recent constitutional conferences; or from a list of names submitted by provincial premiers. It was David Elton, President of the Canada West Foundation, who conceived and argued for the idea of taking out advertisements to invite Canadians from all walks of life to participate in a constitutional conference of their choice; his idea was based on the success with the Canadian Olympic Torch program and with the American system for admitting landed immigrants. Elton had hoped that up to 50 percent of the participants to the conferences could be selected in this fashion, though, with 64 ex officio delegates already committed, that turned out to be ambitious; the actual number of RSPs varied from 8 to 23 percent of total delegates from one conference to another. To ensure that such participants had a "demonstrated interest in, and some knowledge of constitutional matters, and a significant record of service to their communities," these so-called "ordinary Canadians" were asked to prepare a brief outline of their interests in constitutional matters. From there it was up to the institutes to review (and to screen out where appropriate) a "representative" blend of these delegates from the Canadian public. After facing considerable scepticism and questioning in approximately two weeks of negotiations, this modified version of Elton's plan was finally accepted by the leaders of the other institutes and by the government. As it turned out, no element in the planning of the conferences was more important in reviving public confidence in the independence of the process and interest in constitutional reform itself.

In addition to the group of randomly selected participants, there were also leaders and representatives from other organizations and interest groups invited to attend the conferences. Kroeger explains the process that was used to generate these names:

> I signed letters on behalf of the Institutes to nearly 100 organizations representing groups such as visible minorities, the disabled, senior citizens, the fishing industry, students, the arts, women, aboriginal people, the legal profession, and many others, requesting they let us have the names of individuals who might be invited. We also received a large number of unsolicited suggestions. In all, some 1700 names were accumulated in our computer bank, which was then placed at the disposal of the institutes.

These, too, were a critical part of the "representation" of the public at the constitutional conferences and considerable effort was expended on trying to have this group reflect the makeup of the country. Descriptors in participant lists from one conference to another indicate the wide range of representative interests planners sought to have reflected in conference attendants: Aboriginals, youth, students, women, multicultural community, disabled, seniors, business, labour, environment, sports, agriculture, fisheries, mining, real estate, financial, religion, academia, education, arts and cultural community, rights groups, broadcasting, professional, research institutes, health, consumer representatives, voluntary sector, and the like. This kind of smorgasbord of interests virtually guaranteed that on many significant constitutional issues, there would be a clash of opinions and orientations. While many doubted how accurately these representatives could reflect their members in discussion of constitutional proposals that had usually not been debated in their organizations, there was nonetheless little reluctance by most interest group leaders to exploit the opportunity to speak to the Canadian people on live television about their concerns and preoccupations. This, too, made for lively debate.

Under the terms of agreement with the institutes, each of the conferences began with an automatic complement of 64 ex officio participants comprised as follows:

- 30 members of the Joint Parliamentary Committee
- 6 participants from federal party caucuses (two selected by each of the caucuses of the three federal political parties with Parliamentary status)
- 24 participants named by premiers or heads of government (two individuals from each province and territory)
- 4 participants, each selected by one of the four national aboriginal organizations.

With total participants ranging from 217 to 256 at any one conference, this decision meant that this largely "government" contingent would always constitute from 25 to 30 percent of total conference participants. Since it was a key objective of the conferences to make an impact on elected people in the parties, on the recommendations of the Joint Committee and ultimately on provincial governments, this ex officio representation appeared to be a logical bridge to the "real world of politics." All participants realized that, following public discussions and reports, it would be governments that would be required to negotiate behind closed doors a final constitutional package, and legislative assemblies to pass any constitutional amendments that might win broad public support.

The final group, usually averaging approximately half of the membership of the government contingent, were specialists or constitutional experts. Many of these participants provided expertise to workshop discussions, served as workshop chairpersons, or in other official capacities. In the Calgary conference, for example, specialists accounted for approximately 14 percent of total conference participants. Since extensive discussion in smaller workshop sessions was seen to be at the very heart of the success of the conferences, these workshop sessions, interspersed with plenary sessions, occupied most of the conference timetable. Each of the institutes selected specialists for this task, trying here as in the other categories, to achieve "balance" in linguistic, regional, gender and other representative dimensions.

In fact, the institutes and Kroeger's constitutional secretariat, which had been swiftly assembled to assist them, faced a daunting task of building "representative" conferences.[4] Although countless hours were spent on this challenge, trying to make conference representation approximate a template of Canada's diversity from Statistics Canada, getting the requisite data on each participant's characteristics was invariably a delicate and often impossible task. Moreover, the earlier decision to leave the institutes in charge meant that there would be considerable variation in representation from one conference to another. Certainly, as Table 2.1 shows, there was no agreement, for example, among the institutes about what ratio of randomly selected participants would apply, nor of most other indicators. Some institutes, like the Canada West Foundation, embraced the idea so that fully 22 percent of their participants were selected in this fashion, while others, such as the Niagara Institute in Toronto, chose a mere 8 percent in this fashion. Clearly, a total gender imbalance of about two to one in favour of males also existed, with only the Vancouver meeting deciding to choose a majority of women among non-ex officio members; there was also a sizeable underrepresentation of francophones at only 20 percent of total conference participants. Given the number of those declining invitations especially from Quebec, it was not easy for planners to make reality conform to the template.

Table 2.1

Participant Attendance Breakdown for Five Conferences:
Randomly Selected Participants, English-French Ratio, Gender Division

Conference	Total Numbers of Participants	Numbers of RSPs	Numbers of Anglophone/ Francophone/ Other	Numbers of Male-Female
Halifax	221	41	187/33/1	150/71
Calgary	256	56	212/40/4	176/80
Montreal	232	30	175/57	170/62
Toronto	246	19	189/54/3	166/80
Vancouver	217	49	162/50/5	132/85
TOTAL	1172	195	925/234/13	794/378

Source: Compiled by author from official summaries of invitation lists.

Moreover, the degree of variation in regional attendance is rather startling. To judge from the figures in Table 2.2, it seems doubtful that effective comprehensive guidelines were in place among the institutes concerning territorial representation. While the number of provinces that had to be represented by a respectable minimum dictated numbers of participants from both the Atlantic and western provinces (and the north) much higher than could possibly be justified by population, this rationale still does not explain the marked predominance of participants from western Canada. In total conference participation, for example, the west outstripped all other regions in attendance, enjoying almost 100 more delegates than Ontario. Some of this overrepresentation was the consequence of the prior decision to hold two of the five conferences in the west, and of the different system of representation of province and territory chosen by the Calgary West Foundation.[5] Note the total western representation at the Calgary conference that quite handsomely outstrips that of Ontario and Quebec combined; indeed, the Atlantic and western regions alone account for *more than twice* the numbers of Ontario and Quebec. These regional figures certainly depart sharply from Canadian population indicators, underplaying significantly Ontario's representation. On territorially sensitive constitutional subjects, such as Senate reform, these patterns could doubtless effect conference outcomes. While representation based on strict faithfulness to Canada's population would scarcely have been appropriate, the absence of credible, comprehensive guidelines on territorial representation among the institutes certainly contributed to the anomalies seen in Table 2.2.

Table 2.2
Participant Attendance Breakdown by Province/Region

Conference	Atlantic	Quebec	Ontario	West	North	Total
Halifax	51	44	54	62	10	221
Calgary	58	40	38	106	14	256
Montreal	39	60	63	62	8	232
Toronto	37	59	72	67	11	246
Vancouver	35	52	46	76	8	217
TOTAL	220	255	273	373	51	1172

Source: Compiled by author from official summaries of invitation lists.

It was clear from the outset that the proceedings would be covered live by Newsworld, and arrangements were being made to accommodate the large number of other media that were expected to attend. In the end, approximately 250 to 350 journalists from the print and electronic media followed the conferences and reported extensively upon them. The conferences had considerable direct and total "reach," especially over live national television. Indeed, the average reach for each of the five weekend conferences on Newsworld was about one million viewers, with the first in Halifax drawing about 650,000 and the Toronto conference approximating 1.3 million.[6] Moreover, the conferences were invariably featured in the national news on both CBC and CTV, and other public affairs programs, reaching many more millions of Canadians. No doubt the novelty of this democratic constitutional experiment appealed to many Canadians, as they saw many so-called "ordinary Canadians" debate the issues with interest group leaders, politicians and experts. But just as interesting was the rostrum of distinguished Canadians who were successfully drawn into leadership of the conferences by the institutes as rapporteurs, chairpersons, and speakers. Of all the critical roles for television, however, none was more important than the conference co-chairpersons who had to synthesize and report on the thoughts of many workshops, and preside over lively plenary sessions throughout the weekends. Laudable performances were turned in particularly by former premier Peter Lougheed and his co-chairperson Monique Jérôme-Forget; by Judge Rosie Abella; and by former U.N. Ambassador Yves Fortier.

The terms of the formal agreement between Ottawa and the institutes were announced by Joe Clark on 2 December. Although the government had attempted to interest native leaders in organizing a conference on their constitutional concerns, the offer had at first not been taken up, chiefly because of the doubts of Ovide Mercredi, leader of the Assembly of First Nations.[7] It was not until early February that native leaders agreed to a subsequent conference on aboriginal issues to be held in mid-March. Hence, initially four conferences from 17 January to 9 February were assigned substantive chunks of the constitutional package as outlined in Table 2.3. A fifth conference that was originally to have focused on aboriginal concerns was instead planned as a concluding conference in Ottawa (subsequently moved to Vancouver) "to draw together the results of the first four conferences and move towards a broad, practical consensus that could help governments act."[8]

Hence, by early December, the framework for a new experiment in public involvement in constitutional revision had been finalized. And, in the end, the need for ensuring a credible independent process had trumped the government's initial fears of losing control of its agenda. While Arthur Kroeger and his hastily assembled secretariat would provide skilled logistical support to the institutes, the conferences were truly in the hands of independent institutes who enjoyed the last word on who would come (excepting only the 64 ex officio Committee, party, and government representatives) and how they would be organized.[9] Politicians were always to be in a minority, and were expected to adopt a "listening" mode. While the negotiations with the institutes had resulted in a conference format that would deflect criticism of stage-managing by Ottawa and promote widely-reported and open-ended discussion of the federal proposals, it was certainly not clear that "saving the process" would necessarily mean "saving the package." Indeed, the complicated federal proposal comprising 28 frequently interrelated recommendations was now to face an unprecedented public trial.

Table 2.3
Conferences

Sponsor	Topics	Place	Date	Chairs/Co-chairs
APEC	Distribution of Powers	Halifax	Jan. 17-19	L. Yves Fortier Rosalie Abella
Canada West	Institutional Reform	Calgary	Feb. 17-19	Hon. Peter Lougheed Monique Jérôme-Forget
C.D. Howe/ IRPP	Economic Union	Montreal	Jan. 31-Feb. 2	Thomas Kierans Monique Jérôme-Forget
Niagara	Identity, Rights and Values	Toronto	Feb. 6-9	Hon. Edward Schreyer Glenda Simms Peter Meekison Louise Vaillancourt
(Secretariat)	Conclusion	Vancouver	Feb. 14-16	Hon. Peter Lougheed Rosalie Abella L. Yves Fortier
(Secretariat)	Aboriginal Issues	Ottawa	Mar. 13-15	Hon. Joe Ghiz Mary Simon

Source: Peter Harrison, *The Constitutional Conferences Secretariat: A Unique Response to a Public Management Challenge* (Ottawa: Canadian Centre for Management Development, 1992) p. 6.

THE CONFERENCES, THE PUBLIC AND THE PACKAGE

By the end of the first conference in Halifax, it was already clear how powerful and unique a vehicle had been constructed to test public opinion upon the government's constitutional proposals. Participants were highly supportive of the conference and its format of providing more than half the time in intensive workshop sessions. Goodwill had been expressed towards accommodating Quebec's needs, if necessary through an asymmetrical division of powers; over two-thirds of the delegates declared in exit polls that they had significantly modified their views over the duration of the conference.[10] The mixing of politicians, experts, interest group leaders, and public in the workshops had also worked remarkably well, with participants insisting on sketching out a broad direction for constitutional change rather than becoming lost in technicalities. Moreover, here and in the following conferences, the debate was carried out in a civilized and moderate tone, with none of the stridencies that had character- ized the earlier Spicer Commission or the first hearings of the Parliamentary Committee. As Jeffrey Simpson remarked:

> Against the odds, these gatherings in Halifax, Calgary, Montreal, Toronto and Vancouver worked splendidly. Indeed, they rescued constitutional reform, at least temporarily. When they began, no one could predict how they would unfold. But they took on a dynamic of their own, and that dynamic was one of intense debate coupled with a genuine desire to find accommodations. Instead of the usual shouting and insinuation, the discussions were civil and constructive, a rediscov- ery of much-ballyhooed but infrequently observed Canadian compromise and tolerance.[11]

The prior screening of RSPs by the institutes to reduce the "yahoo factor" certainly helped ensure that these conferences would not be victimized by the incivilities that had plagued the earlier consultative processes. The screening and selection process of over 1200 applicants took place in early January with representatives from each of the institutes selecting in order (or weeding out) contestants from mail, pre-sorted by postmarks into boxes by province and territory. This was a function that the institutes could and did perform effec- tively without the media criticism that would certainly have arisen were such screening to be undertaken by a government-controlled agency. At the same time, the open-ended nature of admission through application after public advertising preserved the participatory and democratic character of the exer- cise.

This process ensured in fact a more thoughtful and moderate audience for the federal proposals than would any open-hearing process. There was consid- erable irony in this conclusion, given all of the initial worry by federal officials over the novelty of the conference procedure. What had appeared at first to be risky and radical in process was decidedly not so, at least as compared with the more open-ended processes used by the parliamentary committee or the Spicer Commission. Even more ironically, there was an opportunity for a neutral arms-length institute to exercise considerably more control over who might come without the damaging sting of media criticism. The conference format also removed the sterile, two-dimensional, often antagonistic dynamics associated with the usual parliamentary committee structure; here politicians were among the participants in a public deliberative process, not authority figures monopolizing the committee table, listening and questioning intervenors, and then retiring to their own deliberations. The advantages of this consultative mechanism over a wide range of policy issues will doubtless not escape the attention of publics and future policy-makers.

Another reason for the relatively moderate tone of the conferences was undoubtedly the tacit decision of almost all Quebec sovereigntists to boycott the conferences. Such a decision was in part a natural conclusion for those who had little interest in revising federalism, and was also a logical extension of the province's decision to stay out of this process and wait to see what "offers" would be made to Quebec by the rest-of-Canada (ROC). There was also, apart from a few high-profile leaders such as Marcel Bélanger or Claude Castonguay, a relative absence of Quebec nationalists, and of leaders of many nationalist interest groups, especially Quebec labour.[12] Therefore, Quebec representation comprised almost exclusively federalists. Under these circumstances, it was hardly surprising to find the conference mood more accommodating. On the French-English dynamic, it was a debate among and for the moderates.

It should be firmly stated that this nationalist underrepresentation flowed from Quebecers' own choices, and not from the conference planners who had done their utmost to get credible Quebec representation. There were still prominent names from Quebec in attendance, including noted author Christian Dufour and political scientist Guy Laforest, but on the whole, most nationalists were noticeable by their absence. Under these circumstances, it caused many to wonder whether this unreal debate between the nicer people of ROC and mostly moderate Quebec federalists was really beside the point. That was certainly the conclusion of the Parti Québécois in its "counter-conference" protest in Montreal on 2 February. On the other hand, if federal renewal were to have any chance of success, it would depend on the moderate forces of accommodation continuing their high-profile, well-reported dialogue. At issue was the informing and preparation of sceptical and undecided publics on both sides for the need for understanding and compromise in a comprehensive constitutional settlement.

In that exercise, achieving a credible public hearing for the federal proposals on constitutional revision remained an important government objective; so too did the wide dissemination of the proposals to the public in an interesting and accessible form. In both respects, the conferences were an extraordinary success. Very high numbers of Canadians watched the conference on television or read about it in their newspapers. Polling data indicates that Canadians were beginning to adopt a more accommodating approach to some of the elements of a future constitutional package, including the distinct society clause, by the late fall of 1991; doubtless, something of that change was reflected in the tone of the constitutional conferences in the first months of the new year. But the conferences may well have enhanced and accelerated that change in public attitude, as the veteran constitutional sage, Gordon Robertson has argued.[13] Though no polls to my knowledge were taken to monitor the exact effects of the conferences on public opinion, there can be little doubt that, at the very least, they increased public understanding of the government's proposals and contributed to a new spirit of moderation in constitutional dialogue.

One ought not, however, to confuse moderate tone with passivity towards the federal package. The conferences from the outset demonstrated considerable willingness to challenge and reject elements of the federal package. In Halifax, for example, many delegates openly questioned the wisdom of Ottawa's decentralizing policy, arguing that powers might go to Quebec that would not flow to other provinces. In that respect, there was a remarkable divergence in the views of a citizens' conference from that typical in an intergovernmental forum. Similarly, reactions to the proposal for legislative interdelegation were generally negative, reflecting suspicion of government's abuse of this mechanism to achieve a "backdoor route to special status" for Quebec.

The following week in Calgary, there was more of the same, including an almost total rejection of the government's proposal for a Council of the Federation to manage intergovernmental relationships. An elected, effective and equitable Senate was approved, but far more stress was laid upon the need to represent the social diversity of Canadians — multiculturalism, native peoples, gender equality — than merely territorial representation. The extraordinary stress on the mechanism of proportional representation flowed from such considerations. Ironically, these outcomes took place in a conference weighted towards "outer Canada" *despite* presentations by advocates of both the Council of the Federation and the Triple-E Senate to persuade delegates otherwise.[14]

It was the Montreal conference on the economic union, however, that most demonstrated the feisty independence of the conferences. Here, almost the whole of the government's constitutional proposals on the economic union were severely attacked or gutted: the proposed section 92A giving Ottawa powers for the efficient functioning of the economic union; economic and fiscal harmonization; changes to the Bank Act; and even the strengthening of section 121 to ensure the free movement of goods, services, capital and people within the economic union. Even more remarkable, these groups succeeded in placing the social charter on the agenda, despite the fact that it was not among the government's constitutional proposals at all. Here, social interest groups demonstrated what could be achieved by their prior caucusing and by extensive and skillful use of the plenary microphones to advance their own agenda; there was little compensating rhetoric by the corporate interests in attendance. Most business leaders were not enamoured with this kind of politics and failed to counterbalance the rhetoric of labour and other such interest group representatives. Since the media fell for the gambit, the impression was created that there was a national consensus around the goals of certain interest groups. In the end, the effect of this hijacking of the economic agenda was devastating for that part of the federal package, since most of this agenda would not be able to be resurrected again.

Nothing in Halifax or Calgary quite prepared conference planners or the business community for this well-organized drive by labour and social groups: hotel caucus suites had been booked; speeches prepared; and participants carefully primed to seize the advantage on the plenary floor. Even television reporters were invited to the caucus suites to witness the interest groups working out their weekend manoeuvres! But the success of the hijack of the Montreal conference was in part a direct consequence of how the C.D. Howe Institute had insisted on organizing its conference.[15] First, compared to many other conferences, it kept the number of randomly selected delegates to a minimum and consequently overplayed the significance of interest group representation. At the same time, in failing to provide small-scale workshop discussions (provision was made for only three massive groups of approximately 70 participants), there was little time for small-group interaction, changes of view, and consequent complexity to be drawn out on the economic agenda. In such a framework, there was an incentive only for a minority to give "set piece" presentations. All of these organizational errors carried significant consequences for the fate of the package.

This was, of course, the price to be paid for the decision to leave the institutes free to run their own conferences: process and package were both affected by the independent decisions of institutes. In that respect, both the C.D. Howe Institute and the Niagara Institute were more frequent targets of delegate criticism, the latter chiefly for its overuse of professional facilitators untutored in the conference subject matter who employed what several delegates called "touchy-feely" methods. From the taxpayer's standpoint, too, there could be vast and unjustified differences in the price tag for the conferences, with the Niagara Institute costing in excess of $800,000 — almost three times the rate of the other conferences.[16] On the whole, however, despite these failings, there was general agreement that the decision to leave control with the institutes was a wise one and that the consequent downside risks were well worth assuming.

Of course, it is easy for constitutional specialists to show that consideration of the proposals may have often been superficial, ill-informed, or confused.

Conference discussion proceeded with very little knowledge of the details of the subject matter or of the broader implications and ramifications. How many of the participants, for example, actually had a grasp on a system of proportional representation, or the single transferable vote, or the meaning of asymmetrical federalism? Moreover, most of the proposals, despite an apparent accessibility, were in fact a complicated and interrelated set of ideas. The prior decision of the government to carve off chunks of the constitutional subject matter for separate treatment in conferences with different groups of participants, however, prevented delegates from looking at these interrelationships. Hence, conclusions arrived at in one conference would crucially affect the viability of other proposals discussed elsewhere. Nor was the final conference, rescheduled for Vancouver after extensive western lobbying, able to reassess earlier conference conclusions or otherwise play this horizontal integrating role. Indeed, to revisit and possibly undo the work of earlier conferences was a risk that Vancouver conference leaders, such as Rosie Abella, were determined to avoid.

Whatever the admitted flaws of such a process, it is not clear that cabinet or legislative decision making is really any more refined than what occurred at the conferences. Citizens might legitimately ask, for example, how knowledgable are politicians on these kinds of subjects, or how probing and intelligent are cabinet or caucus discussions of constitutional proposals. Nor is it reasonable to criticize the conferences for not examining proposals with academic skill and detachment. That was not their function. It was to give a broad public reaction to the proposals. As Kroeger rightly declared, the conferences in doing so were "like an army: large, somewhat clumsy, often characterized by internal confusion — but you can tell the direction in which it is marching."

IMPACT OF THE CONFERENCES

There were undoubtedly important directions given to the Parliamentary Committee and governments by virtue of this unusual public exercise. The Parliamentary Committee admitted as much, even though it did not always adopt conference outcomes, as in its retention of the property rights provision, for example, despite extensive opposition to it in the Toronto conference. On other charter and values issues, however, the Committee reaffirmed conference outcomes: acceptance of Quebec's distinct society clause alongside strengthened commitments to linguistic minorities; support for a comprehensive Canada clause; support for the idea of a social charter; opposition to changes in the notwithstanding clause.

The evidence shows that the conferences were important too in winnowing down the shape and size of the federal package. Noteworthy in particular were the deletions in provisions for institutional reform and the economic union. Following its decisive rejection in Montreal, the Council of the Federation proposal was not acted upon by the Committee, nor was most of the proposed economic agenda including section 92A and the proposed Bank Act changes. The Committee clung to section 121 only, though even here subsequent multilateral discussions among governments confirmed the uneasiness and reservations expressed by conference participants; in the end, no changes were made to section 121 of the constitution. In each case, however, the conferences failed to suggest other specific alternatives for improving intergovernmental relations and the economic union. There was a clear wish to avoid an excess of government, as well as the dangers of judicial review of many laws under section 121, but there was not corresponding evidence of a wish to grapple with the problems that these proposals were aimed to meet.

But surely the most startling and fateful governmental divergence from the conference outcomes arose over the Senate. In the complicated two-phase discussions among governments and aboriginal leaders that took place from April to the end of August, significant differences arose. In the first phase, which consisted of discussions among aboriginal leaders and all governments *except Quebec*, the decision was taken to adopt a modified Triple-E Senate model, counterbalanced with increased Commons representation for more populous provinces. Provision was made for eight Senators from each province, with the proviso that most Commons legislation could not be blocked with less than a 70 percent vote of that chamber. These multilateral talks also rejected fixed terms and stand-alone election for the Senate; they went further to propose that elected Senators could only play an opposition role and might not serve in cabinet. This insistence on provincial equality, whatever the price, could not have diverged more sharply from the Calgary conference outcome. As it turned out, premiers such as Don Getty and Clyde Wells were far more insistent on the principle of equality even at the expense of effective powers for the Senate than were the conference delegates from their provinces. Moreover, they were also much more focused on questions of territorial rather than social representation — a fact that led Judy Rebick of the National Action Committee on the Status of Women to denounce the governmental agreement as a betrayal of the principles of representation agreed to in Calgary.[17] With Quebec absent from that multilateral bargaining table, the governmental forum was, moreover, even less representative than was the Calgary conference format. It is scarcely surprising then that the modified Triple-E format adopted would have subsequently run into difficulty in Quebec and among delegates representing some interest groups. By the time Quebec had joined the talks for the final constitutional discussions in mid-August, however, the commitment to provincial equality had become the unshakeable E, and Senate powers to block virtually all ordinary legislation had to be sacrificed to preserve this symbolism.[18] In retrospect, the choice of the conference for an *equitable* Senate with *effective* powers may have been the more prudent choice, a compromise better reflecting political realities in the country at large.

On the charter, there was a left-leaning policy direction — hostility to the entrenchment of property rights and its limitations on governmental activity; affirmation of the need, on the other hand, for a social charter setting out citizen entitlements, and ambivalence over the wisdom of further limiting of the notwithstanding clause. In all of these conclusions, the governments subsequently followed the choices of the conferences, leaving to one side everything but the social charter. There was congruence, too, in the support for the inherent right of aboriginal self-government as "one of three orders of government in Canada." All of this suggested that Canadians were again reflecting their more complex approach to rights and the charter — demonstrating once again their willingness to *affirm* the positive role of government and to give at least as forceful a role to collective rights as to individual.

Such was the outcome too of the sixth special conference, hastily assembled from 13 March to the 15th to deal exclusively with the subject of aboriginal rights. It was in fact a tribute to the success of the earlier conferences and their acute sensitivity to the constitutional concerns of collectivities that native leaders reversed their earlier hesitation and entrusted their agenda to a conference forum. Doubtless even Ovide Mercredi had by now come to regret his earlier rejection of an aboriginal constitutional conference, a free 48-hour national television extravaganza devoted exclusively to native concerns; doubtless too the continuous high visibility of Ron George, President of the Native Council of Canada, as champion of aboriginal rights in earlier conferences contributed to Mercredi's belated change of heart. Besides, he had little to fear from a conference debate or challenge to native issues: the constitutional conferences had already endorsed an immediately justiciable inherent right of Aboriginal Peoples to self-government, declaring this to be "more than an empty box." Such a right carried with it not only "jurisdictional powers, but also land, resources and the protection of aboriginal languages."[19] In deference to the collective claims of Aboriginal Peoples, the sixth conference also supported the idea of "an aboriginal order of government, which would exist alongside, and in partnership with, the federal and provincial orders of government." It went on:

> While these Aboriginal governments would constitute a third order of government, it was noted that both in their structures and their powers they would not simply replicate the largely European models of existing Canadian governments. Instead they would embody Aboriginal cultural values, such as consensus decision-making, respect for the role of elders and a different balance between collective and individual rights.[20]

At the same time, however, the conferences were not unmoved by the insistence of aboriginal women on protection of their charter rights prior to any move towards aboriginal self-government. Gender equality and rights of citizenship were all part of this complicated debate. Striking a balance would be no easy matter, but the conference prepared the way for those discussions, anticipating the final compromises applying the *Charter of Rights and Freedoms* to aboriginal governments and retaining the 1983 guarantee of gender equality in existing and aboriginal treaty rights.

The conferences may have made a more enduring contribution to aboriginal issues, however, in their vigorous endorsement of the decision to include aboriginal leaders in any subsequent negotiations with governments. The inclusiveness of the conference format itself and the high visibility and ex officio status the conferences accorded aboriginal and territorial leaders also worked to support the later claims of these leaders to a seat at the government negotiating table. While native leaders could look back to enjoying such a position in pre-Meech conferences, inclusion for territorial leaders was altogether unprecedented. Moreover, in a curious way, the conferences may even have established a more direct bridge to the elite governmental bargaining table in the person of Premier Ghiz who became a vigorous advocate for admitting aboriginal leaders into the multilateral talks among governments. His position was completely in keeping with the conclusions of the aboriginal conference of which he was co-chairperson. In short, in many ways, the conferences made a tangible contribution to the enhanced status of these constitutional actors, opening the way for their entry into the critical second stage of intergovernmental bargaining among first ministers. The constitutional victories won by these leaders in the subsequent agreement that finally emerged from these discussions were the fruit of this more inclusive process.

Finally, it is worth underlining the gesture towards collective rights made in the apparent Halifax conference endorsement of the notion of special powers for Quebec.[21] This position appeared to be the logical result of many English-speaking interest group leaders' sensitivity to Quebec's concerns, on the one hand, and their suspicion of the ambitions of other provincial governments on the other. While it was said special arrangements could be made for Quebec respecting either labour market training or culture, given its unique labour force and cultural requirements, the same was not true for other provinces. There was similar resistance in the conference to any general devolving of legislative powers to the other provinces and a wish to protect the powers of Ottawa to meet the needs of the citizens of the rest-of-Canada. Although the Parliamentary Committee appeared to move modestly towards this notion of asymmetry in its recommendation for special arrangements for Quebec on culture and broadcasting, elsewhere on the division of powers, symmetry among provinces prevailed. In the end, the idea of special powers for Quebec predictably failed to satisfy other provincial governments during the subsequent multilateral talks; moreover, judging by polls, it is doubtful whether special status would have been approved by the Canadian public at large.[22] Such counterbalancing tensions left governments with quite restricted options. In the final constitutional package, the governments retained the principle of formal equality of provinces in the division of powers (with flexibility for provinces to do things differently in fact), while at the same time they limited the scale of devolution by tightening up the intergovernmental agreements, and rejecting legislative delegation, changes to the residual power, and some of the limits on the federal spending power. Here, the final legal architecture reflected the need to make some offer to the provinces on powers, while remaining mindful of the warnings over undue decentralization expressed at Halifax.

It was only a couple of months that separated the Halifax conference's desire to be open to Quebec from darker sentiments reflected in the disastrous meetings of the Dobbie-Castonguay Committee in late 1991. While it is true that polls had indicated that public opinion was beginning to shift towards a more accommodating stance towards Quebec by the end of 1991, there can be little doubt that these conferences accelerated the shift in mood. Participants were serious about tackling the constitutional agenda and in keeping the country whole. Discussions were focused, with participants required to face one another in an honest exchange of views. With so many experts present, it was less likely that ignorance would remain unchecked. In fact, everything about the conference format encouraged the primacy of rational dialogue over a mere venting of the spleen as with the Spicer Commission. Although the plenary sessions of the conferences were always vulnerable to hijack by the prior caucusing and planning of interest groups, as was demonstrated particularly in Montreal, representational balance and effective group discussions in workshops can significantly reduce that risk. Group workshop discussions, unlike the pattern in legislative hearings, can also reduce the likelihood that certain individuals or groups could singly set the tone and agenda by their arguments. In short, the constitutional conferences turned out to be more focused and effective vehicles for the expression of the public on the proposals than any that the government had planned. By the publicity they generated and the extraordinary exchange of views of citizens, they also served to educate the viewing public far more than did the Parliamentary Committee.

Above all, the conferences injected a spirit of accommodation, even of optimism, on the constitutional file. While that rare spirit lasted, even journalists — surely the most cynical among us — were inclined to wax lyrical over the unexpected, "magic incandescent power" of the conference innovation. Take, for example, William Johnson of the *Montreal Gazette*:

> This wandering nation-building innovated on all previous constitutional history. The participants were mostly unelected ... [neither] parliamentary committee [nor] meeting of first ministers.

This was like nothing before, neither constituent assembly, nor town hall meeting. It was an invention of despair when all else seemed doomed to failure; a great national public debate in the age of television; an attempt to find legitimacy for refashioning a country when the federal government and most politicians had lost credibility in the eyes of the citizens.[23]

It was Joe Clark, amidst the post-conference euphoria, who pointed to the longer road ahead, warning that "no one should confuse the success of these conferences with success in the country."[24] In short order, William Johnson and many others were soon to realize that executive federalism was far from dead — that, in fact, the real work of the politicians had just begun. After the two-month whirlwind of these six open constitutional conferences, Canadians witnessed five gruelling months of closed-door governmental bargaining before a final constitutional package was unveiled in early September. A drawn-out and Byzantine affair that taxed public patience, the bargaining process proceeded in two phases: the first led by Constitutional Affairs Minister Clark involving representatives of all provinces but Quebec, together with territorial and aboriginal leaders; the second, a First Ministers' Conference, including Quebec's premier, with aboriginal and territorial leaders. Although unanimity among the negotiators was finally achieved after much posturing and compromising, the process virtually guaranteed disappointments, especially among worried interest groups excluded from the process. This suspicion over process would then feed on doubts over the integrity of the constitutional compromise. It remains to be seen how important these consequences turn out to be in the national referendum on the final constitutional package.

While it is still too early to predict what longer-term effects the conferences might have on the fate of this constitutional round, in the short run, the conferences seem to have functioned quite well as vehicles for public involvement in and testing of the federal constitutional proposals. They offered direction for reshaping the package and for preparing the ground for the secret multilateral bargaining process that followed. Whether a more expeditious period of "in-camera" negotiations among governments would have helped keep alive the spirit of the conferences a little longer is an interesting question for future historians to consider.[25] In the meantime, in the ensuing debate over ratification, we can safely predict "echoes" from the constitutional conferences: not only the reappearance of delegates in the national debate, but undoubtedly of the rhetorical themes that preoccupied the conferences. Whatever the outcome of the package and of the subsequent ratification politics, there can be little doubt that the conferences will have successfully contributed a great deal to both. For that reason, we are likely to see leaders turn to this kind of vehicle as an ongoing part of Canada's constitutional culture.

NOTES

Since this subject is so current, I relied heavily upon interviews with several senior people intimately familiar with the organization and planning of these conferences. They are Arthur Kroeger, former Coordinator of the Constitutional Secretariat, his deputy Peter Harrison of the Canadian Centre for Management Development, David Elton of the Canada West Foundation, Monique Jérôme-Forget of the Institute for Research on Public Policy, and Tim O'Neill of the Atlantic Provinces Economic Council. I am deeply grateful to each and every one of them for kindly agreeing to make time to discuss these matters with me. Of course, none bears any responsibility for the judgements (or errors) that I may have made. Indeed, some may well take issue with my conclusions and arguments. I am grateful, too, to the Niagara Institute for providing information, and for the helpful interview with Dr. Ronald Watts, of Queen's University, formerly with the Federal-Provincial Relations Office of the Government of Canada.

1.   Arthur Kroeger, "The Constitutional Conferences of January-March, 1992: A View from Within," Speech to IPAC, University of Victoria Conference, 23 April 1992.

2.   The Citizens' Forum on Canada's Future (Spicer Commission), too, in pursuit of its independent mandate to test the public mood in 1990 and 1991, proved frequently to be a dubious exercise in the venting of the public spleen and was plagued with organizational and leadership problems.

3.   News Release, President of the Privy Council and Minister Responsible for Constitutional Affairs, 2 December 1991.

4.   Certainly the best account of the logistical difficulties in participant selection and many other management problems is by the Deputy Co-ordinator of the Constitutional Conferences Secretariat, Peter Harrison. See his manuscript on the conferences "through a public management optic" as follows: Peter Harrison, *The Constitutional Conferences Secretariat: A Unique Response to a Public Management Challenge*, (Ottawa: Canadian Centre for Management Development, 1992), 31 pp. plus annexes.

5.   Representation was based on "equitable representation for each province and territory on a formula derived from the representation in the German Bundesrat. That is, on a ratio of three for small provinces; four for medium-sized provinces (British Columbia and Alberta) and five for large provinces (Ontario, Quebec).

6.   It is difficult to get more detailed information on how fully or extensively the proceedings were followed, nor is an information breakdown on a regional basis readily available. The reach is based on responses for a viewer who might watch Newsworld coverage of the conferences at least once for at least one minute over the weekend broadcasting. Many factors can influence total numbers of viewers, including the length of coverage, time zone, and so on. According to some of its data, quite apart from total numbers, the Calgary conference was very actively followed. Source: CBC Newsworld

7.   The original plan was for the aboriginal conference to be run by the Institute for Research on Public Policy. This was not agreeable to native leaders who wished to run their own conference, and naturally the institute was not enthusiastic with

any such assignment under the circumstances. In the end, the IRPP worked jointly with the C.D. Howe Institute on the conference on the economic union in Montreal.

8. Original scheduling plans were subsequently challenged and sometimes modified after a great deal of lobbying and politicking. First, there were attempts behind the scenes to convince the federal government to choose Vancouver instead of Calgary for the conference on institutions, lobbying that was stoutly resisted by the province of Alberta and the Canada West Foundation. Vancouver subsequently replaced Ottawa as the location for the final conference in the series of five, while a special sixth conference on aboriginal concerns in Ottawa was subsequently added at the request of native leaders who had changed their minds about the desirability of a conference on their constitutional issues. The decision on the aboriginal conference was not taken until the weekend of the Vancouver conference, leaving little time for preparation. Indeed, the first terms agreed to by Constitution Minister Joe Clark and native leaders, was for a native conference on the following weekend! After strenuous objections from the conference secretariat and reconsideration of the short time for planning by native leaders, it was agreed to move it forward to mid-March.

9. This was less true, however, of the final concluding conference in Vancouver. Here, though the institutes exercised the formal right to be consulted and to approve the conference planning, they did not get as directly involved. Most of the arrangements were made by Arthur Kroeger's secretariat on behalf of the federal government. The secretariat was also the executive agent for the aboriginal conference, liaising with aboriginal organizations and the conference co-chairpersons. For details, see Harrison, *The Constitutional Conferences Secretariat*. On another matter touched on in this reference, it should also be noted that the institutes were able to resolve the delicate politics of invitations to the Reform Party and to the Bloc Québécois by extending the invitations directly. They did so as they saw fit on their own authority, as the ex officio arrangements for parties did not include them.

10. See, for example, *Renewal of Canada: Division of Powers — Participant Survey: Summary Report*. Corporate Research Associates, for Atlantic Provinces Economic Council, Halifax, January 1992.

11. Jeffrey Simpson, *Globe and Mail*, 17 February 1992.

12. Virtually the whole of Quebec labour ruled out attendance at the conference and quietly informed the institutes that sending out an invitation was pointless, indeed almost an insult.

13. Gordon Robertson's observations on the positive role of the conferences on public opinion are related to us by Kroeger in "The Constitutional Conferences," Speech to IPAC, 23 April 1992.

14. In fact, it would be fair to say that the decision of the Canada West Foundation to permit "advocates" to present the proposals to the plenary sessions most often backfired. In the case of the Council of the Federation, Mel Smith of British Columbia hurt his own cause by presenting what was widely regarded as a one-sided report, as did Gordon Gibson on the issue of Senate reform.

15. Although the Institute for Research on Public Policy also shared responsibility for the conference, it was principally the C.D. Howe Institute as the first institute approached to do this conference that took principal leadership for the conference and especially for the workshop design.

16. Among the reasons for the cost differential was the fact that the Niagara Institute chose to have several expensive pre-conference meetings with its advisory committee of 55 and its extensive use of expensive consultants and paid professional facilitators. The money was on all accounts not well spent, particularly for the professional facilitators who failed in the workshops (in contrast to the success of the other conferences in their use of unpaid specialists and academics as chairpersons to lead workshop sessions). Direct costs of the institutes for the conferences do not, of course, take into account other expenditures assumed by the constitutional secretariat. Final figures on the total cost of the conferences could not be obtained, but an estimate of $8.8 million was offered by a senior conference manager.

17. *Globe and Mail,* 15 July 1992.

18. The requirement for a system of proportional representation and the single transferable vote for Senate elections also disappeared in the final round of discussions among first ministers, territorial and aboriginal leaders.

19. Report of Vancouver Conference, in *Renewal of Canada Conferences: Compendium of Reports* (Ottawa: Constitutional Conferences Secretariat, March 1992), p. 8. This was also very much the conclusion of the Royal Commission on Aboriginal Peoples in its commentary published on 13 February 1992.

20. *First Peoples and the Constitution: Conference Report* (Ottawa: Privy Council Office, n.d.), p. 7. The subsequent grant of the notwithstanding clause over the charter to aboriginal governments flowed logically from this kind of rhetoric.

21. I say "apparent" here because, though the conference report indicates support for special powers for Quebec only, at other points in its report, other versions of asymmetry are indicated. Since there was virtually no plenary presentation of the different versions of asymmetry to handle the division of powers, nor consequent canvassing of delegates' opinions, it is difficult to be categorical. In fact, debate over precisely what version of asymmetry had been agreed to in Halifax continued throughout the subsequent conferences.

22. Equality of provinces with respect to rights and powers is a principle widely endorsed outside Quebec. Moreover, judging from many polls conducted in 1992, there is strong support for devolution of powers to all provinces throughout the country, even in Atlantic Canada and Ontario. See, for example, the Gallup Report on Decentralization in the Constitutional Deal by Lorne Bozinoff and Peter MacIntosh, released 28 May 1992. There is also a corresponding weakness in confidence in federal leadership. The erosion here since the Trudeau years is quite marked. Obviously, the new federal government under Brian Mulroney is no champion of social policy nor slayer of provincialism, but some interest group leaders, caught in a time warp, do not seem to have caught up with this fact.

23. William Johnson, *Montreal Gazette,* 17 February 1992.

24. Joe Clark, quoted in Edison Stewart's report from Vancouver, *Toronto Star*, 15 February 1992.

25. The case for closed door bargaining after public discussion is made in Peter Russell, "Towards a New Constitutional Process," in Ronald Watts and Douglas Brown (eds.), *Options for a New Canada* (Toronto: University of Toronto Press, 1991), pp. 141-56. As noted above, however, this phase should not go on interminably, as it seemed to do in the post-conference period in Canada.

3

Robert Bourassa et la maîtrise du temps

Guy Laforest

In the first 12 months since the defeat of the Meech Lake Accord, the Bélanger-Campeau Commission dominated the Quebec political scene. In 1991-92, this honour belongs to Robert Bourassa. This chapter attempts to provide an account of the role played by Quebec, and especially Robert Bourassa, in the Canada round. In the process we discover an experimental personality, past master in the art of pushing back deadlines and capable, until a new order comes, of getting out of all sorts of impasses. We also learn that what drives Bourassa may also risk becoming the chief weakness in this constitutional gameplan.

La personnalité énigmatique et insaisissable de Robert Bourassa — véritable Houdini du jeu politique — aura incontestablement été l'élément-clé sur la scène québécoise en 1991-1992. Pour donner un avant-goût de l'épaisseur du «mystère» Bourassa, on ne peut trouver de meilleur exemple que la conférence de presse donnée par le Premier ministre du Québec le 9 juillet 1992, deux jours après que les participants aux pourparlers multilatéraux sur la constitution en soient arrivés à une entente qualifiée d'historique par le ministre Joe Clark.

Monsieur Bourassa aurait pu se prononcer dès sa sortie du conseil des ministres, le 8 juillet. Fidèle à son habitude, il préféra reporter le tout au lendemain. En conférence de presse, monsieur Bourassa évita de prendre position clairement, dans un sens ou dans l'autre. Il nota les progrès considérables réalisés par ses homologues provinciaux, vanta leur ardeur au travail et la générosité de Bob Rae (était-ce vraiment un compliment?). Il se félicita de retrouver dans l'entente la «substance» de l'Accord du lac Meech. Mais il n'annonça pas pour autant son retour à la table des négociations. Il prétexta avoir besoin de clarifications et de précisions quant à la plupart des piliers de l'entente: le Sénat triple-E (les provinces dont le Québec possèderaient-elles un veto sur l'entrée de nouvelles provinces?); le droit inhérent à l'autonomie gouvernementale pour les autochtones (est-ce que cela affecterait l'intégrité territoriale du Québec?). Monsieur Bourassa reconnut que son gouvernement se posait aussi des questions à propos des sections de l'entente concernant le partage des pouvoirs et la clause de la société distincte dans son rapport avec le principe de la dualité linguistique. Il rappela que les textes qui lui étaient parvenus demeuraient préliminaires, et qu'il fallait donc attendre les formulations juridiques avant de pouvoir vraiment se prononcer. Il rappela aussi qu'en temps et lieu, les «offres» seraient étudiées par une commission parlementaire, par le cabinet et le caucus de son parti, peut-être même par un congrès spécial du Parti libéral et enfin par l'Assemblée nationale elle-même. Il se réclama de la vision québécoise du fédéralisme, vu comme un pacte entre deux nations ou deux peuples, mais dit aussi accepter le principe de l'égalité des provinces. Répondant aux questions des journalistes, il affirma qu'il pourrait être difficile de vendre l'idée d'un sénat égal aux Québécois. De là à dire que cette idée était inacceptable à ses yeux, il y avait une marche que monsieur Bourassa ne franchit pas. À la fin de la conférence de presse, l'ambiguïté persistait quant aux positions du gouvernement du Québec. Pour Robert Bourassa, toutes les portes restaient ouvertes. Il ne s'était engagé à strictement rien de particulier. Le mystère Bourassa restait entier. Son gouvernement attendrait qu'Ottawa annonce l'étape suivante, soit la convocation de la Chambre des communes ou celle d'une conférence des Premiers ministres. Robert Bourassa irait-il à une telle conférence? Il jugea prématuré de le dire avant de savoir s'il y en aurait une. Une heure après son arrivée, le maître de l'ambiguïté s'esquiva. Il avait encore une fois gagné un peu de temps.

Si Robert Bourassa et sa maîtrise du temps s'imposent à l'attention des observateurs, cela tient pour beaucoup à ce que la variable temporelle fut l'une des principales dimensions de la ronde du Canada. En mars 1991, la Commission Bélanger-Campeau a donné 18 mois au reste du Canada pour repenser la fédération et faire des offres de renouvellement au Québec. Jusqu'en juillet 1992, le reste du Canada n'a cessé de multiplier les délais et de retarder les échéances. Rappelons la conclusion du Rapport du Comité mixte spécial du Sénat et de la Chambre des communes co-présidé par Gérald Beaudoin et Dorothy Dobbie, *Un Canada renouvelé*, publié en février 1992:

> Pour accélérer le processus, nous proposons que notre rapport serve de base de discussion et de point de départ à la réalisation du consensus intergouvernemental. Il serait utile, croyons-nous, de se donner jusqu'au début de mai pour dégager ce consensus de manière que les gouvernements puissent faire le nécessaire pour mettre à contribution leur assemblée et, le cas échéant, leurs administrés avant que ne se mette en branle la campagne référendaire au Québec.[1]

Lorsque les négociations multilatérales sur la constitution se sont amorcées à Ottawa en mars, avec la participation des dirigeants des organisations autochtones et des territoires, de même que celle de tous les gouvernements provinciaux sauf celui du Québec, le ministre responsable du dossier pour le gouvernement fédéral, Joe Clark, prévint tout le monde qu'il faudrait dégager un consensus pour la fin de mai. On venait donc de prolonger d'un mois le calendrier serré prévu par le rapport Beaudoin-Dobbie. Lors de la dernière des réunions multilatérales initialement prévues, à la fin de mai à Toronto, Joe Clark reporta encore une fois l'échéance, cette fois-ci à la fin de juin. On venait de gagner un autre mois. Avant la fin de juin, la date limite pour la définition d'un consensus glissa à la mi-juillet ou encore à la fin de juillet. Les échéances étaient toujours repoussées, le temps passait, rien ne se produisait, l'impasse persistait. Tout le monde attendait. Robert Bourassa attendait des offres. Tout le monde attendait après Robert Bourassa. Dans *Canada, the State of the Federation 1991*, Daniel Bonin écrivit que Robert Bourassa représentait «l'ultime inconnue» de la crise politique et constitutionnelle canado-québécoise. Robert Bourassa, le maître du temps, demeure cette ultime inconnue en 1992[2]. À l'heure où ces lignes sont écrites, et ce malgré l'entente du 7 juillet, tout le monde continue d'attendre. Et Robert Bourassa donne l'exemple.

Maître du temps, Robert Bourassa l'est à plusieurs égards. À l'intérieur des paramètres fixés par la Loi 150, c'est lui qui choisira la date du référendum qui aura lieu au Québec au plus tard le 26 octobre 1992, sur la souveraineté ou sur des offres de renouvellement de la fédération. La Loi 150 n'enlève légalement rien à la marge de manoeuvre de monsieur Bourassa, qui pourrait retarder ou annuler le référendum, s'il jugeait que cela s'avérait nécessaire pour les «intérêts supérieurs du Québec». Maître du temps, Robert Bourassa l'est aussi dans ses rapports avec le gouvernement fédéral de Brian Mulroney. Ce dernier fut réélu en novembre 1988, alors que monsieur Bourassa et le Parti libéral du Québec s'imposèrent de nouveau en septembre 1989. C'est donc monsieur Mulroney — s'il choisit de demeurer en poste — et son parti qui devront rendre des comptes en premier à un électorat canadien et québécois plutôt hostile à l'idée d'accorder trois mandats consécutifs à quelque formation politique que ce soit.

Depuis l'échec de l'Accord du lac Meech, monsieur Bourassa a par ailleurs démontré son aptitude à se servir des vertus réparatrices du temps. Partisan du fédéralisme et de l'intégration dans les grands ensembles, admirateur du modèle européen ou les nations trouvent de la sécurité, Robert Bourassa est également un homme qui pousse à des hauteurs rarement atteintes le culte de la prudence. Son vocabulaire est celui de la paix constitutionnelle, de la sécurité culturelle, du progrès et de la stabilité économiques, de l'ordre social. Il n'aime pas prendre des risques, pas plus qu'il n'apprécie de voir les gens défiler dans les rues. On comprendra donc aisément que cet homme n'a pas accueilli dans l'enthousiasme la ferveur souverainiste qui s'est manifestée dans les rues de Montréal au lendemain du dérapage de Meech, les 24 et 25 juin 1990. Depuis lors monsieur Bourassa, de tergiversation en tergiversation, s'est servi du temps pour reprendre le contrôle de la situation, pour calmer le jeu, pour ramener les

Québécois dans la proximité des valeurs qu'il privilégie, celles du réalisme et de la prudence. Une étude approfondie menée par Crop-*L'Actualité* sur les valeurs et les intentions des Québécois atteste que monsieur Bourassa n'a pas travaillé en vain. Les Québécois — comme les autres Canadiens d'ailleurs — en ont ras-le-bol de l'interminable tragi-comédie constitutionnelle, ils sont très préoccupés par la situation économique et s'identifient pour l'instant beaucoup trop au Canada et à ses symboles pour oser se lancer dans l'aventure d'une rupture politique.[3]

La maîtrise du temps demeure toutefois une affaire bien relative. Selon la perspective que je ferai mienne dans ce texte, Robert Bourassa est aussi le prisonnier du temps, l'otage de son attitude face au temps. Étrange destin que celui de cet homme, naturellement porté vers la gestion de la croissance économique et la planification de grands projets d'infrastructures, qui se retrouve tour à tour aux prises avec la montée du terrorisme et des crises sociales lors de son premier passage à la tête du Québec dans les années soixante-dix, qui a vu plus récemment fondre sur lui une tempête linguistique, le vide constitutionnel créé par l'échec de l'Accord du lac Meech et la crise d'Oka. Dans les situations tendues, Robert Bourassa pactise avec sa variable de prédilection: le temps. Il s'en sert pour remettre au dernier moment les décisions les plus difficiles, pour se garder toutes les portes ouvertes, en bref pour éviter les choix douloureux. Le temps procure à Robert Bourassa la paix et la quiétude qu'il affectionne, mais à fort prix. D'abord, les décisions sans cesse remises ne deviennent pas toujours moins pénibles, bien au contraire. Un jour finit par venir où il faut se résigner à choisir. Il se peut aussi, comme Aristote nous l'enseigne dans *l'Éthique à Nicomaque*, que les habitudes s'incrustent, et qu'à force de pas vouloir choisir on en vient à ne plus être capable de faire des choix, et donc à laisser les autres, ou encore les sondages, choisir pour soi. Dans la crise constitutionnelle canado-québécoise, comme nous le verrons plus loin, cette voie serait par exemple celle d'un référendum fédéral qui se substituerait au référendum québécois, avec la bénédiction de Robert Bourassa.

Les hésitations de Robert Bourassa à choisir une démarche ou une stratégie, sa manie de toujours vouloir gagner du temps, ont selon moi une conséquence fâcheuse pour son gouvernement et pour le Québec. Le comportement de cet homme est tout simplement trop prévisible. Ses interlocuteurs dans la ronde constitutionnelle du Canada ne peuvent pas faire autrement que d'en tirer un immense avantage. Comme bien d'autres avant lui, dont Pierre Elliott Trudeau, Robert Bourassa aurait avantage à se faire lecteur de Machiavel:

> Je ne veux rien ajouter sur les moyens d'endiguer la fortune en général. Mais si j'en viens au particulier, je vois tel prince être aujourd'hui heureux et demain ruiné sans avoir entre-temps changé de politique. Cela vient d'abord, me semble-t-il, des raisons longuement exposées ci-dessus: ce prince s'appuie totalement sur la fortune, et il tombe quand elle tourne. Ensuite, celui qui sait adapter sa conduite

aux circonstances sera plus sûrement heureux que son collègue qui n'a pas appris cet art.

> Très peu d'hommes, quelle que soit leur sagesse, savent s'adapter à ce jeu; ou bien parce qu'ils ne peuvent s'écarter du chemin où les pousse leur nature; ou bien parce que, ayant toujours prospéré par ce chemin, ils n'arrivent point à se persuader d'en prendre un autre. C'est pourquoi l'homme d'un naturel prudent ne sait pas employer la fougue quand il le faudrait, ce qui cause sa perte. Si tu savais changer de nature quand changent les circonstances, ta fortune ne changerait point.[4]

Je ne sache pas de passage, parmi les grands classiques de l'histoire des idées politiques, qui puisse s'appliquer autant que celui-là au destin de Robert Bourassa. Mais n'est-il pas un peu paradoxal d'affirmer, comme je le fais, que Robert Bourassa souffre d'une incapacité chronique à décider, à trancher dans le vif, qu'il s'avère aussi incapable de s'adapter aux circonstances et de substituer la fougue à la prudence qui correspond à sa nature, tout en maintenant qu'il demeure l'ultime inconnue dans la crise politico-constitutionnelle que nous traversons? Nous n'en serions bien sûr pas au premier paradoxe dans l'histoire d'une fédération canadienne qui a vu le même Premier ministre, Pierre Elliott Trudeau, fouler au pied les libertés fondamentales lors de la crise d'octobre en 1970, avant de se faire le promoteur de l'enchâssement d'une Charte des droits et libertés dans la constitution une décennie plus tard. Je pense qu'il est possible de résoudre cette énigme que représente Robert Bourassa et d'élucider le paradoxe de sa prévisible imprévisibilité. Nous savons qu'il fera des clins d'oeil au temps pour retarder la décision finale, que les prochains mois auront sur lui l'effet d'une chambre des tortures médiévale dans la mesure où nous connaîtrons l'apogée de la crise. Mais tant que tout ne sera pas joué, nous conserverons des doutes.

Pour jeter un peu de lumière sur le mystère Bourassa, et pour mieux comprendre ce qui s'est passé au Québec au cours de la dernière année, il faut imaginer le Premier ministre et chef du Parti libéral du Québec en joueur d'échecs, impliqué dans trois parties qui se déroulent simultanément. Le terrain de la première partie épouse les contours du Parti libéral du Québec; c'est l'échiquier partisan. Le deuxième affrontement met aux prises les partis politiques à l'échelle de la province; appelons-le l'échiquier québécois; la troisième joute prend la forme de la ronde du Canada, les pourparlers constitutionnels subséquents à l'échec de l'Accord du lac Meech; c'est l'échiquier canadien. La conférence de presse du 8 juillet a encore une fois été un modèle du genre. Sur le premier échiquier, monsieur Bourassa a tenu en équilibre les principales factions de son parti, vantant le Canada pour plaire aux fédéralistes inconditionnels, tout en reprenant un peu plus loin le vocabulaire du nationalisme québécois. Sur le deuxième échiquier, monsieur Bourassa rappela que c'est le Parti québécois qui avait bradé le droit de veto du Québec en 1981; sur l'échiquier canadien, comme on l'a vu, il ménagea les susceptibilités des uns et des autres. Selon mon hypothèse, Robert Bourassa a été un très bon joueur sur les deux premiers échiquiers, où il a multiplié les succès tactiques. Sauf que chaque fois qu'il a déplacé victorieusement ses pièces sur les échiquiers partisan et québécois, il a affaibli ses positions sur l'échiquier canadien. En d'autres mots, Robert Bourassa a vogué de succès tactique en succès tactique jusqu'à l'impasse stratégique. Il a astucieusement gagné du temps, conservant ses chances de l'emporter sur chacun des échiquiers, mais sans pouvoir éluder les dilemmes qui sont les siens dans la ronde du Canada. En effet, selon les analyses de Vincent Lemieux, Robert Bourassa a absolument besoin d'une victoire sur l'échiquier canadien pour s'imposer sur les deux autres, c'est-à-dire pour préserver l'unité de son parti et conserver le pouvoir lors des prochaines élections au Québec[5].

DE *BÂTIR ENSEMBLE L'AVENIR DU CANADA* AU RAPPORT BEAUDOIN-DOBBIE

L'idée-force du rapport et des recommandations de la Commission est que les Québécoises et Québécois prennent les décisions quant à leur avenir politique et constitutionnel. Le gouvernement du Québec la fait sienne. En temps utile, la population québécoise sera appelée à assumer les décisions capitales pour son avenir. Ainsi, d'une part, le gouvernement du Québec conserve sa faculté d'initiative et d'appréciation des mesures favorisant le meilleur intérêt du Québec; d'autre part, l'Assemblée nationale demeure souveraine pour décider de toute question référendaire et, le cas échéant, adopter les mesures législatives appropriées»[6].

Par le biais de cet «addendum» au rapport de la Commission Bélanger-Campeau, Robert Bourassa et Gil Rémillard délimitaient la marge de manoeuvre — somme toute immense — du gouvernement du Québec. Celui-ci adoptait la stratégie du couteau sur la gorge en s'engageant à faire un référendum sur la souveraineté au plus tard le 26 octobre 1992. Il se plaçait aussi en attente d'offres visant à renouveler le fédéralisme. L'affirmation de la souveraineté de l'Assemblée nationale signifiait en clair que le référendum pourrait porter sur de telles offres, si cela favorisait le meilleur intérêt du Québec. Cette position fut reprise par Robert Bourassa et son gouvernement en juin 1991, dans le débat sur le projet de loi 150, créant deux commissions parallèles sur le processus de détermination de l'avenir politique et constitutionnel du Québec. Le consensus suscité par la Commission Bélanger-Campeau ne dura pas bien longtemps. Croyant que le gouvernement se ménageait trop de portes de sortie lui permettant de se défiler du référendum sur la souveraineté, les péquistes votèrent contre la Loi 150. Une fois adoptée, la Loi 150 créait une commission pour étudier la souveraineté et ses impacts (dans l'entourage de monsieur Bourassa, on l'appela vite la commission sur les coûts de la souveraineté), et une autre sur toute offre d'un nouveau partenariat de nature constitutionnelle.

À l'automne 1990, Michel Bélanger et Jean Campeau en avaient mené bien large à la tête de la Commission sur l'avenir politique et constitutionnel du Québec. Ces deux hommes avaient profité de la maladie puis du relatif silence de Robert Bourassa pour s'imposer et acquérir beaucoup d'autonomie face au gouvernement. Avec la loi 150, Robert Bourassa voulut éviter la répétition d'un tel scénario. Il nomma les députés libéraux Claude Dauphin et Guy Bélanger, respectivement à la présidence de la commission sur les offres et à celle sur la souveraineté. Contrairement à la tradition parlementaire en vigueur à Québec, on ne leur adjoignit pas de vice-présidents à même les rangs de l'opposition officielle.

Fort de sa Loi 150 et de sa stratégie attentiste, le gouvernement du Québec observa avec un certain détachement les préparatifs en cours à Ottawa. Robert Bourassa accueillit assez favorablement en juin 1991 la publication du rapport du comité Beaudoin-Edwards sur la formule de modification de la constitution. Comme les signataires du rapport, il exprima sa préférence pour la formule du veto régional qui avait déjà été mise sur la table à la conférence de Victoria[7]. Le Premier Ministre vit aussi dans le rapport du Forum des citoyens sur l'avenir du Canada présidé par Keith Spicer, une preuve de «l'urgence de procéder à une réforme fondamentale du fédéralisme canadien»[8]. Monsieur Bourassa aurait pu prêter attention à certains passages du rapport, qui annonçaient déjà l'avenir:

> Pour la plupart des participants, ailleurs qu'au Québec, il ne faut pas acheter le maintien de la province dans la Confédération au prix de la destruction ou de l'atteinte à ce qu'ils chérissent le plus, et surtout pas au prix du sacrifice de l'égalité individuelle ou provinciale ... S'il n'est pas impossible que des mécanismes non constitutionnels puissent être trouvés pour satisfaire un certain nombre des revendications du Québec et des provinces, de l'avis des participants hors Québec, ces accords, pour être acceptables, ne pourraient intervenir que dans le cadre d'un pan-canadianisme fort où tous les Canadiens jouiraient de droits égaux, de normes nationales et d'un même accès aux programmes et services.[9]

En insistant sur l'égalité dans les relations entre les individus et les provinces, le rapport du Forum des citoyens prenait le relais de la Commission Bélanger-Campeau, qui avait constaté l'existence d'un choc des visions, des aspirations et des identités nationales entre le Québec et le Canada. La Commission Bélanger-Campeau avait fait ressortir toute l'importance de la Loi constitutionnelle de 1982, qui avait renforcé la perception d'une identité nationale canadienne se manifestant dans des croyances en l'égalité de tous les citoyens canadiens, de toutes les origines culturelles et de toutes les provinces[10]. Par l'entremise de la Loi 150, le gouvernement du Québec avait donné au reste du Canada une obligation de résultat. En attente, les autorités québécoises demeuraient lucides quant à la difficulté de la tâche pour le Canada. Lors d'une conférence prononcée dans le cadre prestigieux des Cambridge Lecture Series, madame Diane Wilhelmy, la sous-ministre responsable du dossier constitutionnel au Conseil exécutif, diagnostiqua de façon réaliste les principales dimensions de la crise: l'obsolescence de la vision dualiste à l'extérieur du Québec, le principe de l'égalité entre les provinces et l'absence de consensus sur la définition des communautés nationales représentaient à ses yeux les principales causes de l'impasse[11].

En attente des offres fédérales, le Québec continua de boycotter les discussions multilatérales. Monsieur Bourassa ne se rendit pas à la conférence des premiers ministres des provinces en août à Whistler. Il reçut néanmoins madame Rita Johnston, Premier ministre de la Colombie-britannique, à Montréal, et lui répéta que le Québec cherchait réparation pour l'affront subi en 1982. Monsieur Bourassa rencontra aussi le ministre fédéral responsable des affaires constitutionnelles, M. Joe Clark, mais fut fort peu loquace quant au progrès des discussions en cours à l'intérieur du cabinet fédéral. Ces rencontres allaient donner le ton à toute l'année: le Québec entretiendrait des rapports bilatéraux intenses avec le gouvernement fédéral et les autres joueurs, sans se commettre sur le fond des négociations multilatérales se déroulant sans lui.

La ronde du Canada fut inaugurée officiellement avec la publication par le gouvernement fédéral d'un document de réflexion, *Bâtir ensemble l'avenir du Canada*, le 24 septembre 1991. Quelques jours auparavant, le quotidien *Le Soleil* offrit à ses lecteurs une longue entrevue de Robert Bourassa avec le journaliste Michel Vastel. Optimiste, monsieur Bourassa nota que ses partenaires canadiens avaient encore un an — c'est-à-dire beaucoup de temps devant eux — pour faire une offre valable au Québec. Si cela se produisait, il n'hésiterait pas à amender la Loi 150 pour faire un référendum sur ces offres. À une question de Vastel, lui demandant s'il pourrait être de l'intérêt des Québécois de tenir un référendum sur la souveraineté, monsieur Bourassa répondit ce qui suit: «Je ne crois pas parce que je me pose des questions sur la portée réelle d'un tel geste»[12]. Dès ce moment, la stratégie du couteau sur la gorge, élaborée par Léon Dion et la Commission Bélanger-Campeau, puis reprise par la Loi 150, commençait à ressembler à un bluff. Pourquoi accepter d'énormes coûts de transition, poursuivit monsieur Bourassa, «pour finalement aboutir à une structure canadienne qu'on peut peut-être atteindre sans casser ...»[13].

Cette entrevue identifie bien les différents échiquiers sur lesquels joue monsieur Bourassa: il doit garder son parti uni, tenir compte de la volonté populaire et faire bouger le Canada anglais, tout en rassurant et en sécurisant les investisseurs. Il souhaite une véritable réforme, annonce qu'il ne pourra se contenter de miettes, qu'il ne cassera pas le système si les offres sont acceptables, mais laisse entendre aussi qu'il hésiterait à tenir un référendum sur la souveraineté. En conclusion d'une récente étude, Louis Imbeau nous aide à voir qu'il est difficile de concilier tous ces objectifs:

> La deuxième suggestion qu'on peut tirer de cette analyse est que, si on veut arriver à un compromis, le Québec et le «reste du Canada» doivent prouver qu'ils sont prêts au compromis, tout en montrant qu'ils sont disposés à sévir aussi, si besoin est, c'est-à-dire qu'ils sont prêts à risquer la séparation du Québec. En 1986-1987, Québec a montré qu'il était prêt au compromis. Le «Reste du Canada» a montré, en juin 1990, qu'il était prêt à sévir. Québec doit maintenant montrer qu'il est prêt à risquer l'indépendance et le «Reste du Canada» doit faire la preuve qu'il est réellement ouvert au compromis. A ces conditions, un compromis stable est possible.[14]

Dès septembre 1991, on pouvait deviner que monsieur Bourassa n'était pas prêt à «risquer l'indépendance», pour reprendre les termes d'Imbeau, car cela aurait effarouché les investisseurs et mis en péril l'unité de son parti. Quant au «Reste du Canada», s'apprêtait-il à montrer qu'il était ouvert au compromis? Le Premier ministre du Québec fut à peu près le dernier à réagir au lancement de la ronde du Canada par le gouvernement fédéral. Il s'exprima, comme de coutume, avec mesure et prudence. Il vit dans *Bâtir ensemble l'avenir du Canada* un document utile mais incomplet. Après avoir énuméré quelques aspects positifs (reconnaissance du Québec comme société distincte, limitation du pouvoir fédéral de dépenser, accord sur l'immigration), il considéra «in-acceptable dans sa forme actuelle» le projet d'union économique[15]. Dans les médias, les analystes lui reprochèrent de ne pas avoir remarqué ou critiqué l'édulcoration de la clause de la société distincte, définie, intégrée dans la Charte des droits et noyée parmi une liste de 14 caractéristiques fondamentales dans la «Clause Canada.» On lui reprocha aussi d'avoir fait passer le droit de veto pour le Québec du statut de condition nécessaire au rang d'objectif important et d'avoir annoncé des reculs ultérieurs en acceptant le principe d'un sénat élu, efficace et équitable. En conférence de presse, monsieur Bourassa eut cette phrase sibylline: «Si je dis non, qu'est-ce qui va se passer?»[16] Comme l'a bien vu Michel David, on retrouve en ces quelques mots le dilemme de Robert Bourassa sur l'échiquier canadien. Monsieur Bourassa trouverait excessive-ment ardu de confronter l'impasse constitutionnelle, ses conséquences et les choix douloureux devant lesquels il serait placé. Mais pour préserver les chances de compromis, c'est encore Louis Imbeau qui le rappelle fort juste-ment, il faut que les joueurs soient transparents. La réaction au dépôt du document fédéral ne laissait présager rien de bon:

> On pourrait ainsi multiplier les exemples ou M. Bourassa aurait dû, fort utilement, rappeler les positions de son gouvernement, établir les balises qui le guideront au cours des prochains mois. Il est des moments où un chef de gouvernement, tout en se disposant au dialogue le plus franc et le plus ouvert qui soit, doit situer les

limites qui sont les siennes, son seuil de tolérance ... Hier, M. Bourassa avait une occasion en or de démontrer, en mettant pleinement les Québécois dans le coup, que son principal souci portait sur l'essentiel et non sur l'accessoire. Il a préféré rester dans le vague et le flou, tentant avant toute chose de ne pas compromettre la solidarité partisane. Ce n'est pas très glorieux. C'est même inquiétant pour l'avenir.[17]

Dans les jours qui suivirent sa réaction initiale, Robert Bourassa se déplaça sur l'échiquier partisan pour dénoncer ceux qui réclamaient un référendum hâtif sur la souveraineté avant que la commission parlementaire n'en eût étudié les coûts. Monsieur Bourassa souligna que la Commission Bélanger-Campeau avait évalué à 8 milliards $ le déficit du Québec dans un scénario de souveraineté. Sur la question du droit de veto, Gil Rémillard et Robert Bourassa firent le premier d'une longue série de pas-de-deux: le premier affirmant qu'aucun gouvernement québécois n'a le droit de signer une entente constitutionnelle qui ne comprendrait pas le droit de veto, le second ramenant l'exercice de ce droit aux institutions fédérales et au droit de retrait sur les transferts législatifs. Après la publication du document fédéral, monsieur Bourassa dut comprendre que la partie ne serait pas facile pour lui sur l'échiquier partisan.

Les ténors de son cabinet, les Claude Ryan, Lise Bacon, John Ciaccia, Sam Elkas et Daniel Johnson, donnent l'impression d'être des fédéralistes inconditionnels. Mais le Premier ministre doit aussi composer avec une Commission-Jeunesse qui aura droit au tiers des délégués lors du prochain congrès libéral. Le président de cette Commission, Mario Dumont, est un fervent défenseur du rapport Allaire, un document adopté en mars 1991 qui représente la position officielle du parti sur les questions constitutionnelles. Il ne manqua pas de constater le gouffre entre la politique officielle du Parti libéral du Québec et le document fédéral de septembre 1991. Monsieur Bourassa doit aussi se préoccuper de l'aile nationaliste dans son caucus. Pour le député Guy Bélanger, qui est aussi le président de la commission parlementaire étudiant la souveraineté, le document fédéral prenait l'allure d'un véritable «piège à cons»[18]. Monsieur Bourassa ne peut ignorer non plus la base historique du Parti libéral, formée de gens qui réconcilient dans une vision dualiste fédéralisme canadien et nationalisme québécois. Le notaire Jean Allaire, qui fut président du Comité constitutionnel du Parti libéral du Québec, me semble assez représentatif de ce courant. Il vaut la peine de citer un extrait du rapport qui porte son nom:

> Au Québec, la Confédération a toujours été perçue par nous comme un pacte solennel entre deux nations, pacte ne pouvant être modifié sans le consentement des deux parties. Le Québec étant devenu par la force des choses «l'État national des Canadiens français», on conçoit facilement le dépit qui a gagné les citoyens du Québec un matin de 1981 lorsqu'on leur a communiqué que leur Constitution,

la loi fondamentale de leur pays, allait être modifiée sans leur consentement. Plus grave encore, on institutionnalisait un processus d'amendement permettant des modifications additionnelles, toujours sans le consentement du Québec. Au surplus, cet aboutissement était le résultat opposé d'une promesse solennelle, non tenue, du Premier ministre du Canada. L'Accord du lac Meech constituait en soi une reconnaissance de l'illégitimité d'une Constitution n'ayant pas reçu l'adhésion du Québec.[19]

Pour tenir tout ce beau monde en équilibre, pour gagner du temps et repousser jusqu'au dernier moment les choix les plus pénibles, Robert Bourassa a pu recourir pendant la «ronde du Canada» aux deux commissions créées en vertu de la Loi 150. Les fédéralistes inconditionnels étaient rassurés par leur présence en force à la Commission sur les questions afférentes à la souveraineté; quant à l'aile nationaliste, elle pouvait se consoler des propos «feutrés» du premier ministre en sachant qu'aucune proposition de renouvellement du fédéralisme ne serait agréée par le gouvernement du Québec avant d'avoir été étudiée par la Commission sur les offres de partenariat. En 1991-1992, monsieur Bourassa se réfugia derrière le mandat de cette dernière commission dans les jours qui suivirent la publication de chacune de initiatives de la ronde du Canada: les propositions de septembre 1991, le rapport Beaudoin-Dobbie en février 1992, le rapport d'étape des négociations multilatérales en juin et l'entente du 7 juillet. Je voudrais maintenant considérer d'un peu plus près le travail de chacune de ces commissions au cours de l'année qui vient de s'écouler.

La Commission sur les offres de partenariat devait selon le rapport Bélanger-Campeau et la Loi 150 se pencher sur les propositions «liant formellement» le gouvernement fédéral et ceux des provinces du Canada anglais. Théoriquement, la Commission n'avait le mandat de faire des recommandations qu'après avoir constaté que les partenaires canadiens s'étaient suffisamment engagés, pour qu'il n'y ait pas de répétition d'un scénario comme celui du dérapage de l'Accord du lac Meech. En attendant les offres, la Commission était aussi chargée de recenser les positions constitutionnelles du Québec depuis les années soixante, de circonscrire les perceptions et les objectifs constitutionnels des interlocuteurs du Québec depuis 1982, d'examiner enfin la question des chevauchements de compétence. Au 14 juillet 1992, cette Commission avait entendu les témoignages de 33 experts en 20 séances publiques, en plus de tenir 4 séances de consultations particulières avec 6 groupes sur le rapport Beaudoin-Dobbie. À l'automne 1991, les témoignages des professeurs Patrice Garant, Nicole Duplé, Andrée Lajoie, Jacques Fortin, Ivan Bernier et Réjean Pelletier, sur les différentes facettes des propositions fédérales (société distincte, sénat, pouvoir de dépenser et union économique), indiquèrent à tous les observateurs intéressés que la barre à franchir serait très haute pour rendre un projet de renouvellement acceptable au Québec[20].

Les deux Commissions ne furent pas à l'abri des conflits sur le deuxième échiquier préoccupant Robert Bourassa, le terrain québécois où rivalisent le Parti libéral et le P.Q. de Jacques Parizeau. Vers la fin de l'automne, le Parti québécois décida de quitter le Commission sur les offres, prétextant que cette dernière tournait en rond en l'absence de véritables propositions. On peut s'interroger sur la pertinence d'une telle décision. En assistant à toutes les séances, les députés du Parti québécois auraient pu contribuer, par leurs questions, à renforcer dans le coeur et l'esprit de leurs collègues libéraux le consensus interprétatif de la Commission Bélanger-Campeau, constatant une impasse profonde dans le régime fédéral et un gouffre majeur dans les perceptions entre Canadiens et Québécois. Je considère particulièrement révélateur à ce propos le témoignage du professeur Alan Cairns, qui vint vanter devant la Commission sur les offres la lucidité du rapport de la Commission Bélanger-Campeau. Selon Cairns, le rapport Bélanger-Campeau avait proposé un résumé succinct des principales tendances de l'évolution constitutionnelle récente au Canada en insistant sur la vision politique nationaliste et égalitaire (en réalité symétrique) promue par la Charte des droits et libertés[21].

S'il faut tancer le Parti québécois pour son attitude à la Commission sur les offres de partenariat, on peut en faire autant pour le Parti libéral de Robert Bourassa à la Commission sur la souveraineté. Le mandat de cette dernière n'était pas mince. Elle aurait à jeter de la lumière sur tous les éléments relatifs à la souveraineté, et notamment le processus d'accession à la souveraineté et la reconnaissance internationale, la succession d'États, les diverses avenues de partenariat économique, les impacts économiques (les coûts, selon le vocabulaire des Libéraux ...), et enfin la transition. Au 14 juillet 1992, la Commission avait entendu 52 experts et 3 groupes autochtones en 37 séances publiques. Si tout le monde avait fait diligence, le rapport aurait pu être publié vers la fin de mai 1992. Le président de la Commission, monsieur Guy Bélanger, et son secrétariat, ne sont pas parvenus à obtenir l'approbation des plus fédéralistes parmi les membres libéraux. Selon une analyse d'André Pépin, du quotidien *La Presse*, certains membres, et notamment le député de Verdun Henri-François Gautrin, remettent en question jusqu'à la toute dernière virgule des ébauches de rapport proposées[22]. S'il l'avait voulu, Robert Bourassa aurait pu faire accélérer les choses. Un rapport reconnaissant la légitimité et la faisabilité de la souveraineté aurait renforcé la crédibilité de sa menace dans le reste du Canada. Sur cette question comme sur bien d'autres, la rationalité de la lutte sur l'échiquier partisan l'a emporté à mon avis au détriment de la rationalité du combat sur l'échiquier canadien. On peut penser aussi que monsieur Bourassa a choisi d'attendre les offres définitives du reste du Canada avant de préciser les contours de l'analyse gouvernementale des coûts et des conséquences de la souveraineté.

Parmi toutes les interventions faites devant la Commission sur la souveraineté, la plus retentissante fut sans doute celle du chef de l'Assemblée des Premières Nations, monsieur Ovide Mercredi. Ce dernier ne manqua pas de toucher quelques cordes sensibles pour Robert Bourassa et la plupart des Québécois, moins de deux ans après la crise d'Oka:

L'autodétermination n'est pas un droit relevant d'une «province», c'est un droit propre à tous les peuples. Le «peuple québécois» est-il un «peuple» au sens du droit international? La population du Québec se compose d'une grande variété de groupes raciaux et ethniques. Elle ne peut être considérée comme formant un seul «peuple» pourvu du droit à l'autodétermination. Autrement le «peuple canadien» serait lui aussi un «peuple» selon le droit international ... Bon nombre de Premières Nations au Québec n'ont jamais signé de traité avec le gouvernement et n'ont jamais cédé leurs droits territoriaux de quelque façon que ce soit. Vous ne pouvez pas présumer que ces territoires reviendraient de droit à un nouvel état souverain du Québec.»[23]

Je voudrais faire remarquer en passant qu'Ovide Mercredi, comme le démontre cet extrait, n'a pas uniquement contesté l'existence du peuple québécois, mais aussi celle du peuple canadien. Monsieur Bourassa et son gouvernement n'ont pas relevé jusqu'à présent l'évidente contradiction entre le discours «nationaliste» des peuples autochtones et les principaux documents fédéraux dans la ronde du Canada, qui postulent l'existence d'une seule et unique identité nationale canadienne[24]. On aurait pu inviter monsieur Mercredi à déployer autant de vigueur contre le concept d'une seule nation, qui est au coeur du régime fédéral depuis 1982, qu'il ne le fait contre la vision dualiste promue par les Québécois. Dans un débat l'opposant à Jacques Parizeau à l'Assemblée nationale le 8 novembre 1991, Robert Bourassa se contenta de signifier aux leaders autochtones qu'ils devront respecter l'intégrité du territoire québécois[25]. La machine gouvernementale québécoise ne semble pas encore avoir décidé d'adopter une politique systématique à l'égard des peuples autochtones, qui vaudrait à l'intérieur comme à l'extérieur du Québec, et qui viendrait compléter les vaillants efforts du ministre responsable du dossier sectoriel, monsieur Christos Sirros. Le Québec est encore à la recherche d'une conception d'ensemble du fédéralisme canadien qui intégrerait ses aspirations nationales et celles des peuples autochtones.

En se servant des séquelles de la crise d'Oka, et en brandissant le spectre des 5 milliards $ d'impôts additionnels que la souveraineté coûterait aux Québécois selon une étude du Conseil économique du Canada, monsieur Bourassa obtint un autre succès tactique contre Jacques Parizeau et le Parti québécois lors de l'interpellation de novembre à l'Assemblée nationale. Le prix à payer pour ce triomphe? L'élimination d'une autre pièce — cavalier, tour? — sur l'échiquier canadien:

Sauf que dans son enthousiasme à pourfendre la souveraineté, il brûle beaucoup
de vaisseaux. Pourquoi le Canada anglais ferait-il des concessions pour garder le
Québec, quand son premier ministre répète tous les jours que la séparation serait
la fin du monde?[26]

Officiellement, le Québec n'est pas monté en 1991-1992 dans le train de la
«ronde du Canada». Il est resté en gare jusqu'à ce que le train et ses passagers
reviennent pour lui présenter des offres. Après le dépôt des propositions
fédérales en septembre, les autorités québécoises ont observé de loin la
désorganisation qui a caractérisé les premières semaines dans la vie du Comité
mixte spécial du Sénat et de la Chambre des communes, sous la responsabilité
conjointe de Claude Castonguay (puis de Gérald Beaudoin) et de Dorothy
Dobbie. Le gouvernement du Québec n'a pas été beaucoup plus actif dans le
processus des conférences thématiques sur le renouvellement du Canada,
organisées par le gouvernement fédéral en collaboration avec des instituts
indépendants pour combler le vide laissé par le dérapage des audiences
publiques du Comité mixte en novembre au Manitoba. De la mi-janvier à la
mi-février, cinq conférences reprirent les différents thèmes de *Bâtir ensemble
l'avenir du Canada*: on se pencha sur la répartition des pouvoirs à Halifax, sur
la réforme des institutions à Calgary, sur l'union économique à Montréal, sur
l'identité, les droits et les valeurs à Toronto, avant de faire le bilan à Vancouver
du 14 au 16 février. Si de nombreux citoyens ordinaires du Québec participèrent
à ces conférences, il n'en demeure pas moins que la présence des milieux
nationalistes, universitaires et gouvernementaux y fut négligeable. Les plus
assidus furent les représentants des milieux patronaux, notamment messieurs
Claude Beauchamp et Ghislain Dufour.

À ceux qui voulaient bien entendre, les dirigeants québécois envoyèrent
publiquement des signaux assez clairs quant à leurs objectifs et intentions. Au
début et à la fin de la ronde des conférences thématiques le ministre délégué
aux affaires intergouvernementales canadiennes, M. Gil Rémillard, prononça
deux discours dans lesquels il réitéra les principes défendus par le Québec: le
17 janvier devant la Chambre de commerce d'Anjou (à la veille d'une élection
partielle perdue par le Parti libéral), et le 24 février lors du congrès hivernal de
l'Association du Barreau canadien à Whistler. Ces principes sont les suivants:

1. Les éléments de l'Accord du lac Meech sont «incontournables dans leur
    substance».
2. «Les pouvoirs de l'Assemblée nationale ne sauraient être diminués sans
    son consentement. Le Québec doit pouvoir dire non à tout amendement
    constitutionnel pouvant affecter les pouvoirs de l'Assemblée nationale
    ainsi que les institutions et les caractéristiques principales de la
    fédération canadienne. Aucun gouvernement québécois ne peut ac-
    cepter un accord constitutionnel sans droit de veto.»

3. La clause de la société distincte est indispensable et ne saurait être réduite à une coquille vide. Elle doit avoir des conséquences juridiques et politiques significatives.

4. L'union économique doit être forte et dynamique, sans que les moyens employés pour la créer ne deviennent disproportionnés.

5. Il faut un nouveau partage des pouvoirs qui respecte les compétences du Québec et le critère de l'efficacité.

6. Le réaménagement de la fédération doit être de nature constitutionnelle plutôt qu'administrative.

7. L'intégrité territoriale du Québec doit être respectée. Québec s'oppose donc à la définition par les tribunaux de la nature et des modalités d'application du droit inhérent à l'autonomie gouvernementale pour les autochtones[27].

Des remarques s'imposent à propos d'un certain nombre de ces principes. Il y a d'abord du flou dans l'exigence québécoise d'obtenir «la substance de Meech». Les cinq conditions doivent y être, mais Québec ne demande pas explicitement que l'on revienne à la formulation spécifique de 1987, par exemple sur le pouvoir de dépenser ou la clause de la société distincte. Réclamer la substance de Meech, c'est ouvrir la voie à des compromis sur ces questions. Il y a du vague aussi dans le lien à établir entre la réforme des institutions centrales et le droit de veto. Tel que formulé, le principe mis de l'avant par monsieur Rémillard est compatible avec un droit de veto octroyé au Québec après une réforme fondamentale d'une institution comme le Sénat. Nous verrons plus loin que cette hypothèse est devenue une réalité avec l'entente du 7 juillet 1992. Dans son discours de Whistler, monsieur Rémillard s'exprima en faveur du fédéralisme asymétrique sur la question du partage des pouvoirs. Le Québec semblait donc placer beaucoup d'espoir dans l'ouverture à l'asymétrie manifestée par les participants à la conférence thématique d'Halifax. C'était oublier le rapport Spicer, précédemment cité, de même que les analyses des sondeurs de la psyché canadienne anglaise:

> The whole notion of asymmetrical federalism has no chance, just none whatsoever. I can't see English Canadian public opinion changing sufficiently to make the prospect of giving Quebec anything that is special, unique, different, politically viable. If it was asymmetrical federalism or no Quebec, right now they would probably choose no Quebec.[28]

Néanmoins, Gil Rémillard avait posé d'utiles balises pour l'examen de la suite de l'histoire, non sans rappeler que la souveraineté était une option légitime et faisable pour le Québec. Il ne restait plus qu'à attendre le rapport du Comité Beaudoin-Dobbie et les réactions de Robert Bourassa, à quelque 240 jours de l'échéance fixée par la Commission Bélanger-Campeau et la Loi 150.

ROBERT BOURASSA ET LE QUÉBEC EMPÊTRÉS DANS
LA RONDE DU CANADA

Un Canada renouvelé, le Rapport du comité mixte spécial sur le renouvellement du Canada, fut rendu public à Ottawa le 29 février 1992, dans la confusion la plus totale. Dans ce document qui respirait presque à chaque page les arômes du nationalisme canadien (on y parle constamment de l'identité nationale canadienne, des programmes nationaux, des normes nationales, etc.), il y avait une petite phrase qui fit sourciller les lecteurs québécois:

> Bref, il nous semble irréaliste de penser qu'on puisse mettre un secteur quelconque totalement à l'abri de l'influence fédérale, non seulement à cause des obligations du fédéral en matière internationale et autochtone et en matière de recherche et de développement au Canada, mais aussi à cause de l'impact de sa politique fiscale et budgétaire sur les divers secteurs énumérés dans la proposition.[29]

Sortant de sa réserve habituelle, Robert Bourassa admit être déçu par le Rapport Beaudoin-Dobbie, dans lequel il dit voir une forme de fédéralisme dominateur. Sur la question du partage des pouvoirs, monsieur Bourassa opina «qu'il n'y a pas guère plus sur la table qu'auparavant, c'est vague et il est difficile de conclure qu'il y aurait un véritable transfert de pouvoirs au Québec».[30] Il faut bien constater que le comité mixte eut toutes les misères du monde à faire l'unanimité autour de la simple confirmation de certaines sphères de compétence provinciale: le tourisme, la foresterie, les mines, les loisirs, le logement et les affaires municipales et urbaines. Dans des domaines revendiqués par le Québec, comme la culture et la formation de la main-d'oeuvre, le rapport Beaudoin-Dobbie recommandait la négociation d'accords intergouvernementaux et le maintien des responsabilités «nationales» du gouvernement fédéral. Dans un éditorial, la directrice du journal *Le Devoir*, madame Lise Bissonnette, traduisit bien l'état d'esprit au Québec:

> Pour obtenir un statut qui lui convienne un peu, pour reprendre des champs de compétence devenus territoires occupés, il devra négocier pouce à pouce avec des gouvernements fédéraux toujours coriaces, de quelque couleur qu'ils soient, comme l'ont démontré depuis un an les pourparlers sur l'immigration ou sur la formation de la main-d'oeuvre. Il devra ensuite quêter l'approbation des Communes et du Sénat, donc d'une majorité qui représente une opinion massivement opposée à un statut particulier pour le Québec. Et il devra continuer à vivre avec chevauchements, dédoublements, envahissements qui accompagnent le pouvoir de dépenser d'Ottawa, auquel on propose une entrée royale dans la Constitution.[31]

Quelques semaines avant la publication du rapport Beaudoin-Dobbie, monsieur Bourassa de passage à Bruxelles avait évoqué devant des journalistes la nature de la question qu'il soumettrait en référendum aux Québécois si les offres fédérales s'avéraient inacceptables. Il leur demanderait s'ils veulent remplacer le régime en place par deux États souverains, associés dans une union économique, responsables à un parlement élu au suffrage universel. Lors du même voyage, réfléchissant à la situation du fédéralisme en Yougoslavie et en Tchécoslovaquie, monsieur Bourassa rappela que dans les fédérations où plusieurs communautés nationales vivent ensemble, chacune d'entre elles devrait être appelée à consentir aux changements constitutionnels fondamentaux.[32] Le Premier ministre laissait sous-entendre dans cette déclaration que le Québec représentait une communauté nationale au sein du Canada, et qu'il n'avait pas consenti à la réforme constitutionnelle de 1982. Pris ensemble les discours de Gil Rémillard à Anjou et Whistler, les propos de Robert Bourassa à Bruxelles et sa réaction initiale au rapport Beaudoin-Dobbie, offrent l'image la plus cohérente de la position québécoise sur l'échiquier canadien en 1991-1992. Tout cela établit des critères pour les choix, annonce la préférence du gouvernement pour le fédéralisme renouvelé et précise la solution de rechange si les offres sont inacceptables. Autour de cette stratégie, l'attentisme du Québec pouvait se justifier. Il n'était pas passif. Mais Robert Bourassa avait d'autres préoccupations, notamment partisanes, et d'autres habitudes que celle de son franc-parler lors de ses voyages en Europe, notamment le besoin qu'il ressent de toujours vouloir gagner du temps. Depuis la mi-mars 1992, grosso modo depuis le début des négociations multilatérales à seize, le Premier ministre du Québec semble obnubilé par la question de l'unité au sein de son parti. La conséquence sur l'échiquier canadien me paraît assez évidente: le Québec s'est placé dans une situation de dépendance par rapport aux choix stratégiques du gouvernement fédéral et des autres provinces.

Au début mars, au moment où à Ottawa Joe Clark et Bob Rae facilitaient l'entrée d'Ovide Mercredi et des autres leaders des territoires et des peuples autochtones à la table constitutionnelle, Robert Bourassa choisit de s'absenter de l'Assemblée nationale avant le vote où péquistes et libéraux s'unirent pour désapprouver le rapport Beaudoin-Dobbie. Une semaine plus tard, le 18 mars, en présence de monsieur Bourassa, libéraux et péquistes firent encore front commun pour réaffirmer la détermination du Québec à poursuivre, «dans les circonstances actuelles», son boycott des négociations constitutionnelles multilatérales.[33] Pour rétablir l'équilibre entre les factions de son parti, le Premier ministre fit le lendemain, lors du message inaugural lu aux parlementaires, un plaidoyer dithyrambique en faveur du fédéralisme canadien. Il évoqua même la possibilité du report du référendum prévu pour octobre, et nota que le rapport Beaudoin-Dobbie offrait un nombre sans précédent de pouvoirs au Québec.[34] Dans les jours qui suivirent, monsieur Bourassa poursuivit sur cette lancée lors d'un conseil général du Parti libéral du Québec tenu à Montréal. Il promit à ses militants qu'il ne tiendrait un référendum qu'à condition d'être sûr de le gagner, pour ne pas affaiblir le Québec. Si les offres fédérales s'avéraient acceptables, elles seraient soumises à la population. Dans le cas contraire, il faudrait expliquer à la population «qu'un référendum sur la souveraineté pourrait affaiblir l'économie canadienne».[35] Monsieur Bourassa surenchérit en soulignant le caractère long, complexe et coûteux que prend immanquablement la désintégration d'une fédération. L'impact de la désintégration du Canada sur les marchés financiers internationaux, qui ont prêté 260 milliards $ aux Canadiens, serait selon lui catastrophique. Dès ce moment-là, il était possible de comprendre qu'il n'y aurait pas de référendum sur la souveraineté au Québec en 1992. La stratégie du couteau sur la gorge ne tenait déjà plus qu'à un fil.

Dans une entrevue qui eut beaucoup de retentissement au Québec, publiée par le quotidien français *Le Monde* en avril, monsieur Bourassa confirma ce que tout le monde pressentait depuis déjà un bon moment: s'il y avait un référendum au Québec à l'automne, il porterait sur les offres fédérales.[36] Refusant toujours de participer aux discussions multilatérales qui se poursuivaient aux quatre coins du pays, le gouvernement du Québec n'envoyait pas, c'est le moins que l'on puisse dire, des signaux susceptibles d'amener les Getty, Wells et Rae à lui faire des concessions. D'autant plus que l'on restait volontairement vague, à Québec, à propos des différents consensus qui émergeaient petit à petit à la table constitutionnelle. Les autorités québécoises préféraient se réfugier derrière la répétition de leur position de base: récupérer la substance de Meech, obtenir un nouveau partage des pouvoirs et un droit de veto sur les changements apportés aux institutions centrales.

Robert Bourassa n'a certainement pas renforcé la position du Québec sur l'échiquier constitutionnel en accueillant somme toute assez favorablement l'initiative référendaire du gouvernement fédéral. Vu que son gouvernement considère illégitime la réforme de 1982, il aurait pu s'opposer au principe même d'un référendum fédéral sur le territoire du Québec. Monsieur Bourassa ne fit rien de tout cela. Après avoir laissé entendre qu'un référendum fédéral devrait à tout le moins respecter la loi 150 et fonctionner selon la règle de la double majorité — une pour le Québec, et une autre pour le reste du Canada — monsieur Bourassa resta muet lorsque la loi référendaire ratifiée à Ottawa écarta cette question de la double majorité tout en laissant libre cours à la multiplication des comités et des dépenses.[37] Obsédé par le temps, il vit même dans toute cette affaire une occasion en or pour réduire de 84 à 47 jours la durée d'une campagne référendaire québécoise, reportant ainsi au 9 septembre l'échéance définitive pour le dépôt de la question à l'Assemblée nationale. Cela ouvrirait par le fait même une brèche importante pour la tenue d'un référendum fédéral au Québec.

Alors que le rythme des discussions multilatérales s'accélérait, au début mai, messieurs Bourassa et Rémillard entreprirent un «pèlerinage en vrai Canada» (pour reprendre une expression d'André Laurendeau). Ils firent des arrêts successifs dans toutes les capitales des provinces de l'ouest. Les discussions avec les Harcourt, Getty, Romanow et Filmon ne débouchèrent sur rien de concret. Gary Filmon restait réticent quant à la clause de la société distincte et à l'octroi d'un droit de veto au Québec. Don Getty sortit de sa rencontre avec monsieur Bourassa avec la certitude que le sénat égal n'était pas la préférence du Québec, mais aussi avec l'assurance que ce dernier n'y était pas opposé d'une façon absolue. Avant même que la question du partage des pouvoirs n'ait été abordée à la table multilatérale, monsieur Bourassa calmait les craintes du Canada anglais. Dans les médias, la critique se faisait de plus en plus cinglante ;

> Cette semaine, avant même qu'il ne prenne l'avion pour Vancouver..., le Premier ministre donnait la pénible impression d'être disposé à tous les compromis et marchandages imaginables, pour ne pas dire maquignonnages (à propos du Sénat, par exemple, échangeable contre une concoction sur la société distincte et la moitié d'un veto).[38]

Les réunions multilatérales sur la constitution furent interrompues le 11 juin. Toute lecture du rapport d'étape établit clairement que la question du sénat, notamment le problème de la répartition des sièges, restait en suspens. Sur la question du partage des pouvoirs, il n'y avait d'un point de vue québécois aucun déblocage en comparaison avec le rapport Beaudoin-Dobbie. Sur la clause de la société distincte, les textes demeuraient préliminaires et évasifs. Réagissant à tout cela avec énormément de prudence au terme des travaux de l'Assemblée nationale, monsieur Bourassa exprima des réserves sur le volet autochtone du rapport d'étape, indiqua que le Québec attendait toujours un texte final sur la clause de la société distincte et conclut que le gouvernement fédéral avait jusqu'à la fin de juillet pour lui présenter des offres. Visiblement, monsieur Bourassa avait hâte de quitter le terrain miné de l'Assemblée nationale, les questions de l'opposition, les microphones et les caméras des journalistes. À l'intérieur de son parti, les tensions s'accentuaient. Les jeunes libéraux, défenseurs du rapport Allaire, piaffaient d'impatience et préparaient un congrès pour le début juillet. Pendant ce temps, à la Commission parlementaire sur l'étude des questions afférentes à la souveraineté, les fédéralistes les plus durs empêchaient toujours le progrès des travaux et la publication du rapport. Au-dessus de toutes ces manoeuvres le maître du temps trônait:

> Le Premier ministre laisse faire, laisse dire, tentant de faire plaisir à tout le monde en même temps, gagnant du temps, cette denrée si précieuse et rare en politique. Il reste le seul maître d'une stratégie et d'une tactique qui n'ont pour seul et unique but que de sauvegarder les «convergences» libérales et de glisser sous le tapis, le plus longtemps possible, les divergences profondes qui minent les deux ailes militantes, jeunes et ainés, les deux ailes ministérielles, ultra-fédéralistes et nationalistes de tout poil, et même, dans une moindre mesure, les ministres eux-mêmes.[39]

Comme je le soulignais au début de ce texte, la maîtrise du temps ne libère pas un dirigeant politique de l'obligation de faire des choix. Le visage de monsieur

Bourassa a dû s'assombrir lorsqu'il a appris que, contre toute attente, les participants à la table constitutionnelle multilatérale en étaient venus à un accord le 7 juillet, qualifié d'historique par le ministre Joe Clark. Cet accord, en plus de se prêter à la plupart des autres réserves et critiques émises par les dirigeants et analystes québécois à propos des ébauches précédentes dans la ronde du Canada, entérinait le principe d'un sénat élu, efficace et égal. L'égalité du sénat, c'est l'égalité des provinces, un Québec ramené au rang de province comme les autres dans une grande nation canadienne. C'est le complément institutionnel de la culture politique nationaliste promue par la réforme de 1982 et la Charte des droits et libertés. Cela signifie aussi la fin de la thèse des deux peuples fondateurs, des deux nations ou deux sociétés distinctes prônée par les politiciens et les intellectuels du Québec tout au long du vingtième siècle. Robert Bourassa a dû comprendre rapidement que l'entente du 7 juillet serait invendable au Québec, qu'il ne pourrait aller en référendum sur des offres auxquelles cette entente servirait de fondement. Quand les sénateurs conservateurs et fédéralistes comme Claude Castonguay, Solange Chaput-Rolland et Gérald Beaudoin lui-même se joignirent au tablé de protestations contre l'entente, Robert Bourassa dut se rappeler le cauchemar vécu à Victoria vingt ans plus tôt, lorsque Pierre Elliott Trudeau le somma d'accepter ou de refuser clairement un projet de révision constitutionnelle. Le 22 juin 1971, dans les pages du journal *Le Devoir*, l'actuel ministre Claude Ryan, alors directeur du quotidien, avait fait des commentaires qui n'ont rien perdu de leur pertinence:

> Au cours de la dernière fin de semaine, l'étau dans lequel M. Robert Bourassa s'est laissé enfermer à Victoria a paru se resserrer sensiblement... À la suite de ces interventions divergentes, une question se pose: «De quel côté penchera M. Bourassa?» Le Premier ministre, selon son habitude, cherche sans doute une solution qui lui permettrait de contourner l'obligation où on l'a placé de répondre par un oui ou un non. Cette prouesse semble toutefois devoir être impossible... Nonobstant les nombreuses concessions particulières que M. Bourassa a pu obtenir sur tel et tel article précis, la charte de Victoria, dans son ensemble, est un document qui tend à consolider la prépondérance du gouvernement central dans les affaires canadiennes et à ramener le Québec au rang de province comme les autres, sans égard à ses problèmes et à ses urgences propres.[40]

L'entente du 7 juillet consolide l'emprise du gouvernement central dans la fédération canadienne et ramène le Québec au rang de province comme les autres. M. Bourassa ne veut pas tenir de référendum sur la souveraineté. J'ai l'impression qu'il n'osera pas en tenir un sur des offres qu'il ne pourrait défendre selon les critères répétés à maintes reprises par son gouvernement. Il sait que Brian Mulroney hésite à s'aventurer sur le terrain d'un référendum fédéral ou d'une initiative unilatérale. Il lui reste donc quatre possibilités:

1. Reporter le référendum québécois à 1993, pour attendre que des offres lient formellement les autres gouvernements. Les Québécois seraient

invités au réalisme. Si la conférence constitutionnelle qui s'est amorcée le 18 août 1992 à Ottawa se termine par un accord politique entre les participants, c'est la voie qu'empruntera monsieur Bourassa.

2. Tenir des élections anticipées où il demanderait un mandat pour poursuivre les négociations. Ce serait une répétition du scénario de 1976.

3. Faire un référendum sur une contre-proposition du genre de la question évoquée à Bruxelles, menant à la création d'une union économique entre des États associés.

4. Invoquer des raisons de santé pour démissionner.

Je voudrais que monsieur Bourassa choisisse la troisième option. C'est ce qu'il ferait s'il pensait surtout à sa place dans l'histoire. Toutefois, j'ai bien peur qu'il finisse par adopter la première. Ce serait la voie tracée par des habitudes contractées en 25 ans de vie politique. Comme Robert Bourassa le suggéra lui-même il y a quelques mois, «C'est l'avenir qui devra trancher»[41]. L'avenir va trancher. Et Robert Bourassa reste l'ultime inconnue. S'il pense à l'Histoire, il va oser. S'il suit son instinct, il va essayer de mettre le couvercle sur la marmite constitutionnelle. On ne peut en dire plus pour l'instant.

NOTES

1. *Un Canada renouvelé*, Rapport du comité mixte spécial sur le renouvellement du Canada, Ottawa, ministère des Approvisionnements et Services du Canada, 1992, p. 97.

2. Daniel Bonin, «Le Québec de l'après-Meech: entre le beau risque nouvelle manière et la souveraineté», dans Douglas M. Brown, *Canada: The State of The Federation 1991*, Kingston, Institut des relations intergouvernementales, 1991, p. 50.

3. Voir *L'Actualité*, juillet 1992, vol. 17, no. 11, pp. 22-28

4. Nicolas Machiavel, *Le Prince*, Paris, Librairie générale française, 1972, ch. XXV, p. 133.

5. Vincent Lemieux, «Le positionnement des partis dans les débats sur l'avenir politique du Québec», dans Louis Balthazar, Guy Laforest et Vincent Lemieux, *Le Québec et la restructuration du Canada 1980-1992*. Enjeux et perspectives, Sillery, Les Éditions du Septentrion, 1991, p. 279.

6. *L'avenir politique et constitutionnel au Québec*. Rapport de la Commission sur l'avenir politique et constitutionnel du Québec, Québec, Éditeur officiel du Québec, 1991, p. 97.

7. *Le Soleil*, 21 juin 1991, p. A-5.

8. *Le Devoir*, 28 juin 1991, p. 4.

9. Le Forum des citoyens sur l'avenir du Canada, *Rapport à la population et au gouvernement du Canada*, Ottawa, ministère des Approvisionnements et Services, 1991, pp. 61 et 66.

10. *L'avenir politique et constitutionnel du Québec*, pp. 38-41.

11. Diane Wilhelmy, «Reforming the Constitution», *Cambridge Lecture Series*, 16 juillet 1991, pp. 7, 9 et 11.

12. *Le Soleil*, 22 septembre 1991, p. A-9.

13. Ibid, p. A-9.

14. Louis Imbeau, «Le compromis est-il encore possible? La négociation constitutionnelle de l'après-Meech à la lumière de la théorie des jeux», dans Louis Balthazar, Guy Laforest et Vincent Lemieux, *Le Québec et la restructuration du Canada 1980-1992*, Sillery, Les Éditions du Septentrion, 1991, p. 307.

15. *Le Devoir*, 26 septembre 1991, p. 1.

16. Michel David, «Le dilemme de Robert Bourassa», *Le Soleil*, 26 septembre 1991, p. A-16.

17. Imbeau, p. 306.

18. *Le Soleil*, 25 septembre 1991, p. A-1.

19. *Un Québec libre de ses choix*, Rapport du Comité constitutionnel du Parti libéral du Québec, Montréal, 28 janvier 1991, p. 66.

20. Patrice Garant, «Bâtir l'avenir du Canada avec ou sans le Québec» (24 octobre); Réjean Pelletier, «La réforme des institutions politiques centrales: plusieurs points restent à préciser» (7 novembre); Ivan Bernier, «Les propositions fédérales sur l'union économique» (14 novembre); Jacques Fortin, «Les propositions du gouvernement fédéral sur l'union économique» (14 novembre), Andrée Lajoie, «Contribution aux travaux de la commission parlementaire sur les offres fédérales (Pouvoir de dépenser)» (11 décembre); Nicole Duplé, «La société distincte dans les propositions constitutionnelles du gouvernement fédéral» (12 décembre); mémoires présentés à la Commission d'étude sur toute offre d'un nouveau partenariat de nature constitutionnelle, Assemblée nationale du Québec, 1991-1992.

21. Alan Cairns, «English Canada» and Post-Meech Constitutional Change», A Presentation to the Committee to Examine any Offer of A New Constitutional Partnership, Assemblée nationale du Québec, 23 mars 1992, p. 4.

22. *La Presse*, 30 mai 1992, p. C-7.

23. *Assemblée des Premières Nations*, Mémoire à l'intention de l'Assemblée nationale, la Commission parlementaire étudiant les questions afférentes à l'accession du Québec à la souveraineté, 11 février 1992, pp. 5 et 7.

24. Voir par exemple *Bâtir ensemble l'avenir du Canada*. Propositions constitutionnelles du gouvernement du Canada, Ottawa, ministère des Approvisionnements et Services, 1991, p. 2. La première section du document porte le sous-titre suivant: «L'identité canadienne: des valeurs communes». Selon la vision de ce document, et de l'annexe sur l'identité et les valeurs qui l'accompagne, les Autochtones et les Québécois sont réintégrés dans la mosaïque nationale canadienne.

25. *Le Devoir*, 9 novembre 1991, p. A-4.

26. Michel David, «Bourassa haut la main», *Le Soleil*, 9 novembre 1991, p. A-16.

27. Voir Gil Rémillard, Les Québécois comme les autres peuples sont aujourd'hui forcés de se redéfinir», *Le Devoir*, 17 janvier 1992, p. B-8. Voir aussi Gil Rémillard, «Notes pour une allocution au Congrès du Barreau canadien», Secrétariat aux Affaires intergouvernementales canadiennes», Québec, 24 février 1992.

28. Allan Gregg, «Rootless and Rudderless», dans Knowlton Nash, (dir.), *Visions of Canada*, Toronto, McClelland & Stewart, 1991, p. 58.

29. *Un Canada renouvelé, op.cit.*, p. 71.

30. *Le Devoir*, 4 mars 1992, p. A-1

31. Lise Bissonnette, «Le volet Québec», *Le Devoir*, 3 mars 1992, p. A-8.

32. *Le Devoir*, 8 février 1992, p. A-5.

33. *Le Soleil*, 19 mars 1992, p. A-4.

34. *Le Soleil*, 21 mars 1992, p. A-2.

35. *Le Soleil*, 23 mars 1992, P. A-1.

36. *Le Devoir*, 22 avril 1992, p. A-1.

37. *Le Devoir*, 8 avril 1992, p. A-1.

38. Gilles Lesage, «Gare à la substance de Bourassa», *Le Devoir*, 2 mai 1992, p. A-10.

39. Gilles Lesage, «L'auberge espagnole des libéraux», *Le Devoir*, 10 juin 1992, p. A-8.

40. Claude Ryan, «Le dilemme de Robert Bourassa», *Le Devoir*, 22 juin 1971, p. A-4.

41. *Le Soleil*, 5 mars 1992, p. A-14.

Towards the Final Package: Comments on the Proposals

4

The Importance of the Language Issue in the Constitutional Crisis*

Stéphane Dion

Le mouvement nationaliste au Québec doit pour une large part son existence à la fragilité de la langue française en Amérique du Nord. De fait, à chaque fièvre linguistique au Québec, on est témoin d'une remontée de l'option souverainiste dans la population. Pour obtenir l'aval des Québécois, il importera que la réforme constitutionnelle prenne d'abord en compte l'insécurité linguistique des francophones, bien avant d'autres questions telles que, par exemple, le partage des pouvoirs. Les dispositions de la Loi 101 ayant trait à la langue d'instruction et à la langue de travail devront jouir d'une protection accrue dans la constitution canadienne si l'on veut pallier à la fois au sentiment d'insécurité linguistique et à la tentation souverainiste des Québécois.

Le lien du langage est peut-être le plus fort et le plus durable qui puisse unir les hommes.

Alexis de Tocqueville, 1835

At the time of writing, the most likely outcome of the Canadian constitutional crisis is the *status quo*. The proposals put forward by the English-Canadian premiers have been massively rejected by Québécois commentators and politicians.

All across the political spectrum, the judgement is that the gains offered to the province fail to compensate for the losses implied by a Senate in which Quebec would be massively under-represented and by aboriginal governments which throw into question Quebec's territorial integrity. Compared to the existing situation, the proposals represent a net loss.

Even if these proposals were somewhat improved, they would likely be rejected in a referendum. Yet, in a referendum on sovereignty, Quebec voters

---

* July 1992.

probably would reject that option as well. The majority support for the adventure of independence is fragile and reversible: in large measure it rests on the ambiguity that has gradually come to blur the differences between "sovereignty," "renewed federalism," and "special status."

In sum, I venture the prediction that readers of this volume are still living in a Canada of which Quebec is a part, and under the *Constitution Act, 1982*, which the government of Quebec still has not endorsed. Obviously I may be wrong.

But in any case, the task of a political scientist is not only to predict, or to propose solutions, but also — mainly, in my view — to explain. It seems to me that political scientists have rather neglected this last responsibility, so preoccupied have they been with rewriting the constitution.

What is worth explaining here is an extraordinary phenomenon. Why is it, in this era, that so many Québécois are so nationalistic that they wish to exit from a country that is envied around the world? Were this to occur, it would be unprecedented among democratic systems. It would be the first case of secession in a modern, industrialized, welfare state. What are the closest comparable cases — Norway and Sweden in 1905? Ireland and Britain in 1922? In neither instance did there exist a modern welfare state with a mixed economy and about 45 percent of gross domestic product shared among all levels of government.

Obviously, such an intricate and complex phenomenon as the strength of the secessionist movement in Quebec is not explicable by a single factor. Factors other than language — history, culture, territory — are also important parts of the nationalist credo in Quebec. But if I had to choose *the* main reason to explain why nationalist feeling has fueled a powerful secessionist movement, (without any hesitation) I would select the fragility of the French language in North America.

Secessionist movements generally are rooted in two antithetical feelings: *fear* and *confidence*. The fear is that a linguistic or ethnic group will be weakened or even disappear as a distinct people if it stays in the union. The confidence is that it can perform as well, or even better, on its own. To these two conflicting feelings, I would add a third: a feeling of *rejection*, the sensation of no longer being welcome in the union.

In Quebec, the feeling of rejection is a sporadic phenomenon, expressed most recently in the June 1990 Meech Lake crisis. The feeling of confidence grew steadily over the last three decades, with secularization, the economic advancement of francophones, the consolidation of a francophone business class, and the strengthening of provincial state institutions, along with external factors like free trade and the various difficulties of the federal government. All this led to optimistic perceptions about sovereignty. The feeling of fear is a structural one, clearly connected with the linguistic issue. Simply enough, Quebecers are afraid that their language may be dissolved in an English-speaking ocean.

After stressing the importance of language in the course of the Canadian constitutional debate, and showing that the linguistic cleavage is important as such — not simply as the reflection of a broader cultural conflict — I will explain how I think the language issue could be addressed.

LANGUAGE MATTERS

Francophone Quebecers account for only 2.4 percent of an overwhelmingly English-speaking North America. In 1986, francophones accounted for less than 5 percent of the population in every Canadian province except Quebec and New Brunswick. The rest of Canada is increasingly English. The demographic weight of Quebec is decreasing within the federation. Everything suggests that those two trends will continue in the foreseeable future. Thus, it is hardly surprising that the francophone population of Quebec has a strong feeling of linguistic isolation in Canada and North America, and a sense that the French language is threatened.

In this context, the crucial area is Montreal. Quebec's anglophone and immigrant populations are concentrated there (in proportions of 75 and 90 percent). Historically, the anglophone population was powerful, and the attraction of the continental language is very strong for the immigrant population; so francophones fear losing control of their metropolis. If Montreal were to become English, the rest of Quebec would no longer be in a position to shape a strong French community.

Nationalism finds its central roots in this structural situation. The entire history of Quebec is haunted by the fear of anglicization, obsessed by the examples of Louisiana and parts of Canada where the French presence survives now only as folklore. The manner in which other Canadian provinces historically denied their francophone minorities any bilingual facilities, particularly regarding the language of educational instruction, did nothing to cool Quebec's linguistic insecurity.

Nationalism has always existed in Quebec, but only in the 1960s did the secessionist idea cease being politically marginal. In reviewing the course of the Québécois nationalist movement since that decade, one finds a linguistic crisis at the beginning of each new outburst of nationalism.

The creation and the first progress of the Parti Québécois were greatly helped by the context of linguistic tension at the end of the 1960s, which was focused upon conflict over the control of the Saint-Léonard school board. Recall the spectacular protests mounted against Bill 63, which aimed to maintain parents' freedom to choose a French or English education for their children. Nationalist feeling had never appeared so strong, especially among young Quebecers.

The electoral victory of the Parti Québécois in 1976 was partly linked to the dissatisfaction about Robert Bourassa's ambiguous language policy. It occurred just after a new conflict over the language to be used in controlling air traffic over the territory of Quebec had reinvigorated nationalist feelings.

Linguistic insecurity has triggered all of the outbreaks of nationalist fervour since the 1960s. Conversely, periods of linguistic security are not favourable to the secessionist movement. The cooling of linguistic insecurity following the implementation of Bill 101 decreased secessionist sentiment, and so was an important factor in the defeat of the pro-sovereignty position during the 1980 referendum. This feeling of linguistic security remained strong during the years following the referendum, and it helped to maintain secessionist support at a very low level.

Today, at a time of constitutional crisis, it is easy to forget how low was the support for secession only a few years ago. A January 1985 CROP poll showed that the most popular constitutional option among Quebecers, supported by 52 percent, was the *status quo*! Between October 1985 and August 1989, support for sovereignty rose from 27 percent to 42 percent.[1] There is no doubt that the Supreme Court decision about commercial signs in Quebec — ruling that the unilinguism requirement violated rights to free expression in the Quebec and Canadian Charters of Rights — is an important explanation of this change. A panel survey taken by Montreal students in December 1988–January 1989 showed that the Supreme Court decision on commercial signs created a strong radicalization of those students.[2] With the emotional and visible issue of language in commercial signs, the storm began.

Indeed, the current constitutional crisis can only be understood when one keeps in mind that everything started, once again, from a language issue. The warning "Ne touchez pas à la loi 101" (Don't touch Bill 101) was visible everywhere in Montreal at the same time as secessionist feelings seemed dead and as the Parti Québécois was trying to put off its sovereigntist option. In the context of the Supreme Court decision about the language of advertising in Quebec, and the so-called inside-outside Bill 178, which countered the decision, the pressure group *Mouvement Québec Français* was able to hold the biggest political meetings and demonstrations since the 1980 referendum, and the pro-sovereignty idea gained significantly in popularity.

The language issue had a tremendous impact in the rest of Canada as well. The federal language policy aimed to promote French outside Quebec, in provinces where the French fact is hard to perceive, and it created a lot of hostility against the French-speaking province, even though Quebec's government had nothing to do with Ottawa's policy. The Government of Quebec's own linguistic policy, aimed at resisting the encroachments of the English language, did not foster popular support for promoting French in the rest of Canada.[3] Quebec's Bill 178 angered English speakers in Quebec and elsewhere in Canada, and it contributed to the growing disenchantment with the Meech Lake Accord in English Canada, and to its ultimate failure in June 1990. The law provided a convenient reason for 62 Ontario municipalities to declare them-selves unilingual English in the first three months of 1990, just before the Meech Lake failure. Bill 178 also helped new parties openly hostile to the French fact to gain popularity. These events were seen in Quebec as instances of rejection, and they had a tremendous effect on nationalist feelings among Québécois.

So, the language issue is the crucial factor. But is it crucial as such, or is it only a result of broader cultural cleavages between francophones and anglo-phones?

LANGUAGE MATTERS AS SUCH

A point of view broadly shared is that the linguistic cleavage is less important in itself than as a manifestation of broader cultural incompatibilities between anglophones and francophones. There is little evidence for this view. On the contrary, all the evidence indicates that the linguistic cleavage is a concrete problem, existing despite an impressive cultural convergence of the two com-munities.

By saying this, I do not imply that a mother tongue is only a way to communicate and is unrelated to a broader cultural background, but only to say that it would be misleading to push this argument too far. On the ground of Quebec's linguistic specificity, nationalists claim a systematic distinctiveness that conveniently justifies sovereignty, or a massive devolution of powers to the Government of Quebec, not only in linguistic but also in cultural, social and economic affairs. Both the Allaire and the Bélanger-Campeau reports are based on this mechanistic reasoning. This logic allowed both reports to claim exclu-sive jurisdictions for Quebec without explaining, policy by policy, in what way the withdrawal of the federal government from these fields would serve Quebecers' interests.

In fact, while language has been a stirring issue among the Quebec popula-tion, the distribution of powers, as such, has never been a widespread concern, or even an election issue. The distribution of powers simply did not move people to action, to the great disappointment of Quebec government officials who tried to get popular support for their struggles with the federal government. In this respect, Claude Morin's recollections of his years as Quebec's Deputy Minister of Intergovernmental Affairs is striking. A few days before Daniel Johnson's death, Morin wrote to the former premier a very depressing note, complaining about the persistent indifference of the population about federal-provincial disputes.[4]

The centrality of the language issue is also striking in opinion polls. A 1988 national survey showed that most French speakers in Canada judged the means mobilized to promote French throughout the country to be insufficient, whereas many anglophones (42 percent) considered those means excessive.[5] A 1989 Gallup poll asked, in connection with the Supreme Court's decision about commercial signs, *"What do you think is more important – the rights of English-speaking Quebecers to have freedom of speech or the rights of French-speaking Quebecers to preserve their culture?"* Among anglophones, 72 percent chose English-speaking freedom of speech, and only 16 percent the preservation of Québécois culture. The distribution of the francophones' answers was almost the exact opposite: 15 percent preferred freedom of speech, 78 percent the preservation of culture. No other attitudinal cleavage is nearly as strong as this one. Moreover, when questions about freedom of speech are not connected with the language issue, polls do not show significant attitudinal differences between francophones and anglophones.

We could look one by one at sections of the Canadian and Quebec Charters of Rights and Freedoms and would doubtless find they garner fairly similar levels of approval in Quebec and in the rest of the country, except for the clauses governing language rights. Even the language dispute is not an expression of different values, but rather of different interests: anglophones would certainly be less in favour of individual freedom of choice in this area if their own linguistic security were threatened.

Recently, a controversy arose around the claim of the novelist Mordecai Richler that the Quebec nationalism is deeply racist and, in particular, anti-semitic. In fact, if some polls suggest that francophones may be more racist, others show that francophones are not more intolerant than other Canadians.[6] Regarding anti-semitism, if some polls suggest that it is higher among francophones in comparison with anglophones, it remains true that in 1990, 106 incidents of anti-semitism were reported in Ontario, compared with 36 in Quebec.[7] So, the evidence on the matter is worrying, but mixed. The linguistic cleavage, in comparison, is much more salient. Clearly, Quebec nationalism is rooted in linguistic insecurity, not ethnic intransigence.

In fact, with the fading of other cultural differences, language has become the main source of cleavage between French Quebec and the rest of Canada. Never have anglophones and francophones been so alike. Studies of the attitudes of Canadians[8] show there has been a spectacular cultural convergence between francophones and anglophones. The two linguistic communities now share the same democratic and liberal values, the same concept of rights and freedoms, and the same range of opinions on the role of the state. It is increasingly difficult to find significant differences in these areas. Of course, some differences still exist regarding tastes, behaviours, and attitudes, but many of these differences are declining, and in the end the cultural convergence of French speakers and English speakers is striking.[9]

But language matters as such. It erects a high barrier between francophones and anglophones, even while other cultural differences between the two groups are fading. There are few English speakers in the public-sector bureaucracies of the Government of Quebec, and French speakers' accession to executive positions in business was accomplished essentially in francophone-owned enterprises rather than in English-speaking ones.[10] In other words, the two groups are increasingly similar in their behaviour, but they still live in parallel worlds, broadly ignorant of one another.

The linguistic barrier also has a significant effect on the relationship between francophones and immigrants. Indeed, according to a 1992 CROP poll,[11] English unilingual or bilingual immigrants living in Quebec are more likely to say that Quebecers *de vieille souche* are racist (at a rate of 42 and 40 percent) than are French unilingual immigrants (27 percent).

Since language matters, and matters as such, it should constitute an important part of the package of constitutional reforms that "English Canada" will send to Quebec. Supporters of Canadian unity must find a way to increase the language security of Quebec's francophone population.

QUEBEC'S LANGUAGE POLICY MUST BE SECURED

Bilingualism in federal institutions is perceived positively by Quebec francophones. But this official bilingualism by no means ensures that they will be understood in French in all areas of Montreal, nor does it help to integrate immigrant populations into the French community. The Quebec government does these things. In fact, federal and Quebec language policies are complementary protections for French speakers in Quebec. This partly explains the apparent contradiction of Quebecers simultaneously voting for Trudeau and Lévesque. It was wise politics to support both linguistic protections.

The problem is that the federal government and its institutions unintentionally aided Quebec secessionism throughout the 1970s and 1980s by challenging the Quebec government's legislative efforts to protect French in Quebec. Rarely has a law enacted in Canada been so contested in the courts as was the Charter of the French language, Bill 101. As a result, francophone Quebecers have increasingly perceived the federal government as a kind of intruder state.

It is a great pity that the debate about commercial signs and the outside-inside bill has so harmed the image of Quebec's linguistic policy. A "French necessarily" policy, instead of a "French only" one, would have been sufficient in this area, especially considering similar practices throughout the world. Although the "French only" policy is a small discomfort for anglophones in practical terms, — since it is easy to learn the very basic aspects of a language — it is a needless vexation. At any rate, the issue is hardly important enough to warrant splitting the country. The key issues are elsewhere, in the two major sections of Bill 101 dealing with the language of instruction and the language of the workplace.

With respect to these sections, Quebec's language policy is fair for the anglophone minority. Regarding the language of the workplace, the prescriptions of the law set a "predominantly French," not a "French only" policy. As for the language of instruction, the targets are new immigrants, who are informed of the law when they come to Quebec. None of these legal requests injures the rights and the institutions of anglophones in the province. French Canadians in the other provinces can only dream of enjoying such conditions.

Bill 101 is a soft policy in comparison with those existing in Switzerland or in Belgium. Anglophone institutions are extensively funded by the Quebec government, whereas one will find no public funding for a French school in Flanders, or for a Netherlander school in Wallonia.[12]

Fair for the anglophone minority, Quebec's policies regarding the language of instruction and the language of the workplace are necessary protections for the francophone majority. There is no doubt that without these policies immigrants would massively join anglophone ranks. Yet the contribution of immigration is a necessity for the francophone community, considering demographic trends (low birthrate and aging). In this respect, the effects of Bill 101 are spectacular: the percentage of allophones who went to French schools increased from 38.7 percent to 72.7 percent between 1980 and 1989.[13]

Thus, the provisions of Bill 101 governing the language of work and the language of instruction are vital to ensuring a life in French for future generations, especially in Montreal. Yet the status of these provisions remains fragile from the standpoint of the *Constitution Act, 1982*. A Supreme Court could decide sometime in the future that denying the right of a new immigrant or of a francophone to go to an English school, when anglophones have such a right, is contrary to the Charter of Rights. The Court might invoke to this effect Article 15 prescribing legal equality of all citizens.

Under the current constitution, the province of Quebec may use the "notwithstanding" clause to avoid the consequences of such Supreme Court decisions. But recent experience shows that such a use is politically costly. Something more is needed.

I suggest including in the Canadian constitution a clause assigning to the legislature of Quebec the duty to protect the French-speaking character of the province. Such a clause would secure the interests of the French majority in Quebec without harming English-speaking Quebecers. With such a clause, I do not think the courts would strike down the current policies of the province regarding the language of instruction or the language of the workplace. And since minority linguistic rights are already included in the Charter (in Article 23), I do not see how such a provision could be perceived as offensive.

The aspiration of the French-speaking population in Quebec is to live daily life in French — to work, conduct business, buy goods, and go to the theater, all in French — and to secure the same French environment for future generations. If the signal that Quebecers receive from the rest of Canada is that there is no strong support for this simple aspiration, they will be easily convinced that they would have a more secure future in an independent French-speaking republic.

Language is not always the basis for political identity, which may lie elsewhere, in religion or ethnicity for instance.[14] But in Quebec, language certainly is the primary source of identity. Polls indicate that Quebecers are strongly attached to Canada.[15] Most of them still think that they can secure their aspirations within the federation. There is no doubt that increasing their language security would consolidate this attachment and lower their separatist fervour to far below the majority level.

I am aware, however, that the whole of my proposal is unrealistic in the present situation. Even were the Government of Quebec prepared to reduce its constitutional demands to this single linguistic provision, the west would take the occasion to put its Senate on the table, the First Nations their autonomous and subsidized governments, the Left its social charter, the Right its economic union ... and once more it would all become a veritable stew and the result would be impasse. So it seems that for the foreseeable future, francophone Quebecers will have to be satisfied with the notwithstanding clause as their constitutional protection of linguistic security.

Still, I will hazard a last prediction. The next nationalist wave in Quebec will result, again, from a crisis of insecurity about language. And this will occur, so long as English Canada has not afforded to the homeland of French in North America the linguistic certainty without which it will never feel entirely Canadian.

NOTES

This chapter is a revised version of a speech delivered at the opening symposium "Language as the Basis for Political Identity," at a conference at the Ontario Institute for Studies in Education, Toronto, Thursday, 2 July 1992. Many comments are borrowed from my "Explaining Quebec Nationalism," in R. Kent Weaver (ed.), *The Collapse of Canada?* (Washington DC: Brookings Institution, 1992). The author is indebted to Alain Noël and Robert Young for comments on an earlier version of this paper.

1. Edouard Cloutier, Jean H. Gay et Daniel Latouche, *Le virage: l'évolution de l'opinion publique au Québec depuis 1960* (Montreal: Québec-Amérique, 1992), pp. 62-63.

2. Ibid, p. 64.

3. Robert A. Young, "How to Head Off the Crisis," *The Globe and Mail*, 10 January 1991, p. A17.

4. Claude Morin, *Mes premiers ministres* (Montreal: Boréal, 1992), pp. 598-602.

5. André Blais, "Le clivage linguistique au Canada," *Recherches sociographiques*, 32, 1 (1991): pp. 43-54.

6. Paul M. Sniderman et al., "Liberty, Authority and Community: Civil Liberties and the Canadian Political Culture," paper prepared for presentation at the 1988 annual meeting of the Canadian Political Science Association; Paul M. Sniderman et al., "Anti-semitism in Quebec," manuscript, April 1992.

7. "Jews Secure in Quebec, Group Told. Professor Decries Richler Remarks," *The Globe and Mail*, 25 May 1992, A-1.

8. For a review of these studies, see Stéphane Dion "Explaining Quebec National-ism," in R. Kent Weaver (ed.), *The Collapse of Canada?* (Washington, DC: Brookings Institution, 1992), pp. 99-101.

9. "Qui nous sommes: anatomie d'une société distincte," *L'actualité*, January 1992.

10. Robert Grenon, "présence francophone dans la haute direction des entreprises employant entre 500 et 999 personnes au Québec en 1988," Montréal: Office de la langue française, December 1988.

11. "Un immigrant sur trois trouve les Québécois racistes," *La Presse*, 15 January 1992, A1-2.

12. Kenneth McRae, *Conflict and Compromises in Multilingual Societies: Belgium* (Waterloo: Wilfrid Laurier University Press, 1986); Kenneth McRae, *Conflict and Compromise in Multilingual Societies: Switzerland* (Waterloo: Wilfrid Laurier University Press, 1983); and Jean Laponce, *Languages and their Territories* (Toronto: University of Toronto Press, 1987).

13. Conseil de la langue française du Québec, "Indicateurs de la situation linguistique au Québec," April 1991, pp. 2-3.

14. Pierre A. Coulombe, "Justifying Strong Language Rights in Quebec," paper presented at the 64th annual meeting of the Canadian Political Science Associa-tion, University of Prince Edward Island, Charlottetown, 31 May-2 June 1992; John Edwards, *Linguistic Minorities, Policies and Pluralism* (London: Academic Press, 1984).

15. "Le Canada dans la peau: un sondage CROP-L'Actualité-TVA révèle l'attachement profond des Québécois au Canada," *L'Actualité*, July 1992.

5

The State of Senate Reform:
What Might it Mean for Canada?*

Thérèse Arseneau

La réforme du Sénat aura occupé, étonnamment, une place on ne peut plus significative au sein de la ronde du Canada. A cette occasion, on a pu voir, certes, les partisans traditionnels du Sénat triple E défendre leur credo; mais on vit aussi des groupes non territoriaux revendiquer un Sénat qui soit vraiment représentatif de la société canadienne. Toutefois, toute amélioration dans la représentation d'un Sénat réformé se verrait menacée dans l'hypothèse ou la discipline de parti continuerait de faire défaut à la Chambre haute. Prenant l'Australie comme exemple type, l'auteur démontre comment l'équivalent du Sénat triple E dans ce pays est devenu à toutes fins utiles une "chambre des partis". Les propositions adoptées en juillet 1992 ayant trait à la réforme du Sénat canadien comportaient des éléments clés pour limiter la domination des partis au sein du nouveau Sénat; cependant, les Canadiens ne doivent pas s'attendre à ce que cette réforme mette un terme à l'omniprésence des partis politiques au Sénat. On peut donc prévoir que la réforme augmentera les tensions au sein du Parlement fédéral, sans toutefois les comparer à celles, plus aiguës, qu'on observe en Australie, entre la Chambre basse et la Chambre haute.

Canadians are undoubtedly suffering from constitutional fatigue. Political leaders have been wrestling with the constitution, off and on, for the past seven decades. Yet as a political scientist I must confess to a fixed, but increasingly jaded, fascination with the current round of negotiations. A point of interest is the issue of Senate reform or, more specifically, what might be called the "surprises" of Senate reform. One such surprise is the extent to which Senate reform is on the agenda this time around; the issue has made significant advancement since the Meech Lake Accord. Few, if any, constitution watchers

---

* 15 August 1992.

predicted that the call for Senate reform would progress so far in such a short time.

It is not a surprise that western and Atlantic Triple-E supporters are in the vanguard of this movement. Roger Gibbins wrote in 1983, and other academics concurred, that "the objectives of Senate reform cluster around a single core, that of enhancing the quality of regional representation within national political institutions by national politicians."[1] But what is of interest here, and what has shocked many observers, particularly many of the traditional supporters of Senate reform, is the extent to which non-territorially based groups have adopted reform of the upper house as their own. The "new and improved" Senate envisioned by these non-territorial interests, however, is not a duplicate of the Senate proposed by those concerned with enhancing provincial or regional representation in the federal government. These different, yet not necessarily incompatible, visions of Senate reform warrant further examination.

This commentary will therefore focus on the reform of the Senate as outlined in the July 1992 constitutional package proposed by nine premiers and Joe Clark, and more specifically, on some of the many interesting issues and questions arising from this proposed reform. What should and would be the role of, and basis of representation in, the new Senate? What would be the place of parties in this reformed Senate? And, if it is a party house, can it also be a house of the provinces, minorities and of effective review? Finally, what implications would the reformed Senate have on responsible government in Canada?

SENATE REFORM: WHAT ROLE FOR THE NEW SENATE?

The most frequently cited roles for upper houses are the second chamber as a house of the provinces or states, a house of minority interests and/or a house of review. Of the three the Senate as a federalizing house, representing provinces or regions, equally or equitably, is the role most commonly advocated in Canada. At the root of this territorially-based vision of the Senate is the belief that a federal system has a special need for an upper house,[2] and more particularly one that is provincial or regional in composition and operation, because in a federation there are dual principles that must be protected. On the one hand is the liberal democratic principle of representation by population; this is normally enshrined in the lower house, in Canada, the House of Commons. The second principle, which is seemingly in collision with the first, is the federal principle that each state or province, irrespective of demographic weight or resources, is essentially equal or at least entitled to weighted representation in the federal government. In most federations the upper house is designed to incorporate this federal principle. In Canada the Senate, with its roughly equal regional representation, was formed to be the central institution that would incorporate the federal representative principle. However, because of the Senate's appointive nature, it has always lacked legitimacy and has thus become a mere appendage of the centrally dominated lower house. The demands for a reformed, more federalizing Senate are now quite widespread in the eight provinces of "outer Canada."

The second, and less common, role envisioned for a revised Senate is one based on a more fundamental societal, transprovincial view of Canada. Leading this call for the representation of non-territorial based interests in the upper house are women, Aboriginal Peoples, ethnic minorities, the disabled and other marginalized groups. These groups are highly critical of any Senate model that defines representation in exclusively territorial terms. If the Albertan justification for Senate reform is that the province is "left out" of central decision making, then, according to these groups, the grounds for a Senate composed of more women, First Peoples, the disabled, and ethnic minorities is stronger since these groups claim even greater peripheralization.

Although the advocates of the traditional, territorially-based model of Senate reform seemed taken aback by these groups' attempted usurpation of their project, this development was predictable. According to Alan Cairns, Canadians, largely stimulated by the adoption of the *Charter of Rights and Freedoms*, increasingly see themselves as heterogeneous, and relate to alternate, spatially diffuse civic identities.[3] The Charter also established a new, more direct constitutional relationship with Canadians; it by-passed governments and recognized instead individuals as the possessors of rights.[4] In a sense then the Charter introduced new constitutional actors into the process — individual Canadians and, in particular, the so-called "Charter Canadians." There was the expectation, which did not exist prior to the Charter, that they would actively participate as political actors in not only the constitutional process, but in the broader political process as well.

These groups have seized the opportunity afforded by possible Senate reform to attempt to gain greater access to Parliament, in this case the upper house. But is their vision of non-territorially-based representation necessarily incompatible with the more traditional models of Senate reform? It depends on the extent to which the Senate would be expected to mirror the societal composition of Canada. The National Action Committee on the Status of Women, for example, advocates a Senate wherein 50 percent of the Senators would be women. If this scenario is taken to its fullest extreme the Senate would be expected to be an exact microcosm of Canadian society. It would be very difficult to harmonize this with a Triple-E Senate. Others advance a more modest vision of group representation in the Senate. This more moderate view incorporates the adoption of an elected Senate in which a system of proportional representation (PR) would be used, an electoral system thought to help rather than hinder the election of a broader cross-section of Canadian society. In Australia, a parliamentary system with a Triple-E Senate, the adoption of the single transferable vote (STV) in the late 1940s eventually led to the election of more minor parties and independents, and correspondingly more women, Aborigines and people representing special interests. The Australians have managed to combine regional (in that there is an equal number of Senators from each state) and non-territorially-based representation.

This "combined" approach to Senate representation would be beneficial to Canada, especially given the already strong centrifugal forces in Canadian federalism. The combination of representation roles could actually be a unifying force, for rather than merely emphasizing the already strong regional divisions, the Senate would also represent cleavages that cut across regional lines. Furthermore, such a Senate would be an example of what Cairns calls a "creative constitutional symbiosis between the various identities we all carry ... accommodat[ing] the historic territorial realities of federalism, reinforced by an emerging aboriginal third order of government, and the contemporary reality of constitutionally recognized, trans-regional identities given substance by the Charter."[5]

The third role sometimes promoted for a reformed Senate is as a house of review and check on the government. But while in some countries, such as Australia, great emphasis is placed on this role, in Canada supporters of Senate reform rarely rely on it as a justification for their cause.[6] As Donald Smiley suggests, if the Senate is to be effective in this role, it must have powers commensurate with the House of Commons. In section 53 of the Australian constitution, the Senate was given equal stature with the House of Representatives. The only limits placed on the Senate were that it would not be a confidence house and that it could not originate money bills or impose taxation. (Most constitutional experts believe, however, that the Australian upper house does have the power to defer or reject money bills.) The Senate currently being contemplated in Canada, commonly referred to as an example of Triple-E, would *in practice* be more powerful than the present Senate but its powers would *not* be equal to, or even close to equal to, the powers of the House of Commons. Unlike their Australian counterparts, Canadian Senators would only be allowed to delay for 30 days legislation relating to taxation, borrowing, and appropriation. A vote of 70 percent would be needed to defeat "ordinary" legislation outright. If the vote were between 60 percent and 70 percent opposed to such legislation then the final decision of whether to pass the bill would be made in a joint sitting of both houses, where House of Commons MPs would outnumber Senators by more than three to one. Only in the case of legislation affecting natural resources and fundamental tax policy changes would a normal majority of 50 percent be needed to defeat legislation.

The inequality of lower and upper house powers would limit the provisional Senate's ability to act as an effective house of review. Yet this inability may not be overly damaging to the case for Senate reform, for this role alone would not justify significant change anyway. As Australian political scientist Joan Rydon states:

> it is difficult to perceive of any functions claimed for a second chamber as a house of review which could not be performed within one (if necessary enlarged) chamber. It would be possible to devise rules for delay between the stages of legislation, to prescribe that certain matters must be sent to investigative committees, that on others interested bodies must be given time to submit opinions, that special majorities be required on certain types of decision, etc. A system of rules might be developed in a single chamber which would guarantee a closer review of legislation than any second chamber has ever provided.[7]

POLITICAL PARTIES IN A REFORMED SENATE

These conceptions of the proper role and basis of representation for the Senate all include a concealed underlying assumption: that they would not be supplanted by party loyalty. But people who dream of an upper house with no or even weak party influence will likely be disappointed. If the Senate has *any* power then parties would want to be there, and in our constitutional democracy banning partisan involvement is impossible. It is more important at this stage though to ask: to what extent would they dominate, and if parties are strong, does this necessarily preclude the Senate from acting as a house of provincial interests? of non-territorial representation? as a house of review?

In reference to the first question, the proposed constitutional package of July 1992 does contain certain disincentives for political parties. First, the upper house would not be a confidence house. This lessens the need for parties to maintain strict party discipline therein. Second, as was previously discussed, the Senate would not be as powerful as the House of Commons. Parties tend to focus on loci of power. This should lead therefore to the parties concentrating more on the lower house. Third, the current plan is that the PR system of STV is to be employed in Senate elections.[8] This is significant since a PR system would virtually guarantee that no one party would have a majority therefore preventing the one-party government domination so common in the House of Commons. And, the form of PR chosen, the STV, is also notable since it is meant to be a system that minimizes the powers of political parties over the nomination and election process. Unlike the party list form of PR, which normally offers the voter a party — selected *fait accompli* ranked list of their candidates, PR-STV allows the voter to essentially rearrange the parties' rankings of the candidates by judiciously assigning his or her votes. Last, Senators would not be eligible for Cabinet. Since this means that the most powerful party leaders would be concentrated in the House of Commons, it should make the party less dominant in the Senate.

Although significant, the proposed disincentives are not as far reaching as some might have liked. Ernest Manning, Peter McCormick, and Gordon Gibson, for example, suggested in their 1981 *Regional Representation* study that Senators should also be prevented from caucusing with their House of Commons partisan colleagues, that Senators must, on a regular basis, caucus on cross-party regional lines, and that all votes in the upper house should be free votes.[9]

Political parties would be present in a reformed Senate, but, due to the PR-STV electoral system, they would probably be more numerous and perhaps less domineering than in the House of Commons. The exact extent of their control is still speculation. Would it prevent, however, the second chamber from playing the roles of provincial house, non-territorial house and house of review? Once again it is useful to look at the Australian experience. There, the Senate as "states'" house was arguably the role originally thought to be the most significant and the role most difficult to combine with a party house. It was evident to the founding fathers, especially those from the smaller states, that the larger, more industrialized eastern states, by virtue of their population, would dominate the House of Representatives, the lower house organized on the representation by population principle. In an attempt to counterbalance this dominance and to enshrine the federal principle in the central government, the Senate was established with an equal number of Senators from each state, regardless of population size. For many of the founding fathers this meant that the Senate's main role was to be that of guardian of states' rights. But post-1910, the emergence of modern parties led to party discipline taking precedence over loyalty to state: "loyalty to party meant that, with few exceptions, the potential for the Senate to act as a federal house reflecting coalitions between various state blocs of Senators was not realized."[10]

The popular academic opinion in Australia is that if party discipline is prevalent then this automatically precludes the Senate from acting as a states' house.[11] Defenders of this view argue that, even with the PR-STV electoral system, parties still control the nomination and election of Senators: the candidates are grouped by party; parties rank the candidates within these respective groupings; and parties distribute "how to vote cards" which are frequently the basis for how the electorate votes. All of these are significant. The PR-STV electoral system has the effect of more evenly dividing the votes between the major parties, resulting in safe seats for both the Labor and Liberal-National groupings, and, since Australian voters do not tend to make use of the opportunity afforded by PR-STV to rearrange the ranking of candidates within the party groupings, the result is that, in practice, parties' chosen top candidates are virtually guaranteed seats. This makes Senators, it is argued, more party-people than state-people. According to Smiley:

As in Canada, a member of the [Australian] House of Representatives may build up a local following and retain his [or her] political position through effective and visible service to the individuals and communities in his[/her] constituency. For a Senator this is not so, the constituency is the State executive of the party. Thus the overtly individualistic and anti-party bias of the electoral system for the Senate has reinforced the dominance of parties over the electoral process.[12]

It is also argued that the Senate *operates* as a party house in terms of structuring Senators' votes and that in the past, when the upper house has clashed with the House of Representatives, it has been over conflicting partisan, not state, interests.[13]

Sharman on the other hand contends that this popular view fails to recognize the extent to which partisan activity in the Senate is modified by the upper house's structure and, in particular, its overrepresentation of the smaller states.[14] This smaller state representation, he argues, has an impact in the party rooms and although the smaller states may not always use this to push a regional view in party priorities, the Senate significantly improves their ability to do so.[15] Furthermore, the part of the party that controls the nomination and election of Senators is the *state* executive, making Senators beholden to the state, rather than a national organization. Again Sharman argues that this is a regionalizing force. He believes that overall the state basis of the Senate sensitizes it, and therefore the national political process, to state concerns.[16] In sum, the Australian Senate's greatest influence as a states' house might best be described as a restraining one: because it has the capacity to act as a protector of states' rights, governments are deterred from introducing legislation harmful to the states.

The repercussions of strong parties on the Australian Senate's ability to act as a house of minorities and a house of review are less negative, tempered mainly by the adoption of PR-STV. This system does not penalize visible minorities, Aborigines, women and special-interest advocates who run as independents or under a minor party label. The chances of such groups being elected under PR-STV are considerably better than if the single member plurality system were used. The introduction of PR-STV in the 1949 election also arguably *improved* the Senate's performance as a house of review. Prior to this, one party or party grouping would commonly acquire a majority in the Senate. When the same party grouping held a majority in both houses, which was more the norm, the Senate became a "yes" house for the government. In times of differing partisan majorities the hostility between the two houses was intense. The situation was therefore one of long periods of calm broken by short bursts of Senate opposition based on partisan lines.[17] Since the adoption of PR-STV, the distribution of seats in the Senate is more even, one-party majorities and drastic shifts in support for the major parties are rare, and the number of independent and minor party Senators has increased. The effect has been a revitalization of the Senate as a house of review, particularly since the growth of an effective committee system in the 1970s. It now routinely, rather than sporadically, challenges the government and acts as an independent legislative body.

How likely is it that the Australian experience with parties in the upper house and that house's ability to play the roles of states' house, minority house and house of review would be repeated in a transformed Canadian Senate? Although the exact details of reformed Canadian Senate are yet to be finalized, if what is eventually adopted is close to the Senate proposed in the July first ministers' constitutional package then a degree of comparability can be expected. Foremost of these Australian-Canadian similarities is that, as was previously stated, Canadians should expect relatively strong political parties to be present in their upper house. As Smiley observed in his comparative study of the Australian and Canadian Senates:

> It is naive to contemplate an elected Canadian Senate of Independents — of persons who in a judicious and forceful way press the interests of their provinces and regions unencumbered by party ties and allegiances. Aspirants for the Senate, even those who are well-known in their respective provinces and who can draw on considerable personal resources to mount a campaign, would in all likelihood find it impossible to advance their causes successfully without the endorsation of and access to the much greater resources of one of the parties. And if the Senate emerges as a powerful institution it is unreasonable to believe that the parties themselves will refrain from attempting to determine the persons who compose it.[18]

But as was the case in Australia the vital question is not "would there be parties" but rather "what impact would their presence have on the roles envisioned for the reformed Canadian Senate"? Since the constitutional proposals advocate the adoption of the same PR-STV electoral system used in Australia, similar effects can be expected in terms of the Senate as a house of minorities. In reference to the Senate as a house of review, on the one hand, PR-STV should prevent the upper house from becoming a partisan mirror-image of the lower house, thus enhancing the chances of the Senate acting as a check on the government. On the other hand, since the powers of the proposed Senate are inferior to those of the House of Commons, the Senate would be handicapped in its operation as a house of review. In terms of the Senate as a house representing provincial interests, particularly those of outer Canada, the presence of political parties is likely to cause a conflict of interests. But as in Australia, the Canadian Senate as a party house does not necessarily preclude it from also acting as a provincial house. What is vital is who controls the selection of the party nominations. Would it be the national or provincial organizations? It is important to note that Canadian parties have stronger national organizations than their Australian counterparts. However, there has been a strong trend of late for provincial wings of parties to separate themselves, formally or informally, from their federal wing. If it is the provincial wing that nominates and ranks candidates, the result would be a provincializing force.[19] This could also give the provincial governments more direct access to the day-to-day running of the federal government. If the national party organizations have control, or even a veto, over the pre-selection process, then it is conceivable that this would give the prime minister and Cabinet an opportunity to influence the operation of the Senate.[20]

When trying to ascertain the Canadian Senate's likelihood of acting as a provincial house, based on the Australian experience, it is critical to acknowledge a vital difference between the two countries — Canada is far more decentralized and has stronger provincial identities and provincial governments than does Australia. This could effect a more regionally-based Senate than exists in Australia. Since state particularisms were weak to start with in Australia, it made it easier for party loyalty to supplant state loyalties in the Senate. Given the stronger Canadian provincial allegiances, they might be more resistant to party supplantation.

CONCLUSION

Whatever role is envisioned and incorporated for the "new" Canadian upper house, this reformed Senate would undoubtedly greatly alter the operation of Parliament. Furthermore, considering the Australian experience, the operation of a reformed Senate is also likely to lead to questions concerning the validity of modifying the liberal democratic principle of representation by rival views of representation — minority and provincial rights, and the need for an effective check on the government. Some Australian political scientists, for example, are critical of their country's upper house on these "democratic" grounds. Even though the Senate there is directly elected, it is argued that, democratically, it is the inferior of the lower house due to the constituency of election — representation by population for the House of Representatives versus the overrepresentation of certain "arbitrarily chosen," vastly unequal regional minorities in the Senate.[21] Similar complaints would likely arise in Canada.

Again, if the Australian experience is *a propos* to Canada, questions could also be raised concerning the compatibility of a more powerful upper house and the parliamentary system of government. Sharman raises this issue in reference to Australia.[22] Whenever major conflicts arise between the two houses in Australia, even when based on partisan clashes, Sharman states that more wide-reaching crises also develop:

> An executive based on a partisan majority in the lower house has been faced with an upper house controlled by a hostile partisan majority. The problem has not been one simply of political disagreement between components of the legislature but has involved a clash between competing views of both constitutionalism and the

legitimacy of executive dominance of the legislative process. The executive has called on the right of popular support and the canons of responsible government, while the upper house has claimed the right of legitimate opposition based on the full use of its constitutional power.[23]

The fundamental problem as Sharman sees it is that a powerful, popularly elected second chamber is more compatible with the American style of government which embraces the dispersal of power and expects that conflict, partisan or otherwise, will be frequent and is even desirable. By trying to link such an upper house with a Parliamentary system, which emphasizes the fusion of the legislature and the dominant executive, conflict is inevitable and what is at issue is the legitimacy of the executive's dominance.

This clash is unlikely to be as strong in Canada if the Senate adopted is the one contained in the July constitutional package. Simply, the Canadian version would not be as powerful as the Australian model and would therefore not challenge the executive in the way the Australian one does. Still, the proposed Senate does have powers significant enough to alter drastically the Canadian political system. Even a small change in government structure can have major ripple effects. The Senate reform proposed constitutes a substantial alteration. Significant aftershocks should therefore be expected. At the very least the House of Commons, the Cabinet, the Governor General, political parties and the provincial governments would feel the effects of this change. In conclusion then it is vital to recognize that by advocating significant Senate reform, the proposed constitutional package is also promoting a revolutionized system of government in Canada, the full extent of which will only become clear once the reformed Senate is operational.

NOTES

1.   Roger Gibbins, *Senate Reform: Moving Towards the Slippery Slope*, Discussion Paper no. 16 (Kingston: Institute of Intergovernmental Relations, Queen's University, 1983), p. 8. See also Donald Smiley, *An Elected Senate For Canada? Clues From the Australian Experience*, Discussion Paper no. 21 (Kingston: Institute of Intergovernmental Relations, Queen's University, 1985), p. 37.

2.   See Campbell Sharman, "Second Chambers," in Herman Bakvis and William Chandler (eds.), *Federalism and the Role of the State* (Toronto: University of Toronto Press, 1987), p. 82; and K.C. Wheare, *Federal Government*, 3d ed. (London: Oxford University Press, 1953), p. 93.

3.   Alan Cairns, "The Case for Charter-Federalism," *The Network*, 2, 6-7 (June-July 1992): 25.

4.   Alan Cairns, "Citizens (Outsiders) and Governments (Insiders) in Constitution-Making: The Case of Meech Lake," *Canadian Public Policy*, XIV, Supplement (1988): S 122.

5.   Cairns, "The Case for Charter-Federalism," p. 25.

6. Smiley, *An Elected Senate*, p. 65.

7. Joan Rydon, "Upper Houses — the Australian Experience" (Perth: The Australian Study of Parliament Group, 1982), p. 13.

8. For an in-depth evaluation of PR-STV in a Canadian context see William Irvine, *Does Canada Need a New Electoral System?* (Kingston: Institute of Intergovernmental Relations, Queen's University, 1979).

9. Peter McCormick, Ernest Manning and Gordon Gibson, *Regional Representation* (Calgary: Canada West Foundation, 1981), pp. 115-33.

10. Sharman, "Second Chambers," p. 93.

11. See L.F. Crisp, *Australian National Government,* 4th ed. (Melbourne: Longman Cheshire, 1978) for such an opinion.

12. Smiley, *An Elected Senate*, p. 45.

13. See Crisp, *Australian National Government*, p. 324.

14. Campbell Sharman, "The Australian Senate as States House," in Dean Jaensch (ed.), *The Politics of 'New Federalism'* (Adelaide: Australian Political Science Association, 1977), p.67. The "smaller states" include South Australia, Queensland, Western Australia and Tasmania.

15. Ibid., p. 68.

16. Ibid., p. 73.

17. See Sharman, "Second Chambers," pp. 93-94.

18. Smiley, *An Elected Senate*, p. 52.

19. Ibid., p. 53.

20. Ibid.

21. See Crisp, *Australian National Government*, p. 336; and Sharman, "The Australian House as a States House," p. 64.

22. See Sharman, "Second Chambers."

23. Ibid., p. 86.

6

Constitutional Politics, the West, and the New Political Agenda*

Roger Gibbins

La création apparente, en juillet 1992, d'une réforme du Sénat, selon le modèle du triple E, aura été le fruit de la détermination obstinée du gouvernement de l'Alberta et des autres élites politiques de cette province, combinée au large appui suscité par ce concept à travers le Canada. Dans l'ensemble, les Canadiens de l'Ouest ne manifestent pas, par rapport aux autres Canadiens, un soutien tellement plus ferme à l'égard du Sénat triple E; en fait, l'association qui est faite habituellement entre ce dossier et les gens de l'Ouest apparaît avant tout symbolique en ce qu'il incarne le désir inassouvi de ceux-ci de prendre la place qui leur revient au sein de la fédération canadienne. Selon l'auteur, le Sénat triple E ne compte pas d'alternatives valables dans la mesure où l'on ne trouverait nulle part d'équivalent au principe pourtant avantageux, d'après lui, de l'égalité des provinces. La réforme du Sénat est prônée dans l'Ouest afin de rendre efficiente la politique traditionnelle de ressentiment régional propre à l'Ouest. La conséquence la plus importante de la réforme du Sénat pourrait être d'accorder une représentation régionale plus effective au sein d'un gouvernement fédéral plus puissant. Ce faisant, on prendrait en compte la volonté politique des Canadiens de l'Ouest en rendant plus efficace la politique nationale dans des domaines tels que l'environnement et l'éducation.

It may appear to most observers that western Canadians and their governments have been prominent players — some might even say potentially destructive players — in the current constitutional round that stretches from the death of the Meech Lake Accord into the indefinite future. The reason for this is the centrality of Senate reform to the current round. Despite considerable Atlantic support for institutional reform, particularly from Newfoundland Premier Clyde Wells, the pursuit of Senate reform has always been most closely

---

*   15 August 1992.

associated with the west. Joe Clark's prominent role as constitutional pointman for the federal government has also added to the appearance of western strength even if, from within the region, the Minister of Constitutional Affairs has often seemed more preoccupied with selling Quebec's aspirations to the west than with selling western aspirations to Quebec. And indeed it appeared, at least until Quebec's formal return to the constitutional negotiations, that the west had accomplished its primary constitutional objective when Joe Clark and the nine non-Quebec premiers agreed on 7 July 1992, to a reform package that included a reasonable approximation of a Triple-E Senate. The 7 July agreement called for Senators to be elected by proportional representation, and for the Senate to be composed of eight Senators from each province and two Senators from each territory. The Senate would not be a confidence chamber, but would have substantial powers and, subject to the type of legislation, would be able to block measures passed by the House of Commons.

Of course, it is by no means certain that the Senate component of the package will survive the growing assault from Quebec nationalists inside and outside the Mulroney Cabinet, and from increasingly vocal opponents beyond the borders of Quebec. Given Quebec's initial and emphatic rejection of the Triple-E model, and given Quebec's informal yet effective dominance of both the timing and content of the constitutional process, the survival of the Triple-E model and perhaps of any significant Senate reform is at best unlikely. Nonetheless, the west's temporary 7 July victory on Senate reform provides a useful opportunity to step back and reflect upon some broader western Canadian perspectives on the constitutional agenda, both current and future.

Perhaps the first point to make, although it is by no means original, is that the contemporary "west" is not characterized by a great deal of regional consensus on anything. There are strong partisan and ideological cleavages running across the region, with both the New Democrats (NDP) and Reform Party mounting impressive political organizations. The growing crisis of prairie agriculture is of little interest to the residents of British Columbia, nor to most residents of Calgary, Edmonton or Winnipeg. There are deep fissures within the region with respect to such issues as environmental protection, abortion, international trade strategies, immigration, and aboriginal self-government, and for virtually all of these issues I would argue that fragmentation within the region has come to overshadow lingering differences between the region as a whole and central Canada. With the exception of its linguistic composition, the west is as heterogeneous and complex a society as Canada. It is therefore unreasonable to expect that a clear regional consensus would have emerged on constitutional issues, and in fact it has not emerged among governmental elites or across the broader public.

But how, then, do we explain the apparent western Canadian fixation on Senate reform in general, and on the Triple-E model — elected, equal, and effective — in particular? First, it is not at all clear that there has ever been a strong regional consensus among political and governmental elites on the virtues of Senate reform, much less on the virtues of the specific Triple-E model. The NDP government of British Columbia has been at best an erratic supporter of any type of Senate reform and, as one of the three provinces with more than 10 percent of the national population, was a late convert to Triple-E. The Saskatchewan NDP government, led by constitutional veteran and aficionado Roy Romanow, has also been less than enthusiastic about Senate reform, although late in the game a new "Saskatchewan model" played an important role in the run-up to the July agreement. The primary leadership on the Senate issue has come from Alberta Premier Don Getty, backed with some reservations by Manitoba Premier Gary Filmon. Yet even the Alberta premier has enjoyed less than consensual support from political elites within the province.

Second, while public opinion polls have demonstrated popular support in the west for both Senate reform and the Triple-E model, Senate reform has stopped well short of being a popular crusade. An Angus Reid-Southam poll conducted in late June 1992, found that over 50 percent of respondents in Alberta, Saskatchewan and Manitoba, and 48 percent of those in British Columbia, favoured an "elected, provincially equal upper chamber with strong powers."[1] However, the level of western Canadian support for the Triple-E model was not all that different from levels of support in other regions; 44 percent of the respondents in Atlantic Canada, 38 percent in Ontario, and 40 percent Canada-wide supported the Angus Reid-Southam depiction of a Triple-E Senate. Only in Quebec did support fall off, although even there 27 percent supported the Triple-E or "some form of compromise."[2] The point to stress is that western Canadian opinion on Senate reform is not wildly out of line with Canadian opinion, or at least non-Quebec opinion, as a whole. In going beyond the evidence in the Angus Reid-Southam poll, I would also argue that western Canadian opinion is similar to opinion elsewhere in Canada in another important respect; western Canadians support Senate reform and the Triple-E model, but their support is tempered with a good measure of caution and political realism. Western Canadians are not yet prepared to rush to the barricades to defend Senate reform, although they may well be prepared to use the federal ballot to punish reform opponents.

Western Canadian support for Senate reform is best explained by the role of symbolic politics and, secondarily, by the political muscle of the Reform Party which has championed Senate reform since the party's inception. The Reform Party and more specifically the electoral threat that it posed to incumbent Progressive Conservative MPs in the west were instrumental in getting Senate reform into the September 1991 federal constitutional package. However, although not unrelatedly, political symbolism has played a more important role and one that most likely stretches beyond the confines of western Canada.

Senate reform has become the symbolic key that western Canadians use to unlock any constitutional proposals; it tells them whether the package contained anything for their region. (The role of symbolism also explains why *equal* has been of much greater importance than the murkier and infinitely fudgable issue of *effective*; virtually anything can be sold as effective, whereas only equal can be sold as equal.) This symbolism was picked up in the federal government's 1991 constitutional proposals in which Senate reform was given a central role. The promise of Senate reform, like the promise to address aboriginal aspirations, was used to get western Canadians to the constitutional table, to convince them and other Canadians that more than Quebec's concerns would be addressed. The trick is to keep western Canadians at the table now that Quebec's aspirations are again dominating the process to the near exclusion of other concerns and issues. Senate reform was the lure, but there is little evidence that reform was taken seriously by Quebecers within the federal and Quebec governments.

But I digress. The argument being developed here is not that most western Canadians were convinced about the virtues of Senate reform, or about the virtues of any particular model, but rather that they saw the inclusion of Senate reform in the package as symbolic of the west's inclusion in Canada. In a sense, Senate reform became for western Canadians what the distinct society clause became for Quebecers; nobody was sure what it would mean in practice, but there would be a sense of betrayal if it were not included. The dilemma for the federal government and the premiers was to address this need for symbolic inclusion in a way that could be sold to the rest of the country, including Quebec. The Quebec government's decision not to participate in the constitutional process, and indeed not even to discuss the Senate reform issue, made this task much easier in the short run.

The west's temporary success on the Senate reform issue, and especially the achievement of a Triple-E Senate, came about because a small group of western Canadians, spearheaded by Alberta's Don Getty and backstopped by the intellectual sophistication of the Canada West Foundation, had a clear objective in mind and were able to link that objective to a principled argument. The proponents of an equal Senate were able to seize the principled high ground because they could link the notion of equality to federalist theory, and because of the powerful institutional precedents provided by Australia and the United States. (While linkages to American practice are always dangerous in Canadian political debate, and were used with some effect by the opponents of Senate reform, the strategy was on balance successful.) For their part, the opponents of a Triple-E Senate were never able to coalesce around a single alternative. They thrashed around blindly among a wide range of options including abolition and reform of the House of Commons, and conjured up alternatives that often appeared to have been drawn up on napkins over breakfast. The multitudinous models of an "equitable" Senate that were floated from time to time had the common feature of being or at least appearing to be unprincipled. They seemed to be based on little more than crass political number crunching: what would, or would not sell in Ontario and Quebec, and how many seats would be needed to buy off the west? (In this regional auction, it was Atlantic Canada that paid the highest price.) This is not to say that an equitable Senate could not in theory be defended from the high ground of political principle, but in fact it was not. Opponents of Senate reform in general, and of the Triple-E model in particular, lost the day when Ontario Premier Bob Rae, sailing without a compass, threw his support behind the modified Triple-E proposal.

It should also be noted that the opponents of the Triple-E model lost valuable ground by advancing alternatives based on a faulty understanding of Canadian demography. For example, there was a good deal of talk about Senate models based on regional equality. Given that the four western provinces contain 29 percent of the 1991 national population, it would be a hard sell to convince western Canadians that a regionally equal Senate, in which they would get a quarter or less of the seats, would be an effective counterweight to regional weakness in the House of Commons. A regionally equal Senate would compound and not address the problems of western alienation. British Columbia tried to come to the rescue of the regional model by suggesting that it too, along with Ontario and Quebec, should be treated as a region. This concept of a two tier Senate composed of three "regional provinces" and the rest would not only have been tough to sell on the prairies and particularly to the Alberta government.

In retrospect, it is clear that the initial success of the west in the constitutional process was the direct result of Quebec's decision to stay away from the table. With the Quebec government opting to speak through federal representatives at the table, and with the federal government committed from the outset to including Senate reform as part of the constitutional package, the stage was set for western Canadian premiers and governments. They had relatively clear objectives, they had done their homework, and they enjoyed some enthusiasm for Senate reform among the Atlantic provinces. They benefited from confusion on the part of the Ontario government, and from a federal government committed only to a deal. The mistake, of course, was to assume that the western imprint on the package would persist once Quebec came fully into play. In any direct contest between the west and Quebec, such as that embedded in the Senate reform debate, only a fool would bet on the west.

But what if, by some remote chance, the Senate package survives in a recognizable form, then will western Canadians be content with the constitutional package? And will they be well-served? Unfortunately, the answer in both cases is probably no. The problem stems only in part from what many might see as the insatiable character of western demands and aspirations, although here it is instructive to compare western Canadians with Quebec nationalists. Just as the latter are unlikely to be satisfied with a constitutional package that moves Quebec towards but not to independence, alienated westerners are unlikely to find complete solace in Senate reform. Irritants will inevitably arise and western alienation will continue. Of much greater importance is the fact that the political agenda has been changing rapidly in the west, as indeed it has been changing elsewhere in Canada. Yet, when we look at the emerging constitutional package, it seems to be directed more to the grievances of the nineteenth century than to the priorities and concerns of the twenty-first. It is a document directed to founding peoples and founding communities which pre-date the settlement of the west, and which have little resonance within the contemporary western Canadian electorate. In this respect, the growing indifference of western Canadians to the debate over the distinct society clause does not signify that western Canadians are now convinced about the clause's merits. It reflects more a growing weariness over a debate that seems irrelevant to the problems of the next century, a debate over tribalism when western Canadians are trying to come to grips with a new international order and trading environment.

The concerns and issues that dominate the emerging political landscape in western Canada — environmental protection, the quality of post-secondary education, the challenges of increasingly competitive international trade, immigration, and the globalization of human rights — have little to do with regionalism. Moreover, they energize political identities based more on gender, race and ideology than on geographical location. Even the Reform Party has been moving to a less regionalized platform, one that stresses an array of fiscal and ideological issues with relevance and potential appeal to many Canadians regardless of where they might happen to live outside Quebec. However, if the proposed constitutional package remains intact, it will provide little leverage on the concerns that dominate the new political agenda. The federal government's environmental role will extend little beyond posting warnings about the thickness of the ozone layer and the dangers of suntanning. Interprovincial barriers to trade will gain constitutional protection, rather than being torn down. A national education and labour force strategy will be precluded.

The responsibility for most of the concerns dominating the new political agenda will rest with the provinces. While western Canadians can probably live with this outcome, it should not be mistaken for their preferred outcome, which would be a relatively strong national government coupled with effective regional representation within national institutions. The decentralist thrust of the current proposals is true to nationalist sentiment in Quebec, but it fails to reflect a quite different nationalist sentiment in the Canadian west. Western Canadians have always been supporters of a relatively strong central government, and this underlies their historical support for institutional reform. They have sought a strong national community, knit together by national institutions in which regional interests could find effective expression. While strong provincial governments were not precluded by this vision, neither were they central to it. At least on the prairies, proponents of decentralization such as former Premier Peter Lougheed have been the exception rather than the rule.

It is not surprising, then, that Senate reform has emerged as the key to the western Canadian constitutional vision, to the extent that such a vision exists. Senate reform has been seen as the means by which western Canadian interest in a strong central government could be reconciled with a history of regional neglect by that same government; Senate reform, it was hoped, would ensure that the powers of the national government would not be exercised in a manner that was indifferent or even hostile to regional aspirations. Senate reform is therefore fully compatible with a shift to a new political agenda in which regional concerns would be less central, but in which regional sensitivities would still have to be taken into account. This is particularly the case if Senate reform were to encompass a system of proportional representation which would give electoral expression to nonterritorial interests and identities.

The tragedy is that we may end up with either no Senate reform or with the wrong kind of Senate, one that weakens rather than strengthens the national government, and that the cost for achieving this Senate may be to weaken the national government even further by the wholesale devolution of powers to the provinces. The irony is that western Canadians will be seen as playing a key role in orchestrating a constitutional package that may ultimately weaken the national government which western Canadians, through the quest for institutional reform, have been trying to protect. Canada may well end up with a system of government in which the only effective *national* government will be found in Quebec. Such an outcome would not only be completely at odds with western Canadian constitutional visions; it would also leave all Canadians outside Quebec ill-equipped to deal with the challenges and opportunities of the twenty-first century.

NOTES

1. "Easterners quite like Triple-E," *The Calgary Herald*, 2 July 1992, p. A1. This survey, which showed strong support outside the prairie west for the Triple-E model, is reputed to have had a significant impact on the content of the 7 July constitutional package.

2. An additional 21 percent of Quebec respondents wanted the Senate issue set aside, and 26 percent were "not sure."

7

The Great Canadian Crap Shoot*

J.L. Granatstein

La crise constitutionnelle actuelle doit être attribuée à Brian Mulroney pour avoir réouvert, sans raison, la boîte de Pandore. Le processus en cours depuis l'échec de l'Accord du lac Meech fait courir le risque de porter un coup encore plus fatal aux pouvoirs du gouvernement fédéral que Meech ne l'aurait fait. L'accord conclu en juillet 1992 pourrait avoir pour conséquence d'amoindrir davantage le Canada d'une triple façon: par l'entremise de la réforme du Sénat triple E; en garantissant une représentation sénatoriale basée sur l'équilibre entre les sexes; et en instaurant la règle de la double majorité francophone au Sénat. Nul n'est en mesure, d'après l'auteur, de préciser au juste la portée des dispositions relatives à l'autonomie gouvernementale des autochtones, ainsi que le coût lié à de telles demandes. Mais, par-dessus tout, personne ne s'est montré capable d'assurer la protection des compétences fédérales. Le mieux qu'on puisse espérer désormais serait de maintenir le statu quo, une option qui, au Québec comme dans le reste du Canada, recueille un appui bien plus important que d'aucuns tentent de nous le faire croire.

Canadians have been engaged in the world's longest-running, floating, permanent, established constitutional crap game for more than 30 years. Ever since Jean Lesage and his Liberal Party won election in Quebec and launched the Quiet Revolution that changed Canadiens into Québécois, Canada has been subjected to endless agonizing, to blackmail and threats, and to almost non-stop negotiations aimed at unravelling Confederation. I graduated from university near the time the Quiet Revolution began and for my entire professional life the issue of Quebec's place in or out of Canada has dominated the public stage. Frankly, I am fed to the teeth with the whole question.

This undoubtedly explains my sharp reaction to the whole process that has been underway since Brian Mulroney set out to bring Quebec willingly under

---

* 21 July 1992.

the constitution. The 1982 constitution with its Charter of Rights had taken years to negotiate, and while I disliked large parts of it and believed it to be much inferior to the *British North America Act* it had incorporated and partially replaced, I was more than willing to let it function. What other option did I have? But the prime minister had an option, and he exercised it. By declaring the 1982 constitution not worth the paper it was written on and by giving credence to the separatist argument that Quebec had been stabbed in the back during the climactic negotiations that produced the package in 1981, Brian Mulroney opened Pandora's box and once again let loose the *indépendantiste* goblins. Our current travails are his fault and no one else's.

Mulroney's motives for acting as he did were mixed. There was a genuine desire to bring a satisfied Quebec back into the Canadian fold, and we can admire the spirit with which he sought to do this. But he also aimed at solidifying the Progressive Conservative party's hold in Quebec, at entrenching his own position at its head, and in eradicating the image and memory of Pierre Trudeau in the province. Those latter reasons, while politically potent, were more than slightly self-serving. No one, in other words, should accept Mulroney's endlessly repeated claims of virtue on constitutional questions at face value.

The prime minister's efforts at constitutional renovation produced the Meech Lake Accord. Through an extraordinary process in a long, wearing "Quebec Round," agreement was reached — sort of — between the federal government and the provinces on a package that declared Quebec a distinct society and put that declaration into the constitution so as to ensure it would affect future judicial interpretation in decisive ways. As I viewed the deal, it was a hammer blow at the idea of federal powers, at the ability of Ottawa to play a major role in directing Canada's future development. It gave Quebec much of what it wanted, enough in fact to set it on the road to independence within or without Canada, and with few of the costs that ought to be associated with such a choice.

Worst of all, and usually forgotten in accounts of the Meech Accord, the agreement provided for an annual constitutional conference. This was a lunatic proposal, one that opened the federal-provincial process to endless blackmail and threats, and not only from Quebec. A constitution, to me, ought to be a document carved in stone, one that lays down principles and one that evolves over time through the process of interpretation. Not in Canada, however, where we slap clauses into our constitutions that no one understands when they are written and then, to bowdlerize the process all the more, we make the process of negotiation permanent.

Meech was a disaster. It transferred power outward from the centre and it dealt the idea of central government a sharp blow. What made it worse, of course, was that the Meech Accord was in process at precisely the same time that the Free Trade Agreement (FTA) was in negotiation. The FTA's merits or faults are all not yet clear, though thus far the results suggest that the critics had more telling arguments than its Tory and business proponents. But what the FTA did without doubt was to remove much of the federal government's power to shape and influence the national economy. It too was a hammer blow at Ottawa, and Meech and the FTA together pointed to the death of Confederation. The Meech Lake Accord collapsed in 1990, thanks to native protest in Manitoba and Clyde Wells in Newfoundland, but the FTA goes on.

And the current process, frogmarched towards a tentative conclusion under the threat posed by Quebec's deadline, threatens to deal an even greater blow to the federal power than Meech did. Meech, at least, left our institutions of government alone; the "Pearson" accord, with its aim of Meech plus, gives Quebec most of what it sought under the earlier package and simultaneously turns our system of government upside down in ways that are still incalculable.

Incalculable, but not in any way propitious. The Triple-E Senate argument, started by a prairie farmer in a region long known for fringe political parties and innovative, if slightly batty, political ideas, had little to recommend it. Nonetheless, it largely prevailed. What it is, of course, is a prairie and Newfoundland power grab, an attempt to reverse Canadian history by shifting power to the regions and away from central Canada. Proponents of the Triple-E idea, however, claim only to be seeking fairness on the basis that all provinces were created equal. But the idea that provinces are equal, the heart of the Triple-E argument, has no legal or moral weight and is sanctioned nowhere in our constitution or practices. Nonetheless, it has acquired a life of its own since being pressed by Clyde Wells and Don Getty. But provinces are not equal and there are more people living within two kilometres of where I write in downtown Toronto than in all of Prince Edward Island. That Ontario should have equal weight in the Senate with P.E.I. is simply ludicrous, even if the premier of Ontario, in act of supreme political foolishness that guarantees that his will be a one-term government, accepts it; to his credit, Premier Joe Ghiz seems fully aware of this and has never supported the Triple-E argument.

What has been forgotten out west and in St. John's is that even majorities have rights. It is not the fault of Central Canada that more people live here than in Moose Jaw or Athabasca; it just simply is. But that does not mean that those Ontarians should see their electoral rights diluted. In truth, this diminution of the rights of the majority to favour minorities is a widespread trend in Canada in other areas. Our legislators scurry to entrench multiculturalism ever deeper in our polity and, as minority groups increasingly are favoured with quotas to guarantee them rights to jobs or school entrance, for example, the rights of the majority become less and less important.

There is yet more. The Triple-E Senate adapts an American model to the Canadian parliamentary system. The fact that no state in the Union has anything like the population weight that Ontario or Quebec do in Canada matters not at all. The fact that there are 50 states as opposed to ten provinces, and that different alliances are possible in the U.S. Senate, scarcely enters into the discussion. The simple truth that in the United States the distribution of powers is different and that checks and balances are in place to withstand attempts by any one level of government to usurp power is never mentioned. Nor is the fact that the Senate in the United States is not exactly a perfectly functioning instrument. If the Triple-E proponents prevail, we will have a bastardized system of government that will be highly unlikely to work and that might — it is impossible to tell at this point — lead our government into paralysis. And since the Pearson accord proposes to give each province a veto, the chances of ever being able to rid ourselves of this incubus will be slight. In a word, this is political madness in pursuit of a principle that exists nowhere in our past or present lexicon.

To make matters worse, we are going to elect this Senate by a modified system of proportional representation. Whether the lists will be province-wide (thus making it appallingly expensive for anyone to seek election in the large provinces) is still unclear. But it is now said — in an amendment to the texts released in late July — that the Senate will aim for gender balance. I believe in equal rights, really I do. But I also believe that sometimes women may want to be represented by men and vice versa. And I most certainly do not want the government using the constitution to tell the political parties — and ultimately the voters — that they must produce Senate lists balanced for gender. This is nothing less than national fragmentation at work, and it is of a piece with the argument of francophone groups outside Quebec that every province should have a francophone Senator and that each voting issue will require a determination to establish if it is of francophone interest in which case double-majority rules come into effect. Can we expect Italian-Canadians or Jews or plumbers eventually to demand representation and double-majority protection too? If not, why not? In a curious, mindless way, we seem to be reeling backwards to the Group Government ideas of the Prairie Progressives.

The process of fragmentation is also enhanced by the proposals to create a new level of government for natives. As do most Canadians, I feel terrible guilt about the appalling poverty of the reservations and the plight of urban natives. Their condition is a national disgrace that must be resolved.

But the current proposals are simply extraordinary. Ordinarily when nations draw up constititutions, the draftsmen believe that they know what they are doing at the time they craft the clauses. Most nations recognize that the process of judicial interpretation will, over time, modify or change the meaning of the constitutional provisions. Surely, then, Canadians must be unique in crafting sweeping clauses for a constitution without anyone in the negotiating chamber or outside it having the slightest idea what they mean now, let alone how they will be interpreted by the courts in the future. We are to have a native justice system. How? Will it apply to natives outside reservations? No one knows, but the native leaders want it to. We are to have native self-government. How? Who will pay? How will it interact with existing municipal, provincial and federal governments? Will Toronto with 50,000 natives have a separate ward for them in municipal politics? No one knows, but the native leaders expect self-government in the cities. What will the impact of these changes to the natives' place in Canada be on land-claims negotiations? No one knows, but you can be certain the lawyers will claim inherent self-government gives the natives all of Canada. And will the separate tribal homelands, scattered across the country like paint splattered on the floor, in truth be any different than the "self-governing" native homelands that Canadians so rightfully condemn in South Africa? No one knows, but I fear the worst.

And when queries like these are raised, the answer from Ovide Mercredi and his phalanx of lawyers and from Bob Rae is that the natives have made compromises (where? did they ask for the moon and and the stars and settle only for the moon?) and that we should have faith that the process will work. There are times when the world seems surreal, when we are left gasping for air and clutching at shreds of rational thought. The natives' claim to an undefined but inherent right to self-government and the utterly craven way the provincial and federal negotiators inflicted this pig in a poke upon us is one of those times. And because it is politically incorrect to say anything against native rights, it has been left to the Quebec government to raise objections that are, if truth be told, shared by every government except Ontario's ideologically-driven one and, once they realize what may well be involved, by large numbers of Canadians.

The Pearson accord, like the Meech Lake Accord before it, also fosters decentralization of powers from Ottawa to the provinces. At this writing, the list of powers to be handed over is not long — though more will likely be offered as sweeteners to Quebec — but it includes some significant measures. Culture is offered to the provinces, an incredibly foolish handover that completely neglects the fact that Canadian culture is national or regional, not provincial. Federal cultural institutions are to be preserved, we are assured, but I suspect their lifespans — and finances — are living out numbered days. Housing is to go to the provinces, as is job training. The Central Mortgage and Housing Corporation, which has played a useful role for more than a half century, is presumably now to be scrapped. Job training, one area where federal initiative seems vital if we are to compete internationally, is now fragmented, and many union leaders feel that unemployment insurance, as a result, will be in jeopardy. This might have been barely tolerable if the economic union clause was strong; it is, however, a simple travesty that leaves Ottawa powerless.

What makes all this insufferable is that these measures are proposed directly in the face of the expressed wishes of the people. The Spicer Commission's report made crystal clear that Canadians want a strong central government; every opinion poll since Spicer has said the same. No matter, our federal and provincial negotiators, existing in the dream world of their own making, know better. So much for the openness and responsiveness of this process, put in place to correct the perceived flaws of the closed-door bargaining that gave us the Meech Lake Accord.

It is also absolutely clear that no one of the negotiators through this long process has defended the federal government's powers. Brian Mulroney, searching for a deal, any deal, did not in the Meech process; and Joe Clark, hard-working and weak-willed as he is, simply failed to stand up for the government and country he was expected to represent. Some of us remember Clark impaling himself on the bayonets of a peacekeeping force's honour guard in the late 1970s. This time he has hoist us all on his petard.

Now let us suppose the Pearson deal stands up and wins approval in the required number of legislatures with the magic 50 percent of the population. Then what? Does anyone believe that Quebec or Alberta will be satisfied? With its list of 22 powers that it wants for its very own, Quebec's Liberal government will be back at the table before the ink is dried. And if Parizeau and the Parti Québécois come to power in a future election, as they are almost certain to do, then the drive for sovereignty, whatever that may mean, will begin once more. The constitutional game will go on forever.

And if the Pearson accord fails? As I write, it is still unclear whether Quebec's complaints about the "historic" Meech conditions, as drafted in the accord, and the changes to the Senate and the rights proposed for natives will be accommodated. If Quebec and the other provinces can be temporarily satisfied, the deal may hold — providing the provinces that must have referenda support it, something that I find highly unlikely. But if, as I suspect, Quebec will not be accommodated and the deal collapses, that will leave Mulroney scrambling to make an offer on his own and then, possibly, to submit it to a non-binding national plebiscite. Alternatively, the Pearson accord will collapse, and Bourassa will try his luck in a provincial election that, if he prevails (something highly uncertain given his well-proven propensity for shooting himself in the foot), will be followed by a *de facto* moratorium. The status quo, the 1982 constitution, will then continue in force, and Quebec, unhappy as it may be with that document, will nonetheless continue to live under it. In truth Quebec's unhappiness is overblown, both in Quebec and outside it. The 1982 constitution imposes nothing terrible on Quebec and the province continues to thrive — or as much as any province can thrive in a bleak economy.

I am not one who wants to drive Quebec out of Canada. I take the view that independence for Quebec would be bad for Canada and disastrous for Quebec and, just as I feel I must act if I see someone trying to commit suicide, so I must try to keep Quebec in Canada. I desperately want Quebec to remain because I continue to believe that the best hope Canada has of survival as an independent nation in North America is to remain different from the United States in as many ways as possible. The presence of a strong francophone province is our most telling difference and it must be preserved.

I want my Canada to include Quebec, as the bumper stickers say. But not at any price. Not if it means decentralization to such an extent that the federal government becomes merely a tax collector that transfers the cash to the provinces. Not if it means asymmetrical federalism that sees Quebec get virtual independence and still keep members of Parliament in Ottawa. Not if it means that the rights of English-speaking Canadians are trampled and denied. Quebec is not a province "commes les autres," to be sure, and it is a cultural nation distinct from the rest-of-Canada. But it is not and cannot be a political nation-state within Canada. That is the point beyond which I cannot go. That is the point beyond which no Canadian should go.

8

The Multilateral Agreement:
A Betrayal of the Federal Spirit*

Alain-G. Gagnon and François Rocher

De tout temps, les Québécois sont restés attachés à une conception du fédéralisme articulée autour de la thèse des deux peuples fondateurs. En contrepartie, il appert de plus en plus que, dans le reste du Canada, l'idée qu'on se fait de la fédération canadienne laisse peu de place à des institutions fondées sur la diversité des cultures et des communautés inscrites sur une base territoriale. Ces deux visions concurrentes sont au coeur de la présente crise constitutionnelle, tout comme en 1982, lors du débat entourant les modifications apportées à la Constitution. L'Accord multilatéral du 7 juillet 1992 tient également peu compte de la réalité québécoise. Ainsi, le Québec n'obtient aucune nouvelle compétence lui permettant de s'affirmer comme société distincte; on légitimise le droit du gouvernement fédéral d'envahir des champs de compétence provinciale par l'entremise de son pouvoir de dépenser; et les modifications institutionnelles (notamment la réforme du Sénat) entraîneront, avec le temps, une centralisation du pouvoir politique à Ottawa.

To evaluate the agreement reached on 7 July between the federal government, the provincial first ministers and territorial representatives of English Canada and the aboriginal leaders, it is important, on the one hand, to go beyond the written text to discover its spirit and, on the other, to identify the dominant visions of federalism that feed Quebec and the rest-of-Canada.

The repatriation of the constitution in 1982 and the failure of the Meech Lake "agreement" represent two key moments in recent history. They reveal cleavages which illustrate the extent to which the societal projects proposed by the two principal communities living within Canada are clearly in opposition. First, the dominant vision in Canada-outside-Quebec wants all citizens to be similar and interchangeable, without paying respect to differences in culture and

---

* 20 July 1992.

values. Second, the dominant vision in Quebec wishes not only that the inherent differences of the communities be respected, but that they be expressed in concrete terms in the political arena.

From time immemorial, the Québécois have agreed to work in the Canadian context as long as it is possible for them to express their specificity. The respect of Québécois specificity is at the heart of the experience of Canadian "federalism"; however, it has been fundamentally called into question, since the constitutional conference of November 1981, by Canadians-outside-Quebec and by the federal government. It seems that Canada-outside-Quebec and the political power in Ottawa gradually confused the principles associated with the establishment of a federation with those underlying the respect and expression of federalism.

CANADIAN FEDERALISM: A FICTION

Federalism and federation do not necessarily go hand in hand. A federal society, with the social diversity that is implied, can sometimes evolve in a unitary type of institutional framework, or it can evolve in a totalitarian way, as in the case of the Soviet Union. The Québécois have never rejected the fundamental principles of federalism; what they have rejected is the interpretation given them by Canadians-outside-Quebec, a definition that denies the right to diversity.

In Canada-outside-Quebec, "federalism" and "federation" are used without distinction while inside Quebec, these concepts refer respectively to societal elements and institutions. In Canada-outside-Quebec, federalism is defined as an institutional arrangement rather than as a societal characteristic. Canadians-outside-Quebec, moreover, are not interested in what it otherwise might mean, for this would acknowledge that Quebec has an essential role in protecting the interests of the Québécois nation. The Québécois are in fact true federalists while the Canadians-outside-Quebec betray the "federal spirit" since they do not accept the right to diversity.

In short, federalism is primarily seen by Canadians-outside-Quebec as a type of political organization (read federation) while for the Québécois it essentially corresponds to the actual foundations of society. This difference in interpretation is at the centre of the controversy which is being played out in Canada. First, Canadians-outside-Quebec believe that any solution to the Canadian problem must pass through the restructuring of key political institutions and of "national" standards permitting Ottawa to act in fields as diverse as education, culture and labour market policy. Second, the Québécois insist above all else that a way be found to respect the diversity upon which Canada was founded. In the same manner, federalism requires a clear division of powers, respected by the two orders of government. As the lawyer Andrée Lajoie reminds us, authority cannot be divided, authority is not divisible.[1] Canadians-outside-Quebec do not want a Canada where there are several collective identities competing side by side and rubbing shoulders, involving regional variations in the application of policy. We will come back to this point.

Quebec's approach is clearly distinguished from Ottawa's in that it rejects "intrafederalism" in favour of "interfederalism" or "bilateral federalism" as a guide for its actions.[2] The Government of Quebec has largely favoured bilateral solutions to problems confronting Canada. The reciprocity agreements relating to language policy proposed by the Lévesque government at the 1977 Provincial Premiers' Conference in St. Andrews, New Brunswick are one example. The different interpretations of federalism offered by experts, contingent upon their adherence to the Quebec school of thought or the English Canadian school, complicate the analysis. Alan C. Cairns and Edwin Black recognized at the beginning of the 1960s the existence of these two traditions in Canada. According to them, the main difference opposes a "continental" vision, *à mari usque ad mare*, to a "national" vision resting on two founding peoples.[3]

In documents dealing with this question, anglophone specialists have largely ignored the Québécois vision of federalism, contenting themselves to present the narrow reading of Quebec reality offered by Trudeau. *Le fédéralisme et la société canadienne-française* became the political catechism of Canadians-outside-Quebec seeking a practical solution to the Quebec issue. Trudeau raised the alleged lack of respect of the Québécois for democracy and proposed, as a panacea, their integration into the Canadian whole. He dreamt of a unitary federalism which would have established the principle of the equality of the provinces in order to put an end to any pretensions Quebec had about its distinct character.

For many years, the federal government has betrayed the federal spirit that inspired the construction of Canada. Ottawa uses, for example, its spending power to impose its dictates on the member states of the Canadian federation. It should be mentioned that this sometimes happened with the acquiescence of the Quebec government, since politicians could not always break away from the seduction of money. But here is why the repatriation of the constitution and its repercussions on Quebec society — and this without the decency of having ensured that the Quebec National Assembly would give its support — fundamentally calls into question the confederal pact and casts a new light on the true intentions of the federal government and the anglophone provinces. It is not only a matter of arriving at new arrangements; it is also necessary to accommodate Quebec on the economic, cultural and social fronts.

Contrary to what one might expect, the federal government is not neutral in this conflict which opposes the two principal visions of Canada, since it made one of these visions its own and has attempted for several years to impose it on Quebec. The vision proposed by the federal government is inspired by the

American tradition, according to which federalism is to construct first and foremost a nation-state, without respect for diversity, while the vision proposed by Quebec is based upon the European tradition, in which the building of a country is established on the respect of communities and diversity. Unity within diversity accurately summarizes the vision the Québécois have of federalism, but it is miles away from the vision of Canadians-outside-Quebec.

CONVERGENCE OR DIVERGENCE

From the beginning of the 1960s, the Government of Quebec has defended the idea that the province is nothing less than a political entity whose linguistic, cultural and social specificities are unique in North America. Political and economic tools are required to allow for the preservation and promotion of these essential characteristics.[4] Any constitutional reform which does not take into account the obligations of the National Assembly with respect to the protection of the only predominantly French national community in North America cannot be satisfactory and would not offer a final solution to the Canadian constitutional crisis.

Quebec did not consent to the changes that were imposed on it with the 1982 repatriation because cultural duality, upon which the country was founded, was thrown out. The changes introduced to the constitution were of four types. First, the concept of federalism no longer refers, according to Quebec's partners in the federation, to a watertight division of powers between orders of government; it refers instead to a sharing between levels of government, with Ottawa viewed as the superior authority. Second, regionalism has become a defining element of the federation. According to this interpretation, Quebec is no longer a spokesperson for a nation; instead it speaks for a regional entity. Third, the principle of the equality of the provinces is making rapid headway in Canada, as was demonstrated by the constitutional negotiations surrounding the failure of the Meech Lake "Accord." Under the pretence that it is necessary to have a more equitable process, the anglophone provinces say that they are now ready to renounce the principle of representation by population of the member states. Hence a formula that would give Prince Edward Island, Quebec and Ontario the same representation in a reformed Senate has been contemplated. In a country like Canada, with its historical compromises, this change is unacceptable for Quebec because it will diminish its presence and influence in the new upper chamber. Fourth, the imposition of the *Canadian Charter of Rights and Freedoms* onto Quebec — which gave itself one in 1975 — sought less to protect the citizens of Quebec than it did to weaken the National Assembly, by allowing the federal government to interfere in areas as diverse as culture, language and training.

Quebec will not be able to maintain its distinctiveness unless it controls the economic, cultural and political levers that measure up to this responsibility. In the past, Quebec was satisfied with a type of asymmetrical federalism that Ottawa and the anglophone provinces accepted, although sometimes they did so with great reluctance. The formula that responds to the different needs of member states, the weighted representation of the provinces in the Senate, or the recognition of Common Law and the Civil Code in the exercise of justice, confirm the existence of asymmetrical federalism in Canada. The use of an asymmetrical formula is also found in the administration of many governmental policies, as in the case of immigration, regional development, telecommunications and the management of the pension program.

The issue is no longer that of accommodating Quebec, for example, by forcing the other member states of the Canadian federation to make concessions; rather it is to find out if Quebec and Canada-outside-Quebec can continue to live together. If this is not possible, then we must contemplate living, in a constructive way, side-by-side.[5]

CONTINUITY AND RUPTURE

For many years, specialists in federalism, federal-provincial relations and intergovernmental relations sought to bring out the element of continuity in the Quebec-Canada dynamic. For the past few years, however, it is the image of rupture between Quebec and the rest-of-Canada that has become clear and indeed is being strengthened. Two visions of political reality, anchored in the daily experience of citizens, are confronting each other.

Quebec does not have the right to prevent its partners in the Canadian federation from doing what they think is beneficial for them, but it cannot accept these same partners dictating a course of action that does not respect Quebec's ambitions and does not recognize its societal project. The comments of Jean-Louis Roy, following the election of the Parti Québécois in 1976, still seem fair today:

> The most decisive event that has occurred in the relations between Quebec and Canada since 1960 is the general acceptance, by a majority of Québécois, of the status of nation for their collectivity. The refusal of English Canada, at least of its spokespersons at the federal level and that of the anglophone provinces, to recognize this precipitated the psychological rupture of Canada.[6]

Québécois have spent many years stating that this rupture was irreversible and that sooner or later political space would have to be reinvented. The confederal pact to which the Québécois had adhered in 1867 has crumbled away over the years, with its substance removed. While the shell remains in place, the operating rules have been so profoundly transformed that they are at the point of being unrecognizable. However, it is up to the Québécois alone to decide their political future, free from all threats and constraints which certain political actors might wish to use against them.

The respect of diversity has always been central to the Québécois' vision of the country they live in. This diversity is no longer acceptable for Canadians-outside-Quebec, as is revealed in their desire to apply the *Canadian Charter of Rights and Freedoms* without paying much attention to diversity. This is also seen in the growing popularity of the concept of the equality of the provinces and in the wish to create a strong central government to counter the expression of centrifugal tendencies.

THE MULTILATERAL AGREEMENT: CONSTITUTIONAL POLITICS AS USUAL

Our intention is not to evaluate in detail all of the clauses of the 7 July 1992 agreement following the end of the multilateral discussions. The path that the rest-of-Canada seems to prefer is far from responding to the reservations expressed by Quebec following the September 1991 proposals and the recommendations of the Beaudoin-Dobbie Committee. On the contrary, all evidence seems to suggest that the guidelines remain the same. This can be approached from several angles. Does the agreement respond to Quebec's five conditions for rightfully adhering to the 1982 constitution? Is it more or less generous towards Quebec than was the Meech Lake Accord? What place will Quebec occupy in this new constitutional setting? While we do not doubt the pertinence of these questions, two other issues deserve attention. First, what is the agreement's underlying vision of federalism, and is it compatible with the conception of the federal system favoured by Quebec? Second, given the fact that the Quebec state has for the last 30 years continually sought to increase its room to manoeuvre, how does the agreement respond to this endogenous dynamic of Quebec-Canada relations?

Debates about the Canadian constitution have always revolved around the centralization-decentralization axis. Quebec has continually sought to broaden the fields in which it could operate and has demanded that the federal government respect provincial jurisdictions. On the contrary, the practice of federalism in Canada has led the central government, through the use of its spending power, to occupy jurisdictions initially granted to the provinces. The 7 July agreement, far from breaking this dynamic, reinforces it and indeed will even have the effect of constitutionalizing it.

Three observations can be drawn from the agreement: (i) Quebec gains no new areas of jurisdiction; (ii) Ottawa gives itself the authority to operate in jurisdictions that are recognized as being exclusively provincial; (iii) far from being decentralizing, the agreement defines the mechanisms through which the centralization of political power will take place in the future.

Even though Quebec has made a new division of powers one of its principal claims over the last 30 years, the agreement proposes a rather timorous reorganization. Essentially, the proposed approach is that the federal government will *withdraw* from a few secondary provincial jurisdictions that it has invaded over the years. But the exercise is conditioned by a desire to accompany this withdrawal with relatively strict conditions. Hence, this recognition of "exclusive" jurisdictions will be accompanied by the obligation to conclude an agreement setting the "conditions" of the federal withdrawal. Moreover, these agreements will only be protected against all unilateral changes for a five-year period. At the very most there is the possibility of a renewal, but it risks being contingent, given the partisan changes which occasionally accompany federal elections. The only new power granted to the provinces relates to culture. The confirmation of this "exclusive" jurisdiction is nevertheless limited by the reminder of the important role that the federal government has played in cultural affairs. It will keep its responsibility with respect to "national" cultural institutions, that is to say those that are relevant to the federal government, and the grants that they dispense. In other words, it will be an exclusively provincial jurisdiction with the exception of "national" institutions. In this context, we can ask what the awarding of "exclusive" competence in matters of culture to the provinces will change, whatever the current reality. The range of such a "decentralization" of power is, in sum, null, except at the symbolic level. The same reasoning can apply for labour market development and training. While recognizing it as being under exclusive provincial jurisdiction, the federal government intends to maintain its role in the establishment of "national" objectives. Moreover, the federal government will only withdraw following the request of a province, with the whole thing having to be negotiated, leading to an agreement where the financial compensation will be conditional on the compatibility of training programs with "national" objectives.

At the time of the Meech Lake debates, the clause relating to the restriction of the federal spending power was criticized for opening the door to too much decentralization. It was quickly forgotten that the "boxing in" of the spending power would only apply to programs jointly financed in areas of "exclusive" provincial jurisdiction. Moreover, the receipt of financial compensation would be accompanied by an obligation to put in place programs compatible with the "national" objectives. Far from being decentralizing, this clause only specified the means through which the federal government can intervene in an area of provincial jurisdiction.[7] The right to withdraw is accompanied by an obligation to meet the set standards, with the federal government still setting broad provincial orientations.

In short, with respect to the division of powers, Quebec still finds itself far away from a restructuring that will confer on it the responsibilities it has claimed, since the political document of Paul Gerin-Lajoie, to ensure economic, social and cultural development compatible with the fact that it constitutes the only territory where there is a francophone majority in North America.[8] The logic that emanates from the agreement, however, is one that wants the primary levers of intervention to be held always by Ottawa. Canada continues to evolve without consideration of Quebec's aspirations. It seeks to put in place an institutional framework which, while offering the appearance of federalism, only grants to provinces recalcitrant to the ascendancy of Ottawa the right to manage federal programs, via the necessity to respect "national" standards, as defined by a federal government which rarely misses the chance to extend its tentacles.

This standardizing vision of Canadian federalism is also present in other clauses of the agreement. It is found as much in the recognition of the distinct character of Quebec as in the proposed reform of the Senate. In the first case, the new Canada Clause which expresses the fundamental values of Canada and which will serve as a guide for the courts in their interpretation of the constitution would now include more than a half-dozen characteristics that will eventually have to be ranked by the courts. Included among them is, of course, the recognition of Quebec's distinct character. However, this characteristic must be interpreted in light of the principle of the *equality of provinces*, a new element included in the Canada Clause, the function of which, one can only suspect, is to make commonplace the specificity of the Québécois. Besides the inclusion of the distinct character in the Canada Clause, it is also foreseen that it will be an interpretive rule of the *Canadian Charter of Rights and Freedoms*. However, Quebec's distinct character is narrowly defined as was the case with the September 1991 proposals and the Beaudoin-Dobbie Report.

The recognition of this characteristic is accompanied by a Siamese twin, the recognition of linguistic duality. The multilateral agreement takes up the definition proposed by Beaudoin-Dobbie, namely that the federal government and the provinces will be responsible for ensuring the vitality and development of the language and culture of the francophone and anglophone minorities throughout Canada. One cannot insist enough on the harmful consequences for Quebec of promoting English on its territory. In effect, this clause can only favour the anglicization of Quebec in that it will allow for the paralysis of all attempts made by Quebec to constitute itself as a society whose fundamental attraction is the French language. In other words, this recommendation obliges Quebec to promote the English language even though it is not threatened. Moreover, it is quite likely that it will allow for the invalidation in due time of the clauses of the French Language Charter related to the francization of the workplace, the status of French as the official language of Quebec and the language of education for the children of immigrants.[9] Finally, while the Canada Clause introduced in September 1991 attributed to Quebec the task of protecting and promoting the distinct society, this preoccupation is not present in the wording of the Canada Clause as concocted in the multilateral agreement.

Beyond the enormous problems caused by these factors, the 7 July agreement also foresees a major restructuring of the upper chamber, inspired by the principles of the Triple-E Senate. The obvious intention of the supporters of this type of Senate is to increase the role of the small provinces in federal institutions to the detriment of the more populous provinces of central Canada, including Quebec. The preferred path thus is that of intrafederalism, increasing in this way the political weight of the peripheral and less populous provinces. Besides the fact that Quebec's representation will melt like snow under the sun, passing from 24 percent to less than 10 percent in the new Senate, the latter will present itself as the principal site for the expression of provincial interests in reaction to measures introduced by the House of Commons. One cannot insist enough on the new legitimacy that will be invested in this new upper chamber. We will probably witness a significant weakening of the ability of Quebec's National Assembly to act as the defender of the interests of Quebec; this role will now be shared by Quebec's representatives in the House of Commons and in the Senate. In this zero-sum game, the Quebec state is the loser. In other respects, federal projects which affect in an important way the French language and culture must be approved by a majority of francophone Senators participating in the vote. As the author of the bill, the federal government, in the great majority of cases, will state if it is a bill that requires such an indication or not. The mechanisms for contesting such a procedure, while supposed to ensure sufficient protection for francophones, have not been defined. In other words, the exercise of the double majority will be dependent on the goodwill of the federal Parliament. In this context, the notion of culture could be very narrowly defined so that a large number of bills do not have to be considered under the double-majority rule. Thus this initiative opposes the Québécois' vision of the Canadian political system that has constantly privileged a reinforcement of interfederalism and bilateral federalism.

On the whole, the constitutional changes proposed, far from strengthening the Quebec state's ability to act, are articulated in terms of an increase in the legitimacy of federal political institutions. The recognition of Quebec's distinct character, while present, is marked out by new rules of interpretation in the constitution, including the equality of the provinces and the obligation to promote Quebec's anglophone minority, which eliminate all the potential for an advantageous interpretation of the constitution for Quebec. The impact of such a clause on the division of powers will be nil, in view of the particulars brought about in the text. As for the redefinition of responsibilities between the central government and the provinces, it must be remarked that there is essentially a return to the text of the *British North America Act* of 1867 without respecting the spirit of the same document. In this sense, the notion of "exclusive" jurisdiction loses all meaning because Ottawa authorizes itself to define "national" objectives to which the provinces must comply. This acceptance of exclusivity constitutes a typically Canadian "invention" which definitely breaks with the spirit of federalism that Quebec has always understood and wished for. In such a setting, Canada will be federal in name only.

(translated by Richard Nimijean)

NOTES

1. See Andrée Lajoie, "Contribution aux travaux de la commission parlementaire sur les offres fédérales," Quebec, 11 December 1991.

2. By intrafederalism, specialists refer to representation of provincial interests at the centre (Ottawa). By interfederalism, experts largely make reference to bilateral relations as a mechanism to resolve conflict. Since the end of the 1970s, Ottawa has favoured the introduction of intrafederalism, which has allowed it to assume greater leadership in the management of affairs of the Canadian state, all the while seeking to represent provincial interests within the federal system. But, as Lise Bissonnette maintains, the federal strategy leads Canadian public opinion "to evacuate the provinces from its imagination." See "La loterie peut mener loin," in *Le Devoir*, 21 January 1992, p. A-8.

3. Edwin Black and Alan C. Cairns, "Le fédéralisme canadien: une nouvelle perspective," in Louis Sabourin (ed.), *Le système politique du Canada: institutions fédérales et québécoises* (Ottawa: Editions de l'Université d'Ottawa, 1970), pp. 50-76.

4. For more information on this period, see Alain-G. Gagnon and Mary Beth Montcalm, *Québec: Beyond the Quiet Revolution* (Scarborough: Nelson Canada, 1990), ch. 7; François Rocher, "Quebec's Historical Agenda," in D. Cameron and M. Smith (eds.), *Constitutional Politics* (Toronto: Lorimer, 1992), pp. 23-36.

5. For a detailed discussion of the considerations surrounding this fundamental choice, see Alain-G. Gagnon and François Rocher, (eds.), *Répliques aux détracteurs de la souveraineté du Québec* (Montreal: VLB éditeur, 1992).

6. Jean-Louis Roy, *Le choix d'un pays: le débat constitutionnel Québec-Canada, 1960-1976* (Montreal: Leméac, 1978), p. 323.

7. The same criticism was raised regarding the Meech Lake agreement. See François Rocher and Gérard Boismenu, "New Constitutional Signposts: Distinct Society, Linguistic Duality, and Institutional Changes," in Alain-G. Gagnon and James P. Bickerton (eds.), *Canadian Politics: An Introduction to the Discipline* (Peterborough: Broadview Press, 1990), pp. 222-45.

8. Reprinted in *la Revue d'études canadiennes*, November 1967, pp. 43-51.

9. This threat is all the more likely since the government of Robert Bourassa has demonstrated great overtures with respect to the Chambers Report, which recommended that "access to the anglophone school system be increased *at least* to all children who have studied in English or if one of the parents is a native of an

anglophone country of the world." Groupe de travail sur le réseau scolaire anglophone, *Rapport au ministre de l'Education du Québec*, January 1992, p. 7 (our emphasis and translation). If Quebec followed this path, the Canada Clause imposed by the 1982 Canadian constitution concerning the admission of children to English schools would be replaced by an international clause already foreseen in the same document. Two things must be emphasized: first, Quebec can no longer take steps backwards; and second, it would have to repeat the bad experience of Bill 22, which obliged children to demonstrate their linguistic competence in order to participate in the English system.

9

Lament for the Canadian Economic Union*

Douglas D. Purvis and André Raynauld

Pour prospérer, l'union économique canadienne nécessite à la fois une "intégration négative" (l'élimination des barrières tarifaires) et une "intégration positive" (l'harmonisation des politiques gouvernementales). Du fait qu'au Canada l'intégration négative est relativement complétée, les futurs gains à réaliser sur le plan économique devront provenir désormais de l'intégration positive. En outre, un lien puissant existe entre l'intégration économique et l'intégration politique. A cet égard, le système fédéral, par l'entremise de ses institutions fédérales, permet le mieux la réussite de cette intégration positive. Les propositions du gouvernement fédéral de septembre 1991 furent durement critiquées dans la mesure où l'on y décela une volonté de centralisation des compétences économiques. Il est malheureux qu'ait été sacrifié, après coup, l'aspect le plus important de ces propositions, c'est-à-dire, en l'occurrence, les moyens d'améliorer la coordination intergouvernementale de l'économie canadienne. Les auteurs regrettent que l'entente du mois d'août n'ait pas adopté des dispositions constitutionnelles propres à bonifier l'intégration positive; ils proposent en revanche qu'on crée, à la suite d'un accord politique entre les parties, un nouveau mécanisme qui s'appellerait La Commission fédérale-provinciale chargée de l'Union économique.

The Great Canadian Constitutional Drama that is currently being played out has a number of important dimensions, many of which are discussed elsewhere in this volume. In this chapter we focus on those dimensions that have an impact on the Canadian economic union. While the constitutional deal that emerged (but not ratified) as of late August 1992 is welcome for many reasons, and is complex enough that its full implications will not be understood for years (or perhaps even generations), our main message is conveyed by our title: we fear that a major opportunity for enhancing the economic union — something that

---

* 1 September 1992.

is essential to ensure for Canadians the kind of prosperity that they have come to take for granted — has been lost.

There are a number of reasons, both substantive and strategic, for introducing measures that enhance the economic union.[1] The September 1991 federal *Proposals* recognized this, and contained an ambitious — but imperfect — first step towards a set of changes for securing a strong economic union.[2] Rather than building on this proposal, the subsequent process essentially jettisoned the substance of the reforms. The Beaudoin-Dobbie Report responded to many of the criticisms of the federal *Proposals*, but also substantially weakened the commitment to enhancement of the economic union.[3] The "Pearson agreement" reached by Joe Clark and the nine premiers in early July 1992 included a set of proposals that worsened the prospects for the economic union and gave legitimacy to existing discriminatory practices.

The "Charlottetown agreement" reached in late August 1992 by Brian Mulroney, the ten first ministers, and four aboriginal leaders plus leaders from the two territories, apparently further reduces the focus on the economic union. However, this is actually an improvement over the Pearson agreement since fewer undesirable elements (in particular, fewer exceptions) are to be locked into the constitution. Further, most changes needed to improve the economic union do not have to be embedded in the accord, and with the constitution off the agenda — at least for a few years — progress on non-constitutional issues might be achieved. Before launching into the details of the current debate, some comments on economic and political integration are in order.

ECONOMIC AND POLITICAL INTEGRATION

Analysis and experience, including that flowing from the European drive towards economic integration under the aphorism *Europe 1992*, suggests that there are two essential dimensions to economic integration: these are referred to as *negative integration* and *positive integration*.[4]

Negative integration is an awkward term that refers to the creation of a single market by *removing* barriers to mobility between regions and/or jurisdictions; negative integration thus restricts or constrains governments. However, it is widely recognized that while the removal of barriers is *necessary* to achieve an economic union, it is not *sufficient*. Spillovers, or the effects of policies taken in one region on the economy of another, must also be taken into account so as to ensure efficient outcomes.

As the name suggests, *positive integration* involves a more *proactive* role for government: in order for the benefits of integration to be fully achieved, key policies of the various jurisdictions must be sufficiently "in synch" to foster the efficient functioning of the economy. To some extent this can be accomplished by coordination of the activities of the various governments, but the collective wisdom of public finance specialists suggests that it also requires that significant economic powers be retained by the central government.

The possible degrees of economic integration between diverse regions can be thought of as occurring along a spectrum, as in Figure 9.1. At one end (the "not integrated" end) is autarky; at the other end (the "highly integrated" end) is a unified economic space in which there are no jurisdictional or policy distinctions between the regions. This taxonomy suggests three propositions about economic integration:

Figure 9.1

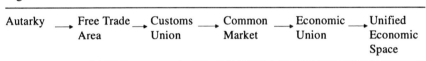

Autarky	Free Trade Area	Customs Union	Common Market	Economic Union	Unified Economic Space

First, as a general proposition, the benefits from economic integration increase with the extent of integration. That is, the benefits increase with a movement along the spectrum from less to more economic integration (although the "shape" of the economic benefits function may vary considerably in different circumstances). Second, at the left end of the spectrum most of the economic integration that occurs is negative integration; one moves along the spectrum towards increasingly positive integration. Third, increased economic integration (and, in particular, increased *positive* economic integration) implies increased political integration. Thus, in this sense, there is a trade-off between economic benefits and political sovereignty.

The first proposition is quite straightforward, and has been argued by a number of authors, in both the Canadian and European contexts. Essentially, it follows from the fact that the opportunities for benefitting from increased specialization, improved resource allocation, scale economies, dynamic learning phenomena, reduced transactions costs, and risk-sharing all increase with the degree of integration.

The second and third propositions are related and warrant elaboration. A *Free Trade Area*, for example, is essentially negative integration since it involves removing barriers to the movement of goods and services. The only positive integration required is a dispute settlement mechanism. (This may be extended to agreement on regulatory and framework policies — such as the "national treatment" principle embodied in the Canada-U.S. Free Trade Agreement.) A *Customs Union* is similar, except that the further step of harmonizing external barriers is necessary, which in turn requires some political cooperation. A *Common Market* involves mobility of capital and labour (and associated services) in addition to the goods mobility of a *Free Trade Area*, and hence requires increased policy harmonization (e.g., tax policies, labour market policies, additional framework policies) relative to what is required in a *Free Trade Area*.

An *Economic Union* represents a higher degree of economic integration. As Harris and Purvis emphasize, an economic union extends mobility rights not only to labour but to people in general; in particular, some broad citizenship rights (not only basic freedoms and rights but access to core public goods and social programs) are guaranteed.[5] An economic union thus requires considerable policy harmonization, including stabilization and social policies geared to income distribution, and the establishment of institutions to support and administer those policies. The need for policy harmonization also arises when one recognizes that monetary union becomes essential somewhere along the economic integration spectrum, and in particular is a necessary component of an economic union. This necessitates a substantial degree of harmonization of fiscal policies, as evidenced by the European experience, and increasingly by the Canadian one as federal-provincial fiscal relations continue to have a prominent role in the Canadian policy debate.

Thus, there is a strong link between economic integration and political integration.[6] For this reason, most economists hold the view that "sovereignty association" involves an internal contradiction: reducing the degree of political integration that would follow from Quebec Sovereignty means that some degree of economic integration would also be sacrificed — and not because the rest of Canada would be "vindictive." This point, which is denied by many Quebec nationalists, was also not fully recognized in the 1991 Economic Council of Canada study *A Joint Venture*; this may account for why that report was not well received by many economists.

THE STATE OF THE CANADIAN ECONOMIC UNION

Evaluating the implications of enhancing the Canadian economic union requires an assessment of the current state of the union. There is a great deal of material to draw on in making such an assessment. Much of the voluminous output of the Macdonald Royal Commission was directed to this issue, the background document on the economic union that accompanied the September 1991 federal *Proposals* provides some useful material on this question, as do many of the contributions in academic writings.[7] While time and space do not allow a detailed review of this material, three broad implications can be identified:

THE CANADIAN ECONOMIC UNION PRODUCES A SURPLUS

There is wide agreement among economists that the Canadian economic union produces a substantial economic surplus which would be lost in the event of

Quebec separation. As noted by J. Maxwell and C. Pestieau, there are four main sources for this surplus.[8] The first is the traditional principle of the division of labour and specialization that gives rise to gains from trade. The second is the presence of economies of scale in the production of private and public goods. The third is the pooling of risks — a more diversified and larger economy is more resistant to external shocks, and federal taxes and expenditures spread the risks among regions. Fourth, a larger economic space increases international bargaining power and leverage, leading to better terms of trade.

It is also worth noting that the losses from fragmentation of the economic union would be greater than the surplus arising in the present situation. This is because the allocation of resources and the present industrial structure in place are only appropriate to past and present conditions. If access to other provincial markets were limited in any significant way, substantial costs of adaptation would have to be borne.

ENHANCEMENTS TO NEGATIVE INTEGRATION ARE LARGELY IRRELEVANT

There are two basic reasons for this view. First, as many economists have stressed, Canada is already highly integrated in this sense, and the welfare gains from further integration are likely to be negligible.[9] This does not, of course, deny the usefulness of measures to prevent fragmentation of the existing union — the costs of disintegration can be high even if the benefits of further integration are small. Second, as Tom Courchene has argued in a number of places, the forces of globalization make domestic agreements for negative integration largely redundant.[10] Pressures from international market forces and institutions (e.g., General Agreement on Tariffs and Trade [GATT]; Bank of International Settlements [BIS], and the Canada-U.S. Free Trade Agreement [FTA]) will effectively constrain the ability of and incentives for governments to introduce policies that impose barriers and impediments to the mobility of goods, services, and factors of production.

THE FORCES OF GLOBALIZATION THAT MAKE NEGATIVE INTEGRATION LESS
IMPORTANT MAKE POSITIVE INTEGRATION MORE IMPORTANT

In the emerging information-based world economy where prosperity is increasingly tied to human capital and the development of what Michael Porter calls a national advantage, one important development that Canada needs in order to enhance the operation of the economy is improved *intergovernmental coordination*. That is, we need enhanced positive economic integration. To avoid being left behind in the race for new sources of high value-added jobs and industries, it is essential that Canada do everything possible to improve coordination and harmonization of structural and stabilization policies. Government policies must stop working at cross purposes, and the duplication and overlap of many regulations that often serve to inhibit innovation must be addressed. The current federal-provincial conflict on the financing and delivery of social policies could not be more costly; again, as Courchene stresses, in the information economy where human capital is key, social policy is economic policy.

FEDERAL INSTITUTIONS AND THE ECONOMIC UNION

The federal government *Proposals*, along with a number of the supporting documents, represented an ambitious package of possible changes, constitutional and otherwise, to Canada's political and economic framework, and attracted considerable attention from economists and other commentators.[11] The debate arising from the federal proposals also served to highlight the importance of federal institutions, which provide a key link in the relationship between economic and political integration. Thus, we now turn to a discussion of these institutions.

SENATE REFORM

Senate reform, and in particular the Triple-E Senate, has emerged as the symbol of an increased voice for regional and provincial interests in Ottawa. We endorse the need for mechanisms to ensure that regional interests are given a voice in national policy formation, while not being allowed to veto policies that are in the national interest but are not in the interest of all regions. But we think that advocates of the Triple-E Senate are mistaken when they suggest that this reform will give more power to the provinces. If by provinces, one means provincial governments, we think that precisely the opposite is true.

Whatever the merits of the Triple-E Senate, we are sceptical that Senate reform of any kind will contribute to the intergovernmental cooperation needed for enhanced positive economic integration. Given this, we would propose augmenting, or even replacing, the Senate with a House of the Provinces, along the lines proposed by Pepin-Robarts more than two decades ago — a proposal that was inspired in part by the German Bundesrat. The federal *Proposals* advocated just this kind of new institution, the Council of the Federation, to which we now turn.

THE COUNCIL OF THE FEDERATION

At present, the principal mechanism Canada relies on to achieve intergovernmental cooperation and coordination involves First Ministers' Conferences, supplemented by countless regular and "spontaneous" meetings of officials, as well as occasional ministerial meetings. First Ministers' Conferences seldom accomplish anything substantive — in part because they are not designed to reach decisions, and in part because there are no mechanisms to implement any decisions that are made.

The federal *Proposals* suggested that an intergovernmental decision-making body be entrenched in the constitution. This Council of the Federation was to be composed of ministerial representatives of federal, provincial, and territorial governments, and it would decide on issues of intergovernmental collaboration. The proposal for a Council of the Federation received, at best, mixed reviews among specialists, and was thoroughly trounced at the "Renewal of Canada: Institutional Reform" conference in Calgary in January 1992. Its acceptability was clouded by what in our earlier paper we called the "federal-centric" nature of some of the proposals, as well as by the controversies over Senate reform. We think this overwhelmingly negative response is unfortunate. The Council is *not* another layer of government, but rather an institution designed to allow us to get better government from existing institutions; to the extent that fears of an additional layer government were the obstacle, the solution should have been to *replace* the Senate with the Council![12]

The Council's role is potentially very important for a wide range of issues pertaining to the functioning of the economic union (e.g., overseeing constitutional authority for managing the economic union, harmonizing fiscal policies, and monitoring limits on the federal spending power). By establishing an ongoing forum of federal and provincial governments, with a mandate to manage the economy and with enough power that one can be confident that governments will introduce the relevant policies and enact the legislation necessary to support its decisions, the Council has the potential to lead to a significant improvement in the operation of the economy.

A FEDERAL-PROVINCIAL COMMISSION ON THE ECONOMIC UNION

A number of commentators, some responding to the federal *Proposals*, have suggested the need for an *agency of experts* to be involved in policies concerned with the economic union. The Beaudoin-Dobbie Committee proposed the creation of an intergovernmental agency to review, assess and report on policies affecting the economic union, and the August agreement gives first ministers the authority to create an independent dispute-resolution agency and decide on its role, mandate, and composition. We support this in principle, and argue that its mandate should be broader than just dispute resolution but should extend to issues related to positive integration. We therefore propose a Federal-Provincial Commission on the Economic Union as part of the options developed below.

The Commission's role would be to provide assessment and advice, to act as a mediator on complaints, and to propose solutions to problems. Its role would be complementary to the Council; it should not duplicate the Council's role. The Council should be an executive (although not a legislative) body representing governments. The Commission would be composed of independent experts who would advise the Council, governments, and perhaps the courts. Commissioners would be appointed by governments but would not be expected to represent governments — much like Supreme Court Justices.

THE ROLE OF THE COURTS

One issue that arises in any discussion of constitutional change and economic integration is the extent to which the courts become involved in adjudicating issues of economic policy. A key role of the constitution is to restrict the powers of government in one way or another; ultimately this involves appeal to the courts to strike down legislation. This, of course, raises immediate concerns about the "supremacy" of Parliament; thus, the relative roles of the courts and elected bodies is a long-standing topic of debate in constitutional affairs.

While constitutional restrictions on governments must ultimately be interpreted by the courts, there is widespread agreement that the role of the courts should be minimized. They should at most be a last recourse, and consideration should be given to mechanisms that reduce the need to turn to that recourse. In addition to the concerns about the supremacy of Parliament, it has to be recognized that appeal to the courts is a costly and uncertain process — which in turn raises the question of the effectiveness of this process in constraining governments. Finally, there is a broad consensus that the courts are not appropriate institutions for settling detailed issues of economic policy.

There are a number of ways of dealing with these concerns. Our proposal is to create an alternative body that would either replace the courts, or act as an intermediate step en route to the courts, for dealing with disputes over policies related to the economic union. A particular appeal of this alternative is that it would allow for providing "expert support" both in assessing damages and in articulating remedies. One possibility is an administrative tribunal similar to those used in international trade disputes. A second is the Council of the Federation, which could reduce the need to refer issues of the economic union to the court, with the Federal-Provincial Commission providing "expert support" to the Council as well as to the courts when recourse to them does occur.

ENHANCING POSITIVE ECONOMIC INTEGRATION[13]

The federal *Proposals* addressed the need for active management of the economic union by proposing the creation of a federal authority to legislate in areas of provincial jurisdiction. This was widely criticized (especially in Quebec) as a federal power grab — even though the new federal authority was significantly restricted. The negative reaction was also in part a reaction to the "federal-centric" wording in the proposed new power (viz., "the Parliament of

Canada may *exclusively* make laws in relation to any matter that *it* declares to be for the efficient functioning of the economic union").

It now appears clear that any constitutional deal that is achieved in the next few months will not contain substantive provisions for enhancing positive integration. However, that does not mean that the serious objective of improving the functioning of the economic union has to be abandoned. We believe that the federal proposal contains the seeds of an effective mechanism that, as developed below, could be introduced as a post-constitutional initiative and do not themselves need to be embedded in the constitution. Our proposal involves two major changes to the September 1991 federal proposal:

- It is essential to recognize (and encourage) the management of the economic union as an area of *federal-provincial co-responsibility*.[14]
- An intergovernmental decision-making body such as the Council of the Federation needs to be established and given a prominent role.

The structure and operation of the Council should be fleshed out in more detail. We would start by indicating the need for an "intergovernmental decision-making body" to manage the economic union, both to help coordinate and harmonize policies of the various governments, and for provincial governments as well as the federal government to bring forward policy initiatives to ensure the efficient functioning of the economic union. We would also propose that a Federal-Provincial Commission on the Economic Union be established and designated as an advisory body to the Council.

By stressing its role as a mechanism for managing the co-responsibility of the various governments, rather than for ratifying the exercise of a contentious exclusive federal authority, the Council might emerge as a vehicle for cooperation and partnership. It would then contribute to the improved harmonization of federal and provincial policies that is urgently needed in the new globalized world economy. As discussed below, the Council would also play a role in dealing with issues concerning the spending power, and perhaps in the legislative delegation discussed in the federal proposals.

A key difference between the shared-power option spelled out above and the federal proposal of September 1991 is that no new authority to legislate outside their jurisdiction is created for either the federal or the provincial governments, at least at this stage.[15] That being the case, there may be no need to try to place the legislative mechanism or the constraints on it in the constitution: the legislative authority of the federal and provincial governments remains unchanged under this proposal.

The mechanism would operate as follows. The Council of the Federation — perhaps constituted at the time by finance ministers and treasurers, or perhaps by other ministers (e.g., Agriculture or Health) — would discuss various initiatives, and if agreement could be reached by the federal government and provincial members of the Council satisfying the 7/50 requirement, legislation would be drafted. However, since the Council is not meant to be a legislative body itself (primarily to avoid a third formal layer of government), the legislation would then be passed by the federal government or the required number of provincial legislatures, depending upon the respective fields of jurisdiction, *each essentially giving effect to decisions taken by the Council.*[16]

In addition, the Federal-Provincial Commission on the Economic Union could perform an "economic auditor general" role. Policies related to positive integration should be the subject of an annual report by the Commission, and that report be tabled in the Parliament of Canada and the legislatures of all the provinces. Debates in the Parliament and the legislatures would subsequently be the basis for open discussion at the Council of the Federation.

OPTING-IN AND OPTING-OUT

A major issue with regard to the above mechanism for generating positive integration is whether policy decisions in areas of exclusive provincial responsibility made by the Council will be binding on all provinces, or only on those provinces that support them in the Council.

Those who are "hawks" on the importance of the economic union will argue that if a law is proposed which has the objective of strengthening the economic union, it would undermine the impact of the law if one or two provinces opted out, especially if one of those opting-out were Quebec or Ontario. Clearly opting-out is to be avoided wherever possible; frequent opting-out would lead to a "checker-board" economic union.

However, advocates of provincial rights will argue that co-responsibility for managing the economic union should not extend to diminishing the legislative authority of provincial governments. Pragmatists will argue that any proposal that threatens to do this will simply be unacceptable in Quebec, and perhaps in other provinces; thus opting-out has to be permitted.

There is therefore an important policy trade-off here — between limiting the powers of the new mechanism but also prohibiting opting-out, or giving the new mechanism very strong powers but permitting opting-out. In "Reconsidering the Federal Proposals for the Economic Union," Raynauld and I discussed a number of aspects of this issue, and in the end we supported an opting-in mechanism related to that proposed by the Regroupement. This proposal requires that any initiative taken by the Council of the Federation be placed before the legislatures of *all the provinces* for approval or rejection. Thus, any province that did not support the initiative in the Council would nevertheless have to explicitly debate and vote on the legislation. Even if the provincial legislature were to reject the legislation, this would be more attractive symbolically than unilateral opting out by the provincial government in question. Further, some positive dynamics might emerge whereby policies in the national interest might receive support in dissenting provinces because of strong support elsewhere. In addition, the opting-in procedure could be reinforced with the "economic auditor general" mechanism suggested above; thus, the annual reports by the Federal-Provincial Commission on the Economic Union would not only address initiatives taken that oppose the principle of positive integration, they would also take up provincial failures to support initiatives designed to promote such integration.[17]

HARMONIZATION OF ECONOMIC POLICIES

The federal government also put forward a proposal that explicitly addressed the issue of the harmonization of economic policies. There is broad agreement that the economic policies of the federal and provincial governments need to be better harmonized and rationalized.[18] There is a perception that many of these policies create wasteful overlap and duplication, and this leads to a lack of accountability. In the context of the economic union, the issue arises primarily with respect to fiscal policies directed at stabilizing the economy, although other policies (regulatory policies with respect to capital markets, for example) might also be viewed as important for the economic union.

With regard to stabilization policies, the concerns are about the interaction of the policies. In some cases, they can have an undesirable cumulative effect. In other circumstances, the policies can work at cross-purposes. The consistency between fiscal and monetary policies is also an issue.[19] Thus, it is widely recognized that Canada's economic performance would be improved if we are able to better manage the interactions between these various stabilization policies.

There is a range of practices and mechanisms that might be put in place to improve performance in this area. There is strong support for some basic changes such as opening up and regularizing the budget processes. However, as the proposed changes get stronger — such as the implementation of policy rules — they are seen to infringe upon the sovereignty of the provinces in this area and support tends to drop.

Our position on this issue, as well as on the proposed reforms to the Bank of Canada, is that these are complex issues of economic policy, and should be dealt with outside the constitutional process. However, we also feel that these issues of intergovernmental collaboration are very important for future economic performance, and that the two institutions proposed above — the Council of the Federation and the Federal-Provincial Commission — could contribute enormously to improvement of policy performance in this area. We would propose, therefore, that the economic auditor general function be extended to this area, so that the Federal-Provincial Commission on the Economic Union would monitor and assess the macroeconomic policies of the various governments, including their medium-term guidelines, and publish its findings in its annual report.

THE FEDERAL SPENDING POWER

In a federal system, the division of powers between the various levels of government is a crucial issue. If such a political system has been adopted in the first place it is because communities have distinctive preferences which are best satisfied at lower levels of government. At the same time, decentralization may jeopardize the national economic union when policy differences become protectionist and discriminatory or simply prevent the reaping of the full profits of the union.

In this area the problems that have arisen over the years have less to do with the constitutional division of powers as such than with the use of the so-called federal spending power. This power has allowed the federal government to intervene in areas of exclusive provincial jurisdiction. The Report of the Special Joint Committee estimated that in 1991-92, 35 percent of federal spending is in areas of provincial jurisdiction.[20] The need for a new set of rules governing the use of the federal spending power is widely acknowledged.

In the Charlottetown agreement, the spending power is circumscribed within framework rules to apply to intergovernmental agreements when provinces wish to opt out with compensation and constitutional protection. The agreement defines national objectives to which the provinces would have to subscribe.

In addition, a number of areas are identified as areas of explicit provincial jurisdiction subject to intergovernmental agreements in all cases. In the field of immigration, there would be a constitutional provision committing the federal government to negotiate such an agreement with each province requesting it. Unemployment insurance and related services remain an exclusive federal prerogative, but labour market development and training is identified as a matter of exclusive provincial jurisdiction subject to agreements on coordination, common occupational standards and on the federal role in setting material policy objectives.

Culture is subject to concurrent powers and the same rule applies to regional development. The following areas are deemed to be under provincial jurisdiction subject to agreements for opting out and compensation: forestry, mining, tourism, housing, recreation, municipal and urban affairs. Finally, telecommunications are presented as an area where the federal government would be committed to come to agreements with the provinces to coordinate and harmonize federal and provincial regulations.

While this agreement does constrain the federal spending power, it does not involve a significant decentralization of powers nor a reinforcement of the economic union. Canadians may suffer as a result of increased opting out.

CONCLUSIONS

Any constitutional deal that emerges over the next few months will likely contain recommendations for negative integration (albeit with enough exceptions that they will have limited effect) but none for positive integration. This is exactly the opposite of what is needed. Mechanisms for enhancing positive integration are essential for preserving the benefits of the Canadian economic union. However, these can be established outside the constitution, and should be a top priority for the post-constitutional policy agenda.

Management of the economic union must be a shared responsibility involving a cooperative effort by the federal and provincial governments. The proposals put forward in this chapter reflect our view that it is better to focus on building institutions and mechanisms designed to foster a spirit of partnership, rather than to use the constitution to impose detailed rules prescribing the behaviour of governments.

By establishing an ongoing forum for federal and provincial governments with a mandate to manage the economy and enough power to issue directives to constituent governments to enact legislation in support of its decisions, the Council of the Federation (or some otherwise constituted intergovernmental body) could contribute to a reversal of recent federal-provincial adversarial relationships. It could build a constructive and positive dynamic, based on the spirit of partnership. Further, by tying economic integration to national institutions, it would make clear the link between economic and political integration, so that national unity would be less likely to be threatened by unrealistic alternatives such as sovereignty-association. Thus, we believe that such institutions provide a constructive step towards economic integration and political reconciliation. That, more than any constitutional limitation on government, would serve to ensure living standards and even democratic rights and freedoms of future Canadians. That is the kind of Canada that we want to live in, and that we want our children to inherit.

NOTES

1. Many of these issues, and others that arise in the next section, are discussed in more detail in Purvis, "The Federal Proposals and the Economic Union," in R.W. Boadway and D.D. Purvis (eds.), *Economic Aspects of the Federal Government's Constitutional Proposals* (Kingston: John Deutsch Institute, Queen's University, 1991).

2. Canada, *Shaping Canada's Future Together: Proposals* (Ottawa: Minister of Supply and Services, 1991).

3. Canada, Special Joint Committee of the Senate and the House of Commons, *A Renewed Canada*, joint chairmen: Hon. Gérald A. Beaudoin and Dorothy Dobbie, MP (Ottawa: Minister of Supply and Services, 1992).

4. These concepts are discussed in detail in Peter Leslie, *The European Community: A Model for Canada?* (Ottawa: Minister of Supply and Services, 1991), a background paper released as part of the federal government's September 1991 constitutional proposals. See also the discussion in André Raynauld, "Les leçons de la construction de l'Europe pour la reconstruction du Canada," miméo (Montréal: Université de Montréal, 1991). Indeed, negative and positive integration were both reflected in the *BNA Act*, now called the *Constitution Act, 1867*. The "Common Market Clause" (section 121) prohibits provincial governments from using tariffs to restrict the inflow of "the Growth, Produce, or Manufacture" of other provinces, and the power to "regulate trade and commerce" given to the federal government under section 91.2 provides some basis for federal management of the economic union.

5. Richard G. Harris and Douglas D. Purvis, "Constitutional Change and Canada's Economic Prospects," *Canadian Public Policy/Analyse de Politiques*, 17, 4 (1991): 379-394.

6. As stressed by Leslie, *The European Community*, and Raynauld, "Les leçons de la construction de l'Europe pour la reconstruction du Canada," the link between economic and political integration is supported by the European experience, where the transition towards increased economic integration as indicated by the aphorism *Europe 1992* has witnessed pressures for increased authority for the European Council.

7. R.W. Boadway, T.J. Courchene and D.D. Purvis (eds.), *Economic Dimensions of Constitutional Change* (Kingston: John Deutsch Institute, Queen's University, 1991); and Boadway and Purvis (eds.), *Economic Aspects*.

8. J. Maxwell and C. Pestieau, *Economic Realities of Contemporary Confederation* (Montreal: C.D. Howe Research Institute, 1980).

9. For a recent statement, see R. Howse and M. Trebilcock, "Proposals for the Economic Union and the Division of Powers," in Boadway and Purvis, *Economic Aspects*.

10. See, for example, his contribution in Boadway, Courchene and Purvis (eds.), *Economic Dimensions of Constitutional Change*.

11. For a detailed discussion of the proposals, see the various papers in Boadway and Purvis (eds.), *Economic Aspects*. The discussion in this and the next section draws on Douglas Purvis and André Raynauld, "Reconsidering the Federal Proposals for the Economic Union," unpublished manuscript, 1992, in which we critically evaluated the federal September 1991 *Proposals* and presented detailed suggestions for modifying the specific proposals set out in that document.

12. Thus we preferred the Triple-A proposal for Senate reform: Abolish, Abolish, Abolish! However, given the key role assigned to the Triple-E Senate in the August

package, we recommend that post-constitutional reforms give a role for some sort of intergovernmental body.

13. For a detailed discussion of proposals for negative integration, including a critical analysis of the federal *Proposals* and in particular of the nature of the exemptions that are permitted see the various papers in Boadway and Purvis (eds.), *Economic Aspects*; and also Purvis and Raynauld, "Reconsidering the Federal Proposals."

14. As we argued in our earlier paper, if a "power" to manage the economic union were to be placed in the constitution, it should be in a new section that recognizes a new kind of *shared* power. A new shared power was also suggested by Purvis, "The Federal Proposals and the Economic Union"; and by Gordon Robertson, Submission to the Beaudoin-Dobbie Committee, December 1991; and by the Regroupement Économie et Constitution, "Amendments Proposed to the Federal Government Proposals on Economic Union," presented to the Beaudoin-Dobbie Committee 12 December 1991. Robertson suggests that, once established, this shared power mechanism might well deal with other federal-provincial frictions that go beyond the management of the economic union. The Regroupement proposal also includes creation of an institution similar to our *Federal Provincial Commission*, but explicitly rejects embedding it in the constitution.

15. One should not rule out the possibility that the Council itself would eventually agree upon an implementation mechanism that would involve, say, the federal government legislating in areas of provincial jurisdiction with an additional mechanism for provincial agreement prior to the federal legislation being effective in particular provinces.

16. The process suggested here is similar to the "directives" approach of the European Community.

17. Since many aspects of positive integration involve the coordination of existing policies rather than the creation of new programs, when opting-out does occur the issues of compensation and national standards would not be expected to arise very often. However, when they do arise, an agreement must be reached between the federal government and the province or provinces involved. This agreement should in turn be consistent with the principles governing opting-out under the federal spending power.

18. For a more detailed discussion, see D.D. Purvis, "Growth and Stabilization Burdens of Government Policy Failures," in H.G. Grubel, D.D. Purvis, and W.M. Scarth, *Limits to Government* (Toronto: The C.D. Howe Institute, 1992).

19. These issues are discussed in detail in the supplement on the economic union issued with the federal *Proposals*, in the various papers in Boadway and Purvis (eds.), *Economic Aspects*; and in Purvis and Raynauld, "Reconsidering the Federal Proposals."

20. Canada, Special Joint Committee, *A Renewed Canada*, p. 63.

10

Packaging Powers*

Katherine Swinton

L'ensemble des modifications apportées, durant la ronde du Canada, au partage des pouvoirs fédéraux-provinciaux est plus complexe que véritablement substantiel dans la mesure où la dévolution de compétences apparaît, tout compte fait, moins ambitieuse que prévue. Les changements les plus significatifs visent à accroître la flexibilité des ententes intergouvernementales; celles-ci ont pour but de déterminer au juste quelles compétences additionnelles seront octroyées aux provinces parmi une liste comprenant la formation de la main-d'oeuvre, la culture, l'immigration et les six sphères de compétence mineure. Globalement, il y a peu à craindre qu'on assiste à une décentralisation radicale. Néanmoins, le Québec pourrait être amené, de facto, à exercer des pouvoirs asymétriques. Or, le recours fructueux à des négociations inter-gouvernementales s'avère, au demeurant, plutôt positif dès lors qu'il permet de repousser à plus tard l'échéance d'une réforme en profondeur de la constitution canadienne. Par ailleurs, les gouvernements qui éprouvent des réserves à l'égard de la Charte canadienne des droits peuvent voir également, dans les modifications ci-haut, des moyens de limiter le rôle confié aux tribunaux. En résumé, les mesures introduites leur souplesse, s'inscrivent parfaitement, en raison de leur souplesse, dans les traditions du système fédéral canadien.

INTRODUCTION

The current round of constitutional negotiations, set in motion by the failure of the Meech Lake Accord, has tried to achieve success by satisfying a number of interests. This was to be the "Canada round," not just another Quebec round, as the Meech process was often portrayed. Nevertheless, in this so-called Canada round, the most important consideration continued to be Quebec's agenda for constitutional reform, because of its self-imposed deadline for change in the requirement of a referendum on sovereignty no later than

* 25 August 1992.

26 October 1992. While other important constitutional actors were concerned with issues such as Senate reform, aboriginal self-government, or a social charter, these were not pressing issues in Quebec. The items high on its agenda were changes to the distribution of powers in the constitution, coupled with the elements of the Meech Lake Accord, including recognition of Quebec as a distinct society, guaranteed representation on the Supreme Court of Canada, and a veto over constitutional amendments affecting national institutions and the creation of new provinces.

Quebec's strategy throughout was to gain "Meech plus," with the "plus" a significant devolution of power to the provinces. This was most dramatically demonstrated in the Allaire Report of the Quebec Liberal Party, with its demand for exclusive provincial power in 22 areas of jurisdiction.[1] But the content of the Allaire Report, while shocking to many in other parts of the country, built on Quebec's traditional demands for powers, as seen, for example, in the "Beige Paper" of the Quebec Liberal Party issued under Claude Ryan's leadership in 1980.

A common thread ran through these and other documents: often, the claim is not for devolution of a new area of federal jurisdiction, but rather the expression of a grievance because the federal government has intruded, through its spending and taxation powers, on areas assigned to the provinces under the constitution. From the perspective of many in Quebec, that federal presence is illegitimate. Therefore, the demand for withdrawal is seen only as an assertion of the constitutional rights of the province.

The difficulty generated by this position is the widespread acceptance of the federal presence and the general support for federal spending in other parts of the country. Coupled with that support has been a longstanding suspicion of "special status" for Quebec, more recently renamed "asymmetrical federalism."

After months of negotiations, the first ministers and aboriginal leaders reached an agreement on the elements of a complex constitutional reform package on 22 August 1992. Focusing only on the powers provisions, one finds much less devolution than might have been expected in light of Quebec's negotiating positions. There is a limitation on the federal spending power that is identical to that in the Meech Lake Accord, allowing a province to opt out, with compensation, from a new national shared-cost program in an area of exclusive provincial jurisdiction, provided it implements a program that meets national objectives. Beyond that, there are numerous areas — immigration, culture, regional development, among others — where a province can require the federal government to negotiate a division of responsibilities, often with an obligation for the federal government to compensate when it withdraws from the field.

A determination of the significance of the package for the distribution of powers is difficult, because its main thrust is to commit the federal government to further rounds of negotiations. Nevertheless, this comment will look at the forces that have shaped this package and speculate on its future significance, a task that is complicated by the absence of a legal text at the time of writing.

POWERS, INSTRUMENTS OR RIGHTS?

The federal government faced a number of difficulties when seeking a position with which to launch the current round with its proposals, *Shaping Canada's Future Together*, issued in September 1991. One was the need to offer Quebec something in the area of powers, while not offering so much that it would offend the supporters of the status quo in other parts of the country. Secondly, it had to devise an offer that could survive the general hostility outside Quebec to asymmetry of powers. And finally, it had to make a determination as to how much to offer, knowing that this was only the beginning of what could prove to be a lengthy round of negotiations. As in any bargaining situation, the initial offer should be modest, since it will likely be met by large demands from other actors in the bargaining process (as the Allaire Report had already indicated), and there must be room to move over time.

Not only were there questions about how much to offer; there was, as well, the dilemma of how to redistribute power and responsibility. One possibility was to reshuffle the legislative powers set out mainly in sections 91 and 92 of the *Constitution Act, 1867*, devising new heads of power and constraining the exercise of some already there, such as telecommunications, broadcasting or the environment. Alternatively, the focus could be on instruments or institutions, either to provide greater flexibility in the federal system (as with interdelegation of legislative power or binding intergovernmental arrangements), or to restrict the flexibility of the system — for example, by imposing conditions on the exercise of the federal spending power in areas of provincial jurisdiction. Finally, the focus could be on rights, rather than government powers, with restrictions on governmental activity through safeguards for market freedoms or recognition of citizens' rights in a social charter.[2]

The initial federal proposal regarding powers was an eclectic mix. Part of the package addressed traditional Quebec demands with regard to the distribution of powers (although without reference to that history). Thus, there was an offer to recognize exclusive provincial jurisdiction over labour market training. However, this was not a big change from the status quo, since both the federal and provincial governments are already active in this area, the former through its jurisdiction over unemployment insurance in section 91(2A) and the latter through its power to deal with education and labour relations under sections 93 and 92(13) of the constitution. Moreover, there was no assurance that federal spending would be curtailed in this area, and this is the major way in which the federal government has been involved in training.

There was, as well, a resurrection of the Meech Lake Accord commitment to negotiate agreements with the provinces regarding immigration, an area of concurrent jurisdiction. These could be given constitutional status.[3] A similar promise was made to negotiate agreements about federal and provincial responsibilities with regard to culture, another area of concern to Quebec. In addition, there was an offer to withdraw from or curtail federal activity in a number of areas already within provincial legislative jurisdiction: tourism, forestry, mining, recreation, housing, and municipal/urban affairs. Thus began a trend that has permeated subsequent stages of this constitutional round: changes will come not by a new delineation of jurisdiction or responsibility spelled out in the constitution, but through promises of future bargaining between interested governments which will likely result in different arrangements from province to province — in short, asymmetry.

Finally, the federal spending power would be constrained, but only in relation to new shared-cost programs in areas of exclusive provincial jurisdiction. Such programs could be established only with the agreement of seven provinces with 50 percent of the population, and provinces could opt out with compensation if they complied with national objectives in their own similar program.

As a counterweight to the perceived decentralizing thrust of the proposals just outlined, the federal government sought to gain something through a demand for a stronger section 121 of the *Constitution Act, 1867*, designed to strengthen the economic union by limiting interprovincial barriers to trade through a guarantee of mobility for persons, capital, goods and services.[4]

Between the proposal in September of 1991, through the Beaudoin-Dobbie committee[5] and the 7 July 1992 agreement reached by the multilateral meetings of all the relevant governments, except Quebec, and the aboriginal leaders, and in the final agreement of first ministers on 22 August 1992, the character of the powers package did not change a great deal. Over the months, though, the powers agenda did expand and contract. A weak form of social charter was added through pressure from the Ontario government and the details of the package changed, sometimes in important ways. There are still provisions relating to the recognition of the provincial role in labour market training and culture, and a federal promise to negotiate withdrawal from the policy areas that came to be called the "six sisters" during negotiations.[6] Added has been a promise to negotiate a regional development agreement with any interested province, and a commitment to eliminate overlap and duplication in the area of telecommunications. A weak form of common market clause, with multiple exceptions, survives, as does a social charter provision. Agreement has also been reached on a constraint on the federal spending power in new shared-cost programs through the province's right to opt out with compensation (a provision similar to that in the Meech Lake Accord). The 7 July constraints on the federal declaratory power remain. There is a mechanism to make intergovernmental agreements binding for up to five years, and reservation and disallowance are to be eliminated.

DAMAGING DECENTRALIZATION OR WELCOME FLEXIBILITY?

While there are some attractive features of the package as it has evolved, especially in its recognition of the value of flexibility, there are some disturbing things about it as well. One concern arises from the process through which proposals for changes to the distribution of powers have occurred — more precisely, the lack of focused discussion about the kinds of changes needed. The list of powers on the table for some degree of devolution has stayed roughly the same since the federal government launched this round (although there has been discussion at various bargaining tables about adding to the list — for example, to devolve marriage and divorce to the provinces). Yet at no time has there been an informed discussion of why these are the key powers to be addressed and what are the criteria for allocating powers in a renewed federal system. While other federal constitutional proposals were accompanied by background papers explaining the area and the context of the debate, the only part of the distribution of powers package treated in this way was the economic union proposals. In contrast, the powers package was supported only by a description of the powers arrangements in various federal systems in the world.[7]

Clearly, there are explanations for the powers package. Quebec has long demanded an expanded role in labour market training and culture, and this demand continued with the Allaire Report. Both items are seen as important to Quebec's development as a distinct society, although there are other powers that nationalists would claim, such as broadcasting and family policy. But why focus on tourism or recreation or forestry? True, they were in the list of exclusive provincial powers in the Allaire Report, but so were many others not mentioned. One can speculate that the reason for the choice was the need to pump up the list — to give the appearance that there is significant devolution to the provinces, without doing major damage to the federal government's ability to act in key areas of public policy.

But this is an explanation, and not a justification for the list. The new arrangements will have an impact on the future functioning of the federal system and will constrain the federal government in the future (although how much depends on a future bargaining process, as discussed below). Therefore, a more systematic discussion of the need for change would have been desirable. Indeed, some would argue that in a rational world, there would also have been discussion of other powers that might be better handled at the federal level — for example, a revised treaty power or an expanded role over the environment. Obviously, the federal government chose not to enter into such a discussion for good political reasons. And, in practical terms, it may not need to do so, for the

Supreme Court of Canada in recent years has given expansive interpretations to federal exercises of jurisdiction under the trade and commerce and peace, order and good government powers that allow it to achieve many of its policy objectives in areas such as trade agreements or environmental regulation without formal constitutional change.[8]

But what of the package arrived at, despite the concerns about the process? Evaluating the significance of the planned changes to the distribution of powers is a difficult task. The first problem arises from the absence of legal language to describe the arrangements, for the words used in a constitutional document can make a significant difference to the outcome. For example, a statement that the provinces have exclusive jurisdiction over labour market training does not, alone, reduce the federal government's ability to attach conditions about training when dispensing benefits under the unemployment insurance power. Thus, the initial federal proposal gave less reason for concern about the magnitude of the change than the 7 July accord, which seemed to confer provincial paramountcy over labour market training. That document, albeit not in legal language, spoke of the province's right to require federal withdrawal from labour market development and training, including the cessation of spending. This is a much more important devolution than the original federal proposal, although this agreement would also be circumscribed by a requirement that provinces comply with national policy objectives relating to labour market development.

A further illustration of the importance of legal language is seen in the culture proposals of the 7 July agreement, which would recognize exclusive provincial jurisdiction over culture within the provinces, but recognize, as well, federal jurisdiction over Canadian cultural matters and Canadian cultural institutions. There is room for much debate about the meaning of "culture," let alone what is provincial and what national. Some commentators fear that the federal jurisdiction is too circumscribed, only "grandparenting" existing national cultural institutions; others would argue that the language of "continuing responsibility" for Canadian cultural matters is an evolving concept that accepts a vital federal role in cultural life. Without the precise language, one cannot be sure of the implications.

Even the proposals regarding matters such as forestry leave questions open without more precise language. While the provinces are said to have exclusive authority over forestry or mining, the major impact would seem to be in the field of federal spending in the province, and not in all areas of regulatory activity. Existing constitutional jurisprudence recognizes that matters of public policy overlap the categories of federal and provincial legislative authority in the constitution, and that "watertight compartments" of policy areas are impossible to design. Thus, even if the provinces have authority over forestry or mining, the federal government will continue to be able to regulate aspects of the industry that interact with areas of federal jurisdiction, such as fisheries or marine pollution. Moreover, it will have continuing responsibility for the "national dimensions" of such matters — that is, some of the international and pan-Canadian aspects of these policy areas.

There are three lessons to be learned from these examples. One is the importance of the legal language to an evaluation of what has been agreed upon. A second lesson is the potential for disagreement (and, therefore, further rounds of discussion) when governments try to capture the 7 July or any subsequent political agreement in constitutional language. A political agreement is only one step forward in the process to constitutional amendment, which should give cause for concern when there are deadlines for achieving an acceptable package of reforms. Third, the language of a constitution is subject to interpretation by the courts and political actors in the future, and past experience indicates that this language will take on its own distinctive content over time.

Another problem in evaluating the powers package as it has been evolving lies in the nature of many of the provisions agreed upon. A reading of the 7 July 1992 agreement reached by the first ministers leaves the impression that the content of much of the powers package is "to be determined." Again and again — with immigration, culture, training, regional development, telecommunications, and the six policy areas — the agreement is to negotiate further. In several of these policy areas, the constitutional commitment is to recognize a domain of exclusive provincial jurisdiction, and thus to acknowledge that the federal presence, especially its spending, may be unwelcome to some degree in some provinces. Therefore, the federal government takes on an obligation to bargain in good faith, with interested provinces, the specific spheres of federal and provincial activity, always subject to an obligation not to derogate from the rights of Aboriginal Peoples or to alter the federal government's fiduciary duty to them. Most importantly — and most controversially when bargaining begins — the federal government is committed to compensate a province when it withdraws from these areas.

From one perspective, this type of arrangement is attractive. Instead of taking on the impossible task of delineating federal and provincial jurisdiction in the constitution for all time (an impossible task both politically and practically), flexibility is provided through negotiations adapted to the different provinces and changing circumstances. As well, those conducting the negotiations in a particular policy area will likely be officials with expertise in the specific subject, rather than the generalists who dominate the intergovernmental process and who often lack the detailed knowledge necessary to a sensible delineation of federal and provincial responsibilities in a policy area.[9]

One aspect of that flexibility will be asymmetry. Quebec will have a much different agenda with regard to culture than will a province like Ontario or Manitoba. Similarly, Quebec, and probably Ontario, will want different arrangements for training than Nova Scotia or Prince Edward Island. For some, asymmetry will be a positive feature for it allows the diversity in public policy, which is one of the major reasons for having a federal system of government. For others, asymmetry is a major defect, for they fear a costly competition among the provinces resulting in "lowest common denominator" public policy. As well, those from the smaller provinces may fear that Ottawa will curtail its activity in certain fields if Ontario and Quebec have withdrawn from them.

In my view, there is little to fear from the package of powers as it stands. This is not the dramatic decentralization that some feared would result from the failure of the Meech Lake Accord. The areas of jurisdiction to be devolved are not ones that impair important federal roles, with the possible exception of training. The federal government will continue to be able to foster a national Canadian culture, or promote tourism internationally, or regulate forestry as it affects the health of the fisheries. As well, it will continue to affect policy in many areas of provincial jurisdiction through the tax system. And while training is to become subject to greater provincial control, there are good reasons to support this result, because of the primary provincial responsibility for education, labour relations, and social assistance. Diversity in approaches to training may result, but this may be positive, leading to emulation in other provinces, as in other areas such as health and safety legislation or health care. Alternatively, if there is an advantage to uniform standards (for example, in the certification of trades), national regulation is not the only answer, as the 7 July accord contemplated with its provision committing all levels of government to negotiate common occupational standards.

Nevertheless, there are further reasons for concern about a package whose content is "to be determined." For many Quebecers, there will be unease that this package is not really "Meech plus," because it does not ensure the major transfer of powers that many have been seeking. This is a symbolic, as well as a practical consideration, because the package relies on future political negotiations. The success of those negotiations, from the province's perspective, depends on the makeup of the federal government. With a federal election expected within the next year, and the very real possibility of a minority government, there is reason for unease. An agreement struck by the current Mulroney government with its strong Quebec representation would be different from that submitted for approval to a House of Commons where the Reform Party held a key number of seats.

This assumes that the agreements will require the sanction of Parliament, as should arrangements of such importance. The fact that the 7 July accord provides that intergovernmental agreements generally will require such approval, and that they will be reviewable every five years, indicates that these special arrangements should be subject to parliamentary oversight as well.

Even without the complication of a differently constituted federal government, negotiations over these powers will be difficult. Most contentious will be the financial arrangements in the agreements. Will the arrangements be a one-time-only deal, or one that is periodically open to review and reconsideration? Undoubtedly, provinces would prefer the first arrangement, so that they have the security necessary for long-term planning. Yet if constitutional flexibility is the rationale for the process, then periodic review is the only method of proceeding. Moreover, concerns for governmental accountability require such review. Otherwise, the federal government would be committed to a financial arrangement for a particular policy area such as training or culture that reflects its policy priorities at this time; yet such an arrangement might well be an inappropriate allocation of resources within a decade, let alone another generation. Therefore, it would weaken severely the federal government if the financial arrangements in today's agreement were to stand indefinitely.

INSTITUTIONAL IMPLICATIONS

The current round of constitutional negotiations commits the country to further rounds of political agreements. Some might decry this as a new variant of "let's make a deal" federalism; others will applaud its flexibility. From an institutional perspective, the result will be that the shape of the federal system continues to be determined, in large part, through the instruments of executive federalism. However, the process will be more open, if agreements need parliamentary and legislature approval, and, at the national level, there will be two sets of regional representatives with watchful eyes on the outcomes: members of the House of Commons and Senators with a potentially much stronger regional mandate than the current incumbents.

Had the process put greater emphasis on a new division of powers spelled out in the constitution, there would have been new responsibilities placed on the Supreme Court of Canada to determine the meaning of the terms. Instead, the details of jurisdiction will be spelled out in the intergovernmental agreements. There may still be a limited role for the Supreme Court in this new arrangement of powers, a role to which it is not well suited. The 7 July accord placed obligations with regard to bargaining on governments, especially the federal level: to conclude an immigration agreement within a reasonable time, to agree to withdraw from labour market training within a reasonable time and with reasonable compensation, to make an agreement with regard to the six policy areas listed earlier within a reasonable time and with reasonable compensation. These commitments are likely to reappear in the first ministers' accord. Hopefully, the components of "reasonable time" and "reasonable compensation" will never reach the courts for interpretation. However, that is a possibility, and the task is not one suitable for adjudication. It is likely, however, that the courts would defer to the political process as much as possible, and it would be relatively easy for them to do so once early bargaining rounds are completed, for these would set guidelines for the future.

This limited role for the Supreme Court is a feature of several other parts of the constitutional package. In the 7 July accord, the preferred form of enforcement for the common market clause is not the Court, but rather a dispute resolution process involving mediation and conciliation, followed by adjudication by a special tribunal, with the Court's role limited to judicial review for errors of law and jurisdiction. The August accord weakens the enforcement mechanism even further, by leaving it to political oversight. Similarly, the social charter would be a statement of objectives monitored by a mechanism to be established by the First Ministers' Conference. Finally, one of the most contentious issues of the negotiations has been the timing of the justiciability of the inherent aboriginal right to self-government, with many governments fearful of the content that the courts might give to this right. As a result, the first ministers' agreement delays justiciability of the right for five years, and constrains the courts to a role of patrolling the negotiation process.

Political leaders seem finally to have recognized the potential scope of judicial power and activism after a decade of experience under the *Canadian Charter of Rights and Freedoms*, and they are wary of giving the judges further opportunity to shape the institutions of Canadian government through a social charter or litigation over the meaning of the right to self-government. Their caution is often well-founded, for judges are not well-positioned in terms of expertise and information to make many of the decisions under discussion in these negotiations about the division of responsibility between governments, whether federal and provincial, or between those governments and a new third order of aboriginal governments.

CONCLUSION

Canada's constitution has been remarkably adaptable over the last 125 years. Nowhere is that more true than with regard to the distribution of powers. Some will oppose the shape of the current proposals for change, but they are well within the Canadian tradition, rather than a departure from it. Admittedly, there is some new constraint on federal activity in some areas, but those areas are already within provincial jurisdiction. More importantly, the constraints are open to negotiation, to adaptation to the needs of different provinces and different circumstances. The emphasis on negotiation and adaptation to changing needs recognizes that a constitution must be a living instrument, while also affirming the premise underlying a federal system — that diversity is a value in some policy areas, unity in others. While Senate reform or aboriginal self-government may change the operation of the Canadian political system quite dramatically (and in unforeseeable ways), the powers package is well within the traditions of the Canadian federal system.

NOTES

1. Constitutional Committee of the Québec Liberal Party, *A Québec Free to Choose: Report of the Constitutional Committee* (Montreal: Québec Liberal Party, 1991).

2. A good overview of the options is found in J. P. Meekison, "Distribution of Functions and Jurisdiction: A Political Scientist's Analysis," in R. Watts and D. Brown (eds.), *Options for a New Canada* (Toronto: University of Toronto Press, 1991), p. 259.

3. The significance of this commitment to give constitutional status to certain agreements is unclear. It seems that the objective is to require a bilateral agreement to change the arrangement and thus to avoid the problems created by the Supreme Court judgement in *Reference re: Canada Assistance Plan (B.C.)* (1991), 83 D.L.R.(4th) 297, which held that the doctrine of parliamentary supremacy allowed the federal Parliament to alter intergovernmental agreements unilaterally.

4. There were other provisions that I have not outlined — one for delegation of legislative powers between governments and repeal of the federal declaratory power. Reference was made to the possibility of repealing the provisions for reservation and disallowance, but only if elements requiring unanimous consent under the amending formula were contemplated. Finally, there was a proposed new federal power to manage the economic union that quickly died because of widespread opposition.

5. Special Joint Committee on a Renewed Canada (Beaudoin-Dobbie), *Report* (Ottawa:Minister of Supply and Services, 1992)

6. The failure to call them the "six siblings" until late in the process after representatives of the National Action Committee on the Status of Women became involved may vindicate some concerns about representation in the process.

7. Contrast "Canadian Federalism and Economic Union" with the study by D. Herperger of the Institute of Intergovernmental Relations, Queen's University, "Distribution of Powers and Functions in Federal Systems" (Ottawa for both: Minister of Supply and Services, 1991).

8. I have discussed these powers in more detail in K. Swinton, "Federalism Under Fire: The Role of the Supreme Court of Canada," *Law and Contemporary Problems*, 55 (1992): 121-45.

9. Indeed, those fearing extensive decentralization from the package should take some comfort that negotiations will be conducted by those with expertise in the area, for those individuals at the federal level will have a strong personal motive to resist dramatic decentralization.

III

Intergovernmental Issues

11

The NDP in the Constitutional Drama

John Richards

Cet article vise deux objectifs: d'abord, évaluer le rôle joué par le NPD dans l'actuelle ronde de négociations constitutionnelles — communément appelée "ronde du Canada — et ce, jusqu'à la conclusion de l'entente multilatérale intervenue au début juillet 1992; puis, décrire dans ses grandes lignes l'évolution historique de la pensée constitutionnelle d'un certain leaderhip néo-démocrate.

Depuis l'échec de l'Accord du lac Meech en 1990, on a assisté à l'élection de trois gouvernements provinciaux néo-démocrates au pays — soit en Ontario, en Colombie-Britannique et en Saskatchewan. Des trois, l'Ontario a assumé de loin le rôle le plus important. Même si les priorités d'Ottawa et de Queen's Park divergent en matière de réforme constitutionnelle, l'auteur estime néanmoins que ces deux gouvernements endossent grosso modo la même approche stratégique: c'est-à-dire, rechercher un compromis qui puisse rencontrer les aspirations essentielles des divers électorats provinciaux à travers le pays. L'article traite en particulier du rôle du NPD eu égard à quatre aspects précis de l'entente multilatérale à savoir: la défense des dispositions relatives à l'autonomie gouvernementale des autochtones; l'engagement formel en faveur d'une charte sociale; la définition du partage des compétences et une déclaration touchant l'union économique; enfin, l'adoption d'une proposition ayant trait à la réforme du Sénat.

En seconde partie, l'article souligne la difficulté du NPD fédéral de faire la synthèse des trois legs constitutionnels hérités du NPD et de son prédécesseur, le CCF (Cooperative Commonwealth Federation). Premièrement, le legs des Fabians britanniques identifié à Frank Scott, appelant ici à un accroissement des pouvoirs du gouvernement central et un enchâssement de la charte des droits individuels. Deuxièmement, l'on renvoie à l'héritage de la gauche populiste de la Saskatchewan, laquelle se distingue par sa propension plus grande en faveur de l'autonomie provinciale perçue comme une condition de base du "fédéralisme coopératif". Enfin, le troisième legs se rapporte à la défense des droits, et en particulier ici de cette volonté d'étendre le concept de droits au-delà des libertés civiles, de manière à englober aussi les droits sociaux des groupes d'intérêts démunis.

LITERARY PARALLELS: *KING LEAR* AND THE FEDERAL NDP

Most politicians espouse most of the time constitutional theories that, at least in the short run, favour their respective constituents. Nonetheless, constitution making invites relatively abstract debate over ideas that for ordinary Canadians are remote from their own definition of their self-interest. The somewhat otherworldly nature of constitutional debates may explain the popularity of theatrical imagery in constitutional discussions. For many, patriation, the Meech Lake Accord and the current Canada round are three acts in a never-endingmelodrama, soap opera, farce or tragedy; politicians have become actors playing their roles either well or badly.

Were I to express the thesis of this chapter theatrically, I would call upon Shakespeare's *King Lear* — with the caveat that Canadians instinctively recoil from playing out the climactic scenes of great tragedies. In the opening scene Lear announces his intent to forsake the "interest of territory, cares of state" by dividing his kingdom among his three daughters. The two elder, Goneril and Regan, greedily accept their father's largesse and shower him with flattery. The youngest, Cordelia, refuses her share, foreseeing the tragedy that will flow from his faith in their statements of love and good intentions. The play's central theme is that naïve faith in the goodness of men — and of women — is an abdication of reason. Such faith induces political leaders to avoid the painful exercise of constraining and reconciling conflicting interests, and without the careful balancing of political interests the result is anarchic chaos.

Since Ed Broadbent's resignation as leader in 1989, the federal New Democratic Party (NDP) has behaved on constitutional matters much like Lear. Its leaders have been reluctant to admit there are difficult constitutional trade-offs to be made or to contribute to making them. "The constitutional debate," Audrey McLaughlin has recently written, "[is] more often the domain of lawyers than of ordinary citizens. [It] has tended to focus on who gets what powers." What is more important to a country than its constitution, she insists, is "how it treats its people."[1]

Broadbent had supported the Meech Lake Accord as a reasonable compromise to secure the Quebec government's endorsation of the 1982 patriation package. McLaughlin, who succeeded Broadbent as leader in 1989, had vigorously campaigned against the Accord ever since the first ministers signed it in 1987. She opposed it because it contained a provincial veto on creation of new provinces and any such veto was "not fair" to her Yukon constituents who thereby faced too high a barrier to obtaining provincial status. "Nor is it fair," she argued, "that Canada's First Peoples have once again been left out of the constitutional settlement." She also opposed the Accord because it might limit equality rights for women and the status of minorities, and because it might constrain Ottawa's ability to spend on new social programs. She did not, however, want to exclude Quebec. Referring to Premier Bourassa's five demands that had served as the basis for negotiation of the Accord, she stated: "I accept Quebec's five minimum demands for agreement to the constitution."[2]

Neither she nor the delegates who elected her leader felt obliged to explain how — once Meech was defeated — these positions were to be rendered consistent. One of Quebec's five demands was for a veto over changes in federal institutions, including creation of new provinces. How would she reconcile it with her support for the position of territorial governments that accession to provincial status should be a bilateral negotiation between the relevant territory and Ottawa? Another of Quebec's demands was a limit to the federal power to launch new programs in areas of exclusive provincial jurisdiction. How would she reconcile it with the opposition to any such constraint as expressed, for example, by women's groups lobbying for a nationally funded child-care program? A third Quebec demand, for a "distinct society" clause, was for a constitutionally entrenched recognition that the Quebec government would enjoy some special powers to promote French within the province, and hence there were limits to the justiciability of minority language rights. It was precisely this — admittedly ambiguous — special status afforded to the Quebec government to which various Charter-oriented interest groups strongly objected. How would she reconcile advocates of Quebec's special status and advocates of the Charter?

To pursue the *Lear* parallel a little further, each of the three NDP governments elected since 1990 has, like Lear's daughters, independently pursued its own constitutional agenda. The federal party has played a negligible role in attempting any reconciliation among them. (This parallel admittedly ignores the fourth NDP government at the bargaining table — that of the NDP in the Yukon.) Since the Ontario NDP has been the most willing to advance constitutional proposals running counter to its short-term interests, it can best lay claim to be Cordelia. I diplomatically refrain from making any parallels between the other NDP governments and either Goneril or Regan.

* * *

In outline, this chapter proceeds as follows. Following this introduction, I summarize the activities of the provincial NDP governments in negotiating four major issues of the Canada round: the social charter, aboriginal self-government, division of powers and the economic union, and Senate reform. The third section is an exercise in intellectual history, discussing three legacies of constitutional thought within the CCF/NDP.

Beyond finding literary allusions, the purpose of this chapter is to explain the contemporary aversion of the federal NDP to address the basic constitutional question of any federal state, what level of government should exercise what powers? A partial explanation is to be found in the simple fact that the federal NDP is in opposition and, like the federal Liberals under Jean Chrétien, has no obligation to implement policy — on the constitution or any other matter. The maxim of the practising politician summarizes this explanation as "don't take an explicit position on anything; inevitably you please some but alienate others." The implication is that the liability of angry voters is more to be feared than the asset of pleased voters.

But during earlier constitutional dramas the federal NDP and its predecessor the CCF (Co-operative Commonwealth Federation), did engage the debate and argue a position. Albeit accompanied by much internal party controversy, the federal caucus supported Trudeau's patriation exercise and Mulroney's Meech Lake Accord. Why the present reticence to engage? An alternate — or supplementary — explanation to political opportunism is the "Americanization" of Canadian left-wing politics. By Americanization I mean here a distaste for government administration with its inevitable imposition of rules, priorities and budgetary constraints, and a tendency to define the positive role of the state in terms of group rights for disadvantaged interest groups — women, Aboriginals, homosexuals, etc. Entrenchment of the 1982 *Charter of Rights and Freedoms* has encouraged this American-style politics by enlarging the prospect of advocacy litigation. The classic constitutional question concerning the allocation of powers is of secondary importance in this rights-based agenda. To the extent constitutional reform is relevant, the central issue is extension of the scope of the Charter to guarantee group rights to a broad set of social services. Hence, the emphasis on a social charter and definition of aboriginal inherent rights.

Audrey McLaughlin's vision for the NDP and Jesse Jackson's for the American Democrats have much in common. The strength of this vision is to articulate clearly the perspective of society's victims; the weakness is to encourage a style of politics that is hostile to the flexible compromises necessary for efficient public sector management. Implicit in a rights-based political agenda is the attempt by aggrieved interest groups to establish certain rights as absolute constraints on government. Those who use the language of rights reject "compromised" rights, are reluctant to accept the concept of a public sector budget constraint, and are suspicious of the exercise of managerial discretion within government. When the rights at issue are basic civil liberties, such instincts are entirely appropriate. But in extrapolating the concept of rights beyond civil liberties — as has been undertaken by the more enthusiastic supporters of entrenched social rights in the constitution — interest groups leaders are denigrating the art of political compromise. The exercise of flexible compromise and efficient public sector management should be as important to the NDP as their analogues are to profit-maximizing firms in the market. Successful welfare states are not, for example, the product of justiciable rights to particular social services; they are the product of historical compromise between those wanting more generous public services and those reluctant to pay the necessary taxes, and of skilled public sector managers seeking to maximize "value for taxpayers."

THE CANADA ROUND, SUMMARY OF PROVINCIAL NDP INITIATIVES[3]

Of the three NDP provincial governments, Ontario has played by far the most ambitious role in this Canada round. This is, in part, explicable by noblesse oblige. Ontario is among the four founding provinces, is the largest province, and has a tradition as an active constitutional player dating back to Oliver Mowat. In part, the explanation lies with Premier Rae's personal convictions. He has consistently championed inclusion of two particular reforms:

- a social charter entrenching the country's commitment to a European-style welfare state, and
- generous provisions for recognition of an aboriginal inherent right to a new third order of government, to be native-controlled.

Rae's ranking of constitutional reforms differs from that of the federal government. The latter's priorities presumably rank highest the realization of reforms acceptable to the moderate Québécois[4] nationalists in control of the Quebec government and to realization of Senate reform that might enable the Conservatives to recapture supporters in the rest-of-Canada (ROC) lost to the Reform Party. Despite these divergent rankings, Rae and Clark have pursued similar strategies, and were the principal authors of the tentative agreement achieved in July 1992. Unlike much of the federal NDP leadership, Rae has consistently argued that the constitutional crisis is profound, and that Canadian politicians cannot turn away from the matter until a solution is reached.

Both Ottawa and Queen's Park have operated on the basis that the country has fractured into several nationalist dialogues, and that preservation of the federation requires accommodation of a rational core within each. In brutal summary the various nationalist constituencies can be summarized as follows:

- Québécois nationalism for which the core demand is some measure of special status for the Quebec National Assembly, in particular constitutional recognition of the province's powers to promote the French character of the province and, the unavoidable *revers de la médaille*, to restrict somewhat the use of English;
- aboriginal nationalism for which the core demand is constitutional recognition of an inherent aboriginal right to form a third order of government, to be native-controlled;
- a right-wing populist nationalism, best articulated by the Reform Party, for which the core demand is a reformed Senate able to provide the eight

peripheral provinces with influence sufficient to block inefficient policies (such as the National Energy Program) that subsidize marginal voters in the central provinces at the expense of productive regional economies;

- a left-wing "Charter nationalism" that comprises a loose coalition of interest groups intent on preserving and expanding the welfare state by means of the Charter, and for which the core demand is constitutional recognition of the welfare state by means of a social charter.

Let us turn briefly to four major items on the bargaining agendas of the three NDP administations during this Canada round.

THE SOCIAL CHARTER

An explicitly non-justiciable social charter is among the elements of the multilateral agreement of July 1992. The Ontario NDP has clearly been the champion of this reform among the governments at the bargaining table, although until early 1992 it was unclear on the matter. Did it favour a powerful version in which interest groups could have recourse to the courts to oblige governments to provide "adequate" levels of a broad range of social services, or a more modest "declaratory" version that would simply extend the list of desirable goals for social policy already present in Equalization and Regional Disparities (section 36 of the Constitution Act)?

The Saskatchewan NDP has a long tradition of government dating back to 1944 and is accordingly less impregnated by the group rights vision of politics that underlies "Charter nationalism." Furthermore, it emanates from the prairie populist tradition which, north and south of the 49th parallel, has been suspicious of an activist judiciary substituting its will for that of elected politicians. For both these reasons, the social charter is an idea on which the Saskatchewan NDP was willing to give only tepid support. The British Columbia NDP also placed a low priority on a social charter and opposed justiciability.[5]

One of the few active interventions of the federal NDP in this Canada round was the role of certain MPs on the Beaudoin-Dobbie Committee in reconciling the various NDP provincial positions on this issue. The result was that Ontario ultimately opted for the more modest "declaratory" version, similar to that recommended by the Beaudoin-Dobbie Committee.[6]

INHERENT ABORIGINAL RIGHT TO SELF-GOVERNMENT

The multilateral agreement of July 1992 is generous on this matter. In considerable detail it obligates both Ottawa and the provinces to negotiate the substance of future aboriginal governments with aboriginal organizations. Ontario played the lead among the nine provinces in promoting this reform and in securing the participation of aboriginal leaders in the current round of bargaining.

All three NDP governments support the inherent right of Aboriginals to self-government as a redress for past racism and as a "leap of faith" that native governments may break the tradition of failure of the federal Department of Indian Affairs. In private, many NDP leaders are sceptical about the unconstrained expectations among aboriginal leaders, and worry about the financial and administrative complexities that a new third order of government will entail. These anxieties are probably highest in Saskatchewan where Aboriginals constitute over 10 percent of the provincial population. Accordingly, the Saskatchewan assessment of these reforms has been more cautious than in the two other NDP jurisdictions. Here is a representative statement from Premier Romanow:

> [M]any worry about [aboriginal] demands ... about the accommodations which are necessary. ... I want to state clearly that our government does not fear this change. We believe that it will be difficult to achieve, that many tough negotiations are yet ahead. ... But we enter this new phase ... determined to succeed with good will and tolerance, secure in our belief that this is a change which is profoundly important and long overdue.[7]

DIVISION OF POWERS AND THE ECONOMIC UNION

The multilateral agreement of July 1992 replaces the existing interprovincial free trade provision (section 121) with a new economic union clause "that prevents the erection of interprovincial trade barriers. ... that arbitrarily discriminate on the basis of province or territory." While highly qualified, this provision does somewhat constrain provincial discretion. In general, however, the multilateral agreement, like the Meech Lake Accord, is designed to satisfy the demands of constitutional decentralists:

- specifying several additional provincial powers, the most important of which is labour training;
- creating a provincial role in Supreme Court appointments;
- allowing provinces to opt out with compensation from any future federal spending in areas of provincial jurisdiction;
- denying Ottawa the ability to amend intergovernmental transfers over the lifetime of specified agreements;
- transforming the declaratory power (section 92(10)(c)) from a federal power into a joint power requiring for its application sanction from both Ottawa and the relevant province(s);
- abolishing federal powers of disallowance and reservation of royal assent of provincial statutes.

The basic reason for this decentralism is pressure from the Québécois nation-alist constituency. But these provisions also reflect fairly closely the interests of other provinces, including Alberta and the three provincial NDP govern-ments. Ontario sided with Ottawa and assured inclusion of a — highly quali-fied — revision to section 121. The British Columbia NDP is currently dominated by a leadership in favour of provincial autonomy over a wide range of economic policies. The Saskatchewan government, given its "have-not" status, has been anxious to preserve federal transfers, but it too was essentially on the side of provincial autonomy.

Accession to increased provincial economic powers was the principal de-mand emanating from the NDP in British Columbia. The tenor of their argument is captured in the following passage from a legislative report:

> The federal role in the economy is to provide international leadership, a sound currency, regulation of interprovincial trade, maintenance of national transporta-tion links, communication and energy infrastructure, and equalization payments to ensure reasonably comparable fiscal capacity in all provinces. But the federal government does not need to be directly involved in labour training, regional economic development, harbours, inland and coastal fisheries, small business development, etc. In these areas, there is not a national interest that must be protected by ... the federal government. In fact, in these areas of the economy, national programs with fixed criteria can hinder the development of local and regional economies by attempting to shoehorn widely disparate service groups into the same size 8 boot.[8]

To accommodate provinces unwilling to assume additional powers, the report went on to recommend concurrency with provincial paramountcy over a class of powers.

The Saskatchewan NDP's principal concern in this area was to prevent erosion of provincial economic autonomy.[9] Saskatchewan argued that a strong economic union clause, combined with the increased importance of federal treaty-making powers in the context of recent international trade agreements (GATT, Canada-US Free Trade Agreement and a potential North American Free Trade Agreement), threatened provincial jurisdiction assured by the Labour Conventions case.[10]

As is discussed more fully below, the NDP is heir to sharply divergent constitutional legacies — nowhere more so than on the subject of decentraliza-tion. Up to, and including the 1982 patriation debates, the majority within the federal NDP were essentially sympathetic to centralist arguments, and many interest groups allied to the NDP still are. For example, union leaders have criticized the transfer of labour training to the provinces. They fear that provinces taking up this new power will obtain funds or tax points that would otherwise finance the federal unemployment insurance system.[11] Many feminist organizations are critical of the constraint on the federal spending power because it renders less probable a nationally funded child-care program.

Those among the NDP opposed to the decentralism of the multilateral agreement have, to date, remained largely mute, but there is no guarantee that they will remain so — particularly during any referendum campaigns on ratification.

THE SENATE

The most controversial element of the multilateral agreement of July 1992 is its provision for a "Triple-E" Senate. It is not necessary to discuss all details of the proposal, but to understand the role of provincial NDP governments in the complex Senate negotiations, it is important to outline the basic elements:

- The Senate would comprise 84 members, 8 from each of 10 provinces plus 2 from each of the 2 northern territories.
- Senators would be elected at the same time as members of Parliament, hence allowing a simultaneous dissolution of both houses of Parliament in the event of a serious political crisis between Commons and Senate over any piece of legislation.
- The Senate would enjoy only a suspensive veto over ordinary revenue and expenditure legislation. It could, however, veto legislation containing fundamental changes in policy (such as legislation introducing the GST), treating it as ordinary legislation.
- The Senate would be able to block, by a simple majority, any legislation bearing fundamentally on resource taxation.
- Any legislation bearing fundamentally on French language or culture would require a double majority — of those Senators voting and of francophone Senators.
- All other bills passed by the Commons (i.e., ordinary legislation) would be subject to Senate approval by either a one-stage or a two-stage process. In the one-stage case, a bill would need at least 40 percent of Senators voting. If a bill secures between 30 and 40 percent approval, its fate would be decided in a second stage by a simple majority in a joint session of Commons plus Senate. Only if opponents rally over 70 percent of Senators would they definitively block a piece of ordinary legislation.

The demand for Senate reform among the general public is highly correlated with support for the Reform Party, and accordingly public support has been strongest in the Prairies and weakest in Quebec. The Reform Party rationale for Senate reform has been a Downsian "median voter" argument.[12] Governments tend to produce policies that redistribute small per capita benefits to the median voters (i.e., residents of Ontario and Quebec) at the expense of larger per capita costs to a small number of outlying voters (i.e., residents of Alberta). Atlantic Canadians have supported Senate reform based on an Olsonian interest group argument.[13] As a regional interest (9 percent of the population) receiving large per capita subsidies from the rest of the country, they want to raise the cost of implementing alternate policies that would lower these subsidies. A Triple-E Senate, allocating 40 percent of Senators to Atlantic Canada, would do just that.

Neither of these public choice arguments impugns the intellectual integrity of Don Getty, Clyde Wells or the other advocates of a Triple-E Senate; they do suggest that voters are rational in choosing their constitutional advocates. In addition to Alberta and Newfoundland, Triple-E supporters have included Nova Scotia, Manitoba and Saskatchewan.

Ontario and Ottawa were the principal opponents of a Triple-E Senate; they were joined in this position by the British Columbia NDP government, and by the governments of New Brunswick and Prince Edward Island. Critics of the Triple-E Senate advanced two basic arguments:

- Given the large differences in population among provinces, equality of provincial representation was too great an affront to the democratic principle of equal voting power of all citizens. Representation should be on an "equitable" basis, weighted towards the smaller provinces but not to the extent of equality of provincial representation.
- The primary role of a reformed Senate was better monitoring of government activity, not the exercise of a definitive veto over government legislation. An overly powerful Senate would weaken the efficiency of the federal government by weakening its accountability to the Commons. Accordingly, they proposed a variety of limitations on the ability of the Senate to veto legislation.

The Senate was the constitutional issue most divisive among the NDP. British Columbia essentially allied itself with Ontario on appropriate Senate powers, but put forward a different formula than Ontario for weighting provincial representation. British Columbia proposed a number of Senators per province that generated equality of representation from five regions: British Columbia (with the northern territories), the Prairies, Ontario, Quebec, and Atlantic Canada.[14] This proposal resurrected a classic British Columbia argument in favour of a five-region model of the federation, with British Columbia not coincidentally as an independent region.

Saskatchewan, on the other hand, represented the pro-Triple-E sentiment within the province. In an attempt to realize a compromise on the Senate, Saskatchewan proposed in June 1992 a variation: an equal number of Senators per province, with the voting of provincial delegations to be unequally weighted, on certain matters, to favour the more populous provinces.[15] While the Saskatchewan model was not adopted, it embodied the principle that underlies the compromise finally realized: maintain provincial equality of representation, but adjust the Senate's voting rules to weaken the power that otherwise would lie with the small provinces. Ontario sought to restrict the Senate to a suspensive veto only. The actual agreement allows for a veto on ordinary legislation, but only if opponents of a bill can rally support of 70 percent of all Senators.[16]

This Senate proposal poses many subtle problems (Who qualifies as a francophone Senator? Who classifies legislation among the alternate categories?), but clearly the central problem is that equality of provincial representation is a symbolic affront to those Quebecers — the vast majority — who subscribe to some variant of Confederation as a compact between two founding peoples. Tactically, a Triple-E Senate is an albatross for those trying to persuade Quebecers to support renewed federalism as opposed to sovereignty. It is now a hypothetical question, but what would have transpired if Saskatchewan had broken the unanimity of Prairie provinces on behalf of a Triple-E Senate and had aligned itself on this issue with the two other NDP governments? Would that have sufficed to produce a Senate more compatible to Quebecers?

On three of the four items discussed, the compromise reached appears acceptable among a majority within all nationalist constituencies across Canada. On the fourth, that is not the case. Quebec opinion on a Triple-E Senate is clearly hostile and this has been the focus of Quebec reaction to the July 1992 multilateral agreement.[17]

On the subject of Senate reform the federal NDP was mute; the provincial sections of the NDP disagreed among themselves. Perhaps all this is more melodrama than Shakespearian tragedy as first suggested, but it is devoutly to be hoped that the Triple-E Senate proposal that actually emerged does not prove to be the focus for conflict that prevents success in this Canada round.

THE NDP, HEIR TO THREE LEGACIES

Having analyzed the role of contemporary provincial NDP governments in the current Canada round negotiations, let us turn to an exercise in intellectual history. The question motivating this exercise remains, why has the federal NDP come to play such a marginal role in addressing the classic constitutional problem of division of powers that inevitably arise in any federal state?

The question may appear a secondary matter, of interest solely to those involved in the internal ideological debates within the Canadian left-wing community. That is a superficial response. The federal NDP has traditionally articulated constitutional ideas for a significant minority of Canada, particularly in the ROC. Since the 1940s, the CCF/NDP has represented between 10 and 20 percent of the Canadian electorate in national elections. The range of support rises significantly if we ignore the poor performance of the party in Quebec and restrict consideration to ROC. At various times in the last decade the NDP has represented the plurality of ROC opinion. Internal NDP debates on the constitution are not marginal; they are themselves part of the constitutional crisis.

An appropriate point of departure is formation of the CCF in the depths of the 1930s depression. The CCF was Canada's first genuinely popular mass-based party of the left. In 1961 it reorganized itself as the New Democratic Party (NDP).

THE BRITISH FABIAN LEGACY

The Regina Manifesto, endorsed by the CCF at its first national convention, in Regina in 1933, is one of the classic documents of the Canadian left.[18] The Manifesto displayed a perfectly understandable hostility to the "inherent injustice and inhumanity" of contemporary capitalism. The central theme of the document was the need to enable a powerful National Planning Commission, operating with the delegated authority of an unfettered national Parliament, to organize the economy. The constitutional orientation was unambiguously centralist:

> What is chiefly needed today, is the placing in the hands of the national government of more power to control national economic development. ... The present division of powers between Dominion and Provinces reflects the conditions of a pioneer, mainly agricultural, community in 1867. Our constitution must be brought into line with the increasing industrialization of the country and the consequent centralizaton of economic and financial power.[19]

The Manifesto was drafted by intellectuals close to the new party who in turn had formed the League for Social Reconstruction, an organization self-consciously modelled on the British Fabian Society.[20] Like many members of the Fabian Society (George Bernard Shaw being an obvious example) the League demonstrated an unbridled faith in the potential of detailed central planning, to be undertaken by intellectuals like themselves. Central planning would not only remove unemployment by stimulating aggregate demand, but also redistribute incomes equitably and enhance industrial productivity. The League spoke with jarringly naïve enthusiasm of Stalin's "remarkable administrative machinery."[21]

The constitutional creed shared by many intellectuals in both the Fabian Society and the League was straightforward: since the power of corporate and financial capital was ever more concentrated, only centralized political power could act as an effective counter force. As democrats, they parted company with communists and accepted the constraint of parliamentary democracy. But they envisioned few other constraints on the power of the national government to plan the economy. As men of the left — very few women were involved in these debates — they wanted no part of imperial traditions. Of particular relevance to this discussion, they were impatient with the Victorian liberalism that permeated the British administrative elite.

Via an altogether different route that same Victorian liberalism had significantly shaped Canadian constitutional evolution. The Judicial Committee of the Privy Council was Canada's final constitutional court of appeal for the first 80 years after Confederation. The British jurists on the Judicial Committee were at the pinnacle of the collective wisdom among the British administrative elite, and many, such as Viscount Haldane, perceived themselves as liberal champions. One tenet of their thought was the value of classic federalism — of a formal division of powers — in administering the Empire. And, in general, British colonial authorities did divide jurisdiction. The British controlled commercial and foreign policy and the legal system, but preserved intact the authority of local elites to determine "local matters" in indigenous political institutions. Application of this doctrine to interpretation of the *British North America Act* resulted in Canadian provinces enjoying far more substantial sovereignty over "local matters" than a reading of the BNA Act would suggest. The CCF and intellectuals within the League were predictably hostile to the Judicial Committee's legacy. They saw it as imperial meddling that had diverted Canadian constitutional practice from the clear intent of John A. Macdonald and a majority of the Fathers of Confederation.[22]

However much one believes in impersonal forces determining political outcomes, it is futile to ignore the unique role of Frank Scott in this debate. He is a genuine *deus ex machina* in Canada's constitutional drama. A renaissance intellectual, a product of the Anglo-Quebec elite, Oxford-trained, his first delight was satiric poetry. The following example is an excerpt from an attack upon the Judicial Committee:

Planning of trade, guaranteed prices, high employment —
Can provincial fractions deal with this complex whole?
Surely such questions are now supra-national!
But the judges fidgeted over their digests
And blew me away with the canons of construction.
"This is intolerable," I shouted, "this is one country;
Two flourishing cultures, but joined in one nation.
I demand peace, order and good government.
This you must admit is the aim of Confederation!"
But firmly and sternly I was pushed to a corner
And covered with the wet blanket of provincial autonomy.[23]

From the 1930s to 1960s Scott was among the small inner circle of national CCF leaders. He also played a central role in key constitutional cases that established the civil liberties of religious and political minorities, rights that were inadequately protected under the conservative Catholic consensus of contemporary Quebec politics. As constitutional law professor at McGill University he exercised a profound personal influence on all prominent CCF leaders, including Tommy Douglas, Premier of Saskatchewan, and David Lewis, leader of the federal NDP. Of greater importance to the actual evolution of Canada's constitution was his impact on Chief Justice Bora Laskin, on Pierre Trudeau, and on many others who came to exercise political power.

Scott was a complex and subtle writer; we cannot do justice to his thought in any brief summary. Despite his subtlety, he consistently and tenaciously clung to a few constitutional doctrines.[24] Here it is worth emphasizing two.

First, as a socialist, he never wavered in his belief in the need for constitutional centralization of economic powers to offset corporate and financial power. This led him to oppose vigorously all "social compact" theories according to which Confederation was a collective contract between two founding nations or among pre-existing colonial governments, with the provinces being the fundamental constituent elements. Scott freely allowed that social compact theories were a reasonable summary of the negotiations that preceded Confederation but, he argued, the Fathers of Confederation, in drafting the *British North America Act*, had not created a classic federation with a rigid division of sovereignty between two levels of government. The BNA Act, if read free of the liberal interpretation imposed by the Judicial Committee, simply did not create a pure federal state. In the following passage Scott cites with approval Wheare's characterization of Canada as having a "quasi-federal" constitution:

> [V]arious provisions [of the BNA Act] give Canada a special form of federalism, unlike any theory of the federal state in existence then or now. Indeed, Professor Wheare has raised the question whether Canada can be said to have a federal constitution at all; he prefers to say that she has a quasi-federal constitution, since, judged by the strict law, it is difficult to know whether it should be called a federal constitution with considerable unitary modifications, or a unitary constitution with considerable federal modifications. Looked at in the light of present [i.e., 1958] Canadian politics, where respect for "provincial autonomy" has been elevated by Privy Council decisions and increasing French-Canadian influence to be a supreme purpose of the BNA Act, the acceptance of the unitary provisions in 1867 appears remarkable.[25]

Second, Scott saw in local majorities acting through provincial governments the primary threat to civil liberties. In particular, he consistently opposed the identification of the rights of francophones with increased provincial autonomy as advocated by Québécois nationalists. Francophones failed to extend their language and culture much beyond Quebec, he suggested, because of the failure of Ottawa to override provincial governments in Manitoba and Ontario that had suppressed minority francophone rights prior to World War I. It was quite natural that Scott be an ardent defender of a constitutionally entrenched bill of rights.

Ultimately, Scott's most significant impact upon the constitution came not through his CCF/NDP associations, but through his friend Pierre Trudeau. Like Scott, Trudeau's constitutional ideas are complex and any brief summary cannot do them justice. Nonetheless, it is quite reasonable to name Scott as the indirect author, via his influence on Trudeau, of the 1982 patriation package. It embodies an entrenched charter of individual rights, as Scott had long wanted. It also reflects Scott's adamant opposition to "social compact" theories according to which the provinces are fundamental building blocks of the federation. Further, the patriation package made no attempt to accommodate moderate Quebec nationalists and allow the Quebec government any unique role in the preservation of the French fact within the province.

THE SASKATCHEWAN LEGACY

The second constitutional legacy of the party has its origins in Saskatchewan. Regina may have given its name to the CCF's first major manifesto, but Canada's most rural province was an unlikely source of constitutional doctrines for a party of the left. The reason that its leaders came, in time, to exercise an influence is obvious: it is the one Canadian jurisdiction in which social democratic politicians have over the last half-century usually been in government rather than in opposition. They accordingly developed a culture of government, as opposed to a culture of opposition.

Viewed broadly, CCF/NDP administrations in Saskatchewan have been a unique hybrid of British left traditions of professional public administration and American left populism. North American populist movements can usefully be classified into left and right variants; the CCF obviously belonged to the latter. Like all populist movements the CCF emphasized the ability of "the people," regardless of class or race, to realize significant collective goals via local democratic institutions. It championed cooperatives more than unions; it championed pragmatic reforms introduced in Regina over hypothetical reforms to be introduced by a future government of the left in Ottawa.

Although the value of its resource base is less than Alberta's, the arbitrarily defined borders of Saskatchewan enclose significant reserves of potash, oil, uranium and other minerals. The commodity price boom of the 1970s triggered a complex conflict over who would get the windfall — resource companies via higher profits, provincial governments via royalties, the federal government via higher taxes, or consumers via prices below world levels. The Saskatchewan government aggressively staked out the claim of Saskatchewan residents as owners (given section 109) of crown resources. The most controversial such "stake out" was nationalization in 1975 of half the potash mines in the province.

In its first two decades in office (from 1944 to 1964) the Saskatchewan CCF had dutifully looked to Frank Scott for constitutional wisdom, but as the Saskatchewan NDP asserted its claim to resource rents in the 1970s, its leaders found themselves resurrecting arguments of the much-maligned Judicial Committee on behalf of provincial autonomy.[26] They argued that provincial rights to manage resources (sections 92(5)) and impose royalties on provincially owned resources (section 109) were relatively clear, and should prevail over the sweeping federal powers to regulate and tax (sections 91(2) and 91(3) respectively).

Resource companies intitiated two important constitutional cases, alleging the province's attempts to regulate production and extract revenues were *ultra vires*. Ottawa entered the proceedings as a co-plaintiff, arguing against the provincial position. The Supreme Court, by ruling against Saskatchewan in both cases, lowered a fog of constitutional ambiguity over a vast body of provincial resource regulation, including that by Alberta of its oil and gas industry.[27]

Premier Blakeney's following comments are typical of the contemporary Saskatchewan response to these matters. They amounted to a "watertight compartments" interpretation of federalism:

> Federalism as we understand it in Canada — or at least as I understand it — means that in a case where provincial interest is paramount under our constitution it stands just as high and unassailable as does the federal power in a reverse circumstance. ... I have become convinced that the present political leadership in Ottawa does not share this view. I have become convinced that their unrelenting attack on our resource policies is prompted — not by a belief that we are acting beyond our powers — as these have been understood for one hundred years — but rather by a desire to extend the central powers of the federal government at the expense of provincial powers.[28]

Much of Saskatchewan's interest in constitutional matters in the 1970s was motivated by redistribution: who would get windfall resource rents? If that had been all there was to it, it invites the accusation of constitutional opportunism. But more was at stake. In1980, Broadbent supported Trudeau's unilateral patriation attempt in exchange for section 92A, a clause that restored much of the provincial resource jurisdiction eroded by the Supreme Court.[29] This compromise did not, however, suffice to prevent a highly public break between the Saskatchewan and federal sections of the party the following year. During 1981, Saskatchewan became one of the "gang of eight" provincial governments in active opposition to unilateral federal patriation.[30]

Saskatchewan representatives spoke of "[parliamentary] politics as the way in which we, in this society, resolve conflicts of values."[31] They were reluctant to extend the scope of the proposed *Charter of Rights and Freedoms* beyond a defence of traditional civil liberties, and they argued strenuously for the "notwithstanding" legislative override (section 33 of the Charter). Ironically, inclusion of this clause was Scott's principal criticism of the patriation package ultimately adopted.[32]

While the provincial government indulged in few conceptual discussions, its leaders realized that their prairie political tradition depended upon maintenance of a classic view of federalism. They had little to gain from either the party's traditional ideas on centralizing economic powers or the emerging tradition of advocacy litigation that prompted many in the NDP to applaud introduction of the Charter. Reduced to their core, the Saskatchewan NDP's constitutional position amounted to two arguments.

The most important is a social democratic version of Breton's argument for "competitive federalism."[33] Provincial autonomy in a federal state is, according to Breton, a political analogue to private firms in a competitive market. Just as the quality of private goods and services is improved by competition in the market, so the quality of public goods and services is improved by entrepreneurial politicians in one province experimenting with new programs independent of the others. As in a competitive market many innovations will prove unsuccessful, but electoral pressure will induce governments over time to copy the good ones.

The market cannot realize its potential without the accountability and reward afforded by the institution of private property. Analogously, competitive federalism cannot function unless provinces retain financial autonomy, allowing electors to hold their provincial politicians accountable for political results. Provinces must be able to tax independently and, while federal-provincial transfers are desirable to increase equity and realize the efficiencies from national exploitation of certain tax sources, such transfers should be unconditional "block grants" that do not distort priorities within provincial jurisdiction.[34] Again, to quote Blakeney:

[T]here is no fundamental reason for Canadians to be further to the left politically than Americans, yet we Canadians have undeniably undertaken more significant political experiments than the Americans. Why? The key to an explanation is that Canadian federalism has preserved enough powers at the provincial level for provinces to serve as social laboratories, whereas American federalism has so reduced states' rights that significant political experiments can only emanate from Washington. ... To launch a major experiment in social policy via the national government requires a majority of a parliament representing the whole country. That is far less likely to occur than that a majority of a state or provincial legislature opt for the experiment. When you talk to an American about medicare, he assumes it must be a federal program and then proceeds to talk about the problems: the inefficiencies of too large a bureaucracy in Washington, the resulting excessive costs, etc. Had a Farmer-Labor government in Minnesota had the power to introduce a statewide medical care insurance program, then, after a decade or so, I suspect citizens elsewhere in the U.S. would have insisted on a national equivalent.[35]

A second argument, implicit in the above quotation but poorly developed by Saskatchewan leaders, is that average cost curves for provision of many public goods and services are (like the microeconomics text cost curves for provision of private goods) "U" shaped. The Atlantic provinces may be too small to realize scale economies in provision of many public goods but, on the other hand, Ottawa may be too big.

Ironically, one of the earliest statements on realizing the agenda of the left by means of competitive federalism was by Pierre Trudeau, writing in a collection of essays published in 1961 to coincide with the reorganization of the CCF into the NDP. He admonished "that Canadian socialists must consider federalism as a positive asset, rather than as an inevitable handicap" and argued the demonstration value of successful socialist experiments at the provincial level.[36] He mocked the subservience of socialist tacticians to the centralizing "theory class" of constitutionalists within the CCF. He went on to deplore the effect upon the CCF's fortunes in Quebec of an excessive commitment to centralization.

By the time of the patriation debate in the early 1980s, Trudeau's constitutional position had evolved a great deal from that of 1961. His conflicts with Quebec nationalists and with western provincial leaders over resource jurisdiction prompted him, upon his "second coming" in the 1980 general election, to espouse a constitutional agenda close to Frank Scott's. Through the *Charter of Rights and Freedoms*, his intent was not only to strengthen individual civil liberties, but to strengthen the commitment of individual Canadians to national institutions and weaken provincial loyalties. (As Scott had consistently argued, the Charter made no concession to a special status for Quebec in promoting French language and culture.) In an ultimately unsuccessful attempt to avoid compromise with the provinces, Trudeau attempted to persuade the Imperial Parliament to "hold its nose" and enact his unilateral patriation package — despite the fact that it enjoyed the support of only two provinces (Ontario and New Brunswick). In so doing, Trudeau was relying on the argument that the BNA Act had not created a truly federal country requiring provincial agreement to any constitutional change, but merely a "quasi-federation."

THE AMERICAN LEGACY

The United States is unique among major industrial countries in having only a limited welfare state. Given the frustration experienced by American reform movements in realizing social program innovation through the political process, many have substituted advocacy litigation. Far more than in western European countries, or pre-1982 Canada, the positive functions of the state have been translated in American discourse into the language of justiciable rights. American reform movements have extended the concept of rights beyond basic civil rights defined by liberal theories of liberty as freedom from state interference. They have elaborated theories of group rights or "collective entitlements" for the disadvantaged.[37]

The third constitutional legacy of the NDP is precisely this American tradition of advocacy litigation, an aspect of social reform that has assumed far greater importance in ROC since introduction of the *Charter of Rights and Freedoms* in 1982. Adoption of the Charter was, in economic terms, a supply-side effect, lowering the cost of litigation relative to parliamentary politics. On the demand side, the severity of the crisis of Canadian public finance has raised fears of "neoconservative budget slashing," and has provided potentially affected interest groups with a strong incentive to translate their stake in the welfare state into collective rights. The Ontario NDP, in endorsing the principle of a social charter, has provided a forum for academics sympathetic to a rights-based agenda to state their case.[38]

To date, Ottawa and the provinces have curtailed spending growth, but there has been no "neoconservative budget slashing." In aggregate, Ottawa and the provinces have reduced public sector spending on programs from the peak reached during the early 1980s recession (an average of 39 percent of GDP in 1982-84) back to the level prior to that recession. In both 1981 and 1989 public sector program spending was 35 percent of GDP; it grew somewhat as a share of GDP upon onset of recession in 1990. Since the public sector remained in deficit throughout the decade, however, debt service payments continued to rise — from 6 percent of GDP in 1981 to 9 percent in 1989 — and the threat exists that spending may be slashed in the future to restore fiscal balance.[39]

An articulate advocate of extension of the concept of rights from individual civil liberties to collective rights is Thomas Berger. Berger can be described as a west coast equivalent of Frank Scott. Like Scott, Berger is a lawyer; like Scott, his has been an impressive, eclectic career — as labour lawyer, as leader of the British Columbia NDP, as head of the federal commission that recommended a moratorium on a Mackenzie Valley pipeline, as justice on the provincial Supreme Court, as advocate of aboriginal rights to self-government. Like Scott, he bases much of his argument on a literal interpretation of the constitution, and is impatient with arguments for classic federalism which accord an importance to the federal division of powers between Ottawa and the provinces. Where Berger has evolved beyond Scott is in arguing that the existing Charter, even without the addition of a new social charter, already provides important justiciable collective rights.[40]

Not surprisingly, many interest groups close to the NDP, and many of the party's leaders, have embraced a similar constitutional interpretation. The National Anti-Poverty Organization (NAPO) has, for example, sought both to expand a collective rights interpretation of the existing Charter and, in this

Canada round, has lobbied to add a strong social charter assuring minimum requirements for a broad range of social policies.[41]

THE NDP'S FAILURE TO SYNTHESIZE ITS THREE LEGACIES

Many NDP leaders are aware of these three competing legacies, of their relative strengths and weaknesses. Given the political difficulty in realizing any reconciliation among them, it is not particularly surprising that the federal NDP has failed at the task. What is less excusable, the party has avoided the debate that must precede any workable compromise. The 1989 federal NDP convention is a clear example. It took place at the height of the debate over ratification of the Meech Lake Accord. Much behind-the-scenes negotiation produced a draft motion that was incomprehensible to all but constitutional lawyers. A floor debate ensued, after which the motion was withdrawn amidst procedural confusion.[42] It was an event that invites allusions to *King Lear*.

Maybe none of this matters. The Ontario NDP has, as earlier discussion demonstrates, filled much of the void created by the absence of the federal NDP from the debate. But a recurring danger to any federal state is that shocks in the political environment produce conflicting political dialogues that seriously fracture the political community. Canada needs institutions, such as its national parties, that serve to heal these fractures by exploring workable compromises. For the federal NDP to abdicate this role is a disservice to the significiant minority of Canadians the party represents, and to the country itself.

NOTES

1. A. McLaughlin, "Mending the ties that bind," *The Globe and Mail*, 21 July 1992.
2. Audrey McLaughlin's positions and the quotations attributed to her in this paragraph are taken from "Meech Lake," a document issued at the 1989 federal NDP convention by her leadership campaign.
3. At the time of writing, August 1992, the constitutional sands have not settled. The nine ROC premiers, the two territorial leaders and the four leaders of the national aboriginal organizations and Joe Clark on behalf of the federal government, have concluded a tentative agreement. The Quebec government has indicated some qualified support for the agreement, but has insisted on amendments — the most important of which are a strengthening of the distinct society clause and a weakening of the Triple-E Senate proposal — before endorsing it as an offer of "renewed federalism" worthy of submission to Quebec voters in a referendum. All references to the multilateral agreement are from the summary of the *Status Report* on multilateral meetings. See, "Summary of proposed constitutional package." Summary of *Status Report* of multilateral meetings on the constitution through 7 July 1992, *The Globe and Mail*, 11 July 1992.

4.   I use Québécois throughout to refer to those Quebec citizens whose maternal language is French. The use of this shorthand does not imply that those Quebec citizens whose language is other than French are any less legitimate citizens of the province.

5.   British Columbia, Legislative Assembly, Special Committee on Constitutional Matters, *British Columbia and the Canadian Federation* (Victoria: Legislative Assembly of British Columbia, 1992), pp. 16-17.

6.   In September 1991 the Ontario government published a general discussion paper on the idea of a social charter. See Ontario, Ministry of Intergovernmental Affairs, *A Canadian Social Charter: Making Our Shared Values Stronger* (Toronto: Ministry of Intergovernmental Affairs, 1991). In a 13 February 1992 news release, "Ontario's Proposal for a Social Charter for Canada" Ontario, Office of the Premier, the government expressed support for a declaratory charter similar to that contained in the report of the Beaudoin-Dobbie Committee published shortly thereafter. See Canada, Senate and House of Commons, *Report*, special joint committee, Senator G.A. Beaudoin and D. Dobbie MP, joint chairmen (Ottawa: Minister of Supply and Services, 1992), pp. 87-88, 122-23. See also S. Delacourt, "Protect six basic social goals, NDP urges," *The Globe and Mail*, 6 February 1992.

7.   R. Romanow, "Statement: Negotiations on the Constitution of Canada," *Debates and Proceedings*, 4 June (Regina: Legislative Assembly of Saskatchewan, 1992), p. 899.

8.   British Columbia, *British Columbia and the Canadian Federation*, p. 15.

9.   Romanow, "Statement: Negotiations on the Constitution of Canada," p. 902.

10.   Lord Atkin, *Attorney General of Canada v. Attorney General of Ontario*, Labour Conventions Case (1937), reprinted in P.H. Russell (ed.), *Leading Constitutional Decisions* (Toronto: University of Toronto Press, 1982).

11.   V. Galt, "Labour says UI at risk in unity deal," *The Globe and Mail*, 15 July 1992.

12.   A. Downs, *An Economic Theory of Democracy* (New York: Harper & Row, 1957).

13.   M. Olson, *The Rise and Decline of Nations: Economic Growth, Stagflation and Social Rigidities* (New Haven, CT: Yale University Press, 1982).

14.   British Columbia, *British Columbia and the Canadian Federation*, pp. 12-14.

15.   Saskatchewan, Legislative Assembly, *House of the Federation: Saskatchewan's Proposal for Reforming the Senate of Canada* (Regina: Government of Saskatchewan, 1992).

16.   To appreciate the compromise consider the effect on the ability of representatives from Quebec or Ontario to ratify ordinary legislation in the current and proposed Senate. Currently, a simple majority — 53 out of 104 Senators — can approve a bill. These provinces, each with 24 Senators, each possess 45 percent of the minimum required for a majority. Under the proposed Senate they each possess 31 percent of the minimum number of Senators (8 out of 26) required to prevent exercise of a Senate veto. Ratification in a joint session requires a minimum of 199 MPs and/or Senators out of a total of 396 (312 MPs + 84 Senators). A condition of the Senate agreement is to allocate Commons' seats more precisely according to population, which increases Ontario and Quebec representation to 109 and 78 MPs respectively. In a joint session Ontario possesses 59 percent of the minimum

required for ratification (109 MPs + 8 Senators out of 199). Quebec possesses 43 percent of the minimum required (78 MPs + 8 Senators out of 199).

17. According to a *Journal de Montréal* poll conducted in July 1992, 44 percent of Quebecers opposed the ROC premiers' agreement; 27 percent accepted it; 28 percent were undecided. See A. Picard, "Quebec negative in poll," *The Globe and Mail*, 14 July 1992.

18. W.D. Young, "The Regina Manifesto," in *The Anatomy of a Party: The National CCF 1932-61* (Toronto: University of Toronto Press, 1969), pp. 39-67.

19. Young, *Anatomy of a Party*, p. 310.

20. M. Horn, *The League for Social Reconstruction: Intellectual Origins of the Democratic Left in Canada 1930-1942* (Toronto: University of Toronto Press, 1980).

21. The League unambiguously approved Stalin's forced industrialization over the market-based development strategy of the New Economic Plan pursued in the 1920s: "After various experiments with different methods of control Russia has led the way in economic planning; the development of a remarkable administrative machinery made possible the formulation and amazingly successful execution of the first Five Year Plan." See League for Social Reconstruction, in *Social Planning for Canada* (Toronto: University of Toronto Press, 1975), p. 217.

22. A.C. Cairns, "The Judicial Committee and its Critics," *Canadian Journal of Political Science* 4, 1 (1971):1-55. See also Horn, *The League*, ch. 6.

23. F.R. Scott, "Some Privy Counsel" (1950), reprinted in W.R. Lederman (ed.), *The Courts and the Canadian Constitution* (Toronto: McClelland & Stewart, 1964).

24. F.R. Scott, "Social Planning and Canadian Federalism," in M. Oliver (ed.), *Social Purpose for Canada* (Toronto: University of Toronto Press, 1961).

25. F.R. Scott, "French Canada and Canadian Federalism," in A.R.M. Lower, F.R. Scott et al., *Evolving Canadian Federalism* (Durham, NC: Duke University Press, 1958), pp. 63-4.

26. See, for example, the favourable references to Lord Watson in a provincial position paper published during the patriation debate. See Saskatchewan, Legislative Assembly, *Canada's Constitution: The Saskatchewan Position* (Regina: Government of Saskatchewan, 1981).

27. J. Richards and L.R. Pratt, *Prairie Capitalism: Power and Influence in the New West* (Toronto: McClelland & Stewart, 1979), ch. 11.

28. A. Blakeney, "Resources, the Constitution and Canadian Federalism," in J.P. Meekison (ed.), *Canadian Federalism: Myth or Reality*, 3d ed. (Toronto: Methuen, 1977), p. 184.

29. R. Romanow, J. Whyte and H. Leeson, *Canada ... Notwithstanding: The Making of the Constitution 1976-1982* (Toronto: Carswell-Methuen, 1984), pp. 116-21.

30. One of the few frank and unscripted public debates within the NDP on constitutional matters took place in a university gymnasium, during the party's 1981 federal convention in Vancouver. It provided one of the most intellectually exciting public exchanges throughout the entire two-year patriation debate. See J.

Richards, "Breaking Away: Constitutional Debates at the Federal NDP Convention," *Newest Review*, 7, 2 (1988): 3-4.

31. Saskatchewan, *Canada's Constitution*, p. 24.

32. S. Djwa, *The Politics of the Imagination: A Life of F.R. Scott* (Toronto: McClelland & Stewart, 1987), p. 436.

33. A. Breton, "Supplementary Statement," *Report*, Royal Commission on the Economic Union and Development Prospects for Canada, Donald Macdonald, chairman, (Ottawa: Minister of Supply and Services, 1985).

34. It is worth noting that the principal author of "block grants" in Canadian fiscal arrangements was Tom Shoyama, a senior policy advisor to the Saskatchewan CCF and one of the administrative elite (the "Saskatchewan Mafia") who in the mid-1960s migrated from Regina to Ottawa after defeat of the CCF government. As federal Deputy Minister of Finance, he responded to the provincial critique that conditional federal grants to finance social programs intruded on provincial jurisdiction by distorting provincial spending priorities. Accordingly, he undertook the complex negotiation to transform them into unconditional block grants under Established Program Financing (EPF). The unconditional nature of most federal-provincial transfers is a major feature distinguishing Canadian from U.S. practice, and a major source of provincial autonomy relative to that of states. Introduction of EPF in 1977 was controversial. Predictably, the federal NDP opposed its decentralizing potential; the Saskatchewan NDP was supportive. See T.K. Shoyama, "Fiscal Federalism in Evolution," in T.S. Axworthy and P.E. Trudeau (eds.), *Towards a Just Society: The Trudeau Years* (Markham, Ont.: Viking, 1990).

35. A. Blakeney, "Decentralization: A Qualified Defence," in J. Richards and D. Kerr (eds.), *Canada, What's Left?* (Edmonton: NeWest Press, 1986), p. 148.

36. P.E. Trudeau, "The Practice and Theory of Federalism," in M. Oliver (ed.), *Social Purpose for Canada* (Toronto: University of Toronto Press, 1961), p. 372.

37. S. Steele, "The New Sovereignty," *Harper's* (July 1992).

38. The most comprehensive NDP statement on behalf of a social charter is that of the Ontario Ministry of Intergovernmental Affairs, *A Canadian Social Charter: Making Our Shared Values Stronger*. See also L. Osberg, *The Economics of National Standards*, research report prepared for the Government of Ontario (Toronto: Government of Ontario, 1992). For a survey of arguments by academics sympathetic to a rights-based view of political reform see several of the articles in H. Echenberg et al., *A Social Charter for Canada? Perspectives on the Constitutional Entrenchment of Social Rights*; the Canada Round, Canada Round, no. 9 (Toronto: C.D. Howe Institute, 1992). For a defence of a justiciable social charter and critique of left-wing arguments for parliamentary supremacy see M. Jackman, "Constitutional Rhetoric or Social Justice: Reflections on the Social Charter Debate," *Inroads*, I, 1 (1992).

39. Statistics in this paragraph were calculated from data in Canada, Department of Finance, "Special Report: Financial Indicators and Reference Tables," *Quarterly Economic Review* (March 1991).

40. T.R. Berger, "Quebec's Rendezvous with Independence," in J.L. Granatstein and K. McNaught (eds.), *"English Canada" speaks out* (Toronto: Doubleday Canada, 1991).

41. National Anti-Poverty Organization (NAPO), "Social Charter Advocates Launch Proposals," *Network on the Constitution*, 2, 4 (1992).

42. G. Paquin, "Le Lac Meech embête le congrès du NPD," *La Presse*, 1 December 1989.

12

La culture au Québec à l'ombre de deux capitales

Daniel Bonin

Over the last 30 years, culture has constantly given rise to a de facto competition between the federal and Quebec governments. In Ottawa as well as in Quebec, culture has been seen as an important way to strengthen the feeling of national identification with one or the other level of government. The government of Quebec, under several premiers, has tried to define precisely its sphere of intervention within the cultural area. In order to comply with the growing expectations of artists, creators, and various people of the cultural and communications milieu, the Bourassa government decided in 1990 to engage in a broad process of public consultation aimed at providing to Quebec its first comprehensive policy in the cultural sector.

A key element of that policy was the need to ensure that Quebec has the lead responsibility for cultural matters. The constitutional saga of 1991-92 has provided several opportunities to the Minister of Cultural Affairs of Quebec, Liza Frulla-Hébert, to express her credo in this regard. In fact, the Charlottetown agreement does recognize Quebec's leading responsibility with respect to cultural matters; but the accord also obliges Quebec to make sure that "the federal government and the province work in harmony." Therefore, it seems that this provincial exclusive power has proven to be, in reality, power to be shared with Ottawa in some fashion.

One can already expect that the cultural issue will continue to lead to a never-ending competition between both Quebec and federal capitals.

Peu après l'échec de l'Accord du lac Meech, le Premier ministre du Québec, monsieur Robert Bourassa, affirmait que la sécurité culturelle des Québécois comptait parmi les priorités absolues de son gouvernement.[1] L'occasion allait lui être fournie dans les mois subséquents de joindre le geste à la parole. Ainsi, dans la foulée des travaux de la Commission Bélanger-Campeau chargée d'examiner l'avenir politique et constitutionnel du Québec, le gouvernement Bourassa confia, en février 1991, à un Groupe-conseil présidé par Roland Arpin, la tâche d'identifier «les priorités du développement de la culture et de l'action culturelle au Québec au cours des prochaines années»[2]. Fort de ce mandat, le rapport Arpin — déposé quatre mois plus tard — aura préconisé l'adoption d'une politique «globale» dans le domaine de la culture et des arts, propre à inspirer des plans d'action sectoriels.

La proposition du Groupe-conseil visait à «accorder à la culture une place à la table des grandes idées, des grands projets, des vastes choix, et lui donner une voix équivalente à celle qu'on accorde aux autres grandes missions de l'Etat», telles les missions sociale et économique.[3] Au demeurant, le rapport Arpin proposait que l'Etat québécois, par l'intermédiaire de son ministère des Affaires culturelles (MAC), se pose en *seul maître d'oeuvre* du projet culturel québécois et ce, «quel que soit le futur statut constitutionnel du Québec».

En juin 1992, soit presque un an jour pour jour après la sortie du rapport Arpin, la ministre des Affaires culturelles du Québec, madame Liza Frulla-Hébert, répondait à l'appel du Groupe-conseil et faisait connaître officiellement la «politique culturelle du Québec» au titre évocateur de *Notre culture, notre avenir.* Reprenant à son compte plusieurs éléments du rapport Arpin, l'énoncé de politique gouvernementale aura notamment fait sien — mais de façon plus discrète — la recommandation du Groupe-conseil relativement à l'exercice exclusif, par le Québec, de la compétence culturelle.

En dehors des liens étroits que la culture entretient avec d'autres secteurs d'intervention telles, par exemple, les communications, l'éducation et la langue, la question culturelle québécoise s'est trouvée également,ces dernières années, inscrite au coeur du débat constitutionnel, à un niveau quasi symbolique cette fois, par l'entremise du concept de «société distincte».

Le présent chapitre entend brosser, dans ses grandes lignes, l'évolution de l'intervention québécoise en matière culturelle depuis ses origines. L'on ne saurait aussi passer sous silence le rôle historique joué à cet égard par Ottawa; de fait, l'intervention publique au Québec, dans le domaine culturel, a été marquée de façon significative par la présence fédérale.

Dans cette optique, il importera d'examiner la rivalité qui a opposé, sur le plan culturel, la plupart des gouvernements québécois et fédéraux au cours des trente dernières années. Chaque camp n'aura d'ailleurs rien cédé de ses prérogatives en cette matière si tant est que l'occupation du champ culturel constitue une condition essentielle, à la fois pour Québec et pour Ottawa, dans leur projet respectif et concurrentiel d'affirmation identitaire.

Nous analyserons enfin le contenu de l'«output» constitutionnel issu de la «ronde Canada» au chapitre de la culture, à la lumière des propositions constitutionnelles fédérales du 24 septembre 1991 ainsi que des recommandations Beaudoin-Dobbie, et de l'entente constitutionnelle dite de Charlottetown.

LES PRÉMICES D'UNE INTERVENTION PARALLÈLE

C'est à partir de la Révolution tranquille qu'on assiste au Québec, avec la création, en 1961, du ministère des Affaires culturelles (MAC), à l'émergence d'une ère nouvelle dans le domaine des activités culturelles. Jusque là, la culture fut tantôt une «affaire privée», laissée aux bons soins de l'Eglise, de mécènes et d'institutions privées d'art, tantôt un domaine d'intervention publique limité, où l'action gouvernementale s'avère avant tout sporadique et ponctuelle, et circonscrite principalement aux domaines du patrimoine et des arts; on pense ici à l'octroi de divers prix littéraires et à la sanction de lois régissant la fondation du Bureau des archives de la province (1920); les monuments historiques et artistiques (1923); l'ouverture du Musée de la province (1933); la mise sur pied des conservatoires de musique et d'art dramatique (1942); et les bibliothèques publiques (1959).

Certes, l'Etat québécois n'est pas absent, comme tel, du champ culturel durant cette période; toutefois, le rôle qu'il y exerce en est un, avant tout, de suppléance face aux intervenants privés, un comportement qui s'inscrit alors parfaitement dans la tradition du libéralisme économique. Entre-temps, un ferment de contestation sociale et politique anime le monde artistique québécois; cela se traduira, en 1948, par la publication du fameux manifeste *Refus Global*.

Au terme de la décennie cinquante, avant donc l'existence du MAC, on compte certes un certain nombre de structures pour encadrer les activités culturelles; mais, à la vérité, il appert qu'alors, «la coordination de l'aide gouvernementale n'est pas assurée et certains secteurs n'y ont toujours pas accès».[4] A cet égard, il convient d'ajouter que le gouvernement du Québec de l'époque, dirigé par Maurice Duplessis, manifestait très peu de sympathie à l'égard des artistes et créateurs que ce dernier qualifiait, avec condescendance, de «joueurs de piano»; cette attitude, selon certains, aura été le lot, jusqu'à tout récemment encore, de nombre de fonctionnaires québécois envers la communauté artistique québécoise.[5] Un phénomène qui ne serait pas étranger au statut mineur dévolu au MAC, historiquement, au sein du Conseil des ministres du Québec.

Le gouvernement fédéral aura devancé le Québec d'une dizaine d'années dans la prise en compte du domaine culturel. L'établissement, en 1949, par Ottawa, de la Commission royale d'enquête sur les arts, les lettres et les sciences (Commission Massey-Lévesque) fut suivi, deux ans plus tard, d'un rapport qui représenta, en fait, la première esquisse de la politique culturelle canadienne.

La création, en 1957, du Conseil des arts du Canada, d'après la recommandation du *rapport Massey*, va marquer un tournant dans le soutien fédéral à la culture et aux communications. Par cette mesure, le gouvernement fédéral se trouvait, pour la première fois, à appuyer la production artistique par l'entremise d'un organisme subventionnaire fondé sur le principe britannique du fonctionnement sans lien de dépendance avec le gouvernement («arm's length»), et qui attribue à des comités de pairs la responsabilité de juger du bien-fondé des demandes de subvention. Au demeurant, le Conseil des arts et l'idée-force qui le sous-tend ont résisté à l'épreuve du temps, mises à part les restrictions budgétaires auxquelles est soumis l'organisme depuis quelques années.

Tel que mentionné précédemment, la création, à l'aube de la Révolution tranquille, du ministère des Affaires culturelles, participe du vaste mouvement de réforme sociale, politique et économique au Québec dont l'Etat provincial se fait alors l'initiateur et le catalyseur. A la même époque, on verra également apparaître ailleurs, que ce soit en France, aux Etats-Unis ou en Ontario, des ministères ou organismes spécialisés conçus pour intervenir plus efficacement dans le secteur des arts et de la culture.

Au cours des trois décennies suivantes jusqu'à la mise sur pied du Groupe-conseil sur la politique culturelle du Québec à l'hiver 1991, les divers gouvernements qui se sont succédé à Québec auront tenté, comme de juste, à des degrés divers, tant par le discours que sur le plan de l'action proprement dite, de favoriser le développement du secteur culturel québécois. Mais aucun n'aura été jusqu'à lui réserver, pour reprendre les termes du rapport Arpin, une «place prépondérante dans les priorités de l'Etat et du gouvernement»[6]. Paradoxalement, ces mêmes gouvernements auront accouché, chacun à leur tour durant cette période, de plusieurs projets de politique culturelle, depuis le *Livre blanc sur la culture* de Pierre Laporte en 1964, jusqu'au *Bilan-action-avenir* de Lise Bacon en 1988, en passant par le Livre vert *Pour l'évolution de la politique culturelle* de Jean-Paul L'Allier en 1976, et surtout *La politique québécoise de développement culturel* de Camille Laurin, en 1978.

Ce Livre blanc du gouvernement péquiste s'est avéré la première réflexion vraiment globalisante sur la culture au Québec; l'on a affaire ici à une conception étendue, voire anthropologique de la culture, perçue avant tout comme un «milieu de vie», et en vertu de quoi «l'ensemble de l'existence est produit de culture».[7] Qui plus est, le Livre blanc de 1978 établit pour la première fois le lien ténu existant entre la culture et les communications. Il appelle aussi à un élargissement des champs d'intervention de l'action gouvernementale en matière culturelle; cela se vérifiera au cours de la dernière décennie alors que les interventions du MAC iront bien au-delà des tâches déterminées dans son mandat originel. Ainsi, durant les années quatre-vingt, le MAC s'emploiera à appliquer la vision holistique, sous-jacente au Livre blanc péquiste, selon laquelle la culture est partout. On verra donc le gouvernement du Québec, via son ministère attitré ainsi que ses instances régionales, s'intéresser à des avenues diverses telles que la commercialisation des arts, le développement des industries culturelles, l'urbanisme et l'aménagement du territoire, etc.

Bien du chemin avait été parcouru depuis la première mission confiée au ministère des Affaires culturelles; il s'agissait alors pour le MAC, outre de favoriser «l'épanouissement des arts et des lettres dans la province et leur rayonnement à l'extérieur», d'assurer la défense de la langue française au Québec et au Canada français, ainsi que de prendre en compte les questions touchant l'éducation. A cet égard, le MAC s'est trouvé à effectuer une sorte de retour aux sources dans sa récente politique culturelle en prônant une plus grande synergie, notamment avec le ministère de l'Education. Au demeurant, les préoccupations linguistiques du MAC ne furent pas uniques en soi; ainsi, au début des années soixante, à Ottawa, «c'est moins la culture que la langue qui constituait l'enjeu le plus significatif, comme en témoigne la mise sur pied de la Commission royale d'enquête sur le bilinguisme et le biculturalisme».[8]

Or, l'on assiste bientôt à un retournement majeur de la part du pouvoir fédéral. Ainsi, c'est au cours du long règne des libéraux, sous Pearson puis Trudeau, de 1963 à 1984, que la culture et son complément naturel, les communications, vont devenir progressivement des secteurs d'interventions stratégiques du gouvernement central. Cette réalité ne s'est pas démentie, incidemment, avec l'arrivée au pouvoir, par la suite, des conservateurs. L'intervention fédérale en matière culturelle aura atteint néanmoins son point culminant sous la gouverne de Pierre Elliott Trudeau. Durant cette période, en effet, le gouvernement Trudeau se sera employé à faire de la culture un vecteur privilégié de son action politique, axée fondamentalement sur la promotion du nationalisme *canadien*.

Le mouvement avait d'abord été amorcé sous Pearson: en firent foi les célébrations du Centenaire de la Confédération qui se traduisirent alors, selon Jean-Guy Lacroix et Benoît Lévesque, par «la plus importante injection de capitaux et la plus importante mobilisation de ressources humaines que le Canada ait connu dans le domaine de la culture et des arts».[9] Il faudra attendre un quart de siècle plus tard, soit à l'occasion des fêtes récentes du 125e anniversaire de la fédération canadienne, pour être témoin d'un tel faste au service de l'unité nationale.

Le développement de la politique culturelle fédérale, pendant l'ère Trudeau, s'effectuera d'abord à la faveur d'une restructuration administrative ainsi que de la mise en place d'appareils et institutions étatiques chargés d'assurer le contrôle canadien dans la sphère culturelle. On retiendra notamment ici la création du ministère des Communications (MCC) et du Conseil de la radio télévision canadienne (CRTC), de même que le rôle imparti au Secrétariat d'Etat en matière de contrôle politique et de centralisation décisionnelle envers les organismes culturels subventionnés par le gouvernement fédéral. Une décennie plus tard — et jusqu'à ce jour —, c'est le ministère des Communications du Canada et les sociétés qui en relèvent qui deviendront les intervenants majeurs en matière de culture sur la scène fédérale. D'après John Meisel, le

MCC pourrait être considéré «de facto» comme un véritable ministère fédéral de la Culture.[10]

UNE AFFAIRE DE CONCURRENCE

Si la politique de canadianisation culturelle prônée par le gouvernement Trudeau a fini par ressembler, au tournant des années 80, à une stratégie de développement des industries culturelles — telle qu'avalisée, en 1982, par le rapport Applebaum-Hébert, il reste qu'au départ, l'occupation du champ culturel par les libéraux participait, comme le reste, de la nouvelle vision nationale canadienne dont Pierre Elliott Trudeau s'est toujours voulu le plus ardent défenseur. Ce dernier aura, de fait, tout mis en oeuvre pour faire de la culture un moyen d'identité et d'unité nationale. Cela dit, le nationalisme fédéral exalté pendant l'ère Trudeau aura commodément servi de fer de lance dans la lutte opiniâtre que le pouvoir central entendait livrer contre le nationalisme québécois, alors en pleine ascension. Le pari trudeauiste consistait alors à investir des «sommes énormes», entre autres dans le secteur culturel au Québec, par l'entremise de l'Etat fédéral, de façon à pouvoir «contrebalancer l'attrait du séparatisme».[11]

Le nationalisme centralisateur défendu par le gouvernement Trudeau sur le plan culturel ne fut pas sans susciter dans certaines provinces canadiennes quelque opposition. Mais c'est le Québec — théâtre privilégié de l'interventionnisme fédéral — qui aura offert la plus vive résistance aux initiatives d'Ottawa. Cet affrontement culmina au cours des années 60-70, dans le secteur des communications, à l'occasion de la fameuse «guerre du câble» entre Ottawa et Québec. Le contentieux à propos de la câblo-distribution, tout comme celui relatif à la radiodiffusion éducative, avaient mis alors en lumière la volonté du gouvernement fédéral d'appliquer une réglementation qui reflète une «vision nationale canadienne» dans ce secteur. Cette approche fut la source, comme on l'a déjà dit, de conflits de juridiction avec les provinces et, en particulier, avec le Québec. L'épisode de la «guerre du câble» aura révélé sans conteste la cohérence remarquable dont ont fait preuve tous les gouvernements du Québec, au-delà de leur allégeance partisane, dans l'affirmation de l'autonomie québécoise eu égard au domaine culturel.

Il serait vain, sauf pour l'esprit militant, de chercher à départager le vrai du faux dans la bataille de compétences qui a opposé, ces trente dernières années, les divers gouvernements fédéral et québécois en matière de culture et de communication. En vérité, il convient plutôt d'analyser le phénomène en terme de rapport de force historique entre deux Etats, l'un central, l'autre fédéré, voyant dans la culture l'objet d'un enjeu stratégique tantôt pour la souveraineté culturelle du Québec, tantôt pour l'affirmation du «nation-building» canadien.

La problématique Québec-Canada à ce chapitre tire en grande partie sa source du vide juridique qui a toujours caractérisé la culture dans la Constitution canadienne. Ainsi, les pères de la Confédération oublièrent de nommer expressément la compétence culturelle dans la *Loi constitutionnelle de 1867*, d'où une absence d'énumération des matières culturelles aux articles 91 et 92 dudit document. Cette zone grise dans le texte constitutionnel fera en sorte que la compétence culturelle ne sera pas attribuée de façon spécifique, à l'exception du droit d'auteur, lequel fut conféré explicitement au gouvernement central. De fait, il aura fallu attendre la *Loi constitutionnelle de 1982* pour que les mots «domaine culturel» soient inscrits dans la Constitution. Mais on n'y trouva, une fois encore, aucun éclaircissement quant au partage des pouvoirs sur le plan culturel entre les gouvernements central et provinciaux[12]. La présence du gouvernement fédéral dans ce domaine se sera imposée progressivement par le moyen de divers instruments, tels que son pouvoir de dépenser à travers ses institutions, ses propriétés et ses programmes de transferts, ainsi que par son pouvoir de légiférer. Sur ce dernier point, mentionnons notamment la *Loi sur le droit d'auteur*, la *Loi sur l'exportation et l'importation des biens culturels*, la *Loi sur le cinéma*, et le projet de loi déposé en mai 1991 sur le statut de l'artiste.

Le Québec, pour sa part, a depuis toujours considéré la culture comme étant une compétence provinciale exclusive, en arguant que les matières contenues à l'article 92 de la *Loi constitutionnelle de 1867* incluait, par inférence, le champ culturel.[13] Depuis Daniel Johnson jusqu'à Robert Bourassa seconde époque, en passant par René Lévesque et Pierre Marc Johnson, un consensus au-dessus de la mêlée partisane s'est créé au Québec autour de la culture; récurrentes à défaut d'être spectaculaires, les «revendications historiques» du Québec en matière culturelle font figure, au cours du dernier quart de siècle, de véritable leitmotive au même titre par ailleurs que l'ensemble des autres demandes formulées par le Québec, à l'occasion de ce processus sans fin de réforme constitutionnelle.[14] C'est également au nom de la défense traditionnelle des «intérêts supérieurs du Québec» que le gouvernement dirigé par Robert Bourassa aura exigé, en 1988, le maintien des lois, programmes et politiques contribuant par la langue, les communications et la culture à la spécificité québécoise, comme gage de son appui aux négociations et à l'Accord sur le libre-échange entre le Canada et les Etats-Unis.[15]

L'Accord du lac Meech, s'agissant de la culture, insistait en premier lieu sur son caractère symbolique, via la reconnaissance du Québec comme société distincte; stricto sensu, le domaine culturel n'émergeait de l'entente que de façon indirecte: soit par l'entremise de la clause générale traitant de la limitation du pouvoir fédéral de dépenser dans des programmes ressortissant à la compétence exclusive du Québec. L'échec de Meech, outre d'amplifier la crise que l'on sait sur le plan constitutionnel, aura amené le gouvernement Bourassa à susciter, auprès des forces vives de la société québécoise, un questionnement en profondeur à propos des grands enjeux sociaux et collectifs auxquels le Québec est confronté.

C'est dans cette perspective que la Commission Bélanger-Campeau fut créée; c'est également sur toile de fond post-meechienne que le gouvernement du Québec convoqua la Commission parlementaire de la culture, à l'automne 1990 puis 1991, afin de discuter de la future politique globale à adopter qui, d'abord au chapitre de l'immigration, qui ensuite dans le domaine culturel.

S'agissant de la seconde commission portant sur la culture comme telle, la ministre en titre, madame Liza Frulla-Hébert, l'avait voulue «ample et féconde, sur fond de débat de société.» Elle disait vouloir rendre la culture «contagieuse»[16]. De fait, à l'exception peut-être de la Commission Bélanger-Campeau qui venait juste de la précéder, rarement avait-on été témoin d'un tel remue-méninges dans l'histoire du parlementarisme québécois: 264 mémoires reçus, 181 intervenants entendus durant les huit semaines d'audiences. Les interlocuteurs clés du milieu culturel étaient réunis au grand complet: artistes, créateurs, institutions culturelles, associations, mécènes, syndicats, industries culturelles, etc.

Autant du côté du parti ministériel que chez l'opposition péquiste, on semblait former le voeu, à l'ouverture des travaux, que la Commission serve à faire le procès du gouvernement fédéral pour cause d'«envahissement» de la «plate-bande» culturelle québécoise. Au demeurant, escomptait-on à tort au MAC que les gens du milieu feraient également chorus derrière la ministre qui faisait sienne la recommandation 94 du rapport Arpin déposé quelques mois plus tôt, et voulant que «la culture fasse l'objet d'un rapatriement complet avec les fonds correspondants et une pleine compensation financière» de la part du gouvernement fédéral.[17]

Parmi les intervenants qui abordèrent la question de la juridiction gouvernementale en matière culturelle (un cinquième d'entre eux environ), il est vrai qu'une large majorité s'est trouvée à avaliser la revendication en faveur d'une maximisation des pouvoirs du Québec dans ce secteur. Néanmoins, on compta aussi une minorité d'intervenants qui exprimèrent avec force conviction leur opposition fondamentale au rapport Arpin. Mis à part quelques esprits alarmistes assimilant le projet de politique culturelle proposé par le Groupe-conseil à une volonté de l'Etat québécois d'exercer une mainmise idéologique sur la culture québécoise,[18] les adversaires du rapport Arpin insistèrent dans l'ensemble sur la nécessité de conserver la double juridiction actuelle en matière culturelle afin de faire jouer le contrepoids; cette position se voulait aux antipodes du rapport Arpin qui décriait précisément les chevauchements et la concurrence entre Québec et Ottawa dans le champ culturel. Ces tenants du statu quo firent valoir le risque de sacrifier impunément, sur l'autel des «vanités politiques», la source de financement fédéral, laquelle représente au Québec plus de 30% des dépenses totales consacrées par Ottawa au titre de la culture.[19]

Au premier rang de ce dernier groupe, on retrouvait notamment les gens de l'audio-visuel et singulièrement, ceux de l'industrie québécoise du cinéma; habiles à tirer profit de la rivalité entre Québec et Ottawa sur le plan culturel, ces derniers avaient tout à craindre d'un éventuel rapatriement exclusif, vers le Québec, des fonds dévolus à la culture. Dans les autres disciplines artistiques — et notamment dans le domaine de l'édition —, le préjugé favorable à Ottawa est apparu moins manifeste; cela pourrait s'expliquer en partie par le fait que dans ces secteurs, le Québec ne jouirait d'aucun traitement de faveur, que ce soit relativement aux paiements directs aux artistes, ou en ce qui à trait à la part québécoise du budget des grandes institutions dites nationales.

La Commission aura révélé la crise de confiance fondamentale caractérisant les milieux artistiques à l'endroit de l'Etat québécois. Sur ce plan, nombre de pro et anti-Arpin se rejoignirent. L'argument essentiel soulevé par ceux-ci avait trait aux dérobades historiques du gouvernement du Québec quant à ses propres engagements envers le soutien aux arts. Maints intervenants soulignèrent le fait que la portion du budget alloué aux Affaires culturelles plafonne autour de 0,7% depuis cinq ans et ce, en dépit de la promesse solennelle faite par Robert Bourassa en 1985 d'affecter 1% du budget global de 40 milliards $ du gouvernement du Québec aux dépenses culturelles. Devant l'annonce, le printemps dernier — en période de vaches maigres — d'une augmentation de 12,4% du budget du MAC pour l'année 1992-1993 par rapport à 1991-1992, les milieux culturels auront fait montre, au mieux, d'une certaine tiédeur; on appréhendait en effet que la majeure partie de l'augmentation des crédits du ministère aille éventuellement aux grands équipements et aux musées plutôt qu'aux créateurs, aux organismes culturels et aux régions. Néanmoins, l'augmentation du MAC fut obtenue en grande partie grâce à l'opiniâtreté personnelle de la ministre Frulla-Hébert, laquelle dut exercer énormément de pression auprès de ses collègues du cabinet pour arracher ce résultat.[20]

Au cours de la dernière année, la ministre Frulla-Hébert aura dû également s'ajuster à la stratégie constitutionnelle de son premier ministre, connu pour osciller sans cesse entre la circonspection et le geste d'éclat calculé. Robert Bourassa n'aura pas rendu la tâche facile à sa ministre au demeurant; sans jamais désavouer celle-ci, le premier ministre du Québec n'aura, en revanche, jamais pris lui-même publiquement position tout au long du débat sur la place de la culture au Québec. D'aucuns, dans les milieux artistiques, eurent tôt fait de déplorer l'apparente indifférence du premier ministre Bourassa à l'égard de la question culturelle au Québec; silencieux lors du dépôt du rapport Arpin et durant tous les travaux de la Commission parlementaire de la culture, de même qu'au cours des mois subséquents, il était presque dans l'ordre des choses que le premier ministre du Québec en arrive finalement à ne pas assister au dévoilement officiel de la politique culturelle du Québec, le 19 juin dernier, sous prétexte d'un soi-disant «conflit d'horaire».

Laissée en quelque sorte à elle-même, sans paramètres clairs définis en haut-lieu, la ministre Frulla-Hébert aura parfois donné l'impression ces derniers mois de tenir un discours incohérent, notamment en ce qui touche l'épineuse question de l'exclusion du gouvernement fédéral du champ culturel québécois. Après avoir d'abord rejeté sans équivoque les propositions fédérales de septembre 1991 (voir infra), madame Frulla-Hébert aura retraité peu après concernant la pleine souveraineté culturelle du Québec dans ce secteur; elle admit alors, en effet, avoir été «ébranlée dans ses opinions» après qu'un groupe d'artistes eurent affiché leur soutien ferme, durant la Commission parlementaire, à l'égard de la présence fédérale au Québec.[21] Ce revirement momentané fut interprété sur le coup, par plusieurs, comme une véritable palinodie de la part de la ministre. Mais celle-ci ne tarda pas à renouer avec son credo original sur le rapatriement de tous les pouvoirs du gouvernement fédéral dans le secteur culturel, c'est-à-dire en l'occurrence: le pouvoir législatif, le pouvoir de dépenser et la mainmise sur la portion québécoise des organismes et grandes institutions (Téléfilm Canada, ONF, Conseil des Arts, etc.). Elle dut néanmoins se passer de l'aval de Robert Bourassa qui affirmait encore, à la fin mai 1992, qu'il n'était pas en soi contre le maintien d'institutions fédérales comme Radio-Canada.

Au reste, ce dernier pouvait s'accommoder d'une ministre ayant son franc-parler en autant que la rhétorique radicale de cette dernière soit «encadrée» sur le plan officiel. Il est significatif à cet égard que dans l'énoncé de la politique culturelle du Québec dévoilée par le gouvernement Bourassa le 19 juin 1992, de même que dans le document de réflexion déposé par la ministre à la Commission permanente de la culture deux semaines auparavant, les courts passages renvoyant à la maîtrise d'oeuvre, par le Québec, de son développement culturel trahissaient un certain recul en comparaison du rapport Allaire; il n'était plus question désormais, pour le Québec, à la suite d'Allaire et d'Arpin, d'exiger le rapatriement de *tous* les champs de compétence en matière culturelle mais plutôt les «pouvoirs et les leviers en conséquence», voire les pouvoirs exclusifs *«qui lui sont nécessaires»* pour assurer ses responsabilités en ce domaine.[22]

Glissement sémantique subtil ou accidentel mais néanmoins réel qui assure dans tous les cas, au premier ministre Bourassa, le pouvoir du dernier mot sur sa ministre. En vertu de cette règle du double discours gouvernemental, le premier ministre Bourassa pouvait donc, sans trop de risque, laisser la titulaire du MAC défendre l'orthodoxie allairiste et pourfendre, au besoin, les velléités centralisatrices d'Ottawa dans le secteur culturel.

L'occasion lui aura été donnée à quelques reprises durant la saga constitutionnelle, au cours des derniers mois. Du nombre, on retient en particulier la réaction de madame Frulla-Hébert à la publication, en avril 1992, du rapport du Comité permanent des Communes sur les Communications et la Culture; sorte de réponse décalée au rapport Arpin, le document fédéral aura opposé un «non» ferme au principe de transfert de compétences exclusives en matière culturelle vers le Québec. A contrario, le Comité était d'avis que le rôle du gouvernement fédéral dans les domaines de la culture et des communications «doit non seulement être maintenu, mais renforcé». Du même souffle, le Comité recommandait la création d'un ministère de la Culture, lequel serait chargé de promouvoir une «politique canadienne de la culture» en vertu de laquelle le Québec, comme les autres, se verrait confier un simple rôle consultatif.

De facture trudeauiste, le document s'employait enfin à diluer finement le principe de la société distincte en élargissant l'application du concept au-delà du territoire québécois pour englober également les «collectivités d'expression française» de toutes les autres provinces.[23] C'en était trop pour la ministre Frulla-Hébert qui aura jugé «carrément insultante et méprisante» la teneur du rapport, ajoutant sans ambages que «c'était se foutre des demandes historiques du Québec» en matière culturelle.[24] Pour finir la titulaire du MAC s'était employée à nier la légitimité de l'entreprise: prenant pour modèle la Commission parlementaire sur la politique culturelle québécoise, madame Frulla-Hébert insista sur la faible participation publique aux activités du Comité des Communes, boudées quasi totalement dans les faits par les milieux artistiques québécois.

Personnalité complexe voire paradoxale, le premier ministre Bourassa aura de tout temps offert l'image d'un homme politique formellement engagé à garantir la sécurité, voire la «souveraineté culturelle» des Québécois; par contre, celui-ci a toujours paru mal à l'aise dans sa relation avec le milieu culturel comme tel. Néanmoins, Robert Bourassa aura su choisir à la tête du MAC, au cours de ses divers mandats, des titulaires — Jean-Paul L'Allier et Frulla-Hébert pour l'essentiel — qui, d'ores et déjà, auront laissé leur empreinte à ce poste. Rien n'y fit cependant: la clientèle du MAC n'a jamais cessé en effet, durant toutes ces années, de voir en Robert Bourassa un indécrottable «comptable de la culture»; or, lorsqu'on analyse les budgets comparés du MAC et du gouvernement du Québec de 1971 à 1991 — en dollars courants—,[25] force est de constater que les libéraux, au chapitre culturel, n'ont pas fait pire que le Parti québécois au pouvoir, un parti pourtant perçu longtemps comme l'allié naturel des milieux artistiques. En définitive, l'exaspération de ceux-ci, conjuguée au lobby personnel exercé par la ministre Frulla-Hébert auprès de ses collègues du Cabinet, aura finalement convaincu le premier ministre Bourassa de donner le feu vert au dépôt de la première politique globale du Québec en matière culturelle.

En livrant ainsi la «marchandise» aux créateurs et aux gens du milieu culturel, le gouvernement désirait se racheter en fait pour sa période de «dormance» en cette matière, de 1986 à 1990: il y allait de sa crédibilité fondamentale comme gouvernement. Qui plus est, Robert Bourassa souhaitait, à la veille de l'échéance référendaire, ne pas courir le risque de s'aliéner le milieu culturel, hostile dans l'ensemble à son option constitutionnelle. Au demeurant, la publication de la politique culturelle du Québec par le gouvernement Bourassa suscita des réactions généralement positives chez les artistes[26]. Du coup, le gouvernement libéral réussit à damer le pion au Parti québécois sur le plan culturel, ce parti préférant remettre à l'automne 1992 son grand débat sur la politique culturelle dans un Québec souverain.

Société distincte oblige, le gouvernement du Québec, en procédant à son virage culturel, s'est trouvé ainsi à devenir le premier gouvernement au Canada à se donner une politique en matière de culture. Détail de taille: cette politique n'aura pas été définie strictement en terme sectoriel, c'est-à-dire limitée au MAC; de fait, l'énoncé de politique intitulé *Notre culture, notre avenir* dépeint la culture désormais comme une «préoccupation première» du gouvernement, au même titre que le social et l'économique. Question de souligner la rentabilité de l'initiative gouvernementale, la ministre aura souligné le fait que le secteur culturel s'avère, tout compte fait, le sixième employeur au Québec avec 75,000 emplois directs et 125,000 emplois indirects, générant au total une activité économique évaluée à 3,1 milliards \$.[27] Elaborée de concert avec 21 ministères et, au premier plan, celui de l'Education, la politique culturelle gouvernementale prendra forme à la faveur d'un plan d'action triennal, comportant, à la clé, 57 millions d'«argent neuf» injectés dans le secteur culturel au cours des trois prochaines années, dont 9,8 millions dès cette année.

Des trois grands axes d'intervention autour desquels s'articule la politique culturelle québécoise, soit l'affirmation de l'identité culturelle, la participation des citoyens à la vie culturelle, et le soutien aux créateurs et aux arts, c'est peut-être le dernier qu'il faut retenir comme élément central de la réforme. Pressé depuis toujours par les artistes québécois de prendre exemple sur le modèle outaouais en matière d'aide aux créateurs, le gouvernement du Québec aura finalement suivi la même voie en créant un organisme autonome, soit le «Conseil des Arts et des Lettres», qui assumera seul le rôle de «subventionneur» du ministère. Ce faisant, on entendait instituer une structure administrative plus souple, fondée sur un partage efficient des tâches entre le futur MAC — qui sera transformé cet automne en ministère de la Culture — et ce nouveau Conseil; délesté de la gestion des programmes de soutien à la création artistique au profit du Conseil, le MAC revu et corrigé se verra confier un mandat plus large, axé notamment sur les orientations et le suivi de la politique culturelle, ainsi que sur l'harmonisation et la coordination de l'activité ministérielle en région.

En mettant sur pied le Conseil des Arts et des Lettres — qui devrait être opérationnel en avril 1993 — le gouvernement du Québec entendait faire d'une pierre deux coups: il répondait d'abord aux attentes des gens du milieu culturel exaspérés par le «dirigisme» et la gestion de crise permanente typiques du MAC en matière d'aide aux créateurs et aux organismes culturels; observable depuis des lustres, ce phénomène aura, avec le temps, entamé sérieusement la crédibilité du ministère auprès des personnes concernées, forçant ainsi le gouvernement à donner un coup de barre spectaculaire pour corriger la situation. D'autre part, celui-ci comptait rivaliser directement avec Ottawa auprès de cette clientèle-cible, en n'excluant pas, le moment venu, de pouvoir récupérer l'argent du Conseil des Arts fédéral dévolu au Québec à cette fin.

On était enfin résolu à Québec à s'impliquer pour de bon dans ce dossier, sachant par ailleurs que le budget du Conseil des Arts fédéral stagne depuis des années en dépit des demandes toujours croissantes du milieu. L'entrée en force du gouvernement québécois lui aura donc permis de rétablir les ponts avec les créateurs et représentants du secteur culturel, déchirés pour plusieurs entre leur prime attachement au Québec et leur reconnaissance envers le bailleur de fonds canadien.

Par ailleurs, si le volet de la politique gouvernementale consacré à l'affirmation de l'identité culturelle impliquait, comme de juste, une valorisation de la langue française, on fit en sorte également de reconnaître la contribution des Québécois anglophones, des communautés culturelles et des autochtones à la culture québécoise, et de renforcer le soutien que le gouvernement et ses institutions leur apportent.

D'aucuns, comme le Parti québécois et l'Union des artistes du Québec, auraient souhaité que le gouvernement Bourassa fusionne le ministère des Affaires culturelles et celui des Communications, de manière à concentrer dans un seul ministère tout ce qui se rapporte à la culture. Les partisans de cette approche étaient d'avis qu'en créant un ministère unique, le Québec serait plus apte à concurrencer les efforts du MCC et de ses organismes affiliés. En définitive, le gouvernement libéral n'en fit rien; à l'évidence, on ne désirait pas instaurer une lutte de pouvoir entre Mme Frulla-Hébert et M. Lawrence Cannon. Au surplus, on estimait à Québec que les revendications historiques du Québec en matière de communications, tout en étant radicales dans leur essence, laissaient quelque place, comme dans le rapport Allaire, à un partage des pouvoirs, notamment dans le secteur des télécommunications.[28]

S'agissant du secteur culturel à proprement parler, une tâche attendait encore le gouvernement du Québec: enchâsser, sur le plan constitutionnel, la maîtrise d'oeuvre à laquelle il comptait donner forme, résolument, sur son territoire.

On s'emploiera dans la prochaine section à décrire l'évolution de ce que nous appellerons les «outputs» constitutionnels en matière de culture, depuis les propositions fédérales de septembre 1991 jusqu'à la récente entente de Charlottetown.

LA VARIABLE CONSTITUTIONNELLE

Dans un éditorial paru aux lendemains de la publication du rapport Beaudoin-Dobbie au début mars 1992, la directrice du quotidien *Le Devoir*, madame Lise Bissonnette, résumait avec brio la stratégie poursuivie ces dernières décennies par le Québec sur le plan constitutionnel. Ainsi, faisait-elle observer, le Québec n'a jamais cessé d'oeuvrer simultanément sur deux fronts, l'un *passif*, l'autre *actif*. Elle poursuivait en ces mots:

> Le premier (front) est celui de la protection de l'acquis, la consolidation des mécanismes de «blocage», pour empêcher que sa position se détériore à l'intérieur du Canada. A côté de ces protections plutôt passives, le second front, plus actif, le voyait batailler pour obtenir le contrôle de son propre développement, pour élargir la sphère d'activité de son gouvernement. Du côté des protections passives, on peut ranger des chapitres comme le droit de veto sur les amendements à la Constitution, le mode de nomination des juges à la Cour suprême, et plus récemment le souci d'obliger à interpréter la Constitution canadienne en reconnaissant le caractère «distinct» du Québec. Du côté dynamique, on range évidemment toutes les requêtes québécoises pour le respect des compétences provinciales, et l'ajout de nouveaux pouvoirs.[29]

Pour l'essentiel, l'Accord du lac Meech releva du front passif, à l'exception de la clause sur l'immigration qui fit l'objet, après coup, d'une entente Québec-Ottawa. Parmi les quatre demandes de protection passive contenues dans l'Accord, la clause de reconnaissance du Québec comme «société distincte» en vint rapidement à constituer, pour reprendre l'expression de Lise Bissonnette, l'«alpha et l'omega» de la réforme constitutionnelle. Une partie du Canada anglais fit capoter l'entente sous prétexte que le caractère distinct du Québec aurait conféré à cette province un statut «supérieur» et des pouvoirs accrus. Comme on sait, une majorité de Québécois perçurent le fiasco de Meech comme un affront fait au Québec; l'émotion suscitée au Québec à la suite de l'échec de Meech aura été à la mesure du caractère hautement symbolique qui avait investi, avec le temps, la clause de la société distincte, laquelle, en raison de son substrat culturel intrinsèque, interpellait directement les Québécois dans leur identité profonde. Du lac Meech au lac Harrington, ce concept n'aura cessé, depuis cinq ans, d'être au coeur des négociations constitutionnelles entre le Québec et le reste du Canada.

Abordons maintenant le front dit «actif», objet principal de ce chapitre. Durant ce qu'on a appelé la «ronde du Québec», de 1986 à 1990, le front actif des revendications québécoises se ramena à toutes fins utiles à l'exigence de pouvoirs accrus en matière d'immigration. Le gouvernement Bourassa entendait, par là, obtenir des garanties réelles pour conforter la «sécurité culturelle» du Québec. De facon spécifique, l'objectif visait à donner au Québec le pouvoir de planifier entièrement son immigration pour maintenir son caractère francophone en faisant contrepoids ou même en renversant les tendances démographiques qui laissaient présager une diminution de son importance relative au Canada.[30]

Si, paradoxalement, ce front fut assez peu actif durant l'épisode Meech, c'est qu'on avait convenu d'exclure, au départ de la ronde de négociations, l'épineuse question du partage des pouvoirs. Il faudra attendre l'après-Meech et l'ouverture de la «ronde du Canada» pour voir ce front réactivé; au chapitre de la répartition des compétences, le rapport Allaire demeurait, en théorie du moins, la référence officielle du gouvernement Bourassa. Mais sur ce plan, le gouvernement du Québec s'est montré peu à peu disposé à rogner dans les revendications du rapport Allaire — plate-forme constitutionnelle du P.L.Q. — pour peu que le Québec puisse trouver la «substance de Meech», à la faveur d'une éventuelle entente qui consacrerait le renouvellement de la fédération canadienne. L'entente constitutionnelle du 28 août dernier aura, de fait, consacré, le virage stratégique du gouvernement Bourassa à ce chapitre. Or, jusqu'à ce que ce gouvernement se rallie audit accord et que, partant, le rapport Allaire soit effectivement relégué aux oubliettes, les autorités québécoises se montreront très critiques face aux initiatives constitutionnelles provenant d'Ottawa et du reste du Canada.

En ce qui concerne spécifiquement la culture, les «outputs» constitutionnels rendus publics au cours de la dernière année auront révélé, si besoin était, le fossé objectif existant entre Québec et Ottawa à ce chapitre. Comme on l'a déjà vu auparavant, le gouvernement du Québec, par l'entremise de sa ministre des Affaires culturelles, aura fréquemment revendiqué la maîtrise d'oeuvre, voire le rapatriement exclusif par le Québec de l'ensemble des compétences existantes en matière culturelle. A la suite du dépôt des propositions fédérales à la fin septembre 1991, la fermeté des revendications québécoises en ce domaine n'auront laissé d'autre choix, subséquemment, aux interlocuteurs du Québec que d'en tenir compte tant soit peu dans le rapport Beaudoin-Dobbie et l'Accord du 7 juillet 1992.

Après des mois d'intenses débats internes et de discussions serrées avec ses partenaires fédératifs — hormis le Québec —, le gouvernement fédéral fit connaître, le 24 septembre 1991, ses propositions en vue d'une réforme constitutionnelle. Dans un document intitulé *Bâtir ensemble l'avenir du Canada*, on n'y retrouvait, comme telle, aucune proposition insérant formellement la culture au sein d'un partage de compétences. En fait, Ottawa affirmait sans trop de détours son intention de rester présent dans le domaine culturel partout au Canada, y compris au Québec, par le maintien des institutions culturelles existantes vouées à la promotion de l'identité commune canadienne. Ainsi donc, la culture se trouvait exclue de la liste des compétences exclusives que le gouvernement était prêt à reconnaître aux provinces dans certains secteurs (6), soit en l'occurrence, les mines, la foresterie, le tourisme, les loisirs, l'habitation, et les affaires urbaines et municipales. S'agissant de la culture, Ottawa privilégiait plutôt la mise en place d'un mécanisme «souple», les accords bilatéraux, «afin de définir clairement le rôle de chaque ordre de gouvernement en ce domaine.»[31]

Pour le gouvernement du Québec et en particulier la titulaire du MAC, madame Frulla-Hébert, le document fédéral prônait la juridiction partagée en matière de culture: y souscrire revenait selon elle à «travailler sous la tutelle» fédérale.[32] De plus, la ministre s'inquiétait des conséquences possibles qu'entraînerait le projet d'union économique tel que libellé; elle soulignait le risque d'une centralisation à Ottawa des pouvoirs de l'union économique qui permettrait au gouvernement fédéral de porter atteinte à trois législations québécoises: soit la Loi sur le développement des entreprises québécoises dans le domaine du livre, la Loi sur le cinéma et la Loi sur les biens culturels. Conformément à la grille d'analyse retenue par la ministre, la proposition fédérale fut jugée carrément «inacceptable». à la suite de quoi, la ministre des Affaires culturelles du Québec invita le gouvernement «à refaire ses devoirs» à ce chapitre.

Cinq mois après le dépôt des propositions fédérales, soit le 29 février 1992, le Comité spécial mixte du Sénat et de la Chambre des Communes chargé d'en examiner «tous les tenants et aboutissants» rendait public son rapport. Intitulé *Un Canada renouvelé*, le rapport du Comité Beaudoin-Dobbie fut reçu, dans l'ensemble, assez fraîchement au Québec, en particulier chez les observateurs francophones. Le premier ministre Bourassa ne put s'empêcher d'y voir quant à lui l'expression d'un «fédéralisme dominateur», laissant peu de place à un «véritable transfert de pouvoirs au Québec».[33] Au demeurant, le rapport Beaudoin-Dobbie était empreint d'un nationalisme résolument canadien. Sur le plan philosophique, le document rejoignait sensiblement *Bâtir ensemble l'avenir du Canada* pour son attachement aux normes nationales et la nécessité, y voyait-il, de maintenir une présence fédérale dans plusieurs domaines d'activités, dont la culture. Selon les auteurs du rapport, le gouvernement fédéral était justifié d'intervenir, entre autres, dans ce secteur précis du simple fait, affirmaient-ils, que «la vie artistique et culturelle présente bien des aspects qu'on ne peut régler qu'au niveau fédéral», comme par exemple, au chapitre des accords commerciaux, des institutions fédérales, ou encore du droit d'auteur.[34]

Après avoir soigneusement établi les fondements historiques, juridiques et politiques de l'intervention fédérale dans le champ culturel, le rapport Beaudoin-Dobbie se devait ensuite, en toute équité, de souligner le «rôle légitime des provinces» en matière de culture. A la vérité, les auteurs du rapport avaient d'abord à l'esprit les «besoins particuliers du Québec» et de son gouvernement, responsable du destin culturel de la seule collectivité éttique majoritairement francophone en Amérique du Nord. En dépit de ses réserves initiales à l'égard du «cloisonnement strict des compétences législatives», le Comité Beaudoin-Dobbie acceptait néanmoins de reconnaître la compétence exclusive du Québec de légiférer en matière culturelle, en autant que le Québec «le demande». Pareille offre était aussi faite d'ailleurs aux autres provinces qui souhaiteraient éventuellement jouir d'une telle prérogative.

A cet égard, les auteurs du rapport Beaudoin-Dobbie faisaient preuve, sans conteste, d'une plus grande «ouverture», sur le plan de la décentralisation, que leurs prédécesseurs de septembre 1991. Or, cette empathie nouvelle envers les provinces, et notamment le Québec, traduisait pour l'essentiel une prise en compte réaliste des idées-force politiques du moment; six semaines plus tôt, en effet, on avait vu l'intelligentsia anglo-canadienne réunie à la conférence nationale d'Halifax se convertir pour une bonne part au concept de «fédéralisme asymétrique» en vertu duquel le Québec jouirait de certains pouvoirs exclusifs, tandis que le reste du Canada conforterait pour sa part le pouvoir central. Peu après, dans un discours à Whistler, le ministre québécois des des Affaires intergouvernementales canadiennes, M. Gil Rémillard, abondait également dans le sens de la position adoptée par les participants d'Halifax au regard du fédéralisme asymétrique.

Cela dit, dans l'esprit du Comité Beaudoin-Dobbie, le pouvoir législatif du Québec en matière culturelle, tout exclusif qu'il pouvait être, demeurait avant toute chose *prépondérant*. Nuance importante qui banalisait en quelque sorte la notion d'exclusivité, la prépondérance suggérant ici de façon assez nette l'idée d'une compétence partagée dans ce secteur d'activités. Dans cette veine, le rapport Beaudoin-Dobbie reprenait l'idée des accords fédéraux-provinciaux déjà évoqués dans les propositions fédérales de septembre 1991; à l'instar de l'Accord Canada-Québec en matière d'immigration — une compétence partagée en vertu de la Constitution —, on préconisait la négociation d'un accord intergouvernemental dans le domaine culturel afin de déterminer le rôle respectif des deux paliers de gouvernement dans le financement des activités en question, et la part des transferts à verser à la province.

En s'employant à une véritable apologie de l'approche coopérative en matière culturelle entre Québec et Ottawa, le rapport Beaudoin-Dobbie choisissait sciemment de relativiser les griefs historiques du Québec eu égard à la juridiction partagée, et ses conséquences sur les chevauchements de compétences et la concurrence indue. En matière de partage des compétences, et s'agissant spécifiquement de la radiodiffusion, le rapport affichait une orthodoxie centralisatrice en ne proposant qu'un pouvoir de consultation au Québec touchant la réglementation fédérale. L'occasion n'était pas encore venue pour que les auteurs du rapport Beaudoin-Dobbie s'interrogent, en profondeur, sur le bien-fondé de l'omniprésence fédérale dans le secteur des communications, comme en faisait foi le projet de loi C-62 déposé, à la même date, à la Chambre des communes.

L'Accord multilatéral du 7 juillet 1992 conclu entre Ottawa, le ROC et les leaders autochtones avait reconduit assez fidèlement l'«esprit» Beaudoin-Dobbie en tentant de marier, autant que faire se peut, la notion de compétence provinciale exclusive avec l'idée de conserver une présence fédérale en matière culturelle. Le gouvernement fédéral avait pu compter dans l'intervalle sur le soutien ferme des milieux culturels anglo-canadiens hostiles à tout désengagement d'envergure, de la part du gouvernement fédéral, dans le domaine des arts[35].

Une entente constitutionnelle fut conclue à Charlottetown le 28 août 1992. Parachèvement de la première mouture concoctée, à Ottawa, le 22 août précédent, l'entente de Charlottetown consacra la réconciliation entre le gouvernement libéral du Québec et ses autres partenaires fédératifs autour d'une volonté commune de renouvellement de la fédération canadienne. Exception faite du volet touchant les protections passives propres à l'entente, le Québec, au chapitre précis du partage des pouvoirs, n'aura réalisé avec cette entente, aux dires mêmes de certains hauts fonctionnaires fédéraux, aucun gain réel par rapport à l'Accord précédent du 7 juillet.[36] En fait, parmi les modifications apportées au texte de l'accord de juillet dans l'entente de Charlottetown, on compte un ajout qui touche indirectement à la compétence culturelle: il s'agit ici de l'engagement, consenti par Ottawa, de négocier avec les gouvernements provinciaux des ententes dans le but de coordonner et harmoniser la règlementation dans le secteur des télécommunications.[37]

Sous réserve des textes juridiques encore au stade de la rédaction à l'heure où ces lignes sont écrites, l'entente de Charlottetown aura reconnu aux provinces une compétence législative exclusive en matière de culture, tout comme d'ailleurs pour la formation de la main-d'oeuvre. On comblait ainsi une zone grise dans la Constitution laquelle, jusque là, avait eu pour effet de n'attribuer à aucun des deux paliers de gouvernement la responsabilité spécifique dans ces secteurs.

L'octroi aux provinces de la compétence législative exclusive dans le domaine culturel visait, avant tout, à satisfaire de façon spécifique aux demandes répétées du Québec en cette matière. Mais Ottawa n'entendait pas renoncer, de ce fait, à sa vocation nationale eu égard à la culture. A vrai dire, les pressions exercées par le lobby culturel anglo-canadien ne lui laissaient guère de choix. Comme auparavant dans *Bâtir ensemble l'avenir du Canada*, le rapport Beaudoin-Dobbie puis l'Accord du 7 juillet, l'entente de Charlottetown aura donc consacré le maintien des responsabilités du gouvernement» fédéral au regard des questions culturelles canadiennes et des institutions culturelles nationales, y compris à l'égard des subventions versées par celles-ci.

Après la conclusion de l'entente du 28 août, le Premier ministre Bourassa était parvenu, dans un premier temps, à rallier la plupart des membres du caucus libéral ainsi qu'une majorité des délégués présents à l'occasion du congrès spécial du parti, tenu le jour suivant. Mais la dénonciation subséquente de l'entente par les Jean Allaire et autres Mario Dumont aura eu pour effet de jeter une ombre sur la réussite de l'opération constitutionnelle fraîchement réalisée par Robert Bourassa. D'abord soumis à la solidarité ministérielle, quelques ministres, dont Liza Frulla-Hébert, n'auraient, semble-t-il, adhéré à l'entente constitutionnelle du 28 août qu'au prix de fortes réticences.[38] Or, la titulaire du MAC avait jugé bon de se tenir coite aux lendemains de la signature de l'entente de principe intervenue une semaine plus tôt. Dans l'intervalle, Gil Rémillard et Robert Bourassa n'hésitèrent pas, pour leur part, à proclamer que le Québec disposait désormais de la «quasi-souveraineté» dans le secteur culturel. Mais enhardie par l'«effet Allaire», la ministre Frulla-Hébert se résolut peu après, selon des sources sûres, à exprimer franchement ses réserves face à la première version de l'entente de Charlottetown. De toute évidence, ses objections portèrent fruit: elle parvint, en effet, à obtenir du Premier ministre Bourassa, puis ensuite d'Ottawa, qu'on insère ultimement certains ajouts clés dans le document constitutionnel, de manière à bonifier les dispositions touchant la culture.[39]

Avec les ajustements apportés, le Québec se voit d'abord reconnaître explicitement, dans le texte officiel de l'entente, la «maîtrise d'oeuvre» de la culture sur son territoire.[40] L'enchâssement, dans la Constitution, de cette expression fétiche de la ministre Frulla-Hébert apparaissait fondamentale à cette dernière; selon elle, Ottawa prenait ainsi acte de la spécificité québécoise, le Québec constituant de fait la province la plus directement concernée au chapitre culturel. Qui plus est, la ministre Frulla-Hébert aura souhaité à moult reprises que soit mieux balisé, hic et nunc, le pouvoir de dépenser du gouvernement fédéral. La formule des accords bilatéraux, évoquée déjà dans les propositions de septembre 1991 et dans les recommandations du rapport Beaudoin-Dobbie lui semblait répondre en partie à cette exigence. A la requête de la ministre, Ottawa accepta de l'inclure après coup dans le texte définitif de l'entente de Charlottetown.[41] Concrètement, cela signifiait que le gouvernement fédéral devrait désormais négocier un accord avec le gouvernement du Québec avant d'entreprendre quelque projet majeur que ce soit dans le domaine culturel au Québec. Une question demeure encore entière à ce stade: quelle sera la portée réelle de la compétence exclusive du Québec en matière culturelle dès lors qu'en vertu des ententes qui en découlent, la maîtrise d'oeuvre québécoise dans ce secteur doit s'«harmoniser avec les responsabilités fédérales»?[42]

Déterminée à mener à bien la mission culturelle québécoise, Liza Frulla-Hébert entend fermement continuer à revendiquer le rapatriement de tous les fonds destinés à la culture. En outre, elle souhaitait récemment , à titre «personnel», que le Québec puisse détenir un droit de regard sur les décisions touchant les institutions culturelles nationales, comme Radio-Canada. La ministre évoquait la possibilité de pouvoir négocier éventuellement une clause d'«opting-out» relativement à ces institutions.[43] Reste à voir si, dans l'hypothèse éventuelle d'une ratification ultérieure de l'entente de Charlottetown, le Premier ministre Bourassa accordera son plein aval aux futures revendications de sa ministre.

CONCLUSION

Au cours des trente dernières années, la culture a donné lieu à une rivalité quasi-permanente entre les gouvernements fédéral et québécois. Tant à Ottawa qu'à Québec, on aura perçu la culture comme le substrat par excellence pour cimenter le sentiment d'identité nationale autour de l'un ou l'autre de ces deux paliers de gouvernement. Dans l'intervalle, le gouvernement du Québec s'est employé, sous divers dirigeants, à définir précisément sa sphère d'intervention dans le domaine culturel. Afin de répondre aux attentes croissantes des artistes, créateurs et des diverses gens du milieu culturel, le gouvernement Bourassa s'est engagé résolument, voilà deux ans, dans un vaste processus de consultation publique visant à doter le Québec de sa première politique globale en matière culturelle.

Comme élément-clé de cette politique, on comptait la revendication en faveur de la maîtrise d'oeuvre, par le Québec, des principaux leviers de son développement culturel. La dernière saga constitutionnelle aura permis à la ministre des Affaires culturelles du Québec, Liza Frulla-Hébert, de faire entendre plus d'une fois son credo en cette matière. A ce chapitre, l'entente de Charlottetown reconnaît au Québec la maîtrise d'oeuvre au regard de sa culture; mais elle assortit également à celle-ci l'obligation de s'«harmoniser avec les responsabilités fédérales». Une compétence primordiale donc, mais qui, dans les faits, se trouve en partie partagée avec Ottawa.

Selon l'issue du vote référendaire qui portera sur le document de Charlottetown, on peut d'ores et déjà prédire que tout le dossier afférent à la compétence culturelle continuera de susciter, au mieux, une concurrence inextinguible entre les capitales québécoise et outaouaise dans les mois et les années à venir.

NOTES

1.   Voir Michel Vastel, *Bourassa*, Montréal, Editions de l'Homme, 1991, p.287.

2.   Voir Le Groupe-conseil sur le politique culturelle du Québec, *Une politique de la culture et des arts*, Proposition présentée à madame Liza Frulla-Hébert, ministre des Affaires culturelles du Québec, par le Groupe-conseil sous la présidence de monsieur Roland Arpin, Gouvernement du Québec, juin 1991, 2e édition, août 1991, p. 8.

3.   Ibid., p. 295.

4. *Réflexions sur la culture présentées à la Commission permanente de la culture*, par madame Liza Frulla-Hébert, ministre des Affaires culturelles, Gouvernement du Québec, non daté, p. 9.

5. D'après Guy Frégault, longtemps sous-ministre au MAC, tel que rapporté par Laurent Mailhot et Benoît Melançon , «Littérature, Nation, Etat», dans *Question de culture*, (L'Etat et la culture), no 10, IQRC, Québec, 1986, p. 59, note 16, et les divers témoignages des créateurs québécois entendus à la Commission parlementaire sur la culture à l'automne 1991.

6. Le Groupe-conseil..., *op.cit.*, p. 324.

7. Voir Mailhot et Melançon, *op.,cit.*, pp. 55-58.

8. Jean-Guy Lacroix et Benoît Lévesque, «Les libéraux et la culture: de l'unité nationale à la marchandisation de la culture, (1963-1984)», dans Yves Bélanger, Dorval Brunelle et al., *L'ère des libéraux. Le Pouvoir fédéral de 1963 à 1984*, Québec, P.U.Q., 1988, p. 407.

9. *Ibid.*, p. 415.

10. Voir John Meisel, « Flora and Fauna on the Rideau: The Making of Cultural Policy», dans Katherine A. Graham (dir.), *How Ottawa Spends, 1988-1989*, Carleton, University Press, 1988, p. 61. Outre le fait d'oeuvrer au développement de nouvelles technologies d'information et de communications, le MCC s'est vu confier aussi, vers le début des années 80, la responsabilité du secteur des arts et de la culture, confiée auparavant au Secrétariat d'Etat. Selon Meisel, en plus du MCC qui détient la prime responsabilité dans le secteur culturel, il convient de souligner aussi l'influence exercée à «court terme» par le Cabinet du Premier ministre et le Bureau du Conseil privé dans l'élaboration des politiques culturelles du gouvernement fédéral. Cf. Meisel, *op.cit.*, p. 72.

11. Voir Pierre Elliott Trudeau, *Le fédéralisme et la société canadienne-française*, Montréal, Editions HMH, 1967, pp. 204-205.

12. En vertu de l'article 40 de la *Loi constitutionnelle de 1982*, une province pourrait se prévaloir du droit de retrait avec juste compensation financière dans le cas d'une modification constitutionnelle impliquant un transfert de compétence législative provinciale au Parlement fédéral dans des «domaines culturels». Cependant, l'on ignore encore à ce jour la signification réelle et la portée dudit article.

13. Le Québec invoque ici ses pouvoirs exclusifs de légiférer dans des matières plus générales tels que «les ouvrages et entreprises d'une nature locale» — article 92 (10)—, la «propriété des droits civils dans la province» — article 92 (13) — et finalement, «toutes les matières d'une nature purement locale ou privée dans la province» — article 92 (16) —.

14. Pour un résumé chronologique des revendications québécoises, voir Réflexions sur la culture..., *op.cit.*, pp. 14-15. D'aucuns, à l'instar du politologue Stéphane Dion, considèrent que le transfert au Québec de nouvelles compétences exclusives, y compris dans le domaine de la culture, constitue tout au plus un credo politicien sans grande résonance auprès de la population québécoise. Voir Stéphane Dion, «Le Canada malade de la politique symbolique», *La Presse*, 26 février 1992, p. B-3.

15. Cf. *Les positions traditionnelles du Québec en matière constitutionnelle (1936-1990)*. Document de travail préparé par le Secrétariat aux affaires inter-gouvernementales canadiennes, Direction des Politiques institutionnelles et constitutionnelles, Ministère du Conseil exécutif, Gouvernement du Québec, 1991, p. 79.

16. Cf. *Le Devoir*, 22 novembre 1991, p. B-1.

17. Voir Le Groupe-conseil..., *op.cit.*, p. 284.

18. Voir entre autres Louis-Philippe Rochon, «L'abject mariage de l'Etat et de la culture», *Le Devoir*, 19 novembre 1991, p. B-8.

19. En 1990-1991, le budget total des dépenses fédérales au titre de la culture s'élevait à 708 millions $ (à l'exclusion de la radiodiffusion et des télécommunications notamment). Le montant estimé des dépenses pour le Québec se chiffre à 213,4 millions $ (30%). Voir Réflexions sur la culture, *op.cit.*, p. 17. Au reste, selon Statistiques Canada, la contribution fédérale aux dépenses culturelles du Québec s'est accrue de 25% au cours de la dernière moitié des années 80, en comparaison d'une augmentation de 12% pour le Canada dans son ensemble. Cf. *La Presse*, 20 mars 1992, p. A-15.

20. Cf. *Le Devoir*, 28 mars 1992, p. A-4.

21. Citée par Ray Conlogue, «Frulla-Hébert renews stand on culture», *The Globe and Mail*, 27 novembre 1991, p. C-1.

22. Voir Réflexions sur la culture..., *op.cit.*, p. 30 et Ministère des Affaires culturelles (MAC), *La politique culturelle du Québec. Notre culture, notre avenir*, Québec, Gouvernement du Québec, 1992, p. VIII.

23. Voir *Culture et Communications: les liens qui nous unissent*, rapport du Comité permanent des Communications et de la Culture, Chambre des Communes, Ottawa, avril 1992, p. 39.

24. Cf. *Le Devoir*, 9 avril 1992, p. B-3.

25. Cf. Groupe-conseil, *op.cit.*, p. 239.

26. Cf. *Voir*, 2-8 juillet 1992, pp. 5-6.

27. Cf. *La Presse*, 19 juin 1992, p. C-2.

28. Sur la foi d'informations confidentielles livrées par des stratèges fédéraux, Alain G. Gagnon soutient qu'à Ottawa, on ne comprenait pas pourquoi «le premier ministre du Québec n'insistait pas davantage pour exercer la pleine compétence dans le secteur des télécommunications par exemple». Cf. Alain G. Gagnon, «La trahison des élites politiques», *La Presse*, 15 août 1992, p. B-3.

29. Lise Bissonnette, «Le volet Québec», *Le Devoir*, 3 mars 1992, p. A-8.

30. Cf. le discours de Gil Rémillard prononcé à l'occasion du colloque «Une collaboration renouvelée: le Québec et ses partenaires dans la Confédération». Reproduit dans le rapport du colloque, Peter Leslie (dir.), Institut des relations inter-gouvernementales, Queen's University, Kingston, 1987, p. 51.

31. Cf. *Bâtir ensemble l'avenir du Canada*, (Propositions), Ministre des approvisionnements et Services Canada 1991, p. 36.

32. Cf. *Le Devoir*, 2 octobre 1991, p. A-4.

33. Cf. *Le Devoir*, 4 mars 1992, p. A-1.

34. *Un Canada renouvelé*, rapport du Comité mixte spécial du Sénat et de la Chambre des communes, Ottawa, ministère des Approvisionnements et Services Canada, 1992, p. 74.

35. Cf. *The Globe and Mail*, 2 mai 1992, p. C-3; 23 mai 1992, p. C-3 et 3 juin 1992, p. C-2. Pour une bonne analyse des données du problème au Canada anglais, voir notamment Roy Mac Skimming, «Ottawa goes minimalist in its approach to the arts», *The Globe and Mail*, 25 juin 1992, p. A-15.

36. Cf. *La Presse*, 26 août 1992, p. C-16.

37. Cf. *Rapport du consensus sur la Constitution*. Texte définitif. Charlottetown, le 28 août 1992, p. 13.

38. Cf. *Le Devoir*, 3 septembre 1992, pp. 1-2, 4.

39. *Ibid.*, p. 2.

40. Voir *Rapport du consensus sur la Constitution...*, *op.cit.*, p. 12.

41. Cf. *Le Devoir*, 3 septembre 1992, p. 2.

42. Voir *Rapport du consensus sur la Constitution...*, *op.cit.*, p. 12.

43. Cf. *L'Actualité*, 15 septembre 1992, pp.20-22.

13

Agriculture and the GATT:
The Search for Balance in Canadian Trade Policy

Andrew F. Cooper

Ce chapitre examine l'approche privilégiée par le Canada à l'occasion des négociations commerciales du GATT. Tout en situant l'agriculture canadienne dans le cadre d'une économie internationale en pleine mutation, cet article entend analyser tout d'abord les facteurs clés qui ont façonné et déterminé, sur le plan infra-national, la politique du commerce agricole canadien. Cette politique, qui comporte deux facettes, s'explique par les profondes différences structurelles à la base de l'industrie agricole canadienne, laquelle est fondée à la fois sur la région et sur le type de production. Le fait que la base électorale et politique du gouvernement Mulroney dépend largement du soutien apporté par le Québec et les provinces de l'Ouest n'est pas sans exercer également une certaine influence sur l'orientation de la politique canadienne en cette matière. L'imbrication des enjeux rattachés aux négociations du GATT et à la question constitutionnelle canadienne aura eu pour effet de rendre encore plus complexe la nature du débat au pays. L'auteur affirme, pour l'essentiel, que le gouvernement Mulroney s'est employé à gérer le dossier de la politique du commerce agricole par l'intermédiaire d'une approche dichotomique: c'est-à-dire en combinant les éléments d'une stratégie offensive d'ajustement aux impératifs commerciaux internationaux avec une stratégie défensive d'ajustement aux réalités commerciales canadiennes. A court terme, cette approche pragmatique s'est avérée fructueuse. Mais à longue échéance, pareille démarche stratégique laisse entrevoir des difficultés croissantes, tant du point de vue de la politique étrangère que sur le plan de la politique intérieure.

The Canadian approach to the agricultural trade negotiations within the General Agreement on Tariffs and Trade (GATT) has come under sharpened scrutiny. Rather than being portrayed as principled and reasonable, Canada's performance during the Uruguay Round has been viewed as becoming increasingly ambiguous — to the point of hypocrisy.[1] On the one hand, with respect to its market-oriented and export-dependent commodities, Canada has attempted to maintain its position as a strong advocate of liberalization. On the other hand, in regard to its regulated and import-restrictive sectors, Canada has enhanced its efforts to preserve the architecture of supply management.

What makes this dichotomy more intriguing is the tension that this inconsistent approach has introduced between Canada's needs and interests with respect to agriculture and the wider objectives of Canadian diplomacy. From a general foreign policy perspective, the GATT has traditionally served as a useful arena in which Canada could showcase its willingness and capacity to be a good international citizen. In agriculture, as in a variety of other issue-areas, Canada has played the role of an activist middle power in the post-1945 international order. During the so-called "golden age" of Canadian diplomacy, in particular, Canada did its best to see that neither of its Atlantic partners, the United States and the Western European nations in the emergent European Community, broke the values or norms of that order. Considerable effort was made to monitor (and modify) the behaviour of these other nations. In this activity Canada was careful to appear fair and not one-sided; that is to say, its role was that of an "honest broker" or "bridge builder." Breaches of the rules by either the U.S. (the main target being the American methods of surplus disposal) or the EC (particularly with regard to the restrictions on free market access for farm products) were pointed out.[2]

Paradoxically, the Canada-United States Free Trade Agreement (FTA) has reinforced rather than diminished Canada's need to signal its continued commitment to constructive internationalism. Certainly, there has been a considerable incentive on the part of the Mulroney government to show that an institutionalized special deal with the United States has not impaired Canada's autonomy in world affairs or to undermine Canada's capacity "to make a difference."[3] In overall foreign policy terms, as John Whalley has suggested, the FTA's effect has been to increase "the pressure on Canada to elevate its middle-power diplomatic role. The need is to demonstrate that Canada's sovereignty has not been impaired by the agreement, that Canada is a separate country that takes foreign policy positions independent from the United States."[4]

In terms of Canadian material interests, the value of a successful completion of the Multilateral Trade Negotiations (MTN) remains very great. Although the FTA has provided Canada with some margin of preference with respect to access to the large U.S. market, there continues to be a consensus that multilateralism is Canada's first best option in foreign economic policy. Canada has much to gain, specifically, from the establishment of new rules on subsidies and better rules to settle disputes via a comprehensive GATT agreement, not least because these results were not achieved in the FTA. As the (then) Trade Minister John Crosbie put it at a trade ministers' meeting in 1989: "We need the rule of law in trade affairs and we have a lot at stake in this round."[5]

As has become more obvious in the late 1980s and early 1990s, international trade policies have become more tightly intertwined with domestic politics. An ascendant question in the international political economy relates to the heightened tension between the forces of economic integration and the forces of resistance to that change. The growth of interdependence, and the accentuated incorporation of national economies into both global and regional economies, has presented new challenges in terms of national economic statecraft.[6] The test of government's economic performance has progressively become whether it fosters reform and promotes international competitiveness. Yet, inevitably, societal elements within those countries have strongly resisted the process of change, because they foresee bearing its attendant adjustment costs.

The controversy surrounding the Canadian approach to agriculture within the GATT negotiations presents an interesting case study of this phenomenon. To comprehend the dualistic nature of Canada's position requires some basic understanding of the deep and pervasive structural differences within the Canadian agricultural industry. It is important to emphasize, from this contextual perspective, that it is impossible to speak of a monolithic farm community in Canada. Rather it is split by fundamental cleavages based on geography and type of production. Moreover, over the past decade, the pattern has been towards even greater differentiation along regional and production lines.[7]

The structural dimension is a necessary but not sufficient explanation for the contorted nature of Canada's agricultural trade approach. This mode of understanding needs to be supplemented by an examination of important situational factors. For one thing, the fragile nature of the governing coalition needs to be taken into account. The political and electoral base of the Mulroney government has been centred largely on the twin pillars of rural Quebec and the prairie farmers in western Canada. To retain power, therefore, the government has had to accommodate the interests of two groups that have become more polarized on policy matters. For another thing, the internal debate on the GATT negotiations has become increasingly intense because of its developing linkage with constitutional politics. While long associated with western estrangement from Ottawa, the agricultural issue has become pivotal to the question of national survival and the future of Quebec.

This chapter attempts to explain the nuances of the Canadian approach to the agricultural issue within GATT through the adoption of a domestic-centred mode of analysis. While locating Canadian agriculture in a changing international political economy, the primary focus will be to explore the set of internal features that have shaped and conditioned Canadian agricultural trade policy. Through examining the nexus between the international system and domestic political structures and processes in this fashion, the complex relationship between international challenges and domestic constraints may be captured with greater accuracy. As suggested by Putnam in his influential study of two-level games in international relations, what may be "rational" in terms of foreign economic diplomacy may be "impolitic" in terms of domestic strategy.[8]

SETTING THE CONTEXT OF THE DEBATE

The central concern of the Mulroney government in terms of agricultural politics and policy has been to cope with the conflicting interests around the issue of trade liberalization. At one end of the spectrum, the more outward-looking commodity producers have been among the most enthusiastic support-ers of trade reform. This was especially true of the groups representing the western Canadian grain producers, such as the United Grain Growers, Prairie Pools Inc., and the Western Wheat Growers' Association, as well as the red meat industry, such as the Canadian Cattlemen's Association (CCA) and the prairie hog marketing boards. These groups were closer in outlook to agri-business corporations than they were to many of the other segments of the farm commu-nity. Confident that they were efficient enough to compete successfully in the international arena on the basis of comparative advantage, what these groups pressed for were fair and consistent rules of the game in terms of market access and export subsidization. As Charles Gracey, the Executive Vice-President of the CCA expressed it, in 1985: "Canada needs to bring to the next round an adamant and determined stance to dismantle old rights and privileges and to insist categorically on absolute fairness and equity."[9]

The fundamental problem for these competitive exporters stemmed from the serious erosion of the norms and principles of the liberal international economic order. The conflicts found in the international relations of agricultural trade in the 1980s and 1990s reflect, and even highlight, many of the general trends found in the international political economy. The most dynamic change in this issue-area has been the challenge by the EC and other nations to American leadership since 1945. Stimulated by the food "shocks" of the early 1970s, the EC moved from being a net-importer of agricultural goods to a position where its production exceeded self-sufficiency in a wide range of goods. The result was a gradual globalization of the Common Agricultural Policy (CAP), as the surpluses generated internally have been exported outside of the EC through a generous "restitution" scheme. The EC's increasingly assertive approach, in turn, prompted countermeasures from the United States. Generally speaking, the U.S. may be said to have utilized a two-track response. On the other side, in contrast, the U.S. has also employed a more aggressive tit-for-tat approach through the Export Enhancement Program (EEP) and other retaliatory mea-sures.[10]

These changes in the international political economy of agriculture proved to be highly traumatic events for Canada. In terms of agricultural exports, Canada found itself increasingly caught in the crossfire of the "ploughshares war" between the U.S. and the EC. The deleterious impact of American unilateralism on Canadian sales was demonstrated most clearly by the Reagan administration's decision in mid-1986 to negotiate sales of subsidized wheat to the Soviet Union. In terms of the EC's actions, the internationalization of the CAP was strongly felt not only in third markets but in the home market. Most notably, the movement of highly subsidized EC beef into Canada was a serious irritant in Canadian-EC relations in the mid-1980s. The intensity of these irritations was accentuated, furthermore, by the spillover of agricultural disputes into other issue areas. The controversy surrounding the ban by the EC on imports of meat treated with hormones provides just one illustration of this phenomenon.

These new set of external circumstances, and mounting internal pressures to do something about them, provided much of the stimulus for the Canadian initiatives in terms of agricultural trade reform. In addition to working through the G7, the "Quadrilaterals," and other established forums, Canada signed on to a coalition of agricultural "fair trading nations" established at a ministerial meeting in Cairns, Queensland, Australia in August 1986. Significantly, Charles Mayer (the Minister of State for the Canadian Wheat Board, and the Canadian ministerial delegate at the Cairns meeting) was accompanied to Cairns by representatives from export-oriented western Canadian farm organizations.[11]

The Mulroney government was pushed towards what may be termed an offensive adjustment strategy because of the importance of its competitive sectors: approximately 80 percent of Canadian wheat and 60 percent of Canadian grain is exported. But Ottawa has also been pulled back towards a more defensive, protectionist strategy by its uncompetitive and domestic-oriented producers who are clustered in the dairy, egg, poultry, and much of the fruit and vegetable sectors. This distinction is crucial. As conceptualized by John Ikenberry, adjustment strategies can be pursued internationally and domestically on the one hand and offensively and defensively on the other. That is to say, states can adopt a mix of strategies, encompassing offensive international adjustment; defensive international adjustment; offensive domestic adjustment; and defensive domestic adjustment. International strategies can be pursued defensively — by attempting to maintain the benefits from an existing set of arrangements (formalizing special trading relationships or by means of specific reciprocity) — or offensively, by creating new arrangements more suited to changing conditions (the strengthening of multilateral arrangements). Domestic adjustment represents more territorially-centred responses. Again, this can be done either by defensive measures to preserve or reinforce existing arrangements (through subsidies or non-tariff barriers) or by offensive measures that would change existing, or create new structures (restructuring or reducing the level of protectionism).[12]

In terms of Canadian agriculture, the forces favouring a domestic defensive adjustment strategy were heavily concentrated among the eastern Canadian producers whose commodities were under the authority of marketing boards. These groups were wary of change, fearing their needs and interests would be hurt by any push towards trade liberalization. Specifically, they were fearful of any modification in the system of quantitative import restrictions or import quotas allowed under Article XI when an internal system of supply management was in place.

Although they had a mutuality of interest in defending a "way of life" these defensive domestic adjusters did not entirely coincide in terms of their values and goals. Outside Quebec, the major source of resistance to either offensive and domestic international and/or offensive domestic options was sector specific. Utilizing the language or agrarianism, the centrepiece of the strategy of resistance adopted by commodity specific groups and marketing boards was the future survival of the family farm. In a costly educational campaign directed at the wider Canadian public, for example, the Dairy Farmers of Canada attempted to drive home the message that "everytime a dairy farm dies, a part of Canada dies." In a similar vein, a representative of the supply managed industries told a parliamentary committee that agriculture could not be judged "on a narrow set of economic measures" because: "consumers not only want cheap food, [but] safe food in abundant supply ... produced in an environmentally sound manner and with respect to family farms and the rural lifestyle."[13]

A second key strand of resistance was territorially based. The most significant of these forces emanated from Quebec, in the form of the Union des producteurs agricoles (UPA). In common with the resisters outside Quebec, the UPA stressed the virtues of the family farm and the danger of deregulation. Unlike them, however, the strategy of the UPA was based more on the defence of agriculture in and for Quebec. After all, the UPA's newspaper is called *La Terre de chez-nous*. And, as a UPA official put it in 1985: "all national groups tend to consider food self-sufficiency to be an attribute of national political sovereignty and an essential factor in collective stability and security."[14]

The political rationale for the Mulroney government responding to these defensive pressures was compelling. Electorally, Quebec farmers were a formidable force. The farm vote had a disproportionate weight in federal elections, with a third of the Quebec seats being predominantly rural. Given these numbers, in a close contest, the farm vote could make a difference. The UPA's organizational clout had to be taken seriously, too. Not only did it have a large membership (approximately 42,000), a high degree of concentration (close to 50 percent of Quebec farmers were clustered in the dairy sector), and charismatic leadership (Jacques Proulx), but also the organization continually demonstrated that it was willing to use any and all means to achieve its goals. These pressure tactics included mass public rallies and private persuasion through letter writing and telephone campaigns.

MANAGING THE FORCES OF ADJUSTMENT AND RESISTANCE

The Mulroney government has tried to manage the differences between the adjusters and resisters by attempting to treat them as separate but equal entities. Instead of directly addressing the controversial issues head on, by the development of a comprehensive policy, the Conservative government tried to put off any clear choice between the export-oriented western farmers and the import-sensitive eastern producers. In an attempt to maximize competitiveness and minimize the cost of reform,[15] a dualistic approach was put in place which combined elements of both an offensive international adjustment strategy and a defensive domestic adjustment strategy.

This dualistic approach was not only consistent with the Conservatives' aim of holding together the Quebec-western Canada alliance, it also meshed completely with the personal political style of the prime minister himself. Consistent with both the *modus operandi* of a labour negotiator, and political deal-maker, the ultimate question of purpose for Mulroney was not whether a policy was harmonious in terms of its internal components but whether it had wide-spread regional appeal. As such, Mulroney's approach to agricultural policy may be seen as another example of a shift away from the rational management perspective as practised in the Trudeau period and a return to the older tradition of brokerage politics.[16]

In implementing this approach, special emphasis was placed on two devices. The first of these was the use of delaying tactics. As suggested above, key decisions in terms of agricultural policy were either put off or side-tracked onto other agendas. Not only was Canada often late in setting out its proposals on agriculture with respect to the Uruguay Round, but these negotiating documents were not as a matter of course released to the public.[17] To a large degree, of course, this caution reflected the sensitivity among resisters concerning both the GATT talks and the overlapping Canada-U.S. Free Trade Agreement negotiations. Contrary to initial expectations, agriculture had been put on the table in terms of these bilaterals. This is not to say that the FTA deal resulted in what may be termed a "big bang" reform. As the deal was negotiated by the end of 1987, the marketing boards were not scrapped or even radically altered. At the same time, nonetheless, the FTA did provide for a "little bang" (particularly throughout the elimination of tariffs over a ten-year period).[18] This prepared the way for further pressures to build up against the existing architecture via the Uruguay Round. As one American expert suggested, Canada as well as the U.S. "kept their powder dry in the North American talks awaiting the bigger battle in the GATT."[19]

Secondly, transactional tactics were used. When some form of action was necessary to defuse tensions, side payments were offered to both adjusters and resisters. The Mulroney government acted in several ways to allay the uncertainty felt by the producers of supply manager commodities. In late 1987, for instance, the government moved to add yogurt and ice cream to the import control list. It also signalled its intention to take action on other value-added items (such as chicken pies, and frozen pizzas). Conversely, the Mulroney government intervened, through devices such as the Special Canadian Grains Program (1986), to provide compensation to western farmers for the low prices they were receiving in the absence of a completed GATT deal.

In the short run, this brokerage approach paid healthy benefits for the Mulroney government. By juggling the interests of both the adjusters and resisters the Conservatives were able to retain considerable electoral support in their 1984 strongholds. Indeed, in winning another majority in the autumn of 1988, the victorious party was able to sweep the rural seats in Quebec and in Alberta. Notwithstanding this clear success, however, strains were becoming visible within this governing coalition even before the election campaign. The decision to place agriculture onto the FTA agenda was viewed by the UPA leadership as an act of betrayal.[20] Given this stance, Mulroney had to appeal over the head of the leadership for support from the rank and file members. Although less of a factor in the 1988 election, the ad hoc compensation schemes for prairie farmers (intended as one-off measures but becoming entrenched as permanent fixtures), placed Ottawa in an increasingly awkward position as well. Continuing to "throw money at the problem" contradicted the government's stated desire to tackle the budget deficit. To cut back on these programs, though, was politically unattractive because any signal that the government was losing its will to deal with the problems of falling prices and farm incomes contributed to the revival of western Canadian alienation.

The strong ties forged between regionally-centred farm groups and provincial governments made the process of accommodation on agricultural policy even more difficult. As its relations with the Mulroney government deteriorated, the UPA fell back on the Quebec government for support. In many ways this development was surprising. Opposition by the farming community had been instrumental in defeating the earlier Bourassa government. What is more, the Quebec government and the UPA were situated on different sides of the free trade debate. Whereas the Bourassa Liberal government remained strongly on side with the Mulroney government with respect to the overall benefits accruing from a trade deal with the U.S., the UPA had joined with the major trade unions within Quebec in a united front to fight against the FTA. The fall back strategy, therefore, rested on expediency. So as to not lay itself open to criticism by the Parti Québécois, the Bourassa government was careful to couch its support for the bilateral negotiations on the condition that a pact would not allow any erosion of Article XI. As Michel Pagé, the Quebec Agricultural Minister told the UPA annual convention, Article XI must be "inscribed in black on white" in the final text of a deal.[21]

For their part, the western provincial premiers continued to put unrelenting pressure on the federal government to deliver in terms of trade liberalization in agriculture. Premier Peter Lougheed of Alberta had been an early advocate of unlimited free trade with the United States. Not only had he served as a catalyst for mobilizing regional political support on the issue (for example, at the meeting of western premiers in Grande Prairie, Alberta in May 1985), and had continued this active "boosterism" at the national level as co-chairperson (with Donald MacDonald) of the major pro-FTA lobby group, the Canadian Alliance for Trade and Job Opportunities. Grant Devine of Saskatchewan, for his part, was not only a mainstay in the campaign for FTA but also a vocal demandeur with respect to multilateral trade liberalization. Departing from any semblance of an even-handed perspective by the end of the 1980s, Devine argued for more vigorous pressure against the Europeans by way of a boycott or tax on imports from the EC.[22] In the absence of a completed GATT round, however, Devine also pressed hard for an expanded federal government relief effort to meet his more immediate political exigencies. Indeed, it was Devine's early morning phone call to Prime Minister Mulroney in the middle of the 1986 Saskatchewan election campaign that was instrumental in winning prairie farmers the one-billion dollar payout under the Special Canadian Grains Program.

To be fair, the Mulroney government showed a willingness to refine its management techniques to face this delicate situation. Most importantly, to show that agricultural policy was being upgraded in terms of the overall government's priorities, Donald Mazankowski was gradually interjected as a broker in this issue-area. Initially, in an ad hoc fashion, this intervention was justified on the basis of Mazankowski's position as deputy prime minister. By September 1988, however, Mazankowski had taken over the role of acting agriculture minister. And in January 1989 he formally took on the responsibilities of this post.

Mazankowski's appointment was crucial for a number of reasons. As deputy prime minister, "minister of everything," and a key player in the cabinet committee structure, Mazankowski had the authority to deliver what he promised. In this regard, he differed considerably from his predecessor (John Wise) who had little clout in policy terms.[23] Mazankowski could also capitalize on his considerable popularity and credibility with western farmers to be an effective mediator. Indeed, it may be argued, even his perceived bias in some ways allowed him more leeway in working towards some form of consensus on agricultural policy. Finally, Mazankowski was an adroit negotiator. If less publicized than Mulroney's deal-making techniques, his skills of manipulation were arguably more effective.[24]

In taking charge, Mazankowski gradually imposed his own stamp on the policy dynamic. In terms of procedure, he attempted to depoliticize agricultural policy by bringing the disparate groups more fully into the decision-making process. Apart from the existing formal process of consultation with respect to the GATT negotiations (including a Federal-Provincial Agriculture Trade Policy Committee, the Committee on Multilateral Trade Negotiations, and a Sectoral Advisory Group on International Trade) he initiated a more general agricultural policy review through a number of task forces and advisory committees.[25] At the same time, more attention was paid to extending the informal mechanisms for discussion between government and producer organizations. The policy result was a cautious but decided tilt in favour of reform. While the sensibilities of the resisters were taken into account, the government clearly indicated its intent to move vigorously towards a more offensive form of domestic adjustment. The preliminary report of the agricultural review, while not directly addressing the issue of structural adjustment, contained references to the benefits accruing from greater flexibility in income support programs, a shift towards a "second generation" of marketing boards, and a more "market-oriented" framework for agricultural policy.

Mazankowski attempted to interject similar subtlety into the formulation of the Cairns Group's negotiating approach. Indeed, his grip at the reins of agricultural policy was signalled when the government had to deal with the deepening rift between Canada and its allies on the proposal for a short-term reform package for the Uruguay Round involving proposals for a "freeze" on new access barriers, a ban on the introduction of new non-tariff barriers and trade-distorting barriers, immediate across-the-board cuts in subsidies by agreed percentages, and the establishment of targets for reducing support and protection over a ten-year period. Australia had originally put forward the idea at the Bariloche meeting of the Cairns Group in February 1988, and the rest of the "fair trading" group were firmly on-side with this set of confidence-building measures. But Canada was unwilling to accept any package that involved significant political and economic costs, especially at a sensitive time in the FTA negotiations and also in the run-up to the general election. To try to defuse the situation, therefore, Mazankowski took advantage of the opportunity of his visit to Australia in June-July 1988 to engage in some high level crisis management.[26]

These diplomatic efforts papered over the differences between Canada and the other members of the Cairns Group for a short time. Australia, although reluctant to damage its image as a progressive force in the international political economy of agriculture, settled for the somewhat awkward compromise of deleting the specifics with respect to the short-term proposals in the Cairns Group's "Time for Action" reform program of July 1988.[27] But it did submit a separate proposal of its own with detailed recommendations concerning the specifics with respect to a "downpayment" on a longer-term reform package. Canada, although willing to agree to a freeze on further trade distorting initiatives and prepared to accept an overall reduction of 10 percent over the next two years, remained adamantly opposed to any commodity-specific measures, particularly those directed towards the domestic-oriented sectors. In other words, Canada continued to want to liberalize in its own way rather than on the criteria of a strict formula drawn up by other actors.

THE WIDENING OF THE DEBATE

Despite the international pressures, the reform process at both the international and domestic levels were stalled in Canada by the political and constitutional circumstances associated with the Meech Lake imbroglio. As in so many other spheres, Meech marked a watershed in terms of agricultural policy. Prior to Meech it was possible to contemplate a negotiated settlement on the basis of some regional compromise; in the post-Meech period this possibility seemed far more remote. Rather than the impetus being towards the depoliticization of agricultural policy, the momentum was swinging back towards a more acute form of fragmentation.

Several factors led to this change of atmosphere. As noted above, the grievances of the UPA had been building up against the Mulroney government and the federal system since the 1988 election. Exacerbated by growing suspicions that a combination of the federal reform proposals from inside and intensified pressure for adjustment from outside (illustrated by the rapid and successful U.S. challenge to the Canadian action on yogurt and ice cream) would lead inevitably to a complete "sell out" of Quebec farming, the UPA moved to wrap agriculture more closely in a nationalist cloak. Galvanized by the forceful rhetoric of Jacques Proulx that Ottawa was "bartering away the subsidies to Quebec dairy farmers, in order to secure export markets for prairie grain growers at the GATT bargaining table,"[28] the UPA pushed harder in demanding that agricultural policy be given over completely to the Quebec government. As another UPA official stated at the organization's annual convention in December 1989: "If the federal government is not taking into account the Quebec farmers' position, the Quebec government should patriate as much power as it can in this field. We no longer believe the assurances of the federal government."[29]

What was new, in the aftermath of Meech, was that agriculture took on a much more profound symbolic importance in Quebec with respect to the perceived failure of the federal system. Because of the profound feelings of hurt and humiliation arising out of the failure of Meech, the agricultural issue became more salient to the sovereigntist forces in Quebec. Arguing that its agriculture could be better protected in an independent Quebec, both the Parti

Québécois and the new Bloc Québécois seized the opportunity to thrust this issue into the forefront to politics. This point was underscored by the fact that the first question that Lucien Bouchard asked in the House of Commons, after his break with Mulroney and the Conservative Party, related to the future of Quebec agricultural producers: "as a result of the positions which the federal government will take in the current round of GATT negotiations in Geneva."[30]

The UPA reinforced this sense of realignment by their own activities. The Quebec farmers' organization severed some of its ties with farm organizations outside Quebec. The UPA withdrew from the Dairy Farmers of Canada ostensibly because of financial problems. Although it remained in the Canadian Federation of Agriculture, by the end of 1990, "il n'y a pratiquement aucune communication entre les dirigeants de UPA et de la FCA."[31] Reinforcing this impression of delinkage, the UPA acted with pronounced autonomy in its efforts to defend Article XI under the GATT. Most tellingly, it paid greater attention to building alliances of resisters on an international rather than a trans-Canadian basis. While marching with the European farmers in a show of agrarian solidarity at the December 1990 GATT meetings, for example, the UPA chose not to join with the Ontario Federation of Agriculture in a collective lobbying effort "to save marketing boards" in late 1991.[32] In contrast, the UPA's own enthusiasm for Quebec sovereignty became even further accentuated. In a brief to the Bélanger-Campeau Commission on the future of Quebec, the UPA reported that 99.2 percent of the organization's farm union delegates and 72 percent of its general membership supported independence.[33]

In response to this marked shift in Quebec, an inevitable backlash developed in western Canada. This reaction was partly a result of the Quebec farmers breaking ranks with Canadian farmers to march with "the enemy" in Brussels. As Harvey McEwen, the president of the Western Canadian Wheat Growers Association, stated: "When someone goes out and supports the very same people who are putting you out of business, I have a very hard time considering someone like that an ally."[34] However, the hardening of the stance of many prairie farmers also developed out of their concern with the spillover effect of the constitutional debate. Convinced that a breakthrough in the reform process would become even more improbable as the agricultural issue became intertwined with the larger question of the survival of a united Canada, some prairie farm representatives were prepared to jettison Quebec entirely. In McEwen's words again: "Any farm group that says it wants to separate from the country, fine, let them run their own programs."[35]

So long as the overall GATT negotiating process was immobilized, much of this debate over agricultural reform had a hypothetical flavour to it. What brought the controversy to a head in late 1991 and early 1992 was the agreement by both the U.S. and the EC that the so-called Dunkel text (with its emphasis on the conversion of quotas into tariffs subject to future reductions)[36] provided a basis for compromise in breaking the deadlock on the farm conflict. While providing a building block for some form of negotiated consensus between the majors at the international level, however, the Dunkel proposals made the policy predicament at the domestic level more acute. For Canada's international commitments to reform remained extremely difficult to reconcile with the domestic imperative of maintaining much of the status quo on domestic political grounds.

The justification for placing domestic convenience ahead of international commitment was based on two types of argument. The first of these was centred on a realist view of the world, where the declared national interest of individual states remained paramount. As Mazankowski forthrightly put it, just prior to the Brussels 1990 meeting: "What's wrong with staking a Canadian position? I thought we were sovereign in staking out our own trade policies. We did it with respect to the free-trade agreement. And we're doing it now. We should be applauded for that."[37] Alternatively, Canadian politicians and officials contended that Canada stood out as an "exception" in agricultural trade relations because the architecture of supply management did not constitute trade-distorting measures. Because they were not export-oriented, it was maintained, these structures were not part of the problem. Canada should therefore not be expected to offer tariff equivalents for its supply-managed products under the type of proposals featured in the Dunkel text.

Regardless of their domestic political attractiveness, these types of rationales were ineffective in gaining Canada manoeuvrability vis-à-vis the international negotiating process. If a balanced approach between the forces of adjustment and resistance minimized the dilemma of governance at home, the contradictions contained in this approach did not make it easy to sell abroad. As Canada's chief negotiator told the House of Commons Agriculture Committee in February 1992: "We owe it to you ... to tell you the facts of life — we just can't come to you and pretend that we don't have a tough time defending this."[38] Even Canada's constitutional problems, dramatized by the prospect of an October 1992 referendum in Quebec, elicited very little sympathy in a world facing a proliferation of "nationality questions."[39]

More to the point, support for Canada's position among its traditional allies weakened appreciably. Canada insisted that it not only be given due allowance under Article XI for import quotas of supply management but that Article XI be "clarified and strengthened." This alienated it almost completely from its erstwhile Cairns Group partners. While Canada continued to be nominally a member, in terms of policy substance it was no longer a player within the group. The situation with the United States was aggravated by a number of serious bilateral irritants between them, and the U.S. also became more frustrated with the Canadian attempt to maintain a dualistic approach with respect to agriculture and the GATT. Ignoring the contradictory elements in the U.S.'s own policy, American officials continually criticized Canada's approach as having all the consistency of *Jell-O*.[40]

Gradually this sense of isolation produced an air of desperation in Canadian agricultural trade diplomacy. Detached from "like-minded" allies, Canada began to search frantically for support of its demands on Article XI from non-traditional sources. One focal point of this lobbying effort was the EC, ironically the target of so much of Canada's own criticism with regard to illiberal trade practices in agriculture. While Canada had not tried to isolate the EC in the Uruguay Round, much of its foreign economic diplomacy had been directed to making the Community "more forthcoming" in terms of making concessions on agricultural trade. Complicating matters further, many of the attempts Canada had taken to keep to the "middle path" between the U.S. and the EC had hurt rather than helped Canadian-EC relations. A perception of bias against the EC, for instance, came to the fore during the prime minister's tour of the major European capitals prior to the Toronto G7 Summit in 1988. What was intended to serve as a showcase for Canadian diplomacy, ended up as an embarrassing episode featuring mutual recriminations concerning the comparative levels of farm subsidies.[41] Given this background, therefore, the bemusement with which the Europeans received the Canadian overtures on Article XI was not surprising.

Canada also targeted another, more diffuse group of potential allies. This was the collection of countries including Japan, Korea, and the Nordic countries, which were interested in maintaining their own national systems of agricultural protection. The association that Canada established with these countries, nonetheless, remained extremely loose. Each had its own distinctive preoccupations. If they were all attempting to preserve elements of the status quo of the agricultural trading system, they differed considerably with respect to their specific interests in doing so. As such, this grouping of countries had far less potential for becoming an effective multimember coalition than did the Cairns Group.

CONCLUSION

This chapter seems to confirm that in the agricultural dimension of trade policy there has been a retreat from internationalism. Certainly, the gap between Canadian rhetoric at the beginning of the Uruguay Round and Canadian practice during the GATT negotiations has grown. Claims of leadership were discarded as the burden of costs necessary to undertake that leadership role in a credible fashion became more apparent. Rather than persisting as a prime mover for "necessary" reform in an offensive mode, Canada became a cautious advocate for domestic adjustment when possible.

In many ways this retreat on agriculture, as in other areas of Canadian foreign economic policy, may be criticized as representing a withdrawal from a more visionary and creative approach to one concerned more with "safety first" mechanisms for coping with parochial concerns.[42] In alternative terms, though, Canada's highly nuanced approach on agricultural trade may be seen as a pragmatic recognition of the fact that international reform is not just an economic process but a political process, and a mainly domestic process at that. As Michael Aho, among others, has pointed out: "Trade negotiations are as much domestic negotiations as they are negotiations among countries."[43]

This internalization is reinforced by the special nature of Canada's regionalism. For all of the change apparent through the Uruguay Round there is a great deal of continuity exhibited in Canadian policy making on agricultural trade. To a considerable degree, the means by which the Mulroney government has attempted to manage agriculture and GATT in the 1980s and 1990s may be viewed as an accentuated extension of the "federal style" of Canadian foreign policy making going back to the 1950s and 1960s. When confronted with serious regionally-based differences during that earlier period, the federal government adopted a negotiating approach that emphasized the management process itself rather than the rationality of the outputs of that process.[44] While a messy style, it was a style that worked to the point of tempering if not resolving differences.

The difference in the 1980s and 1990s is that with the rising stakes involved in trade issues such as agriculture, the political system has been pushed to the limit. The challenges of international competitiveness have made the struggle over the form and scope of adjustment an increasingly fundamental and sensitive one, with clear winners and losers depending on the choice between offensive and defensive, and international and domestic strategies. This re-ordering in the international system has also contributed to limiting Canada's flexibility in foreign economic diplomacy. Notwithstanding the dexterity with which the internalization of trade policy has been handled by the Mulroney government, and the imperative for buying more time to allow some settlement of the constitutional question, the pressure to meet new international obligations under a negotiated GATT agreement may eventually be too overwhelming for the maintenance of a dualistic approach. If Canada is cornered by such a multilateral agreement, the techniques of domestic statecraft will be increasingly concentrated on cushioning the impact of change on the losers (and deflecting the responsibility for it) while facilitating other producers' adjustment to market signals. Although trade policies will continue to be rooted in domestic realities, therefore, those domestic realities will be made more compatible with the international political economy. Unfortunately for Canada, however, much of this ongoing debate about efficiency and social protection in agriculture will be played out in a fashion that both reflects and accentuates regional cleavages.

NOTES

1. See, for example, Jeffrey Simpson, "A two-headed agricultural policy," *Globe and Mail*, 17 November 1989; Hyman Solomon, "Canada's contortions on supply management," *Financial Post*, 15 March 1990; Barry Wilson, "Canada takes on two roles at the same time," *Western Producer*, 14 December 1990.

2. For background see Theodore H. Cohn, *The International Politics of Agricultural Trade: Canadian-American Relations in a Global Agricultural Context* (Vancouver: University of British Columbia Press, 1990); A.F. Cooper, "Agricultural Relations Between Western Nations; Canadian Perspectives," in I.S. Knell and J.R. English, *Canadian Agriculture in a Global Context: Opportunities and Obligations* (Waterloo: University of Waterloo Press, 1986), pp. 69-85.

3. John English and Norman Hillmer (eds.), *Making a Difference? Canadian Foreign Policy in a Changing International Order* (Toronto: Lester, 1992).

4. John Whalley, "Comments," in Jeffrey J. Schott and Murray G. Smith (eds.), *The Canada-United States Free Trade Agreement: The Global Impact* (Washington, DC: Institute for International Economics and the Institute for Research on Public Policy, 1988).

5. Darryl Gibson, "Crosbie fears GATT failure will 'badly smash' Canada," *Winnipeg Free Press*, 14 November 1989.

6. See David Baldwin, *Economic Statecraft* (Princeton: Princeton University Press, 1985).

7. See, for example, A.F. Cooper, "Between Integration and a Way of Life: Trade Liberalization and the Political Economy of Agriculture," in Leslie A. Pal and R.-O. Schultze, *The Nation-State Versus Continental Integration: Canada in North America — Germany in Europe* (Bochum: Universiatsverlag Dr. N. Brockmeyer, 1991), pp. 115-30.

8. Robert D. Putnam, "Diplomacy and domestic politics: the logic of two-level games," *International Organization* 42 (1988): 434.

9. C.A. Gracey, "That Spade is a Shovel," remarks to the conference, "Canadian Agriculture in a Global Context," University of Waterloo, 22 May 1985, p. 6. See also Alex Graham, Chairman, Prairie Pools Inc., "GATT and the Western Grain Industry: Framework for Discussion," paper presented to a workshop on "The GATT Agricultural Trade Negotiations," Centre for Trade Policy and Law, Carleton University, 22 November 1990.

10. See, for example, Robert Paarlberg, *Fixing Farm Trade: Policy Options for the United States* (Cambridge, MA: Ballinger, 1988).

11. See Clyde Graham, "Farm and trade officials to meet in Australia," Halifax *Chronicle Herald*, 23 August 1986.

12. G. John Ikenberry, "The State and Strategies of International Adjustment," *World Politics* 29 (1986): 53-77.

13. Alex Craig, chairman, Sub-Committee on Trade of the Supply Managed Commodity Committee, CFA, testimony before the House of Commons, Standing Committee on Agriculture, 15 June 1989, 14:13.

14. Jean-Yves Couillard, second vice-president, UPA, testimony to the Special Joint Committee of the Senate and the House of Commons, Canada's International Relations, 22 July 1985, 7:25.

15. Ikenberry, "The State and Strategies of International Adjustment."

16. Peter Aucoin, "Organizational Change in the Machinery of Canadian Government: From Rational Management to Brokerage Politics," *Canadian Journal of Political Science* 19 (1986): 3-27.

17. See opposition complaints about the delay in tabling the Canadian negotiating proposal on agriculture in October 1987. Canada, House of Commons, *Debates*, 27 October 1987, pp. 10189-10191.

18. For a good overview see G. Bruce Doern and Brian W. Tomlin, *Faith and Fear: The Free Trade Story*, (Toronto: Stoddart, 1991).

19. Jeffrey J. Schott, *United States-Canada Free Trade: An Evaluation of the Agreement* (Washington DC: Institute for International Economics, April 1988), p. 24.

20. Suzanne Dansereau, "L'UPA entend accentuer son opposition au libre-échange," *Le Devoir*, 2 December 1987, p. 9; Richard Cleroux, "PM faces fight with Quebec farmers over free trade deal," *Globe and Mail*, 30 August 1988, p. A8.

21. Robert McKenzie, "Quebec wavers on free trade for farmers," *Toronto Star*, 4 December 1987. The importance of Article XI was reiterated by the Quebec government in *Les négociations commerciales multilatérales de l'Uruguay Round: Perspectives Québécoise* (Quebec: March 1990), pp. 29-36.

22. Peter Morton, "Angry farmers seek revenge in GATT flap," *Financial Post*, 8-10 December 1990.

23. To give just one illustration, Wise had had serious reservations about free trade. In a speech in 1985 Wise had pointed to the inconsistencies in the American stance on trade liberalization: "We hear a lot of talk about free trade and so on. That is fine. But it appears that certain people are not always as free in their trading as they would like to lead people to believe they are." House of Commons, Standing Committee on Agriculture, 4 February 1985, 5:16. In fact, it has been commonly accepted that Wise resigned as minister because of his critical views on the impact of the FTA.

24. Bill Redekop, "Mazankowski gets farmers' nod," *Winnipeg Free Press*, 30 December 1988; Barry Wilson, "Mazankowski clout makes big difference," *Western Producer*, 10 August 1989.

25. Agriculture Canada, *Growing Together: A Vision for Canada's Agrifood Industry* (Ottawa: Minister of Supply and Services, Publication 5269/E, November 1989).

26. For a fuller discussion see Richard A. Higgott and A.F. Cooper, "Middle power leadership and coalition building: Australia, the Cairns Group, and the Uruguay Round of trade negotiations," *International Organization* 44 (1990): 589-632; A.F. Cooper, "Like-Minded Nations and Contrasting Diplomatic States: Australian and Canadian Approaches to Agricultural Trade," *Canadian Journal of Political Science* 25 (1992): 349-79.

27. Cairns Group, "Time for Action: A Proposal for a Framework Approach for Agriculture," MTN. GNG/NG5/W/69.

28. Benoit Aubin, "Quebec farmers plan to besiege Tory MPs," *Globe and Mail*, 11 May 1989, p. A5. On Proulx, see Danielle Thibault, "M. Agriculture," *L'Actualité*, December 1988, pp. 78-86.

29. Jean-Yves Duthel, quoted in "Market boards that stabilize rural incomes are under fire," Barry Wilson, *The Montreal Gazette*, 8 January 1990, p. B 6.

30. Canada, House of Commons, *Debates*, 24 September 1990, p. 13212.

31. Claude Turcotte, "Le Président de l'UPA croit a un compromis au GATT," *Le Devoir*, 6 December 1990.

32. Alan Freeman and Drew Fagan, "Quebec silence loud at GATT," *Globe and Mail*, 29 November 1990.

33. Union des producteurs agricoles, *Eléments d'analyse sur les relations actuelles entre le Québec et le Canada*, Commission sur l'avenir politique et constitutionnel du Québec, 2 November 1990.

34. "Western farmers lash out at Quebec's GATT stance," *Globe and Mail*, 11 December 1990.

35. Ibid.

36. Draft Final Act Embodying the Results of the Uruguay Round of Multilateral Trade Negotiations, MTN.TNC/W/FA, GATT, 20 December 1991.

37. Madelaine Drohan, "Canada at odds with trade group," *Globe and Mail*, 24 October 1990.

38. Germain Denis, testimony to the House of Commons, Standing Committee on Agriculture, 11 February 1992, 24:10.

39. See Madelaine Drohan, "Canada can't get any sympathy," *Globe and Mail*, 20 November 1991.

40. Peter Morton, "Jell-o jibe angers Canadians," *Financial Post*, 6 December 1990. See also Edward Greenspan, "Canada teased for its farm trade," *Globe and Mail*, 14 April 1990.

41. Using a hockey analogy, understood by few Europeans, Prime Minister Mulroney stated that European farmers enjoyed NHL-level subsidies, whereas Canadian farmers received only Junior B-level subsidies. "PM blames reports for gaffe," *Winnipeg Free Press*, 28 May 1988, p. 14.

42. See, for example, Cranford Pratt, "Canada: An Eroding and Limited Internationalism," in Cranford Pratt (ed.), *Internationalism Under Strain: The North-South Policies of Canada, the Netherlands, Norway, and Sweden* (University of Toronto Press: Toronto, 1989).

43. Michael Aho, "Foreword," in Robert L. Paarlberg, *Fixing Farm Trade*, p. viii. See also Henry R. Nau (ed.), *Domestic Trade Politics and the Uruguay Round* (New York: Columbia University Press, 1989).

44. Thomas Hockin, "Federalist Style in International Politics," in Stephen Clarkson (ed.), *An Independent Foreign Policy for Canada?* (Toronto: McClelland & Stewart, 1968), p. 119.

14

Political Autonomy in the North:
Recent Developments

Peter Clancy

Au cours des trois dernières années, les initiatives menées en faveur de l'autonomie politique des Territoires du Nord se sont déroulées sur plusieurs fronts. L'auteur du présent article est d'avis que malgré la complexité des questions en jeu, les autorités des territoires nordiques font preuve d'une grande ingéniosité pour définir la substance et le processus propres à l'application de cette autonomie. Le chapitre passe en revue la tournure récente des négociations touchant les revendications autochtones, de même que le processus constitutionnel au sein des Territoires du Nord-Ouest et les actions entreprises par le nouveau gouvernement communautaire durant ces dernières années. Il est question aussi de l'interaction entre les contraintes d'ordre territorial et national. L'aggravation de la crise fiscale constitue précisément l'une de ces contraintes majeures. Elle fait déjà sentir ses effets sur le peuplement autochtone, la dévolution des compétences, et la redéfinition du gouvernement communautaire. Hormis l'ampleur des défis qui les attendent, il faut souligner la capacité des gouvernements nordiques à prendre en charge les intérêts de leur région.

INTRODUCTION

This chapter reviews recent developments, trends and issues in the field of northern self-government. At a moment when constitutional futures dominate the political agenda throughout the nation, the northern territories may well offer some instructive experience. Despite their modest populations and peripheral location, both Yukon and the Northwest Territories face difficult challenges in fashioning institutions and political processes for their diverse and dynamic constituencies.[1] On balance, it could be argued that both territories are doing better than their southern counterparts — in creatively bridging an intricate complex of social and political demands, and in generating processes for constitutional evolution involving both legislative bodies and popular consultation. In contrast to the logic of the "seamless web," the territorial approach suggests a quilt in which separately fashioned patches are continually being arranged and adjusted. While this may be a product of necessity more than choice, its achievements are nonetheless notable.

Given the dense cluster of issues on the northern political agenda, it is difficult even to demarcate the contemporary period. For present purposes, the past three years will form the basis of review. It was, after all, during the spring and summer of 1990 that three of the last decade's major comprehensive land claims reached a point of decision: two of these won interim approval, while one was abandoned. On the intergovernmental front, 1990 also saw the negotiation of a new financial transfer arrangement between Ottawa and the Northwest Territories, one that presaged grave fiscal consequences. On the national scene, the year marked the expiration of the Meech Lake process, and the confrontation between the Mohawk peoples of Kahnasetake and Kahnawake and the Governments of Canada and Quebec. This had implications for federal aboriginal policy and for the aboriginal role in the national constitutional processes that followed.

The forces unleashed by these events have done much to structure the current political agenda in the north. This is not to deny the many continuities with northern politics past. At least in the Northwest Territories, a veteran observer might be struck by the parallels to one decade earlier. Then, an increasingly acrimonious national constitutional dispute had forced both territorial governments and aboriginal groups to sharply defend their interests from compromise at the first ministers' table in the south. A northern plebiscite posed the question of dividing the N.W.T. and creating two new territories. A series of comprehensive claims negotiations generated mixed signals from governments and citizens, and regional cleavages emerged within the aboriginal movement. Finally, an Aboriginal-led Legislative Assembly fashioned significant progress on political development within the north. All these have recurred.

At the same time certain distinguishing contemporary features must be noted. Unlike a decade earlier, the current redefinition of northern policy is shaped profoundly by the fiscal crisis. In the north this has surfaced a decade later than in the provinces, and it will pose mounting complications through the 1990s. Also by contrast to the earlier period, northern authorities are now engaged in a dual negotiation of the political contract in the north. On one dimension, this involves the social relationship between ethnic and racial groups, while on a second it involves central-local relations, in both the aboriginal and the general political communities. One overriding feature prevails as strongly today as it did in the past. Political autonomy is the goal. As ever, there remain many prospective routes to it. These are introduced in the next section, and are taken up in more detail in those that follow. While the mix of paths remains to be determined, it may be possible here to identify some forces that will operate in the future.

THE CROWDED NORTHERN AGENDA

The growth of indigenous political capacity in the north has advanced in a number of ways. Yet any review of autonomy measures begs two prior questions: who sponsors each autonomy proposal, and who benefits? Such a formulation can sharpen our understanding of how institutional changes work to the advantage and disadvantage of social and political groups. At least four broad institutional initiatives vie for priority.

One is the aim of attaining provincehood in the north. This time-honoured goal affects, at least formally, all residents of the Northwest Territories or Yukon Territory. Its advocates suggest that it completes the evolution of responsible government in Canada's federal system by bringing the fullest measure of citizenship to northern society. Moreover, its inclusive character treats equally all resident individuals or groups. This places it squarely within the liberal democratic tradition in Canada. To the northern governments, it offers full executive and legislative powers entrenched in the constitution, remedying the deficiencies long associated with "territorial" status and its colonial attributes. Two decades ago the elected Councils in both the Northwest Territories and Yukon unequivocally declared provincial status to be their number one goal.

In the period since, there has been far greater debate on whether provincial status, on its own, would be a major gain for either territory. One line of argument suggests that such small societies on the economic periphery are not well matched to the provincial role in the Canadian federation. For example, their tax bases and therefore fiscal capacities are insufficient to support full provincial regimes. Furthermore, it is possible that the federal-provincial redistributive system would be less advantageous for the north than is the status quo. Gordon Robertson has suggested that northern governments reap a fiscal *benefit* from their territorial status, capitalizing on a special relationship to Ottawa that would not survive the transition to provincehood.[2] This argument can be generalized to suggest that an enriched arrangement of territorial autonomy offers long-term advantages that should not be minimized. A self-governing territory in association with Ottawa may offer many of the prerogatives of provincehood without some of the severe liabilities.

This denotes a second arrangement, in which northern governments should continue to press for provincial-*style* structures, regardless of whether sovereign provincial status is achieved now, later or ever. During the past decade, such a devolution of powers has been pursued, with differing degrees of commitment, by governments in Ottawa, Yellowknife and Whitehorse. The process is still incomplete, though the progress made to date is virtually irreversible.[3] In part it has been achieved by the transfer of federal programs to territorial control. In other fields, such as sub-surface resource jurisdiction, the devolution process awaits fulfilment. In future, legislative competence may be transfered from the Parliament of Canada to the Territorial Legislatures. As devolution proceeds, the federal government withdraws from fields that the constitution generally assigns to provinces, and legislative and administrative competence moves physically to the north. Certainly this lacks the dramatic sweep, or more importantly the secure constitutional grounding, that accompanies the creation of new provinces. Instead it is measured by the slower and more subtle processes of intergovernmental negotiation; fiscal, personnel and asset transfers; and shortened spans of political control. Nonetheless, some studies have suggested that this less exalted form of political autonomy can make a difference. Power in northern hands will dictate outcomes that differ materially from those emanating from central authorities in southern Canada.

A different critique of the provincialist agenda is based on the overriding priority of alternative political claims. Since the Berger Inquiry of the mid-1970s, aboriginal political groups have demanded that their rights and title be addressed and confirmed before any other constitutional changes occur in the north. The struggle over this principle has pervaded northern politics over the past 20 years. It was endorsed by (then) Justice Thomas Berger, and has been periodically acknowledged by successive ministers of Indian and Northern Affairs. It was articulated, in a historic shift of orientation, by the Ninth Legislative Assembly of the Northwest Territories in 1979, as it was by the Yukon Territorial Government (YTG) after the 1985 election which brought the New Democrats to power. Nonetheless, aboriginal groups have continually found it necessary to resist *de facto* constitutional change flowing from federal-territorial devolution or territorial-local restructuring.

Without question, the aboriginal struggle to claim title and rights has emerged as the most important political initiative of the contemporary period. The history of culture contact, together with the character of the colonial occupation in the far north, have left Aboriginal Peoples with strong legal and political claims for autonomy. Defined as continuing rights that are conferred by territorial occupancy and use, aboriginal title remains intact throughout most of the far north. Since the federal government reversed its position in 1973, and recognized the continued existence of comprehensive aboriginal rights, the politics of negotiating claims settlements has touched all corners of northern public life. The Government of Canada has reached settlements with the Inuvialuit of the western arctic (1984), and the Gwich'in Tribal Council of the lower Mackenzie region (1992). It has also concluded Final Agreements (which remain to be ratified) with the Council of Yukon Indians (CYI), representing both status and Non-status Indians, and the Tungavik Federation of Nunavut (TFN), representing the Inuit of the central and eastern arctic. Negotiations are presently underway with the Sahtu Tribal Council, representing Dene and Métis of the mid-Mackenzie region. There has been discussion, though no formal move to date, about another regional claim by the Tli Tribal Council, representing the Dogrib people of the North Slave region. As will be seen below, this domain of aboriginal rights and self-government (bolstered by judicial findings and supportive public opinion) raises thorny questions about the extent of legislative sovereignty held by modern governments over Aboriginal Peoples. Pursuing it constitutes a full-blown political autonomy strategy, because aboriginal title obliges the Crown to acknowledge and to deal with the First Peoples in a unique fashion.

Over the past 20 years, some novel and innovative political arrangements have emerged from the claims negotiating process.[4] For example, comprehensive settlement agreements, the product of bilateral negotiations between the Crown in right of Canada and aboriginal claimant groups, have established a plethora of new institutions in the north. Some of these are new joint decision-making bodies for wildlife, land and water management, and environmental protection. Others involve the future form of tribal and territorial government. They have also placed a variety of new assets in aboriginal hands. These include financial resources, land, water and sub-surface resource ownership, and rights on public land use. In return, Ottawa has sought to secure its remaining jurisdiction by extinguishing certain aspects of aboriginal title over land and resources. Moreover, since all existing as well as future aboriginal claim settlements have constitutional standing, this process has the effect of creating a new order of government in northern society, albeit one encompassing aboriginal residents alone.

Fourth and finally, there is a set of autonomy initiatives that designate the local or regional community as the preferred decision-making level. This has been variously advanced under the label of de-centralized government, prime public authority, and enhanced community government. Its essence is to push both political control and program delivery capacity from the central to the local level. In this the GNWT may have launched an initiative nearly unique in the country. Its fullest expression could see the constitutional recognition of local community governments as the institutional anchor of northern politics.

These sweeping and contested avenues of political innovation, occuring simultaneously and on many different fronts, illustrate the prospects as well as the difficulties in settling the autonomy question. The N.W.T. Cabinet acknowledged as much in a recent policy paper where it observed:

> The very particular challenge to the people of the Northwest Territories as they address questions relating to land claims, division, extinguishment, devolution, self-government and our future in Canada, is to assess the relevance of each question to the larger context.

> Indeed, it is likely that the degree of interconnection between these elements is so high that progress on any one element will be extremely difficult, if not frequently impossible, unless it is coordinated with most if not all of the other elements.

In addition, in the absence of effective coordination with national constitutional reform, we may find that our objectives are inconsistent with or do not take advantage of new constitutional arrangements at the national level.

A comprehensive and integrated — as opposed to a piecemeal — approach must be taken if we are to experience progress.[5]

It follows that any interpretation of autonomy initiatives will need to trace a bundle of distinct analytical threads. This task is addressed in the sections below, which review recent developments on a number of political fronts.

ABORIGINAL CLAIMS SETTLEMENTS

The year 1990 marked a political watershed in several respects. In the field of land claims, a settlement paradigm that had been evolving for several years faced intense scrutiny on a number of fronts. Not since 1984 had a settlement been ratified and entrenched. During the intervening period, sustained negotiations were conducted on the three remaining northern claims in Yukon, the Mackenzie District, and the Nunavut region. In each case, the aboriginal claimant group conducted talks with negotiators named by Ottawa, in an effort to build a comprehensive settlement package. Rather than deal with all issues at once, it became the practice to formulate a roster of discrete topics, which could be addressed in sequence according to a mutually accepted schedule. Once negotiations were successfully concluded in a subject area, the parties initialled a "sub-agreement," and the discussions turned to new topics. Over a number of years the scope of the draft texts mounted, and on completion they formed the basis of a draft Agreement-in-Principle (AiP). With the endorsement of the sponsoring parties, this interim document was then revised into a draft Final Agreement (FA) which required formal ratification on all sides.

Although the settlement parameters were defined, and periodically amended, by Ottawa, each negotiating process began at the initiative of the claimant group.[6] Despite obviously unequal opening positions, the process was far from static. Each aboriginal group entered the process with its own priorities, not all of which could be fit within the stipulated federal criteria. At the same time, Ottawa could not compel each aboriginal group to accept identical terms (because their bargaining strength and concerns varied from issue to issue). Consequently, a dialectical process emerged. Advances or breakthroughs by aboriginal groups at one negotiating table, manifest in a sub-agreement, offered precedents that could be utilized at other tables. For example, in 1983 the TFN achieved a breakthrough on powers to be exercised by the Nunavut Wildlife Management Board, the joint Inuit-government policy-making body for the Nunavut Settlement Area. While Ottawa sought to confine such bodies to an advisory role, the TFN won agreement for a limited executive role. By 1990, similar boards were part of the Dene-Métis and CYI claims as well. Though they continued to differ in key respects, many of the draft agreements shared general features, as each precedent became a potential common denominator.

In 1990 all three draft agreements faced review by their respective aboriginal constituencies. After negotiating for 16 years, the Council of Yukon Indians had initialled an AiP in 1989, and an Umbrella Final Agreement in March 1990.[7] This included over 41,000 square kilometres of land, and \$282 million (1988 dollars) in capital payment. In addition to the financial, land and institutional terms of compensation, the CYI had chosen to build self-government provisions into its agreement. This would take the form of separate First Nation agreements to be negotiated with each Yukon band, just as the specific land selections would have to be negotiated with each band.[8] The CYI argued that the two sets of institutions were intrinsically related, and should be implemented (and constitutionally protected) together. The March 1990 approval confirmed the momentum of the CYI claim, which was strongly supported by the Penikett Government. Since that time, a model self-government agreement has been negotiated. This opened the way for acceptance of the Final Agreement by all First Nation bands late in 1991.[9]

Almost simultaneous with the CYI endorsement of its Final Agreement, the leaders of the Tungavik Federation of Nunavut signed an Agreement-in-Principle covering the Inuit territories of the central and eastern arctic. Composed of 43 sub-agreements, the TFN claim had been eight years in the making. Its terms included Inuit land ownership of 350,000 square kilometres (36,000 with sub-surface rights), \$580 million dollars in capital payment, a share of resource royalties in the settlement area, and equal membership (with public appointees) on a variety of wildlife, land, and environmental management boards which would exercise decision-making and advisory powers.[10]

This claim also included a self-government dimension, but unlike the CYI, the Inuit opted for the creation of a public government in a separate Nunavut Territory. This would be accomplished by the division of the existing Northwest Territories along a north-south boundary. In December 1991, the TFN approved a Final Agreement with Ottawa and the Government of the Northwest Territories. Once again, political development provisions were incorporated in the commitment to hold a boundary plebiscite, and to negotiate a separate Political Accord covering the transition to the Nunavut Territory.[11]

A plebiscite on the principle of division had passed in 1982. The plebiscite on the proposed boundary occured a decade later, on 4 May 1992. It resulted in a 54 percent majority in its favor, thus clearing the way for eventual division.[12] Significantly, the margin of approval in the eastern arctic was almost 90 percent, while in the western N.W.T. the level of support was only 28 percent.[13] This, together with the differential turnouts of 74 percent in the eastern arctic and 47 percent in the west, suggest that political division is very much an Inuit project.

In contrast to the regional splits which now characterize the Dene-Métis claim area in the Mackenzie region, the results also suggest a continuing consensus on the unified Inuit claim in the east. The degree of popular support for the actual TFN settlement will be evident when the ratification vote is held in early November 1992.

The parallel negotiation of the *Nunavut Political Accord* was tentatively completed in April 1992.[14] It provides for federal legislation to create the new territory by 1999. It also stipulates a transitional planning process to handle administrative design, the negotiation of financial structures for the new government, and training measures in anticipation of Nunavut's employment needs. All of these will be formulated in the interim.[15]

In stark contrast to this steady progress is the recent claims experience in the western N.W.T. Here in 1983 the Dene and Métis peoples decided to pursue jointly their Denendeh claim. In September 1988, an Agreement-in-Principle was initialled. This package featured elements similar to the TFN and CYI claims. It included a capital transfer payment of $483 million (1988 dollars), a land quantum of 66,000 square miles of surface land (with another 3900 square miles including sub-surface rights), resource royalty sharing provisions, and joint management boards covering wildlife, land and water management, and environmental impact, among others.[16]

This package proved to be far more controversial among the Dene than had been the case with other aboriginal groups. For example, there was criticism from both the band level and from the Dene Nation leadership, challenging the adequacy of the lands acquired in fee simple ownership, when compared to the vast expanses on which title was being forfeited. The joint management bodies were also challenged as a poor substitute for aboriginal powers of self-government. Ultimately it was the "extinguishment" provision, which eliminated any further aboriginal title to lands and resources, that proved to be the *coup de grace*. The latter two points appeared all the more critical after May 1990, when the Supreme Court of Canada ruled in the *Sparrow* and *Sioui* cases that section 35 of the constitution (affirming existing aboriginal and treaty rights) should be generously interpreted in protecting aboriginal rights from erosion by governments.[17] For the Dene this raised a prospect that self-government might already be included under section 35, thus rendering many of the settlement terms marginal, irrelevant or damaging.[18]

Events came to a head at the Joint Dene-Métis Special Assembly convened to consider the package in July 1990. After extensive debate it was clear not only that the delegates were sharply divided on the advisability of acceptance, but also that the differences were arrayed along two lines of cleavage. First there was considerably more support for the AiP among the Métis delegates than the Dene. Second, people from the more northerly regions of the Mackenzie Valley and Delta leaned in favour while the people from the more southerly Great Slave region were opposed. This developed into an acrimonious split, with the northern tribal groups contemplating the pursuit of a separate "regional" claim, leaving the southern tribal groups convinced of the fatal flaws of the failed proposal. This marked a serious rift within and between the memberships of the two constituent organizations, which has not yet been completely overcome.

Indeed, the claims politics in the Dene-Métis region have increasingly diverged. Within months of the 1990 Assembly, the Gwich'in Tribal Council approved an application for a regional claim in the Mackenzie Delta region, to be modelled on the rejected AiP. After an interlude of several months, the Minister of Indian and Northern Affairs agreed to this course, so marking a major departure from the past commitment to umbrella talks. With the GTC designated as the negotiating body for a combined group of some 2,000 Dene and Métis, claims funding began in December, negotiations proceeded through the winter, and an AiP was initialled in July 1991. Its compensation terms included over 22,000 square kilometres in fee simple land (with 6,100 square kilometres of sub-surface rights), $75 million in capital transfer over 15 years (with $1 million to purchase municipal lands), and exclusive hunting and trapping rights over 60,000 square kilometres The AiP also included an extinguishment clause covering "lands and waters."[19] The September ratification vote was approved by 94 percent of the voters on a turnout of over 90 percent.

The entire process bore parallels to the Inuvialuit Settlement of 1984. This had been concluded after the western arctic organization split from the wider Inuit claim, with the goal of reaching an early settlement in the face of the Beaufort energy boom. For both groups, the positive gains in political and economic capacity were judged sufficient to accept an extinguishment provision. The Gwich'in Settlement exerted a demonstration effect of its own as a third group, the Sahtu Tribal Council approached Ottawa early in 1991 requesting regional negotiations. A joint Dene-Métis organization was formed by the fall, and negotiations began in the spring of 1992.

The political future of the Dene Nation and the Métis Association remain questionable. Formally, the motion rejecting the 1990 AiP called for a reopening of negotiations to replace the extinguishment clause with a positive statement of treaty and aboriginal rights. Since the regional fragmentation of the claims process, the Dene Nation continues to demand the renegotiation of treaty rights. The objective here is to use treaty renewal as a vehicle to devise political institutions along traditional lines. In this sense, Dene interests are most closely tied to the national scene, where new constitutional amendments (and the influence of the Royal Commission on Aboriginal Peoples) offer one of the best chances for achieving this goal.[20] It is significant that the Assembly of First Nations has been outspoken in its critique of extinguishment provisions, to the point of triggering internecine tensions. Former Grand Chief George Erasmus predicted in August 1990 that the Inuit would reject the TFN agreement on these grounds. Then TFN President Paul Quassa responded that extinguishing land and resource rights did not affect other categories of aboriginal rights. In a similar vein, AFN Grand Chief Ovide Mercredi has castigated the TFN Final Agreement and offered to campaign in the north against it. This was quickly dismissed by Inuit Tapirisat President Rosemary Kuptana.

TERRITORIAL CONSTITUTIONAL REFORM

If 1990 was a pivotal year for aboriginal claims, then it might be said that 1991 saw the Government of the Northwest Territories reclaim some initiative in both the constitutional and the fiscal realms. In considerable degree this flowed from developments detailed above. While the federal government takes the lead in settling comprehensive aboriginal claims, the territorial governments play a central role in determining institutional change *within* their borders. This includes shaping an agenda for northern constitutional change, and for any internal devolution, self-government, or power sharing within territorial jurisdictions. Any such initiatives were framed in the context of the aboriginal settlement process, which both territorial governments monitored closely through their participation in the federal caucus, their negotiators at each table, and their role as signatories to each successfully concluded agreement.

The GNWT has an extensive history of involvement in northern constitutional issues.[21] Since 1979 its ongoing efforts have been anchored in a dual commitment: first to support the prompt and equitable settlement of aboriginal claims, and second to maximize the extent of northern self-government in directions that enjoy broad support within the territory. This implies a dual process of fashioning a consensus within the N.W.T., while simultaneously acting as a government to defend northern interests in Ottawa and in the national constitutional arena where these interests are constantly exposed. For over a decade these goals have been advanced through a continuing sequence of legislative committees, position papers, public consultations and task forces.[22]

The most recent of these rounds is rooted in the 1990 aboriginal claims developments. Put simply, the initialling of the TFN claim signalled the advance not only of the settlement package, but also the commitment to territorial division and the creation of the Nunavut Territorial Government. The latter issue had been virtually dormant since 1987, when the aboriginal and GNWT leadership had concluded the Iqaluit Agreement (through the agency of the two constitutional forums). This agreement both confirmed the plan for ultimate territorial division, and set out a number of principles and processes by which the result could be achieved. However, the Iqaluit Agreement was left in limbo by the continuing differences between the Dene Nation and the TFN over the actual boundary of separation. Since this line was to be set by the limits of their respective claims areas, progress under the Iqaluit Agreement was a function of agreement at the land claims table. For several years, the unresolved boundary lingered.

The boundary was revisited, however, in 1990 as the AiPs neared draft form. When Dene-Inuit negotiations failed to produce a deal, the Minister of Indian and Northern Affairs appointed first a fact finder and then an arbitrator in aid of a solution. The demise of the Dene-Métis AiP considerably lessened the urgency for a solution on the Dene side, though the Inuit remained anxious for a resolution. The boundary was finalized in 1991, when Northern Affairs Minister Tom Siddon accepted the arbitrator's proposal. Although the Dene protested this outcome, it closed a major gap in the TFN proposal, while simultaneously clearing the way for the revival of Nunavut.

By 1991 the need for a review of northern constitutional options was increasingly pressing. To the new trajectories in claims politics, and the prospect of territorial division, was now added Ottawa's post-Meech constitutional initiative. The Spicer Citizens' Forum was tasked to report by June, the Parliamentary Special Joint Committee on the Amending Formula (the Beaudoin-Edwards Committee) was already deliberating, and Ottawa's broader package for the renewed "Canada round" was due for release later in the year.

While the GNWT intervened actively in all of these settings, its most critical challenge was to bring some order to the indigenous constitutional agenda and to focus on future options for the western territory which would co-exist with Nunavut. To this end, the Cabinet met with the western aboriginal group leadership (Inuvialuit Regional Corporation, Gwich'in Tribal Council, Sahtu Dene-Métis Council, Dene Nation, and Métis Association) and established a Commission for Constitutional Development. Consisting of five members, each nominated by a constituent group, and chaired by Jim Bourque, the Commission's mandate called for the formulation of "a comprehensive constitutional proposal for those regions of the Northwest Territories remaining after the creation of Nunavut for consideration by way of a plebiscite."[23] The first phase called for a report on potential options to be released before the boundary plebiscite, while Phase II involved the design of a formal constitutional proposal.

The first report offers several basic proposals. First, it responds to aboriginal anxieties about their declining place in a divided electorate. Indeed the position of the First Nations is central to the statement. The Commission endorses the northern constitutional entrenchment of aboriginal self-government as an inherent right, and calls for guaranteed aboriginal representation in future legislative bodies. Second, it proposes entrenching a "District" level of government "which may be public, exclusively aboriginal, or a combination of both."[24] Clearly the need to recognize a plurality of community governments, while avoiding duplication and overlap, underlies this discussion. It suggests one means by which present territorial functions can be fulfilled alongside land claims authorities and any future self-government settlements with federal Indian Affairs.

THE FISCAL CRISIS AND STRENGTHENING OF COMMUNITY GOVERNMENT

Once again the roots of the present policy can be traced to 1989-90, when the GNWT recorded the first of a succession of budget deficits. Although the shortfall could be covered by the accumulated surplus of past years, it signalled that the deficits already endemic in provincial circles had belatedly arrived in the north. On the revenue side, the root of the problem is the extraordinary dependence upon federal transfers of funds. Approximately 85 percent of territorial revenues take this form, with a full 75 percent provided by the unconditional federal grant calculated according to a five-year Formula Financing Agreement.[25] Only 10 percent of revenue is derived from taxes within the N.W.T. Overall, the revenue constraint will become increasingly severe under the new agreement signed in April 1991. As it has with the provinces, the federal government has acted to share out (or "offload") its fiscal shortfall through cuts in transfers. Ottawa has also attempted to persuade the GNWT to levy personal income and corporate taxes at rates approaching the provincial average, by inserting into the formula a "tax effort factor," which penalizes the Government of the Northwest Territories for "a perceived lack of tax effort."[26]

It is true that territorial tax rates fall short of the provincial average (43 percent basic tax compared to 54 percent in the provinces, and 10 percent corporation tax compared to 15 percent in the provinces).[27] However, the GNWT has argued that no increases are possible in the context of a northern energy slump and the federal Goods and Service Tax phase-in. With transfers and taxes constrained, the pressure for a solution shifts to the expenditure side of the budget. Administrative growth measured in person-years averaged less than 1 percent over the 1987-91 period, and the gains from "normal" restraint measures had largely been reached. Moreover, the long-term trends in social program expenditures are ominous. With a domestic birth rate almost twice the national level, the pressure on health, education and social services will continue to mount in the 1990s and beyond. Consequently, given its greater direct control over program spending, the GNWT has chosen to attack its fiscal crisis on the expenditure side of the budget. This has emerged as the single most important policy initiative of the past 18 months, and it is a foundation for the present Cabinet which took office after the 1991 election. Its application may also strengthen Yellowknife's hand in future revenue negotiations with federal authorities.

In January 1991, the Financial Management Board of Cabinet established a Project Group for the Review of the Operations and Structures of Northern

Government. Eleven months later the Project Group submitted a two volume Report (described widely as the Beatty Report), which outlined a comprehensive strategy for reorganizing the formulation and delivery of government services. It emphasized the search for administrative efficiencies by halving the number of departments, cutting staff, and applying means tests to social programs. This was combined with a separate, and in many respects far more ambitious, proposal to restructure government roles between Yellowknife and the communities. The title of the Beatty Report, *Strength at Two Levels*, aptly captures its overall thrust.[28]

This proposal must be seen as an adroit synthesis of themes that have been advanced over several years. Sketching an over-bureaucratized state, it described a $1 billion public service employing 6,200 officials to deliver 375 programs to a society of 55,000 people. Furthermore, it confirms that the GNWT is top-heavy with senior managers located largely in Yellowknife, as opposed to dispersing responsibility and job opportunities to the communities where two-thirds of northerners (and the majority of Aboriginal People) live. In addition it supports the concept of empowering community governments, making them the "prime public authorities" in the territory. This thrust is congruent with Yellowknife's efforts to contain the expansion of regional councils as a potential third level of government, by focusing on re-invigorating the local level. The Beatty Report also fits easily into the concept, advanced subsequently by the Constitutional Commission, of extending constitutional recognition and priority to a "District" order of government which could be local or regional, public or aboriginal in character.[29] The appeal of a fiscal blueprint which dovetailed with the GNWT's commitments about personnel, affirmative action, local economy and even the constitution commitments, seemed irresistable. It was sufficient to prompt the Government Leader, Nellie Cournoyea, to greet the new Legislative Session with a Cabinet endorsement of a report only weeks old.

As the 1992 session unfolded, it became evident that not all MLAs shared the Cabinet's enthusiasm. For example, proposals to merge the departments of Health and Social Services, to rationalize hospital services, and to abandon many of the 800 boards and agencies and commissions identified by Beatty, drew fire from the affected interests. The Standing Committee charged with reviewing the boards declared that it would not be stampeded into precipitous decisions. And on the floor of the Legislature, MLAs staged a three day filibuster by reviewing the Beatty Report page by page, until the Cabinet invited three MLAs to join the Cabinet Working Group. [30] While there certainly will be political refinements to the scope and timing of implementation, it is clear that this report has provided a framework policy to accommodate the two dominant issues of the contemporary period: fiscal reform and political self-determination. As another government statement reads:

Reshaping Northern Government is designed to transfer government programs and responsibility for decision-making closer to the people, so that program design and delivery will reflect more clearly the needs and traditions of the people. It involves ensuring that sufficient resources are provided for the efficient and effective delivery of programs and services and it involves planning for and co-ordinating a long-range implementation strategy.

However since the government's fiscal position will not permit us to accomplish all this while continuing our current practices, we must both reduce our operations in some areas and increase our efficiency in others. At the same time, we must consolidate or eliminate programs that we no longer need or cannot afford.[31]

Significantly the government aims first to establish its fiscal parameters before addressing the question of local control. While Phase II still awaits policy clarification, it offers the potential to harness land claim institutions, aboriginal self-government institutions, or local community governments, to the cause of community self-sufficiency. Communities will be allowed to progress as quickly or as slowly as they choose. The varying grades of Community Transfer Agreement can range from the local delivery of existing programs to the local formulation of alternative programs within the financial parameters which Yellowknife would otherwise apply. In such a scheme the future shape of a Western Territorial Government might be discerned, as might the prospective Nunavut Government.

THE NATIONAL CONSTITUTIONAL PROCESS

Throughout the period under discussion, the federal-provincial deliberations on constitutional reform have addressed issues of great salience to the north. From the Meech Lake package to the spring and summer negotiations of 1992, territorial governments and aboriginal groups have closely monitored the play of at least four issues: the procedure for approving the creation of new provinces; the role of new provinces in future amending formulas; the constitutional entrenchment of aboriginal self-government rights; and the role of territorial governments and national aboriginal groups in future first ministers' conferences on the constitution.

The Meech Lake resolution drew the antagonism of territorial governments over the proposed formula for approving constitutional amendments creating new provinces.[32] From the prevailing rule requiring the consent of Ottawa and seven provinces representing 50 percent of the population, Meech proposed a change to require the unanimous consent of all eleven governments. Northerners recognized that many provinces feared the impact of new provinces on the "seven of ten with fifty" calculation, since the addition of northern provinces allowed new permutations of the "seven" which many existing provinces would resist so as to avoid diluting their leverage. Accordingly, the chances of winning unanimous consent diminished or vanished. Consequently the demise of this aspect of Meech was met with satisfaction in the north. When the 1991 federal proposals revived the Meech provision the territories again took aim, for Ottawa was willing to return to the unanimity rule. The northern opposition to this was well expressed by Yukon Government Leader Tony Penikett: "to have this matter remain in the constitution at a time when the northern territories, the federal government, and the First Nations here have concluded land claims agreements and are concluding self-government agreements is frankly ridiculous."[33]

The preferred northern option of amending by territorial and federal consent alone was adopted by the Beaudoin-Dobbie Report, which outlined a *quid pro quo* that may have eased provincial anxieties. In return for the more flexible formula, the new provinces could be omitted from the general amending calculation until a mutually satisfactory adjustment to the formula could be found.[34]

On the issue of aboriginal self-government, the distance travelled since Meech is much more dramatic. Struck in the immediate aftermath of the failed 1987 Aboriginal Conference, the Meech Accord had entirely ignored these questions. However, three years later the combined impact of Elijah Harper's intervention in the Manitoba legislature and the Oka events in Quebec brought aboriginal policy sharply into focus. In his House of Commons statement of 25 September 1990, the prime minister described one of the four pillars of the government's new "Native Agenda" as "the enlargement of aboriginal capacity for self-government, within the framework of the Canadian Constitution."[35] Ottawa's concrete proposals appeared one year later in the constitutional paper *Shaping Canada's Future Together*.[36]

A detailed tracing of the aboriginal provisions in the 1992 constitutional round is beyond the scope of this chapter. Yet even a brief recitation of the themes under discussion at the time of writing suggests some potential ramifications for First Nations in the north. The multilateral negotiation process in the spring of 1992 produced a draft agreement by which the aboriginal right of self-government would be accepted as an inherent right and entrenched in section 35. This would be "described" (though not "defined") as a "system to guard and develop native languages, cultures, identities, and traditions." It would establish a third constitutional order of government, with access to programs and financial resources. While negotiations will determine the pace and extent of the powers taken up, the inherent right would become justiciable three years (later extended to five) after the amendments take effect, thereby offering all parties early recourse to the courts. National First Nations groups would be guaranteed participation and right of consent, in this and any future constitutional issues affecting aboriginal affairs. A national treaty with the Métis First Nations would provide them with a land base.

Regardless of the ultimate outcome, the very fact that such provisions have been formulated in draft form will colour the future of self-government in Canada. Should they be enacted in a form consistent with the general sketch above, they are more likely to accelerate than to completely re-direct the trajectories of aboriginal claims settlement in the north. They would fulfil the longstanding aim of northern groups to include self-government provisions alongside land claims settlements on the constitutional plane. For the southern region Dene and Métis, whose position is the most indeterminate today, the advantages may be greatest. The provisions may well assist the Dene Nation in its professed goal of a self-government model based on the re-negotiation of treaties, relying heavily on traditional processes and values. Finally, by reinforcing the constitutional position of the Métis, it heightens their standing in the N.W.T. and Yukon.

LOOKING FORWARD

In closing, a number of points can be made about future directions of autonomy efforts in the north. Two quite different processes are being utilized to formulate and legitimize new institutional arrangements. On the one hand is the elite-centred, top-down pattern. This is evident both in the national first ministers' arena, where critical compromises are taken in the closed environment of mutual accommodation and trade-off, and also in fiscal policy strategies such as the Beatty exercise and the federal-territorial negotiations over transfers. In each case, excluded interests are free to reject the definition of the problem or the form of solution, as well as to protest their non-involvement. Even for those interests that are centrally involved, there is a risk that the stakes and the outcomes will be poorly understood and judged. This is a special concern to aboriginal claims negotiators, for despite the extensive research and exhaustive discussion involved, the impact of these processes at the settlement level remains quite limited until ratification gives way to implementation.

Alternatively, outcomes can be formulated, or at least ratified, with significant popular input. Here the *northern* constitutional process compares favourably over the past decade. The formal political authorities of the GNWT continually have been willing to open the consultation process, by means of convening occasional "leadership summits" with the aboriginal organizations, by striking commissions and forums, and by involving northerners by plebiscite. Similarly, the standards set for aboriginal ratification for claims settlements are notably stringent, requiring the consent of special majorities within a majority turn-out of eligible voters. The discrepancy between these two kinds of political process will continue to shape the "fit" of issues in this crowded northern agenda. Here it is instructive to contrast the relative ease with which the boundary plebiscite was arranged, against the significant resistance generated by the Beatty Report.

The question of representation can be extended to consider the overall configuration of group interests in the north. One might ask whether it has been permanently split into a two-tier hierarchy? Northern First Nations, given their centrality to the constitutional debate, are routinely recruited to political "summits," either to set consultative mandates or seek strategic agreements. Here the aboriginal leadership participates, together with the NWT Cabinet and Legislative Assembly, in very exclusive exercises with profound framework-setting implications. By contrast, a lesser order of interest groups is routinely overlooked for such purposes. This includes business groups such as the Chamber of Commerce, Federation of Independent Business, Chamber of Mines, and a broader array including the Municipalities Association, Status of Women Council, and the Federation of Labour. For such groups, consultation is limited to "normal policy," when they debate a narrower array of issues with their sectoral counterparts. These groups are destined to appear at the public hearings which have been arranged at the "higher" plane. Nowhere are the constitutional prerogatives of elected politicians less closely guarded than in the north; yet there are definite limits of access to the privileged circle.

Another factor that seems destined to shape both claims settlements and future self-government is the fiscal squeeze, which is now structural. To date, Ottawa's desire to offload program responsibilities can be seen in the shape of the federal devolutions to territorial governments, the current aboriginal self-government schemes such as Alternative Funding Arrangements, and the newly negotiated financial transfer terms. In the future, this same impulse will play a critical role in the implementation phase of aboriginal claims settlements. The growing scarcity of federal funds threatens to lead to extended implementation periods, proposals for aboriginal cost sharing and self-taxation, and increased pressure (directly or indirectly) for territorial government contributions. But all N.W.T. authorities are now wrapped in their own austerity regime. Moreover, their fiscal dilemmas can only mount in subsequent years. Demographic trends show the N.W.T. with the highest birthrate in the nation, and the cost of delivering social programs is destined to mount along with the needs of the youthful northern population.

Clearly the present N.W.T. strategy involves coupling a fiscal review to a process of community devolution. As far as possible, this will be done in concert with northern claims settlements, thereby merging the territorial with the federal stream of programs in a single set of multi-purpose local agents.

Northern politics will continue to revolve around the competition to define priority and position among several distinct "publics." What may be new is the level of active involvement by those publics, and the greater proximity of tangible material results.

NOTES

1. This challenge is not a new one. For detailed discussions of northern political development see Gurston Dacks, *A Choice of Futures* (Toronto: Methuen, 1981); and Mark O. Dickerson, *Whose North?* (Vancouver: University of British Columbia Press, 1992).

2. Gordon Robertson, *Northern Provinces: a Mistaken Goal* (Montreal: Institute for Research on Public Policy, 1985).

3. For a survey of the devolution process see Gurston Dacks (ed.), *Devolution and Constitutional Development in the Canadian North* (Ottawa: Carleton University Press, 1990); and *The Northern Review*, 5 (Summer 1990), "Special Issue: Devolution in the North."

4. For discussions of the process, see Office of Native Claims, "Perspectives on Land Claims Policy," in Canadian Arctic Resources Committee, *National and Regional Interests in the North* (Ottawa: CARC, 1984), pp. 87-106; and *Living Treaties, Lasting Agreements: Report of the Task Force to Review Comprehensive Claims Policy* (Ottawa: Indian Affairs and Northern Development, 1985).

5. Government of the Northwest Territories, Executive Council, "A Position Paper on Political and Constitutional Development," 25 February 1991, p. 7.

6. See for example, the Indian and Northern Affairs' papers: *In All Fairness* (Ottawa: Minister of Supply and Services Canada, 1981); and the subsequent *Comprehensive Land Claims Policy* (Ottawa: Minister of Supply and Services Canada, 1987).

7. *Yukon Indian Land Claim, Framework Agreement* (Whitehorse: Yukon Territorial Government), February 1989.

8. Vic Mitander, "Commentary," in Frank Cassidy (ed.) *Aboriginal Self-Determination* (Victoria: Oolichan Books, 1991).

9. *The Press Independent*, 20 December 1991.

10. Tungavik Federation of Nunavut, *Agreement in Principle Between the Inuit of the Nunavut Settlement Area and Her Majesty in Right of Canada* (Ottawa: TFN, 1990).

11. Tungavik Federation of Nunavut, *Agreement Between the Inuit of the Nunavut Settlement Area and Her Majesty in Right of Canada* (Ottawa: TFN, 1991).

12. The proposition, presented in ten languages, read as follows:

> On April 14, 1982, a majority of voters in an N.W.T.-wide plebiscite voted to support the division of the Northwest Territories so as to allow the creation of a new Nunavut Territory with its own Nunavut government. The N.W.T. Legislative Assembly and the Government of Canada accepted this result.
>
> In the Iqaluit Agreement of January 15, 1987, the Nunavut Constitutional Forum (NCF) and the Western Constitutional Forum (WCF) agreed that the boundary for the division of the N.W.T. would be the boundary separating the Tungavik Federation of Nunavut (TFN) land claim settlement area from the Inuvialuit and Dene-Métis land claim settlement area. On April 19, 1991, the Government of Canada endorsed the compromise boundary shown on the map below.

Division will occur in such a way as:
- to maintain adequate levels of public services;
- to respect the opportunity of residents of the Mackenzie Valley and Beaufort areas to develop new constitutional arrangements in the future part of the western N.W.T.;
- to respect the employment status and location preferences of GNWT employees.
ON THESE UNDERSTANDINGS, DO YOU SUPPORT THE BOUNDARY FOR DIVISION SHOWN ON THE MAP ABOVE?

The Press Independent, 27 march 1992, p. 2.

13. *The Press Independent*, 8 May 1992. It is interesting to compare these proportions to the 1982 plebiscite, when 56 percent supported the principle of division and 44 percent opposed. Frances Abele and Mark O. Dickerson, "The 1982 Plebiscite on Division of the Northwest Territories: Regional Government and Federal Policy," *Canadian Public Policy*, 11, 1 (March 1985): 1-15.

14. *News North*, 27 April 1992.

15. *Nunavut Political Accord*, 27 April 1992.

16. *Comprehensive Land Claim Agreement Between Canada and the Dene Nation and the Métis Association of the Northwest Territories* (Ottawa, 1990).

17. *R. V. Sioui*, [1990] 1 SCR; and *R. V. Sparrow*, [1990] 1 SCR.

18. Bill Erasmus, "Commentary," in Frank Cassidy (ed.), *Aboriginal Self-Determination* (Lantzville: Oolichan Books, 1991), p. 123.

19. *News North*, 23 September 1991.

20. See George Erasmus, "Commentary," in Frank Cassidy (ed.), *Aboriginal Self-Determination* (Lantzville: Oolichan Books, 1991), p. 22.

21. For a review see Peter Clancy, "Politics by Remote Control: Historical Perspectives on Devolution in Canada's North," in Dacks *Devolution*.

22. For an excellent summary of events, see Steve Iveson and Aggie Brockman, *Western Constitutional Forum: Chronology of Events, 1982-1987* (Yellowknife: Western Constitutional Forum, 1987).

23. "Terms of Reference," *Interim Report*, Commission for Constitutional Development (Yellowknife: Government of the Northwest Territories, 1992).

24. Commission for Constitutional Development, *Working Toward a Common Future* (Yellowknife: Government of the Northwest Territories, 1992), p. 26.

25. Northwest Territories, Financial Management Board Secretariat, *Main Estimates, 1991-1992* (Yellowknife: Government of the Northwest Territories, 1991).

26. Northwest Territories, *Annual Report, 1991* (Yellowknife: Government of the Northwest Territories, 1992), p. 24.

27. *News North*, 8 January 1990.

28. Northwest Territories, Project to Review the Operations and Structure of Northern Government, *Strength at Two Levels*, 2 vols. (Yellowknife: Government of the Northwest Territories, 1991).

29. Commission for Constitutional Development, *Working Toward a Common Future* (Yellowknife: Government of the Northwest Territories, 1992).

30. *The Press Independent*, 6 March 1992.

31. Government of the Northwest Territories, *Reshaping Northern Government* (Yellowknife, February 1992), pp. 5-6.

32. For a discussion of these issues, see Bernard W. Funston, "Caught in a Seamless Web: The Northern Territories and the Meech Lake Accord," *The Northern Review*, 3/4 (Summer-Winter 1989): 54-84.

33. Canada, Special Joint Committee of the Senate and the House of Commons on a Renewed Canada, *Proceedings*, 55 (28 January 1992), p. 55:6.

34. Special Joint Committee on a Renewed Canada, *Report* (Ottawa: Minister of Supply and Services, 1992), pp. 94-95.

35. Canada, House of Commons, 2d Session, 34th Parliament, *Debates*, 25 September 1990, p. 13321.

36. Canada, *Shaping Canada's Future Together* (Ottawa: Minister of Supply and Services, 1991). The aboriginal sections should be read together with the background paper released two months later, *Aboriginal Peoples, Self-Government, and Constitutional Reform* (Ottawa: Minister of Supply and Services, 1991).

IV

Chronology

15

Chronology of Events July 1991 – June 1992

Anne Poels

An index of these events begins on page 279

3 July 1991 *Aboriginal Peoples* *– Land Claims*	A blueprint for a new relationship between the British Columbia Indians and the federal and provincial governments is released in Vancouver. The report of a seven-member task force recommends an overhaul of the land claims process and an independent treaty commission to monitor it. There is to be no limit on the number of claims being negotiated at any given time and ownership of land, sea and other resources is to be resolved by agreement of the three parties.
3 July 1991 *Regional Develop-* *ment – Northwest* *Territories*	In Yellowknife, The Northwest Territories and the federal government sign a five-year, $38.5 million agreement on support for industry and culture designed to boost the northern economy. Ottawa will assume 70 percent of the cost.
4 July 1991 *Agriculture*	The federal and provincial agricultural ministers meet in Kananaskis, Alberta to focus on ways to help farmers hurt by low grain prices, high interest payments and the huge subsidies paid to European producers. The ministers agree on the establishment of a government-industry advisory group on farm finance policy.

5 July 1991 *Aboriginal Peoples* *– Constitutional* *Change*	Constitutional Affairs Minister Joe Clark agrees to a process that gives Canada's Aboriginal Peoples an unprecedented role in constitutional reform and opens up the way for aboriginal participation at future First Ministers' Conferences. Following a meeting with Grand Chief Ovide Mercredi and other members of the Assembly of First Nations in Morley, Alberta, Clark approves a parallel reform process designed by Aboriginal People to define their place in a new Canada. This signifies a shift in federal policy that had long envisaged only an advisory role for Aboriginals.
10 July 1991 *Environment –* *Quebec*	Federal Environment Minister Jean Charest orders a global environmental assessment of the proposed \$12.6 billion Great Whale hydroelectric project in northern Quebec, and meets with opposition from the provincial government, environmental and native groups. Quebec Energy Minister Lise Bacon makes it clear that Quebec considers the federal initiative an intrusion into provincial jurisdiction, while environmentalists and the Cree of James Bay express their disappointment that Charest did not stop further development of the Great Whale project, pending the outcome of the report.
12 July 1991 *Fiscal Policy*	Finance Minister Don Mazankowski unveils draft legislation to keep federal spending increases to an average of 3 percent a year over the next five years. The legislation will make it illegal for the government to spend more than the set amounts except for emergencies and special circumstances. It will also prohibit the government from raising taxes to cover expenditures, although this can be circumvented by passing amendments to the bill.
13 July 1991 *Aboriginal Peoples* *– Land Claims*	The Gwich'in Indians of the Mackenzie Delta reach a land-claim settlement with the federal government covering 15,000 square kilometres of land in the Northwest Territories, and providing \$75 million over 15 years, as well as the right to manage wildlife resources and economic development incentives. The settlement was reached after the failure of negotiations with the umbrella group of the Dene Nation and Métis covering all of the Western Arctic. Ottawa has agreed to negotiate with each aboriginal group separately.

20 July 1991 *Premiers –* *British Columbia*	Rita Johnston becomes leader of the Social Credit party, and next premier of British Columbia, replacing Bill Vander Zalm who resigned 2 April 1991 over conflict of interest charges. In Vancouver, Johnston wins on the second ballot of the convention, defeating contender Grace McCarthy 941 votes to 881.
6 August 1991 *Aboriginal Peoples* *– Ontario*	Ontario becomes the first province to recognize the aboriginal inherent right of self-government. In Thunder Bay, Premier Bob Rae signs an historic agreement with 12 First Nations chiefs that commits the province to negotiate the devolution of government powers on a nation-to-nation basis. The agreement could give Aboriginal Peoples more control in such areas of provincial jurisdiction as policing, courts, medical care and natural resources.
10 August 1991 *Progressive* *Conservative Party* *of Canada*	Delegates at the federal Progressive Conservative Party's biennial convention in Toronto vote overwhelmingly in favour of the Quebecer's right to self-determination. Delegates also approve other policy resolutions, among them motions to impose user fees on health care, to privatize the CBC and to abandon the policy of multiculturalism.
15 August 1991 *Supreme Court –* *Federal-Provincial* *Fiscal Relations*	The Supreme Court of Canada rules that Ottawa has the right unilaterally to reduce Canada Assistance Plan payments to the three richest provinces: Ontario, British Columbia and Alberta. Politicians and social groups worry that the decision could mean tax increases, spending cuts or bigger deficits at the provincial level, all of which would contribute to the deterioration of social programs.
18-20 August 1991 *Free Trade –* *North America*	Trade ministers from Canada, Mexico, and the U.S.A. end three days of negotiations for a North American free trade deal. No decisions are made, but the ministers make progress on issues such as:

- services
- investment
- protection of intellectual property such as copyrights
- level of local content required for cars to be shipped duty free across the border

• timetables for phasing out tariff barriers.

20 August 1991 *Environment –* *Saskatchewan*	Environment Minister Jean Charest announces that Ottawa will not order a halt to further construction of the Rafferty-Alameda dam in southern Saskatchewan. A consultant's report commissioned by the federal government said a shutdown could cause the dam to be breached next spring, posing a possible safety hazard to people downstream. A full federal environmental review is expected to be released next month.
26-27 August 1991 *Premiers – Annual* *Conference*	Provincial premiers, with the exception of Quebec's Premier Robert Bourassa, wrap up their annual conference in Whistler, B.C. The Premiers call on the prime minister to organize a First Ministers' Conference on the economy before the end of the year. Economic worries, the premiers say, hinder their ability to concentrate on the country's constitutional problems. The premiers also meet, for the first time at their annual meetings, with the leaders of the major national aboriginal organizations.
27 August 1991 *Aboriginal Peoples* *– Royal Commission*	Prime Minister Brian Mulroney appoints George Erasmus, former Grand Chief of the Assembly of First Nations, and Judge René Dussault of the Quebec Court of Appeal as co-chairmen of the Royal Commission on Aboriginal Peoples. The Commission's mandate will be to examine issues from aboriginal self-government to justice and land claims, and, in the words of the prime minister, "deal with centuries of injustice."
27 August 1991 *Energy – Quebec*	Premier Robert Bourassa announces that construction of the Great Whale hydroelectric project in northern Quebec will be postponed for a year due to reduced demand for power in New York. The delay will allow time for the full environmental assessment announced earlier this month.
28 August 1991 *Health Policy –* *Quebec*	Quebec passes health-care reforms designed to decentralize and modernize the present system. Some of the new measures include a limited user fee for non-emergency visits to the hospital and a requirement that new doctors work in understaffed parts of the province before being able to practice in major cities.

29 August 1991 *Aboriginal Peoples* *– Justice –* *Manitoba*	The Manitoba Aboriginal Justice Inquiry releases its report recommending sweeping changes to the legal system. The Inquiry calls for a separate native legal system based on generations of tradition, and endorses aboriginal self-government. The report recommends that natives run their own criminal, civil and family legal systems similar to arrangements found in various American states. It also calls for more native judges, police officers and court officials, and training in aboriginal culture for nonaboriginal officers of the justice system. The report follows nearly three years of hearings and study by Associate Chief Justice Al Hamilton of the Manitoba Court of Queen's Bench and Associate Chief Judge Murray Sinclair of the Provincial Court.
30 August 1991 *Aboriginal Peoples* *– Land Claims –* *Alberta*	The federal government signs a $19.6 million land-claim agreement with the Stoney Indians in Morley, Alberta. Recognizing that the Stoneys lost potential revenue from mineral rights when valleys in the area were flooded and reservoirs built for power projects, the settlement establishes a $12 million trust fund, to be administered by the tribal council, and a $4 million economic investment fund. The claim is the second largest to be settled in Alberta.
3 September 1991 *Free Trade –* *Canada-U.S. –* *Disputes*	Canada terminates the softwood lumber "memorandum of understanding" with the United States. In 1986 Canada agreed to charge a 15 percent tax on all softwood lumber exported to the United States. The U.S. lumber lobby maintained that Canada was unfairly subsidizing softwood. In the past five years, however, most provinces have introduced forest management measures, including higher stumpage fees which, coupled with the reduced demand for Canadian lumber south of the border, have contributed to higher costs for forest companies. Ottawa now feels that the 15 percent tax is no longer warranted.
5 September 1991 *Education – Quebec*	Quebec Education Minister Michel Pagé announces the formation of a task force to study the future of English schools in the province. Enrolment in Quebec's English schools fell by 57 percent between 1972 and 1990, while enrolment in French schools fell only 24 percent during

the same time. Journalist Gretta Chambers will chair the task force.

7 September 1991
*Aboriginal Peoples
– Justice*

In Whitehorse, federal Justice Minister Kim Campbell tells a conference on native justice that she is prepared to give natives more control over police and the courts. Native leaders demand a separate native justice system with their own police, prosecutors and judges.

10 September 1991
*Environment –
Saskatchewan*

The three-member independent panel set up by Ottawa to study the Rafferty-Alameda dam concludes that the project is relatively harmless to the environment. In its report the panel also finds that the partly completed project will not meet its original objectives such as irrigation and recreation. It may also have some effect on upstream water quality and wildlife habitat.

12 September 1991
Justice

A tentative 20-year agreement regarding RCMP services is reached between the federal government and a committee representing provincial governments that use the force. There will be no change in the existing cost-sharing arrangement: the provinces will continue to pay 70 percent and not the 75 percent Ottawa wanted them to pay.

13 September 1991
*Energy –
Saskatchewan*

The federal government and the province of Saskatchewan sign a memorandum of understanding under which Ottawa will study the feasibility of building a nuclear power station in the province and establishing a research and technology program, as well as possibly storing nuclear waste.

14 September 1991
*Aboriginal Peoples
– Land Claims –
Saskatchewan*

Saskatchewan Premier Grant Devine and Indian Affairs Minister Tom Siddon sign an agreement on sharing the $431 million cost of fulfilling outstanding land entitlements of Saskatchewan Indians. Twenty-seven Saskatchewan bands may now get compensation for land to which they were entitled, but never received, under treaties signed between 1871 and 1910. Ottawa will initially pay 70 percent of the cost and Saskatchewan 30 percent, but this will change over the next 15 years with Saskatchewan coming to assume 49 percent of the bill.

18 September 1991
Health Policy

Canada's health ministers meet in Winnipeg and pledge to uphold universal medicare. Federal Health Minister

Benoît Bouchard says he cannot guarantee that Ottawa will maintain the current level of funding to the provinces in light of the federal restraint measures. The ministers also examine ways of improving the efficiency of the present health-care system.

20 September 1991
Constitutional Change; Social Charter

Speaking at a press conference in Toronto, Ontario Premier Bob Rae announces that he is going to seek support for a charter of social rights to be included in the constitution. Rae argues that access to medicare, social assistance, unemployment insurance and basic education is a fundamental right of every Canadian. Federal Constitutional Affairs Minister Joe Clark responds that a social charter may prove to be unworkable.

23 September 1991
Elections – New Brunswick

Frank McKenna and the Liberal Party win a landslide victory in New Brunswick. Prior to the vote, the Liberals held all 58 seats in the legislature; they now have 46 elected members. The antibilingualism Confederation of Regions Party becomes the official opposition with eight seats while the Conservatives elect only three members, and the NDP, one.

24 September 1991
Constitutional Change – Federal Proposals

In the House of Commons, Prime Minister Brian Mulroney presents Ottawa's reform proposals, *Shaping Canada's Future Together*. A 30-member committee chaired by Manitoba Conservative MP Dorothy Dobbie and Quebec Senator Claude Castonguay will take the proposals across the country in an effort to invite citizen participation. Among the 28 government proposals are:

• Quebec would be recognized as a "distinct society" by including a new section in the *Charter of Rights and Freedoms*, with a definition of distinct society confined to Quebec's French-speaking majority, unique culture and civil law tradition;

• a Canada Clause defining what it means to be a Canadian in the constitution;

• aboriginal self-government within ten years;

• a reformed Senate that is elected, with more equitable provincial representation and with powers somewhat less than the current Senate;

• a broadened common market clause;

- a new federal head of power to manage the economic union;
- some transfer of powers to the provinces, and streamlining of other powers;
- a new Council of the Federation composed of federal, provincial and territorial representatives to decide on uses of the federal spending power, and the new economic union power;
- inclusion of property rights in the Charter;
- making it harder for legislatures to use the Charter Notwithstanding clause (section 37); and
- more free votes in the House of Commons.

Across Canada, reaction to the government's proposals is generally favourable, although Quebec and aboriginal leaders express opposition. Quebec Premier Robert Bourassa demands a veto over changes to federal institutions and rejects the proposal for economic union. Ovide Mercredi calls the proposals a "betrayal of natives" for not recognizing the immediate and inherent aboriginal right of self-government.

26 September 1991
Constitutional Change – Federal Proposals

Finance ministers meet in Ottawa to discuss the federal government's constitutional proposals. The provinces express concern that Ottawa might use the proposals to gain control of their economies. The federal government wants to strenghten the economy through coordination of fiscal policies and the elimination of interprovincial barriers to trade. Speaking from Quebec City Robert Bourassa again demands a veto over constitutional changes affecting Quebec.

30 September 1991
Constitutional Committees – Prince Edward Island

A committee of the Prince Edward Island legislature issues a report in which it supports the federal proposals to recognize Quebec as a distinct society and to reform the Senate. The report opposes the entrenchment of property rights in the constitution and calls for recognition in principle of the aboriginal right of self-government.

1 October 1991
Constitutional
Change – Monetary
Policy

Bank of Canada Governor John Crow criticizes the federal constitutional proposal that would give the provinces a role in Bank of Canada policy. Crow says that monetary policy is indivisible and that it would be inadvisable to give provinces, motivated by their own agendas, the power to determine national policy.

4 October 1991
Fisheries

Fisheries Minister John Crosbie announces $39 million in emergency aid to fishermen in the Atlantic provinces. Most of the money will be directed to make-work projects to help workers qualify for unemployment insurance.

10 October 1991
Agriculture –
Financial Aid

The federal government announces it will provide an extra $800 million in emergency aid to farmers. Grain farmers suffering from the lowest grain prices in 20 years will get most of the aid, $700 million, with the remaining $100 million going to producers of other commodities. Officials in Ottawa say the funds for the program will come from spending cuts and tax increases. Spokesmen for the farmers, who held a rally of 7,000 people at the Manitoba legislature 9 October, are not enthusiastic.

17 October 1991
Elections –
British Columbia

Mike Harcourt becomes Premier of British Columbia, defeating Rita Johnston's Socreds, as voters in the province elect an NDP government. The New Democrats take 51 of 75 seats. The Liberals become the official opposition with 17 seats, while the Socreds elect only seven members. The NDP has been in power only once before in British Columbia, from 1972-75.

21 October 1991
Elections –
Saskatchewan

Roy Romanow's New Democrats are elected with a majority government in Saskatchewan. The NDP takes 55 of 66 legislature seats. The Conservatives elect only ten members and the Liberals one. Saskatchewan's new leader, Roy Romanow, was a former deputy premier and Attorney-General in the NDP government of Allan Blakeney from 1971-82.

22 October 1991
Taxation

Manitoba abandons plans to harmonize its provincial sales tax with the GST. In August, Prince Edward Island also announced that it was no longer interested in coordinating the federal and provincial sales taxes. Quebec decides to delay the final step in its harmonization by postponing for six months the implementation of an 8 percent tax on services in the province.

23 October 1991
Senate Reform –
Newfoundland

Speaking in Toronto, Newfoundland Premier Clyde Wells advocates a Senate reform that would see an elected Senate based on the U.S. model with equal regional representation. The previous day, in what is generally perceived as a softening of his position, Wells tells the Newfoundland Constitutional Committee that Quebec should be given distinct society status, as well as the power to override the *Charter of Rights and Freedoms*, in order to preserve and promote its culture, language and civil code within the province.

25 October 1991
Free Trade –
Canada-U.S. –
Disputes

In Geneva, a panel of the General Agreement on Tariffs and Trade finds that Canadian provinces unfairly price and distribute imported beer from the United States. Key issues in the GATT decision are the limitations Canada imposes on where imported beer may be sold and the fees it charges for its distribution. In 1987 GATT ruled (against Canada) in a similar dispute launched by the European Community over beer and wine. As a result of that ruling most provinces have since lowered markups on imported wine.

28 October 1991
Constitutional Com-
mittees – Manitoba

An all-party committee of the Manitoba legislature releases its report on Manitoba's position on constitutional negotiations. The committee agrees to have Quebec's uniqueness recognized in the Canada clause. It also supports a strong central government, an elected Senate, and the aboriginal right of self-government.

29 October 1991
Premiers –
Atlantic Premiers'
Conference

Atlantic premiers meet in Summerside, P.E.I., and adopt a series of measures designed to save their provinces money. The premiers pledge greater economic cooperation and the possible integration of some government services. The meeting was called after provinces learned that they would receive about $145 million less in equalization payments this year. To avoid costly duplication, the provinces are considering the creation of single agencies that would deliver programs and services to all Atlantic provinces.

4 November 1991 *Regional* *Development –* *Ontario*	In order to boost northern Ontario's economy, the province signs a four year, $95 million, shared-cost agreement with the federal government. The deal will help fund programs in the forestry, mineral and tourism sectors.
7 November 1992 *Constitutional* *Committees –* *Castonguay-Dobbie*	The Special Joint Committee on a Renewed Canada chaired by Claude Castonguay and Dorothy Dobbie is recalled to Ottawa from its cross-Canada, consultative tour, amid allegations of mismanagement and disorganization. Constitutional Affairs Minister Joe Clark promises changes to the committee's scope but stops short of saying whether he will fire Dorothy Dobbie who has been blamed for much of the committee's trouble.
8 November 1991 *Constitutional* *Change – Federal* *Proposals*	Speaking during a special two-hour debate in the National Assembly, Quebec Premier Robert Bourassa urges Quebecers to consider Ottawa's constitutional proposals. Admitting that at present the federal proposals fall short of Quebec's expectations, Bourassa says that he expects modifications. Bourassa's bottom line remains unchanged — recognition of the distinct society for Quebec, a new division of powers between the provinces and Ottawa, and respect for Quebec's territory. For his part Parti Québécois Leader Jacques Parizeau scorns Ottawa's latest offerings and accuses the federal government of making a grab for Quebec's economic powers.
13 November 1991 *Constitutional* *Change – Public* *Conferences*	Constitutional Affairs Minister Joe Clark announces that the federal government, together with leading public policy organizations, will sponsor five regional public conferences to discuss the government's proposed constitutional package.
19 November 1991 *Social Assistance*	The National Council of Welfare releases a report in which it concludes that people on welfare need inflation protection. The report partly blames the federal government for the drop in income received by welfare recipients in the last year. It is the responsibility of the provinces to set welfare rates, but because of recent federal restraint measures they have failed to keep up with increases to welfare benefits.
21 November 1991 *Labour Training*	In Montreal, the federal and Quebec governments end months of dispute over manpower training and sign a

labour agreement by which Quebec's professional training commission will coordinate all labour force development in the province. Ottawa will spend $685 million
over two years, with Quebec contributing $365 million.
The agreement will stay in place until a new constitutional deal is reached.

25 November 1991
*Constitutional Com-
mittees –
Castonguay-Dobbie
Committee*

Citing health reasons, Claude Castonguay resigns as
co-chairperson of the Special Joint Committee of the
Senate and House of Commons and is replaced by Senator Gérald Beaudoin.

28 November 1991
*Regional
Development –
Quebec*

The federal government announces a $300 million, five
year federal-provincial program designed to help boost
Quebec's economy. The federal government will contribute $160 million to the program. The media outside
Quebec accuse the federal government of pandering to
Quebec in light of the current constitutional crisis, but
political leaders claim the agreement is routine.

28 November 1991
*Constitutional
Committees –
Nova Scotia*

Nova Scotia's advisory committee on constitutional reform, chaired by Eric Kierans, releases its report. The
committee endorses distinct society status for Quebec,
the inherent right of aboriginal self-government, an
elected Senate, and electoral reform that would allow for
proportional representation in the Commons. In its report the committee also stresses that Nova Scotians are
tired of a federal government so engrossed in the constitutional debate that it fails to address the pressing economic situation in the country.

6 December 1991
*Free Trade –
Canada-U.S. –
Disputes*

Canada accepts a report by the General Agreement on
Tariffs and Trade that accuses the provinces of unfairly
restricting the sales of U.S. beer. Federal Trade Minister
Michael Wilson says provinces must start to make their
markets accessible to U.S. beer in order to comply with
the international ruling.

7 December 1991
*Aboriginal Peoples
– Land Claims –
Yukon*

Yukon Indians accept an agreement on land claims and
self-government which was first negotiated in March
1990. The agreement addresses issues common to all 14
Yukon First Nations and provides a mechanism by which
land-claim agreements can be negotiated on an individual basis. The agreement also outlines a self-government

model that gives Indians the ability to govern themselves, administer their own programs, raise money through taxation and pass their own laws for settlement lands.

9 December 1991
Education

In Toronto, provincial education ministers reach an agreement on national educational testing. The testing is designed to provide a better idea of how Canadian students perform in literacy and mathematics. All provinces and territories except Saskatchewan have accepted the plan.

9 December 1991
Aboriginal Peoples
– Land Claims –
Ontario

Ontario and the federal government sign an agreement with the Nishnawbe-Aski First Nation. The deal provides $60.5 million for housing, roads, sewers and other necessities as well as 608 square kilometres of Crown land, with resource rights, to be used as reserves in northern Ontario. This is the first time a province has surrendered resource rights and land without seeking compensation from the federal government.

11 December 1991
Aboriginal Peoples
– Justice

The Law Reform Commission of Canada advises the federal and provincial governments to start negotiating with native communities the possible establishment of an aboriginal justice system. It also recommends that interim measures be adopted to make the present system more accessible to Aboriginal People.

12 December 1991
Economy –
First Ministers'
Conference

Prime Minister Brian Mulroney agrees to hold a First Ministers' Conference to discuss the troubled economy, but warns that Ottawa is not prepared to spend more money, run up the deficit or cut interest rates.

12 December 1991
Social Assistance
Reforms

A federal House of Commons subcommittee reports on child poverty in Canada. It recommends reforming the child tax credit system and family allowances to make more money available to low income families. The report also calls for Ottawa, in cooperation with the provinces, to develop a universally accessible day-care system as well as national welfare standards.

18 December 1991
Health Policy –
Quebec

Quebec's Health Minister Marc-Yvan Côté releases a discussion paper of proposals on how Quebec can continue to fund its $12 billion-a-year health-care system. Among the controversial proposals are some that, if implemented, would violate the Canada Health Act. These are: charges for room and board in hospitals, a \$5 user fee for basic consultations with a physician, and a tax on medical services according to the user's ability to pay. Quebec feels its position is justified in view of Ottawa's declining contributions to provincial medicare programs.

9 January 1992
Language Policy –
Alberta

Alberta Premier Don Getty calls for an end to official bilingualism and multiculturalism. Getty's comments provoke angry responses across Canada from federal as well as provincial politicians.

10 January 1992
Aboriginal Peoples

The federal government announces that it will spend \$8 million to build Canada's first prison on an Indian reserve. The minimum security prison will be for Aboriginal People, operated by Aboriginal People. It is hoped that such an institution will reduce the cultural shock native prisoners often experience when they become incarcerated.

14 January 1992
Constitutional
Change –
Aboriginal Peoples

Prince Edward Island Premier Joe Ghiz proposes a treaty of reconciliation between the federal and provincial governments and the Aboriginal Peoples of Canada. Ghiz believes the treaty would provide the basis for negotiations on such matters as self-government, transfer payments, taxation, and resource development. Ovide Mercredi, Grand Chief of the Assembly of First Nations, welcomes the proposal.

14 January 1992
Constitutional
Committees –
New Brunswick

New Brunswick's Commission on the Constitution releases its report. It endorses the Triple-E Senate as a means of achieving greater regional equality. The committee supports recognition of Quebec's distinct society, official bilingualism, the inherent right of self-government of Aboriginal Peoples, as well as the entrenchment of social programs in the constitution.

17-19 January 1992
Constitutional
Change – Public
Conferences

As announced 13 November 1991, the first of five federal constitutional conferences, entitled "Renewal of Canada: Division of Powers," is held in Halifax. Participants include the Beaudoin-Dobbie Committee, federal and provincial representatives, interest-group leaders, and "ordinary Canadians." Among the points of consensus are:

- a strong federal government is needed in order to ensure that basic benefits are equally accessible to people across Canada, regardless of shifts in federal-provincial power-sharing arrangements;
- "asymmetrical federalism," which would allow provinces to negotiate their own power-sharing arrangements with Ottawa, is acceptable. Asymmetry is seen as a way to accommodate Quebec's demands for more powers without extending them to other provinces; and
- national standards, affecting all provinces and territories in domestic and external matters, are a necessity. The prevailing feeling among the delegates is that this should be achieved through cooperation and consultation between the federal government and the provinces.

23 January 1992
*Supreme Court –
Environmental
Reviews*

The Supreme Court of Canada rules that the federal government has a constitutional right to hold environmental reviews on any project with wide environmental implications, even if it falls under provincial jurisdiction. At issue is the Oldman River dam in Alberta. In an 8-1 ruling the high court says that the federal government has the power to order environmental studies on any project that impinges on any aspect of federal jurisdiction. Ottawa did not order environmental hearings on the project until it was almost completed. Alberta, together with six other provinces, challenged the federal government's right to interfere, claiming the dam was a provincial matter. Following the Supreme Court judgement, environmentalists and native groups, long opposed to the Oldman project, express their satisfaction with the court's decision.

23-26 January 1992
*Constitutional
Change – Public
Conferences*

The second federal constitutional conference, "Renewal of Canada: Institutional Reform," is held in Calgary. The main issue under discussion, Senate reform, receives strong support as delegates endorse an elected and effective upper house. Two specific proposals are discussed: equal representation, demanded by Newfoundland and Alberta, which would see an equal number of Senators elected from each province, and equitable representation, proposed by the federal government, which would weight representation in favour of the smaller provinces.

24 January 1992
Environment

Delegates do not come to a consensus between the two. Women's groups, Aboriginals, the disabled and visible minorities also demand greater representation in the reformed Senate. Ottawa's proposal for the creation of the Council of the Federation is rejected overwhelmingly by the delegates.

Ottawa, Quebec, the Cree and Inuit agree on an environmental review process for the $12.6 billion Great Whale hydroelectric project currently under construction in Quebec. Under the agreement, environmental and native groups will receive $5 million to finance their interventions, and a series of public hearings will be held to examine possible alternatives. Finally, upon examination of all the issues, a recommendation will be made as to the acceptability of the project.

28 January 1992
*Aboriginal Peoples
– Justice –
Manitoba*

Justice Minister Jim McCrae rejects Manitoba's aboriginal justice inquiry recommendation for a separate legal system for natives. McCrae makes it clear that the federal government is not likely to change the constitution to accommodate such a system. He does promise, however, to make improvements so that natives in conflict with the law are better served by the present system.

28 January 1992
Health Policy

Federal and provincial health ministers meet in Banff and approve an eight point set of policy directives including:

• establishing rigid health-care budgets;
• relying less on the present fee-for-service method of paying doctors;
• eliminating the physicians monopoly in certain procedures;
• developing national clinical standards designed to eliminate unnecessary medical treatments;
• reducing post-graduate medical positions by 10 percent; and
• restricting the number of immigrant doctors.

The ministers hope that these measures will help to reduce skyrocketing health-care costs.

30 January 1992 *Federal-Provincial* *Fiscal Relations*	Federal Finance Minister Don Mazankowski announces that Ottawa plans to give an extra $622 million to the seven poorest provinces over the next two years. The Atlantic provinces, Quebec, Manitoba and Saskatchewan will receive the money under changes to the equalization formula. Quebec will receive $198 million, Saskatchewan $60 million, Manitoba $55 million, New Brunswick $39 million, Newfoundland $31 million, and Prince Edward Island $5 million.
31 January- 2 February 1992 *Constitutional* *Change – Public* *Conferences*	The third federal constitutional conference, "Renewal of Canada: The Economic Union," is held in Montreal. Delegates reject most of the federal government's proposals which they feel would give Ottawa too much power over the economy. There is wide support for a social charter to be included in the constitution, and the idea of Canada as an economic and social union finds favour with the delegates. Ultimately, as important as the economic and social issues are, the consensus remains that most important is the preservation of the Canadian political union.
7-9 February 1992 *Constitutional* *Change – Public* *Conferences*	The fourth federal constitutional conference "Renewal of Canada: Identity, Rights and Values" is held in Toronto. The prevailing feeling is that of goodwill as delegates fully support the need to recognize Quebec as a distinct society. Participants also endorse the idea that the Aboriginal Peoples' inherent right of self-government should be entrenched in the constitution. Due to the complexity and importance of the issue, delegates recommend that a special conference be held dealing exclusively with aboriginal rights.
10 February 1992 *Economy –* *First Ministers'* *Conference*	Canada's first ministers (absent Premier Bourassa of Quebec) meet with Prime Minister Brian Mulroney in Ottawa to discuss the economy. They agree to hold further ministerial meetings on training, the social safety net, interprovincial trade barriers, external trade, agriculture, fisheries and capital spending for roads and sewers. The first ministers will meet again next month.

10 February 1992	A preliminary ruling, released by the U.S. Customs ser-
Free Trade –	vice, contends that more than 96,000 Honda cars pro-
Canada-U.S. –	duced in Alliston, Ontario in 1989 and 1990 do not
Disputes	qualify as being North American-built under the Free

10 February 1992
Free Trade –
Canada-U.S. –
Disputes

A preliminary ruling, released by the U.S. Customs service, contends that more than 96,000 Honda cars produced in Alliston, Ontario in 1989 and 1990 do not qualify as being North American-built under the Free Trade Agreement. The cars were exported to the United States duty free. If the preliminary ruling is confirmed, Honda will have to pay $22 million in back tariffs. In Barrie, Ontario, Prime Minister Brian Mulroney accuses the Americans of harassment and orders Canadian Ambassador Derek Burney to launch an appeal under the Canada-U.S. Free Trade Agreement.

11 February 1992
Free Trade –
Canada-U.S. –
Disputes

Canada wins a victory when a panel of the General Agreement on Tariffs and Trade finds that American states unfairly restrict the distribution of Canadian beer and wine. Ironically, last December another GATT panel found that the provinces unfairly restricted the sales of American beer in Canada.

12 February 1992
Free Trade –
Canada-U.S. –
Disputes

In light of the recent GATT ruling on the distribution of American beer in Canada, provincial trade ministers meet and decide to begin removing internal barriers that restrict the movement of domestic beer among the provinces. It is hoped that this will help Canadian breweries compete with the expected influx of cheaper American beer to Canada.

13 February 1992
Election Reform

The Royal Commission on Electoral Reform and Party Financing, set up in 1989 and headed by Pierre Lortie, tables its report in the House of Commons. Among the Commission's recommendations are:

- shorter election campaigns;
- limited advertising by lobby groups;
- guaranteed representation in the Commons for Aboriginal Peoples;
- staggered voting hours across the country to reduce the time difference between the closing of polls in the east and west;
- banning the publication of polls in the last two days of a campaign;
- lifting the limit on liquor sales on election day;

- allowing workers to take a leave of absence to run as a candidate;
- setting up mobile voting booths to facilitate voting for the disabled; and
- making it easier for parties and candidates to obtain public financing.

Although the Commission's recommendations are not binding on the government, Conservative House Leader Harvie Andre promises to set up a special parliamentary committee to examine the report.

13 February 1992
Constitutional Change; Social Charter

Ontario tables its proposal for a social charter with the parliamentary committee on constitutional reform. The main features of the NDP government's proposals are to expand section 36 of the constitution, which also guarantees equalization payments to Canada's poorer provinces, to require governments to provide primary and secondary education, protect the environment, and ensure universal access to health care, housing, food and other necessities of life. These principles would be monitored by an independent commission, but would not be enforced by the courts. The Ontario proposals would also provide constitutional protection for intergovernmental agreements for financial arrangements.

14-16 February 1992
Constitutional Change – Public Conferences

The last of five Renewal of Canada constitutional conferences is held in Vancouver. Delegates examine findings from the four earlier regional meetings and recommend:

- distinct society status for Quebec,
- the inherent right of aboriginal self-government,
- reform to the Senate to make it elected, effective and more representative, and
- a commitment to social goals.

Participants fail to find a way that would give Quebec more powers to protect its distinctiveness and at the same time satisfy the rest-of-Canada's desire to maintain a strong central government. Constitutional Affairs Minister Joe Clark announces that a conference dealing specifically with aboriginal issues will be held 14-15 March.

15 February 1992
*Aboriginal Peoples
– Nova Scotia*

The federal government signs an agreement with the government of Nova Scotia to allow the Micmacs in Cape Breton to form their own police force. The all-native police force will provide services to all Micmac communities. Ottawa agrees to pay 52 percent of the cost and Nova Scotia the remainder. The agreement comes in the wake of the Royal Commission investigation into the wrongful conviction for murder of Donald Marshall Jr., a Micmac Indian.

26 February 1992
*Social Assistance –
Reforms*

Federal Health Minister Benoît Bouchard announces that Ottawa will not introduce the long-promised national child-care program. Instead the federal government will proceed with a tax-based child benefit package geared to an estimated 3.1 million low- and middle-income families. The new package will replace the universal family allowance system.

1 March 1992
*Constitutional
Committees –
Beaudoin-Dobbie*

The Special Joint Committee of the Senate and House of Commons, led by Conservative Senator Gérald Beaudoin and Conservative MP Dorothy Dobbie, presents its report in the Commons. The all-party committee of 10 senators and 20 MPs held public hearings across the country and examined hundreds of submissions, as well as the results of the five Renewal of Canada conferences, before arriving at the following conclusions:

- Satisfying Quebec must be a priority. Quebec's traditional veto over constitutional change must be restored and its distinctiveness — defined by language, culture and civil law — enshrined in the constitution.
- Quebec should be able to negotiate an agreement with Ottawa on cultural jurisdiction and to improve provincial participation in broadcasting.
- The Supreme Court of Canada should be entrenched, including a guarantee of three judges from the Quebec civil bar.
- Through negotiated agreements with Ottawa, the provinces should be given the opportunity to assume responsibility for regional development, energy, mining, tourism, forestry, recreation, housing, family policy and urban affairs.

- The provinces should be able to opt out of federal shared-cost programs, with compensation.
- The Senate should be elected, effective and equitable.
- Aboriginal Peoples' inherent right of self-government should be enshrined in the constitution and aboriginal representation in the reformed Senate guaranteed.
- An economic union should guarantee the free flow of people, goods and services across Canada.
- A social covenant should make governments responsible for the provision of health care, education and social services.

Prime Minister Brian Mulroney praises the report, while Quebec's Premier Robert Bourassa expresses his disappointment, contending the proposals illustrate a "domineering" federalism. Bourassa says he remains optimistic that a satisfactory solution will be reached but warns that time to reach a constitutional deal is running out. Elsewhere, the reaction is mixed. Ontario reacts favourably while the western provinces, Newfoundland and the Assembly of First Nations Grand Chief Ovide Mercredi express some reservations.

6 March 1992
Fisheries

Fisheries Minister John Crosbie announces that all commercial salmon fishing in Newfoundland, with the exception of Labrador, will be banned for five years to protect dwindling resources. Fishermen affected by the ban will be elegible for part of a $40 million federal-provincial compensation package.

6 March 1992
Free Trade –
Canada-U.S. –
Disputes

In a preliminary ruling, the U.S. Commerce Department finds that Canadian provinces unfairly subsidize lumber through low stumpage fees on Crown land. Until the final decision, expected later in the summer, the ruling requires importers of lumber from British Columbia, Ontario, Quebec and Alberta to post a bond promising to pay a 14.48 percent duty. Lumber from the Atlantic provinces and Saskatchewan remains exempt from duty, as the industry there was judged to be too small to have a significant impact on the U.S. market.

10 March 1992 *Constitutional* *Committees –* *Alberta*	Alberta's constitutional all-party committee issues a report. The committee supports Quebec's quest for distinct society status in language, culture and civil law but only if this does not lead to special powers. The committee feels that any special powers granted to Quebec beyond control over culture, language and law, should be offered to other provinces as well. The report also endorses aboriginal self-government and a Triple-E Senate.
10 March 1992 *Education – Alberta*	Alberta's Premier Don Getty agrees to comply with a 1990 Supreme Court ruling and introduce legislation giving the province's francophones their own school boards and, in effect, control over French-language schools.
12 March 1992 *Constitutional* *Change*	Constitutional Affairs Minister Joe Clark meets with provincial (except Quebec) and territorial intergovernmental affairs ministers as well as with representatives of the four major national aboriginal organizations. Together they agree to a "multilateral," negotiation process which will take place over the next ten weeks. The main objective of the negotiations is to produce a constitutional reform package acceptable to all Canadians.
18 March 1992 *Environment*	Meeting in Vancouver, federal and provincial environment ministers agree to speed up elimination of ozone-depleting chemicals. Recent findings indicate that the atmosphere's protective layer is thinning faster than anticipated. Following the meeting, federal minister Jean Charest announces that the production and importation of the offending chlorofluorocarbons (CFC) will now be phased out by 31 December 1995 instead of by the year 2000. In addition, all provinces agree to begin CFC recycling and recovery programs by the end of this year.
19 March 1992 *Environment*	The House of Commons passes environmental assessment legislation which has been before Parliament since June 1990. The legislation sets out rules by which major projects affecting areas of federal jurisdiction, such as dams or paper mills, can be assessed. Claiming it invades provincial jurisdiction, the Quebec Legislature unanimously condemns the federal legislation. The bill is

supported by the federal Liberals and Conservatives while the NDP and the Bloc Québécois vote against it.

24 March 1992
Telecommunications

Ottawa sells its 53 percent stake in Telestat Canada to Alouette Communications Inc., a consortium of 11 major telephone companies, and Spar Aerospace Ltd. giving the telephone companies a virtual monopoly over the telecommunications industry. The agreement gives Telestat exclusive rights to provide fixed-satellite services in Canada or between Canada and the United States for the next ten years.

24-25 March 1992
Economy –
First Ministers'
Conference

Prime Minister Brian Mulroney meets with the provincial premiers in Toronto. Quebec's Premier Robert Bourassa does not attend but is represented by Finance Minister Gérard-D. Levesque.

The first ministers agree to dismantle interprovincial trade barriers within three years. They also agree to work together to prevent "destructive competition" among provinces for new investment.

27-30 March 1992
Aboriginal Peoples
– Constitutional
Change

The Native Council of Canada Constitutional Review Commission reports to the First Peoples' Congress. In its report the Commission makes a broad set of recommendations including:

- entrenchment of the inherent right of Aboriginal Peoples to self-government;
- constitutional protection of the principles of equity of access to implementation of rights for all Aboriginal Peoples; and
- inclusion of the Métis in section 91(24) of the constitution.

The Commission also feels the following elements should be included in the Canada Clause:

- recognition of Aboriginal Peoples as the original peoples of Canada;
- recognition that the treaties are the source of French and British rights and institutions in Canada;
- any referral to language and culture must also include land, resources, and political institutions; and
- the obligation of Parliament and the government of Canada as well as of the Aboriginal Peoples and

governments to protect and promote their original jurisdiction over lands, languages, cultures and institutions.

31 March 1992
Free Trade –
Canada-U.S. –
Disputes

Federal Trade Minister Michael Wilson announces the end to barriers imposed on imported beer within three years. On 25 October 1991, a panel of the General Agreement on Tariffs and Trade ruled that Canadian provinces unfairly priced and distributed imported beer. Wilson also asks the provinces to eliminate interprovincial barriers on the distribution of beer by 1 July 1992. Ontario, Prince Edward Island, Alberta, Saskatchewan, British Columbia and the two territories say they will comply.

31 March 1992
Energy – Quebec

In Montreal, Quebec Energy Minister Lise Bacon announces changes to the planned development of the Great Whale hydroelectric project in northern Quebec. Citing the deferral of a $17 billion export contract with New York State, Bacon announces that the project will now be broken down into three phases. Phase one is scheduled to begin in the fall of 1993 and to be completed by the year 2000. Projected completion of phases two and three is set for 2005 and 2008 respectively. On 27 March 1992, New York Governor Mario Cuomo announced that because of new conservation measures and independent power production, New York State would not need to purchase additional power from Quebec until the turn of the century. Lise Bacon blames the Cree for New York's decision. Aboriginal groups have long been opposed to the development of the Great Whale.

1 April 1992
Constitutional
Change –
Referendum

Prime Minister Brian Mulroney tells the Commons that he is prepared to hold a national referendum on Canadian unity if the first ministers fail to reach an agreement before the 31 May 1992 deadline. Quebec Premier Robert Bourassa says that he does not oppose a national referendum but reminds Ottawa that he is committed to holding his own referendum in Quebec and will not be bound by the results of any national vote.

2 April 1992
*Constitutional
Committees –
British Columbia*

British Columbia Legislature's Special Committee on Constitutional Matters, chaired jointly by J. MacPhail and D. Lovick, presents its report. The committee endorses:

- an elected Senate with equal representation from five regions — British Columbia and the Yukon, The Prairies and the Northwest Territories, Ontario, Quebec and the Atlantic provinces;
- the right to opt for exclusive provincial jurisdiction over labour training, regional development, harbours, inland and costal fisheries and small business development; and
- recognition of Quebec as a distinct society but without special status.
- recognition for the rights of minorities in British Columbia.

7 April 1992
*Environment –
Saskatchewan*

In Regina, the federal government announces plans to rewrite part of the Rafferty-Alameda dam project's federal licence. Last September a federal review panel recommended the change to the licence to ensure that no water from the project was diverted to the United States. The panel's recommendations have been accepted by Environment Minister Jean Charest. Last October, a Federal Court Judge ruled that the recommendations did not take into consideration the economic aspects of the project, which is again being challenged by two Saskatchewan farmers who will lose part of their land to the development.

15 April 1992
*Constitutional
Change*

The multilateral meetings on the constitution continue. Constitutional Affairs Minister Joe Clark reports, following a ministerial level meeting in Ottawa on the issue of Senate reform, that three options are being considered: an equal Senate with limited powers, an equitable Senate, and complete abolition of the Senate (which would be replaced by a new House of the Provinces). Other issues yet to be resolved:

- power sharing between Ottawa and the provinces;
- distinct society status for Quebec;
- aboriginal self-government; and

• the social charter.

Clark again urges Quebec to end its boycott of federal-provincial meetings and join the discussion.

21 April 1992
Aboriginal Peoples
– Constitutional
Change

The Assembly of First Nations releases a report following six months of testimony from natives concerning their place in Canada. Among the recommendations in the report are:

• Aboriginal People should be recognized as a distinct society and their languages should have equal status with English and French;
• the Charter of Rights should not override aboriginal law;
• natives should have the exclusive power to tax themselves; and
• no megaprojects should be constructed without the full consent of the Aboriginal Peoples.

The report also indicates that Aboriginal People want assurances from Ottawa that in the event of any devolution of powers to Quebec they would continue to deal directly with the federal government on issues concerning them.

22 April 1992
Aboriginal Peoples
– Land Claims –
Northwest
Territories

The Gwich'in Indians become the first members of the Dene Nation to sign a land-claims deal with Ottawa. Under the terms of the agreement, signed in Fort McPherson by Indian Affairs Minister Tom Siddon, the Gwich'in will receive title to 24,000 square kilometres of land in the northwestern corner of the Northwest Territories and northeastern Yukon as well as $75 million over 15 years for education and culture. The Indians will also co-manage 60,000 square kilometres of land with the federal and territorial governments.

23 April 1992
Labour Standards

Federal and provincial labour ministers meet in Toronto, agreeing on the need to harmonize health and safety laws in order to increase protection for workers and provide more uniform standards across the country. It is felt that greater harmonization will also save money and result in less confusion.

25 April 1992
Free Trade –
Canada-U.S. –
Disputes

Ottawa and Washington sign an agreement in principle to speed up the removal of provincial barriers to U.S. beer by September 1993. Ottawa originally planned to phase out tariffs by 1995, to give the Canadian beer industry a chance to adjust to the competition. The Americans complained and threatened to retaliate by imposing duty on Canadian beer sold in the United States. The compromise allows Canadians to reserve the right to set minimum prices in return for speeding up the process.

30 April 1992
Constitutional
Change

Participants in the multilateral meetings on the constitution in Edmonton agree to four of the five key elements in the failed Meech Lake Accord. Quebec has always insisted that unless the Meech Lake demands were met it would not join in further unity discussions with the rest-of-Canada. The participants agree to:

• distinct society status for Quebec;
• greater provincial control over immigration;
• the right of provinces to opt out of new federal-provincial cost-sharing programs with compensation; and
• Quebec's right to have three Supreme Court judges.

The issue of a veto for Quebec over future constitutional changes has not yet been agreed to. Alberta together with several other provinces demands Senate reform as a precondition to any further discussions concerning a veto for Quebec. The leaders also agree in principle to a social charter and economic union provisions in the constitution. They would also allow the territories to become provinces by simple agreement with Ottawa.

4 May 1992
Northwest
Territories –
Land Claims

A plebiscite on a proposed boundary to divide the Northwest territories is approved by voters by a narrow 10 percent margin. The vote is split along regional lines as the Inuit of the eastern Arctic, where the territory of Nunavut is to be established, vote overwhelmingly in favour of the division. In the western Arctic the vote is "no" by a margin of three to one. Federal Northern Affairs Minister Tom Siddon appears satisfied with the results and says he expects that Nanavut will be created by 1999. The agreement reached last year with the Tungavik Federation of Nunavut guarantees the Inuit

$1.5 billion over 14 years and ownership of 350,000 square kilometres of land.

4 May 1992
Social Assistance

As part of budgetary measures announced in February, the federal government announces a $500 million program to help needy children in Canada. Welfare Minister Benoît Bouchard says the program is designed to help women and young children who live in poverty. It will provide $50 million for prevention of child neglect through such programs as nutritional guidelines for children; $73 million for promotion, through educating pregnant women on how to reduce the risk of low birth-weight babies, and $17 million for protection such as helping the RCMP with maintaining the missing children registry. A further $200 million will be allotted to local groups delivering health and social programs to high-risk children and $160 million is for programs in aboriginal communities.

7 May 1992
Justice

Claude Morin, former intergovernmental affairs minister in René Lévesque's PQ government, admits to being an RCMP informant between 1974 and 1977. Morin denies giving the RCMP any information about the Parti Québécois and says he agreed to meet with the RCMP only to find out about their activities in Quebec. Morin also says that he informed Lévesque and former Justice Minister Marc-André Bédard about his contacts with the RCMP in 1975 and 1977.

8 May 1992
Environment –
British Columbia

A Federal Court of Appeal rules that Alcan may resume construction of a $1 billion hydroelectric project in northern British Columbia. The court overturns a lower court decision which, in May 1991, ordered Ottawa to hold environmental hearings into the Kemano 2 megaproject. Justice Louis Marceau said Ottawa does not have to review every project that may have environmental effects on areas of its jurisdiction. Ottawa first approved the project in September 1987 and exempted it from independent review in October 1990.

8 May 1992 *Social Assistance* *Job Training –* *New Brunswick,* *British Columbia*	Federal Employment Minister Bernard Valcourt and New Brunswick Premier Frank McKenna announce two joint pilot projects designed to help people get off welfare. The first, called New Brunswick Works, is a six-year $177 million shared-cost project which will provide welfare recipients with literacy and skills training. The second, a $50 million project, will be implemented in New Brunswick and British Columbia. It is designed to supplement wages of welfare recipients who take low paying jobs. If the projects prove to be a success they will be extended to other parts of the country.
15 May 1992 *Constitutional* *Change –* *Referendum*	A bill allowing a national referendum on constitutional reform is introduced in the House of Commons. The results of a vote would be non-binding. House Leader Harvie Andre says the bill does not mean that a national referendum will necessarily be held, but that Prime Minister Mulroney needs the ability to call one should the situation warrant it.
15 May 1992 *Free Trade –* *Canada-U.S. –* *Disputes*	The U.S. Commerce Department sets the duty on Canadian softwood at 6.51 percent, down from the original 14.48 percent imposed in a preliminary ruling in March 1992. Trade Minister Michael Wilson says the duty on Canadian softwood is offensive and unjust. Wilson tells a news conference in Ottawa that Canada will appeal to a Canada-U.S. free trade panel.
21 May 1992 *Environment –* *Alberta*	Federal Environment Minister Jean Charest announces that Ottawa will not shut down development of the Oldman dam in southern Alberta. In July 1991, a federal environmental review panel had recommended shutting down the project until all environmental and social concerns were addressed. Ottawa's position is that environmental issues are being sufficiently addressed and that there is no reason to stop development of the dam. The lobby group "Friends of the Oldman River" say they will seek an injunction from the Supreme Court of Canada to stop development.
30 May 1992 *Constitutional* *Change*	Five days of bargaining on constitutional reform with federal, provincial, territorial and aboriginal representatives conclude in Toronto without agreement. The main stumbling blocks are the issues of Senate reform, a

constitutional amending formula, division of powers and a proposed economic union. However, a degree of consensus was achieved on:

* distinct society status for Quebec;
* Aboriginal Peoples' inherent right of self-government;
* more provincial control in the areas of immigration, job training, culture, housing, tourism, forestry, mining and municipal and urban affairs;
* the right of provinces to opt out of new federal cost-shared programs with compensation;
* three Supreme Court seats for Quebec; and
* some form of social charter.

The ministers will meet again in Ottawa on 9 June, to try to secure a final agreement.

4 June 1992
Constitutional Change – Referendum

The House of Commons approves the federal government's referendum bill by which it could hold a national vote on constitutional reform. However, Constitutional Affairs Minister Joe Clark stresses that the federal government would much prefer to reach a constitutional settlement through a negotiated agreement with the provinces and aboriginal leaders.

12 June 1992
Telecommunications

In a landmark decision the Canadian Radio-Television and Telecommunications Commission decides to break a monopoly of federally regulated telephone companies in Canada over long-distance telephone services. The 4 – 1 ruling will make it possible for other companies to offer competing services. Already two companies, Unitel Communications and BCRL, are set to enter the $7.5 billion annual long-distance market.

15 June 1992
Constitutional Change – Senate Reform

Constitutional Affairs Minister Joe Clark indicates that despite the break in constitutional talks of 11 June 1992, multilateral negotiations at the official level are continuing. Currently under discussion is a new proposal from Saskatchewan's premier Roy Romanow on Senate Reform. The proposal would give each province an equal number of seats but larger provinces would have more power through weighted voting on most issues. Also being considered is a federal proposal, favoured by Ontario, of a regionally equal Senate.

17-18 June 1992
Health Policy

Federal and provincial health and finance ministers meet in Ottawa to discuss the state of the $60 billion national health-care system. To save money the provinces agree to review the work of doctors and hospitals in order to eliminate unnecessary waste and inefficiency. The ministers reaffirm their commitment to universal medicare.

25 June 1992
Free Trade –
Canada-U.S. –
Disputes

The U.S. International Trade Commission votes 4 – 2 to uphold a 6.5 percent duty on softwood lumber imported into the United States from Canada. Canada plans to appeal the ruling, which applies to British Columbia, Alberta, Ontario and Quebec. British Columbia is responsible for 80 percent of the lumber shipped to the United States and its subsidies have been calculated at 7.95 percent compared to .01 percent for Quebec. Federal and provincial officials have agreed to let the provinces appear separately before the appeal panel.

25 June 1992
Supreme Court –
Taxation

In a unanimous decision the Supreme Court of Canada rules that the 7 percent Goods and Services Tax, introduced in January 1990 by the federal government, is legal. Alberta, supported by British Columbia and Ontario, had challenged the validity of the tax on constitutional grounds arguing that it infringed on provincial jurisdiction. Following the Court's decision, Revenue Minister Otto Jelinek said he hoped that the provinces would now begin to harmonize their sales tax with the GST.

29 June 1992
Constitutional
Change –
Senate Reform

Constitutional Affairs Minister Joe Clark and nine provincial premiers agree to meet on 3 July 1992 to try and resolve the Senate reform issue, which continues to be a major obstacle on the path to a constitutional agreement. Alberta, Newfoundland, Manitoba and Saskatchewan support equal representation for all provinces while the federal government, Ontario and Quebec favour weighted but not equal representation for the smaller provinces. Negotiations continue.

Chronology: Index

List of Titles in Print

Institute of Intergovernmental Relations, *Annual Report to the Advisory Council, 1990-91*/Institut des relations intergouvernementales, *Rapport annuel au Conseil consultatif, 1990-1991*. (charge for postage only)

William M. Chandler and Christian W. Zöllner, editors, *Challenges to Federalism: Policy-Making in Canada and the Federal Republic of Germany*, 1989. ($25)

Peter M. Leslie, *Rebuilding the Relationship: Quebec and its Confederation Partners/Une collaboration renouvelée: le Québec et ses partenaires dans la confédération*, 1987. ($8)

A. Paul Pross and Susan McCorquodale, *Economic Resurgence and the Constitutional Agenda: The Case of the East Coast Fisheries*, 1987. ($10)

Bruce G. Pollard, *Managing the Interface: Intergovernmental Affairs Agencies in Canada*, 1986. ($12)

Catherine A. Murray, *Managing Diversity: Federal-Provincial Collaboration and the Committee on Extension of Services to Northern and Remote Communities*, 1984. ($15)

Peter Russell et al, *The Court and the Constitution: Comments on the Supreme Court Reference on Constitutional Amendment*, 1982. (Paper $5, Cloth $10)

Allan Tupper, *Public Money in the Private Sector: Industrial Assistance Policy and Canadian Federalism*, 1982. ($12)

William P. Irvine, *Does Canada Need a New Electoral System?* 1979. ($8)

Canada: The State of the Federation

Douglas M. Brown, editor, *Canada: The State of the Federation, 1991*. ($18)

Ronald L. Watts and Douglas M. Brown, editors, *Canada: The State of the Federation, 1990*. ($17)

Ronald L. Watts and Douglas M. Brown, editors, *Canada: The State of the Federation, 1989*. ($16)

Peter M. Leslie and Ronald L. Watts, editors, *Canada: The State of the Federation, 1987-88*. ($15)

Peter M. Leslie, editor, *Canada: The State of the Federation 1986*. ($15)

Peter M. Leslie, editor, *Canada: The State of the Federation 1985*. ($14)

Canada: L'état de la fédération 1985. ($14)

The Year in Review

Bruce G. Pollard, *The Year in Review 1983: Intergovernmental Relations in Canada.* ($16)

Revue de l'année 1983: les relations intergouvernementales au Canada. ($16)

S.M. Dunn, *The Year in Review 1982: Intergovernmental Relations in Canada.* ($12)

Revue de l'année 1982: les relations intergouvernementales au Canada. ($12)

S.M. Dunn, *The Year in Review 1981: Intergovernmental Relations in Canada.* ($10)

R.J. Zukowsky, *Intergovernmental Relations in Canada: The Year in Review 1980, Volume I: Policy and Politics.* ($8) (*Volume II not available*)

Conference Proceedings

1. Daniel Bonin, editor, *Towards Reconciliation? The Language Issue in Canada in the 1990s/Vers la réconciliation? La question linguistique au Canada dans les années 1990,* 1992. ($20)

Dean's Conference on Law and Policy

2. John D. Whyte and Christopher N. Kendall (eds.), *The Death and Life of Constitutional Reform in Canada,* 1991. ($8)

Research Papers/Notes de Recherche (formerly Discussion Papers)

31. Steven A. Kennett, *The Design of Federalism and Water Resource Management in Canada,* 1992. ($8)

30. Patrick Fafard and Darrel R. Reid, *Constituent Assemblies: A Comparative Survey,* 1991. ($7)

29. Thomas O. Hueglin, *A Political Economy of Federalism: In Search of a New Comparative Perspective With Critical Intent Throughout,* 1990. ($10.00)

28. Ronald L. Watts, Darrel R. Reid and Dwight Herperger, *Parallel Accords: The American Precedent,* 1990. ($6)

27. Michael B. Stein, *Canadian Constitutional Renewal, 1968-1981: A Case Study in Integrative Bargaining,* 1989. ($12)

26. Ronald L. Watts, *Executive Federalism: A Comparative Analysis,* 1989. ($6)

25. Denis Robert, *L'ajustement structurel et le fédéralisme canadien: le cas de l'industrie du textile et du vêtement,* 1989. ($7.50)

24. Peter M. Leslie, *Ethnonationalism in a Federal State: The Case of Canada,* 1988. ($4)

23. Peter M. Leslie, *National Citizenship and Provincial Communities: A Review of Canadian Fiscal Federalism,* 1988. ($4)

22. Robert L. Stanfield, *National Political Parties and Regional Diversity,* 1985. (Postage Only)

21. Donald Smiley, *An Elected Senate for Canada? Clues from the Australian Experience,* 1985. ($8)

19. Thomas O. Hueglin, *Federalism and Fragmentation: A Comparative View of Political Accommodation in Canada,* 1984. ($8)

18. Allan Tupper, *Bill S-31 and the Federalism of State Capitalism,* 1983. ($7)

17. Reginald Whitaker, *Federalism and Democratic Theory,* 1983. ($7)

16. Roger Gibbins, *Senate Reform: Moving Towards the Slippery Slope,* 1983. ($7)

14. John Whyte, *The Constitution and Natural Resource Revenues,* 1982. ($7)